America
and the
Japanese
Miracle

William H. Becker, editor

Aaron Forsberg

America and the Japanese Miracle

The Cold War Context of Japan's Postwar Economic Revival, 1950–1960

The University of North Carolina Press
Chapel Hill & London

© 2000
The University of North Carolina Press
All rights reserved
Designed by Eric M. Brooks
Set in Electra and Badger Medium
by Keystone Typesetting, Inc.
The paper in this book meets the guidelines for
permanence and durability of the Committee on
Production Guidelines for Book Longevity of the
Council on Library Resources.

Library of Congress Cataloging-in-Publication Data
Forsberg, Aaron.
America and the Japanese miracle : the Cold War
context of Japan's postwar economic revival, 1950–
1960 / by Aaron Forsberg.
p. cm. — (Luther Hartwell Hodges series on business,
society, and the state)
Includes bibliographical references and index.
ISBN 9781469613758 (pbk. : alk. paper)
1. United States—Foreign economic relations—Japan.
2. Japan—Foreign economic relations—United States.
3. Balance of trade—United States. 4. Balance of
trade—Japan. I. Title. II. Series.
HF3127.F67 1999 337.73052—dc21 99-34835 CIP

Portions of this work appeared previously, in
somewhat different form, in "Eisenhower and
Japanese Economic Recovery: The Politics of
Integration with the Western Trading Bloc,
1952–1955," *Journal of American-East Asian Relations*
5 (Spring 1996): 57–75, and "The Politics of GATT
Expansion: Japanese Accession and the Domestic
Political Context in Japan and the United States,
1948–1955," *Business and Economic History* 27 (Fall
1998): 185–95, and are used here with the permission
of Imprint Publications and *Business and Economic
History* respectively.

To my mother and father

CONTENTS

Preface *xi*

Abbreviations and Acronyms *xvii*

ONE Introduction *1*

TWO To Keep the Japanese on Our Side *29*

THREE The Economics of Peace *53*

FOUR War in Korea and the China Trade Embargo *83*

FIVE The Fight over Trade Policy, 1953 *113*

SIX Japanese Integration with the Western Trading Bloc, 1954–1956 *137*

SEVEN The Limits of Integration: Foreign Direct Investment in Japan *169*

EIGHT High-Speed Growth and Trade Friction, 1955–1960 *199*

Epilogue *233*

Appendix: Treaty of Friendship, Commerce, and Navigation, 1953 (Excerpts) *241*

Notes *245*

Bibliography *295*

Index *315*

TABLES

- 5   1.1 Japan's Balance of Payments, 1951–1960
- 6   1.2 Japan: Introduction of Foreign Investments, 1951–1971
- 10   1.3 United States Balance of Trade with Japan, 1947–1971
- 14   1.4 Japan's Receipts from U.S. Military Expenditures, 1950–1960
- 14   1.5 Japan's Foreign Trade, 1945–1960
- 15   1.6 Japan's Import Trade with China, 1930–1975
- 16   1.7 Japan's Export Trade with China, 1930–1975
- 18   1.8 Japan's Imports by Area, 1935, 1950, 1955, 1960
- 20   1.9 Japan's Exports by Market, 1935, 1950, 1955, 1960
- 158   6.1 Reductions in Japanese Rates of Duty on Leading Items, 1955
- 159   6.2 Bindings of Japanese Rates of Duty on Leading Items, 1955
- 160   6.3 Reductions in U.S. Rates of Duty on Leading Items, 1955
- 161   6.4 Bindings of U.S. Rates of Duty on Leading Items, 1955
- 180   7.1 Book Value and Percentage Distribution: U.S. Foreign Direct Investments (by Area, Selected Years)
- 182   7.2 Validated Establishments of Joint Business Ventures in Japan, 1950–1965

PREFACE

This study began as an inquiry into the U.S. effort to promote Japan's economic reconstruction after the Second World War. It has ended as a much larger analysis of the connections between American economic and security policies at the Cold War's height, the origins of Japan's postwar economic success, and the character of the relationship between the United States and Japan since 1945. Drawing upon the rich archival record now open to researchers, I argue here that U.S. national security policies and the escalating Cold War played a larger role in promoting Japanese economic welfare and in forging the pattern of postwar economic integration and conflict between Japan and the United States than has previously been recognized.

This book's focus on one decade deserves explanation. Recent releases of governmental records in the United States, the United Kingdom, and, to a limited extent, Japan afford historians the opportunity to reassess the history of the early Cold War years in a way not possible before now. The 1950s also stand out as a distinctive era. Political developments clearly frame the period. In 1950 the United States and Japan began the negotiations to end the state of war between them. In these negotiations, the U.S. government also desired a Japanese commitment to the American side in the Cold War while the Japanese government sought an American guarantee of Japan's external defense. The result was the conclusion of two treaties in 1951 (that entered into force the following year): the multilateral San Francisco Peace Treaty, which brought the Occupation to a close; and the bilateral U.S.-Japan Security Treaty, in which the United States pledged to maintain its military forces in and around Japan. The security treaty was in reality a military base agreement; it did not contain any formal American obligation to act in the event Japan was attacked. Thus, however closely the security treaty reflected the asymmetrical balance of power at the time, it was never popular in Japan. Many conservative advocates of the American alliance wanted both a stronger American commitment to defend Japan and provisions for joint consultation in the implementation of defense measures. Japanese opponents of the Cold War alliance fought against entering into any sort of security pact with the United States at all.

To an extent that is difficult for later generations to grasp, Japanese politics during the 1950s revolved around the issue of the alliance with the United States. Throughout the decade, the U.S. government both worried about Japan's future political orientation, and attempted to shore up the alliance by emphasizing the economic opportunity flowing from close association with the United States. The climax came in 1960 after the two governments concluded a new mutual security treaty. In the face of massive public demonstrations against both the treaty and the government of Kishi Nobusuke, the Japanese National Diet ratified the revised security treaty, thus confirming Japan's position at America's side in the world.

Economic affairs of the decade of the fifties also display a certain unity. In early 1950, Japan's economy was languishing and the nation's industries were unable to produce goods that were competitive in international markets. Later in the year the outbreak of war in Korea brought a flood of American war orders that temporarily alleviated Japan's chronic foreign trade imbalance. Yet no one counted on this windfall to last forever. Throughout the decade both the American and Japanese governments attempted to find markets for Japanese goods and to promote the modernization of Japanese industry. These efforts succeeded beyond all expectations. By 1960 Japan's economy was growing at a rate of about 10 percent per year, and many of its manufactured goods were highly competitive abroad. In short, the fifties was the decade when Japan made the transition from postwar recovery to high-speed growth.

By studying the stories of the Cold War partnership and Japan's economic revival in the context of each other rather than separately, this book attempts to go beyond the boundaries that separate scholars from each another. If historians of the Cold War usually focus on strategy, finding economic matters of interest only when they impinge on diplomacy, the emphasis here is on the economic consequences of national security policy. Far from being mere irritants in the bilateral American-Japanese security relationship, controversies over the issues of trade and investment relate to broad changes in the world since 1945, particularly Japan's economic ascent and the emergence of an increasingly interdependent world economy. Not all economists and political scientists take the institutional structure of this global economy for granted, but most studies of American-Japanese economic relations focus on the workings of the postwar system. Since the fifties was the period during which Japan defined its place in that postwar order, the aim here is to trace the origins of the many economic and political institutions binding Japan to the outside world as well as those separating it from the Communist bloc. Finally, whereas analysis of the Japanese economic "miracle" has focused relentlessly inward on Japan's experience and unique institutions, this study emphasizes the role of the international context in facilitating the nation's high-speed growth and distinctive brand of capitalism.

Japanese and Chinese names in the text appear according to national custom with the surname first (for example, Kishi Nobusuke). The names of Asian scholars who have published in English, however, follow Western custom with the surname last. Similarly, macrons indicating long vowels have been omitted from familiar place names (such as Tokyo) and the names of Japanese scholars who do not indicate them when publishing in English. Since the pinyin system of romanizing Chinese names is now the standard in both journalism and scholarship, all Chinese names are written in pinyin except for Chiang Kai-shek. On first mention, however, the traditional English Wade-Giles spelling is given in parentheses. With apologies to neighbors north and south, the terms "America" and "Americans" are used synonymously with the United States and U.S. citizens respectively for purposes of stylistic variation and succinctness. The terms "Far East" and "Red China" appear intermittently owing to their use during the 1950s. Wherever possible, however, "East Asia" and "People's Republic of China" are employed instead.

I am very grateful for the advice and support of numerous individuals and institutions I received while completing this study. This book began as my doctoral dissertation, and I owe a primary debt to those who guided me at the University of Texas at Austin, particularly Robert A. Divine, my dissertation supervisor, and David L. Howell, who offered valuable direction in my study of Japan. I have also benefited from the encouragement and advice of professors Lewis L. Gould, Peter Trubowitz, and Wm. Roger Louis. Comments from other scholars who read the entire manuscript helped me to sharpen the argument and avoid misstatement. They include Dave Schmitz, Osamu Ishii, Dennis Doolin, Michael Barnhart, and the anonymous readers for the University of North Carolina Press. Dave Schmitz of Whitman College deserves special mention for the thoughtful guidance he has offered since I began research in American foreign relations as an undergraduate student. Conference presentations based on the manuscript elicited helpful pointers from Susan Aaronson, Mira Wilkins, and Burton Kaufman.

Certain passages of this book have appeared in different form in the *Journal of American-East Asian Relations* and *Business and Economic History*. Grateful acknowledgment is made to Imprint Publications and *Business and Economic History* for permission to use this previously published material.

I must thank the Department of History and the Graduate School of the University of Texas for providing me with financial support in various forms while I researched and wrote the dissertation. Travel grants from The Eisenhower World Affairs Institute and the Harry S Truman Library made it possible to conduct research at both presidential libraries. The archivists at both facilities were patient, and more helpful to me than they probably know. The staff members at the Eisenhower library in particular deserve mention for the number of classified documents that they reviewed for public release in timely fashion. The archivists and staff at the National Archives and the Public Record Office drew my attention to countless useful files that I would not have consulted without such direction. I also wish to thank Joseph E. Gagnon at the Department of the Treasury for expediting my Freedom of Information Act request for copies of documents that were in the process of being transferred from the Department of the Treasury to the National Archives. Support from the Asian Division of University of Maryland University College enabled me to investigate the voluminous records from the 1950s declassified after completion of my dissertation. I owe a special thanks to Ted Franck of the Asian Division. His administrative flexibility and encouragement made it possible for me to conduct follow-up research and to finish the manuscript. I also wish to thank Osamu Ishii of Hitotsubashi University for his helpful advice and consistent support in Japan.

It has been a pleasure to work with the staff of the University of North Carolina Press at each step in the process of turning the manuscript into a book. Executive editor Lewis Bateman and managing editor Ron Maner deserve special mention for the care and thoughtfulness they have shown in bringing this project to successful completion.

Fine teachers can motivate a person for a lifetime. I thus owe a great debt to Glen Knight and Steve Betchart, two of my teachers in high school. Of the friends and colleagues with whom I have discussed various aspects of my research, I would like especially to thank Jon Lee, Mark Stout, Hiro and Yuki Hioki, Chris Held, Noriko Yokoi, and Dennis Doolin. I also wish to thank Akiko Miyamoto, my former Japanese teacher, for her tireless patience as I learned to read Japanese government documents. Lastly, I wish to thank my wife and my family, who have always been there for me and tolerated me when I was totally absorbed in my work.

Despite this generous assistance, the responsibility for all matters of fact and interpretation is mine alone.

ABBREVIATIONS & ACRONYMS

BOJ	Bank of Japan
BT	Board of Trade (United Kingdom)
CCP	Chinese Communist Party
CED	Committee for Economic Development
CFEP	Council on Foreign Economic Policy
CG-COCOM	Consultative Group, Coordinating Committee for Export to Communist Areas
CHINCOM	China Subcommittee of CG-COCOM
CIA	Central Intelligence Agency
CIF	cost, insurance, and freight
CP	Contracting Party to GATT
D.	Democratic Party, United States
ESS	Economic and Scientific Section, SCAP
FCN	Treaty of Friendship, Commerce, and Navigation
FDI	foreign direct investment
FEC	Far Eastern Commission
FIL	Foreign Investment Law, Japan
FOB	free on board
GARIOA	Government and Relief in Occupied Areas
GATT	General Agreement on Tariffs and Trade
GNP	gross national product
HCLC	Holding Company Liquidation Commission
H.R.	House Resolution (U.S. Congress)
ICA	International Cooperative Administration
IMF	International Monetary Fund
ITO	International Trade Organization
JCS	Joint Chiefs of Staff
JSP	Japan Socialist Party
Keidanren	Japan Federation of Economic Organizations

LDP	Liberal Democratic Party (Japan)
MFN	most-favored-nation trading status
MITI	Japan Ministry of International Trade and Industry
MOF	Japan Ministry of Finance
MSP	Mutual Security Program
NATO	North Atlantic Treaty Organization
NIE	National Intelligence Estimate
Nikkeiren	Japan Federation of Employers Association
Nisshō	Japan Chamber of Commerce and Industry
NSC	National Security Council
PPS	Policy Planning Staff, U.S. Department of State
PRC	People's Republic of China
PSB	Psychological Strategy Board
R.	Republican Party, United States
ROC	Republic of China (Taiwan)
RTAA	Reciprocal Trade Agreements Act
SCAP	Supreme Command for the Allied Powers
SWNCC	State-War-Navy-Coordinating Committee
TAC	Trade Agreements Committee
TAEA	Trade Agreements Extension Act, United States, 1955
UN	United Nations
USIA	United States Information Agency
USSR	Union of Soviet Socialist Republics
VER	voluntary export restraint

America
and the
Japanese
Miracle

Chapter One
INTRODUCTION

The American-Soviet rivalry and Japan's rise from surrender to economic superpower reshaped international relations during the decades after the Second World War. During the 1950s the relationship between Japan and the United States became the arena where these two great forces intertwined most completely. That crucial decade saw the United States win Japan's alliance in the Cold War while the Japanese economy made the transition from postwar reconstruction to high-speed growth.

The Thesis and Themes of This Book

Studying the diplomacy of the fifties from the inside reveals the many connections between the Cold War and Japan's postwar economic revival. It suggests that the Cold War environment abroad, particularly U.S. diplomacy, facilitated the so-called Japanese miracle during the period. Still, the primary credit for Japan's high-speed economic growth is not due to the United States; clearly, both the commitment to growth and the discipline necessary to achieve it originated in Japan. The American contribution was to foster an international environment in which Japanese effort produced meaningful results. Yet precisely because the relationship between the United States and Japan was so close, postwar relations were replete with friction.

American interest in Japanese revival flowed from origins far removed from any concern for Japan. As the end of the Second World War neared, American planners in the executive branch prepared to restore international order and build the institutions of the postwar era. For those "present at the creation," as Secretary of State Dean Acheson later described their vantage point, the United States had an obligation to take the lead. Fundamental to the internationalism of these officials (most of whom were conservative Democrats and liberal Republicans) was the establishment of a system of multilateral trade and payments. Beyond the obvious commercial opportunity for the United States, the object of such an order was to break the vicious cycle of protectionism, depression, and war, which they held responsible for causing the collapse of peace during the 1930s.[1]

In theory and in practice, the American foreign policy establishment's thinking was predicated upon the integration of Germany into the Western European economy and Japanese economic revival. In 1945, however, most Americans were unprepared to think about rebuilding either power. After postponing many difficult decisions about the terms of a postwar settlement, U.S. president Franklin Roosevelt died suddenly in April, leaving the problems of peace to Harry S Truman. The two imposing military commanders administering the occupied territories after the war's end— General Douglas MacArthur in Japan and General Lucius D. Clay in Germany—faced daunting challenges simply maintaining adequate food supplies, public health, and civil order. Official postsurrender policies reflected rather than reconciled the conflicting strains in 'American thinking. They were not as punitive as popular American sentiment, but civilian and military officials on the ground concentrated on demilitarizing the former enemies and reforming public life. Beginning in 1947, economic desperation in the occupied areas and the growing American-Soviet rivalry afforded executive officials in Washington the chance to seize the initiative and reorient U.S. foreign policy.

Even more than Germany, Japan represented the supreme test of the establishment's vision. During the Occupation, Japan's conservative leaders expressed their eagerness to join the institutions of the emerging order and to trade with the Western powers. But domestic U.S. support for liberal economic principles was thin, and hostility toward Japanese trade ran deep. The same sentiment defined the policies of America's principal allies and trading partners. Whereas postwar European leaders were able to build on long-standing ties linking West Germany and its non-Communist neighbors in Western Europe, postwar East Asia was not an organic economic unit. Only in the context of the escalating Cold War were American leaders able to overcome opposition to Japanese integration into the global economy.

In this story three themes stand out. The first is the prominence of Japanese economic recovery as an objective of American security policy. The second is the many ways that U.S. policy and other external variables worked to Japanese advantage, often in ways not fully evident at the time. Paradoxically, friction was the inevitable consequence of strategic and economic cooperation. Thus, the final theme is the profound undercurrent of friction in the U.S.-Japanese relationship. If Americans saw the benefits accruing to Japan from the Cold War partnership, the Japanese noticed its demands upon them. Deeply rooted protective tendencies on both sides insured that a proliferation of disputes over trade and investment was the natural corollary to economic integration

The prominence of Japanese recovery as an American policy objective reflects how U.S. foreign economic policy toward Japan was inseparable from the broader Cold War strategy of the Truman and Eisenhower administrations. Japan was one of the great stakes in the struggle between the "free world" and the Communist bloc. Just as Germany was the pivotal nation in the European balance of power, Japan was the "ultimate domino" in postwar Asia.[2] Besides denying Japan's industrial base to the Soviet bloc, from 1948 forward Washington planners called for building Japan into a powerful anti-Communist ally. They correctly identified in economic policy a promising means of consolidating the U.S.-Japanese alliance against Communist power. The outbreak of war in Korea in 1950 reinforced their sense of urgency. During the Japanese peace treaty negotiations, the overriding U.S. aim was to maintain the close bilateral association begun during the Occupation. Toward this end, U.S. officials sought to promote Japan's reintegration into the international economy so that the Japanese could make a living by trade.

The contours of Japan's foreign trade were established during the first half of the decade. Virtually cut off from the world, economic conditions in

Japan in 1950 were desperate. Although the Korean War boom provided a powerful boost at a crucial time, it was also a highly disruptive force. By alienating the United States and the newly established People's Republic of China (PRC), the Korean War paved the way for the imposition of severe controls on trade that severed Japan's economy from the Asian mainland. Because Japan was on the U.S. side in the Cold War, Sino-American political antagonism could and did interfere with Japanese efforts to expand commercial ties with the PRC. In compensation, however, U.S. president Dwight Eisenhower pressed for increased Japanese access to the American market and membership in the General Agreement on Tariffs and Trade (GATT). The effect was to reorient Japan's foreign trade westward and to tie Japan to the U.S. economy. In contrast with the prewar period, Japan's postwar economy developed largely apart from that of the Chinese mainland.

The fragility of the U.S.-Japanese alliance throughout the fifties also had important economic consequences. American officials often worried that Japan might try to pursue an independent course in the Cold War much like India. They looked to economic ties to bind the United States and Japan together more tightly in mutual interest. American policy was a political success. The test came when opposition to the conservative government of Kishi Nobusuke, the revised security treaty, and the Cold War alliance boiled over in 1960. The security treaty crisis was a bruising affair for everyone, but the alliance held. To the extent that Japan's close economic ties with the United States persuaded the Japanese of the value of continued partnership, American policy had precisely the effect that U.S. strategists intended.

The second theme, regarding the commercial advantages that Japan reaped from the American alliance, is reflected in both obvious and less apparent ways. During the first half of the fifties the U.S. goal of building a liberal economic order abroad and the Japanese government's desire to expand the nation's economic opportunity largely overlapped. Both governments focused on remedying Japan's ever expanding trade deficit and integrating Japan into the Western trading bloc. They made visible progress toward accomplishing both goals, but American support for trade liberalization was less solid than either government desired, and progress was slow. Still, the momentum was unmistakable. The peace treaty of 1951 entitled the signatories to reciprocal tariff treatment on their trade with Japan for four years. In 1953 the United States and Japan concluded the Treaty of Friendship, Commerce, and Navigation (FCN) that normalized trade relations for the first time since 1939. In 1953, at American insistence, the

Table 1.1. *Japan's Balance of Payments, 1951–1960 ($ million)*

Year	Receipts	Payments	Balance
1951	2,241	1,909	+331
1952	2,239	1,925	+314
1953	2,120	2,314	−194
1954	2,309	2,209	+100
1955	2,668	2,174	+494
1956	3,225	2,931	+293
1957	3,612	3,966	−384
1958	3,441	2,930	+511
1959	3,914	3,575	+339
1960	4,588	4,476	+111

Source: BOJ, *Economic Statistics of Japan*, 1961, 267–68.
Note: The principal differences between Ministry of Finance (MOF) and Bank of Japan (BOJ) data are as follows:

	BOJ	MOF
1. Invisible trade:	Included	Not included
2. Items without drafts:	Not included	Included
3. Quantum statistics:	Not included	Included
4. Value of exports:	Face value (draft)	FOB
5. Value of imports:	Face value (draft)	CIF
6. Accounting date (E):	Arrival of report	Departure date
7. Accounting date (I):	Arrival of report	Date cleared for entry

contracting parties to GATT accepted Japan as a temporary member over British opposition. In 1955 the Eisenhower administration conducted tariff negotiations with Japan as a prelude to full membership in GATT that year.

Japan would not have enjoyed the same access to Western markets in the absence of the Cold War. Even with firm U.S. backing, Japanese membership in GATT remained circumscribed. Rather than extend the same treatment to Japan as to the other contracting parties, the United Kingdom and fourteen other nations invoked Article 35, an escape clause in the General Agreement. Japan's export trade increased, but the nation's balance-of-payments position remained precarious (Table 1.1). Even more than in relations between the United States and the Federal Republic of Germany, the American connection continued to overshadow Japan's relations with other powers.

Despite these constraints on Japanese trading opportunity, the new order was very tolerant of Japan's own restrictions on foreign trade and investment. Japan's resistance to expanding imports is familiar. Tariff negotiations in 1955 and 1956 revealed a deep-seated mercantilistic impulse in Japanese

Table 1.2. *Japan: Introduction of Foreign Investments, 1951–1971 ($ million)*

Fiscal Year	Total	Stocks	Participation in Management
1951	17.3	13.3	11.6
1952	44.4	9.8	7.2
1953	54.2	4.3	2.6
1954	19.3	3.9	2.4
1955	51.4	4.2	2.3
1956	103.2	9.4	5.4
1957	136.2	12.1	7.3
1958	242.6	11.0	3.7
1959	154.9	27.1	14.6
1960	203.6	74.9	31.6
1965	528.5	83.3	44.6
1967	847.8	159.8	29.8
1968	1,836.6	670.0	52.7
1969	3,488.2	2,462.9	53.8
1970	2,811.9	1,579.7	114.5
1971	4,256.8	2,667.3	255.5

Sources: For 1951–1960: BOJ, *Economic Statistics of Japan*, 1961, 266; for 1965–71: Japan, Office of the Prime Minister, *Japan Statistical Yearbook*, 1972, 311. All figures are based on Bank of Japan data.

thinking. The Japanese government was simply reluctant to make any significant concessions. Commercial agreements, such as the 1953 FCN treaty with the United States, allowed for imposition of restrictions to protect the nation's balance-of-payments position. In the hands of ministries in Tokyo they became tools for protecting various sectors of the Japanese economy, among them automobiles and consumer electronics. Even after the return of currency convertibility in Europe in 1958, Japan was able to restrain the pace of liberalization. The effect was to protect various industries as they attempted to become internationally competitive.

Japanese restrictions on foreign direct investment (FDI) were equally significant. Although Japan desired investment capital, both the nation's business community and the economic bureaucrats opposed allowing foreign firms to acquire a controlling interest in Japanese companies, much less an entire sector of the economy. As administered by the bureaucracy, the effect of Japanese laws relating to foreign investment was severely restrictive (Table 1.2). Following the return of currency convertibility, American multinational companies such as Proctor and Gamble, Ford, and Na-

Corporate Debentures	External Bonds Issued	Claimable Assets Arising from Loans
0.0	—	4.0
0.0	—	34.5
0.0	—	49.4
0.0	—	15.3
0.0	—	47.1
0.0	—	93.7
0.0	—	124.0
0.0	—	231.5
0.0	—	127.6
0.0	9.8	128.2
2.7	62.5	379.6
0.1	50.0	637.5
0.0	219.0	947.4
0.5	235.0	789.6
263.5	122.2	845.9
562.0	54.6	971.0

Notes: Data refer to the value of investments validated under the Law Concerning Foreign Investment, including reinvestments. Participation in management refers to the acquisition of shares exceeding 15 percent of the total share issue of the company in the case of designated industries or 25 percent in the case of undesignated industries.

tional Cash Register established a significant presence in Western Europe. Bureaucratic resistance in Tokyo—supported by Japanese business interests—shielded Japan's economy from similar foreign involvement. What pressure the United States did exert on behalf of American firms yielded few results.

The asymmetry was perhaps greatest in the transfer of technology. U.S. national security policy called for making available to Japan the technology necessary for modernizing its economy. Official productivity programs fostered such diffusion of technological know-how, but in American eyes the principal mechanism was the market. In Japan, by contrast, acquisition of technology was not simply left to the private sector. Every purchase required government approval, usually from the Ministry of International Trade and Industry (MITI). Ministry bureaucrats used their position to assist Japanese concerns in driving the hardest bargains possible and to prevent foreign companies from establishing joint ventures that might lead to dominance over the Japanese partners. Against the entire Japanese system, American companies stood at a distinct disadvantage.

The great irony of the postwar period is the U.S. role in reinforcing the power of the bureaucrats who administered Japan's restrictive and nationalistic industrial policy. During the Occupation the Supreme Command for the Allied Powers (SCAP) governed Japan through the existing administrative structure. The effect was to consolidate the power of the bureaucracy and to expand its role in national life. After Japan regained its independence, the United States pressed Japan to maintain controls on trade with the Communist bloc, to impose restrictions on exports to the United States, and to enforce quality controls on manufactures for export. Even negotiations over liberalization of trade and investment enhanced the significance of the ministry bureaucrats. Thus, American policy continued to shape Japan's institutional landscape and the patterns of Japanese interaction with the outside world.

Although this arrangement is now familiar to students of the Japanese economy, the extent of American tolerance for Japanese restrictions on foreign economic opportunity at the time is striking and has yet to be adequately explained. The origins of this acquiescence deserve emphasis because they were inseparable from the Cold War. On a most basic level, the United States failed to recognize the Japanese economic structure for what it was—a different brand of capitalism and a formula for economic success. In part, Cold War strategy distracted President Eisenhower and his administration from commercial considerations. After Japan became a member of GATT in 1955, the president and his advisors shifted their focus to the spread of Communist influence in Latin America and the newly independent nations of Asia and the Middle East. Once Japan's economy was out of immediate danger, Japanese affairs simply did not draw as much high-level attention as before. When they did, the overriding concern was to strengthen rather than to strain the bilateral axis in the Cold War.

By highlighting the conflict between capitalism and Communism, the Cold War also obscured the differences between the many varieties of capitalism. Executive officials naturally recognized the discrepancies between Japanese—and, to a lesser extent, Western European—economic policies and the principles of liberal trade. Their failure was in thinking that the return of prosperity would put Japan's economy on the road to becoming more like that of the United States. To American authorities statism and restrictionism were paths to economic stagnation rather than strength. Such has usually been the case. Even the Japanese did not realize until the 1960s that their model of economic development—combining both heavy state involvement in the economy and a dynamic private sector—would propel the nation forward as quickly as it did. Although the long-range utility of postwar arrangements is dubious, in the short and medium term shielding Japan's economy as the ministries did worked to Japanese advantage.

Tolerance of foreign economic restrictions was an indication of American strength during the early postwar years. For good economic and political reasons, no one in the U.S. government wished to provoke a Japanese balance-of-payments crisis by forcing Japan to absorb more imports than it could afford to pay for. No one seems to have seriously entertained the notion that Japan's economy would catch up and pose a threat to entire sectors of the American economy. These two expectations of Japan—that its economy would become more like that of the United States and that it would lag behind for a long time—were part and parcel of the global order that took shape during the fifties. Much the same can be said with regard to Western Europe. These trading partners' rise to become powerful competitors during the sixties was, therefore, an unpleasant surprise for Americans. It set the stage for the protectionist sentiment of the seventies. The persistence of structural differences between the American and Japanese economies contributed to the sense that Japanese economic practice was "unfair."

The third theme of this work emphasizes how from the beginning an undercurrent of friction accompanied both the alliance and economic integration. Walter LaFeber has recently explored the long-standing pattern of conflict in U.S.-Japanese relations since the mid-nineteenth century in his fine book, *The Clash*. The extensive differences in structure and practice between the two economies guaranteed that conflict would arise. American alarm over Japanese competition in declining industries and Japanese restrictions on trade and investment were the natural consequences of bringing the two nations' economies closer together. Economic nationalism accompanied integration. Such friction also affected relations between the United States and its European trading partners. But the cross-investment linking the U.S. and the Western European economies eased tensions by giving each power a voice in the other's system.

Japanese popular frustration with the demands of the strategic partnership and the unpleasant fact of economic dependence on the United States also mounted as strategic cooperation between the two countries grew. LaFeber's analysis of the 1950s, which flows naturally from his perceptive account of the crisis leading to war the previous decade, correctly emphasizes American-Japanese political differences concerning policy toward China.[3] The most important American demand in the economic sphere was a virtual embargo on trade with the Chinese mainland, the economic

Table 1.3. *United States Balance of Trade with Japan, 1947–1971 ($ million)*

Year	Exports	Imports	Balance
1934–36 average	206	148	58
1947	60	35	25
1948	325	63	262
1949	468	82	386
1950	418	182	236
1951	601	205	396
1952	633	229	404
1953	686	262	424
1954	693	279	414
1955	683	432	251
1956	998	558	440
1957	1,319	601	718
1958	987	666	321
1959	1,079	1,029	50
1960	1,447	1,149	298
1961	1,837	1,055	782
1962	1,574	1,358	216
1963	1,844	1,498	346
1964	2,009	1,768	241
1965	2,080	2,414	−334
1966	2,364	2,963	−599
1967	2,695	2,999	−304
1968	2,954	4,054	−1,100
1969	3,490	4,888	−1,398
1970	4,652	5,875	−1,223
1971	4,055	7,259	−3,204

Sources: For 1934–1970: U.S. Department of Commerce, *Historical Statistics of the United States: Colonial Times to 1970*, part 2, 903–6; for 1971: Kurian, *Datapedia of the United States, 1790–2000*, 357–61 (Department of Commerce data).

component of U.S. containment of Chinese Communist power in East Asia. Japan's long-standing trade deficit with the United States caused the Japanese to be especially sensitive to restrictions on access to the American market.

Despite this friction, the alliance and the emerging economic partnership generated countervailing pressures that facilitated the resolution of disputes. The clash that LaFeber has identified in prewar relations between Japan and the United States has not reappeared with the same force as before. One aim of this study is to show how, underneath the many clashes over economic issues, the fifties witnessed the emergence of an order that was able to contain American-Japanese rivalry. The significance of the alliance to both governments and the growing interdependence of the two economies produced a far more compelling sense of common interest at the heights of power than would have been the case without the Cold War. Rather than being indifferent to Japan's welfare, the U.S. government desired a healthy Japanese economy. In the many conflicts over trade and investment, administration officials often preferred to keep talking rather than risk jeopardizing the strategic partnership. One effect was to reduce American leverage in commercial disagreements with Japan. For its part, the Japanese government held very closely to U.S. demands on issues such as Sino-Japanese trade and "voluntary" limits on exports. In retrospect, since these policies were highly unpopular in Japan, the United States spent a vast store of political capital on such issues. Most trade disputes were more politically sensitive than economically significant. The important economic change was the rapid expansion of bilateral trade[4] (Table 1.3). In short, American-Japanese trade friction during the 1950s marked the beginning of a pattern of conflict and compromise that endured throughout the Cold War era.

To focus exclusively on the element of conflict in the bilateral relationship, however, is to overlook the great achievement of the early Cold War years. In sharp contrast to the failure of the interwar period, the United States, Japan, and the other nations of the non-Communist world constructed an international order that enabled Japan to prosper while living at peace with its neighbors. This outcome was by no means foreordained. The sense during the fifties was that events could turn either way. At times policy makers on all sides exhibited more pessimism than circumstances warranted. But the commitment to building a new order proved stronger than the countervailing forces. In 1945 few could have imagined the course that events would take.

U.S. Strategy and the Problem of Japanese Economic Recovery

In order to situate the story of America and the Japanese miracle in time and to make clear how the interpretation here adds to the existing literature, it is useful to survey the separate bodies of scholarship on the history of the postwar years. Although grounded primarily in the archival record, this study has drawn from the many studies on both American policy and Japan.

The connection between U.S. strategy and foreign economic policy is familiar to those who have studied the Occupation of Japan from 1945 to 1952. In detailed studies based on a wealth of primary material, historians John W. Dower, William S. Borden, Howard B. Schonberger, and Michael Schaller, among others, have traced the course and reorientation of American East Asian policy after the Second World War. These scholars agree, as the Japanese recognized at the time, that when the Cold War escalated in the late 1940s the objectives of American policy shifted from reforming Japan to promoting Japanese revival.[5]

The histories of the Occupation period show that this reverse course in policy reflected the increasing importance of the American-Soviet rivalry in defining U.S. strategy and the growing role of cold warriors in shaping policy. Whereas the initial policy toward occupied Japan emphasized reform, the National Security Council's policy statement NSC 13/2 of 1948 set forth the goal of refashioning Japan into a strong anti-Communist ally much as the United States was supporting the establishment of a separate West German state in Europe.[6] The new policy reached out to business rather than continuing the breakup of Japan's large industrial combines or promoting the labor movement. By the end of the Occupation the Truman administration had even backed away from its demilitarization of Japan and was pressing for rearmament.

At the outset of the Occupation, reformers paid little heed to Japanese economic stability. In both Japan and Germany, American authorities focused almost exclusively on internal affairs. Within two years, the problems of rampant inflation, a persistent trade deficit, and the Japanese economy's failure to recover alarmed Washington just as similar economic conditions prompted the Marshall Plan for Europe and the 1948 currency reform in the Western zones of occupied Germany. The desire for Japanese economic stability and growth found expression in the stabilization program approved by the NSC in December 1948 and implemented the next year by the Detroit Banker Joseph M. Dodge. The Dodge Plan sought to restore fiscal order in Japan and to promote the nation's foreign trade by enforcing austerity at home. The world recession of 1950 undercut the initial gains, however, and the social price of austerity was high. Thus, the State Department experimented with another means to boost Japan's foreign trade: allowing the reestablishment of economic ties with mainland China.[7]

Given the precarious condition of Japan's economy and the tentative beginning toward repairing the fabric of the region's economy, the revolutionary impact of the outbreak of war in Korea in 1950 stands out. The war was a windfall for Japan. By coincidence and then design, the U.S. military became a prime customer of Japan's idle industries. In filling U.S. war orders, American and Japanese leaders found a way to revitalize economic enterprise and balance Japan's payments. But this "gift from the gods" had a price.[8] As many Japanese lamented at the time and scholarly research confirms, the war polarized international relations, alienated the United States and the PRC from each other, and isolated Japan from the Chinese mainland.

Releases of documents from archives in the PRC and the USSR suggest that the extent of this polarization was greater than previously recognized. Scholarly writing during the 1970s laid stress on how mutual (but especially American) misperception needlessly drove the United States and the PRC apart during the early postwar era. Recent work by Jian Chen and others drawing on Chinese and Soviet sources reveals the mutuality of the antagonism as well as a strong conflict of interest in the relationship. "By mid-1950," Chen has written, "Beijing and Washington had firmly perceived each other as a dangerous enemy." Convinced that a Chinese-American confrontation was inevitable, the Chinese Communists were sympathetic to the North Korean offensive and began planning to intervene in the war against the United States.[9]

One contribution of this book is to carry the story of U.S. policy toward Japan forward past the Occupation's end in 1952, a topic that has attracted strikingly little scholarly attention.[10] Events after 1952 are important because when the Occupation ended Japan's economy was unstable, prosperity remained elusive, and the nation was not yet integrated into international economic life. GNP did increase 11 percent in 1952, but, deflated for population, the index of Japanese industrial production that year was just barely above the average for the years 1934–35. Even this growth was not normal, self-sustaining economic activity. It depended on U.S. subsidies in the form of aid (totaling about $2.1 billion during the Occupation) and military purchases for the Korean War (Table 1.4).[11]

The most visible problem was a persistent trade deficit (Table 1.5). Japan's unenviable position as a populous nation with few natural resources is well known. Since industrialization it has been dependent on foreign trade for survival, and the outlook at the Occupation's end was particularly gloomy. In 1952 alone, Japan's commercial trade deficit exceeded $750 million. Shorn of its empire, Japan was importing 20 to 25 percent of its

Table 1.4. *Japan's Receipts from U.S. Military Expenditures, 1950–1960 ($ million)*

Year	Military Expenditure	ICA Procurement
1950	149	
1951	592	
1952	824	
1953	810	
1954	596	
1955	557	
1956	595	
1957	414	128
1958	375	101
1959	353	111
1960	392	147

Sources: For 1950: *Japan Economic Yearbook*, 1956, 31; for 1951–60: BOJ, *Economic Statistics of Japan*, 1961, 267.
Note: ICA = International Cooperation Administration.

Table 1.5. *Japan's Foreign Trade, 1945–1960 ($ million)*

Year	Exports	Imports	Balance
Sept. 1945–Dec. 1946	103.3	305.6	−202.3
1947	173.6	526.1	−352.5
1948	258.3	684.2	−425.9
1949	509.7	904.8	−395.1
1950	820.1	974.3	−154.2
1951	1,354.5	1,995.0	−640.5
1952	1,272.9	2,028.2	−755.3
1953	1,274.8	2,409.6	−1,134.8
1954	1,629.2	2,399.4	−770.2
1955	2,010.6	2,471.4	−460.8
1956	2,500.6	3,229.7	−729.1
1957	2,858.0	4,283.6	−1,425.6
1958	2,876.6	3,033.1	−156.5
1959	3,456.5	3,599.5	−143.0
1960	4,054.5	4,491.1	−436.6

Sources: Japan, Ministry of Foreign Affairs, *Statistical Survey of Economy of Japan*, 1962, 43. All figures are based on Ministry of Finance data.

Table 1.6. *Japan's Import Trade with China, 1930–1975 (¥ million)*

Year	Total	China	China as % of Total
1930	2,006	283	14.11
1935	3,272	350	10.70
1938	3,794	564	14.87
1947	20,265	182	0.90
1948	60,287	1,275	2.11
1949	284,455	5,588	1.96
1950	348,196	14,158	4.07
1951	737,241	7,778	1.06
1952	730,352	5,365	0.73
1953	867,469	10,692	1.23
1954	863,785	14,677	1.70
1955	889,715	29,080	3.27
1956	1,162,704	30,113	2.59
1957	1,542,091	28,794	1.87
1958	1,091,925	19,594	0.79
1959	1,295,817	6,810	0.53
1960	1,616,807	7,462	0.46
1965	2,940,847	80,894	2.75
1970	6,797,220	91,374	1.34
1971	6,909,956	112,683	1.63
1975	17,170,000	455,000	2.65

Sources: For 1930–1960: BOJ, *Economic Statistics of Japan*, 1961, 253; for 1965–71: Japan, Office of the Prime Minister, *Japan Statistical Yearbook*, 1972, 292–93; for 1975: *Japan Statistical Yearbook*, 1985, 336. All figures are based on Ministry of Finance data.

Notes: Prewar trade totals are adjusted to include Korea and Taiwan, which were then Japanese territories. China includes Manchuria and Guangdong (Kwangtung) Province.

foodstuffs. Virtually all of the raw materials on which an industrial economy depends—petroleum, iron ore, salt, cotton, and wool, for example—came from abroad.[12]

Compounding the expense was the Cold War division of Asia. Whereas the Asian mainland was a major prewar source of supply, postwar attempts to revive Sino-Japanese trade proved abortive (Tables 1.6 and 1.7). The U.S.-led embargo on trade with the PRC and North Korea begun in 1950 brought Sino-Japanese trade to a virtual halt. In 1951 Japan's imports from mainland China of $21.6 million amounted to a mere 1.1 percent of total import trade. Denied access to nearby resources, Japan turned to dollar areas for iron ore,

Table 1.7. *Japan's Export Trade with China, 1930–1975 (¥ million)*

Year	Total	China	China as % of Total
1930	1,871	348	18.60
1935	3,276	575	17.55
1938	3,939	1,166	29.60
1947	10,148	761	7.50
1948	52,022	287	0.55
1949	169,841	928	0.55
1950	298,021	7,068	2.37
1951	488,777	2,098	0.41
1952	458,243	216	0.05
1953	458,943	1,634	0.36
1954	586,525	6,875	1.17
1955	723,816	10,277	1.42
1956	900,229	24,242	2.69
1957	1,028,887	21,774	2.12
1958	1,035,562	18,216	1.76
1959	1,244,337	1,313	0.11
1960	1,459,633	981	0.07
1965	3,042,627	88,213	2.90
1970	6,954,367	204,796	2.94
1971	8,392,768	201,875	2.40
1975	16,545,000	670,000	4.04

Sources: For 1930–60: BOJ, *Economic Statistics of Japan*, 1961, 251; for 1965–71: Japan, Office of the Prime Minister, *Japan Statistical Yearbook*, 1972, 292–93; for 1975: *Japan Statistical Yearbook*, 1985, 336. All figures are based on Ministry of Finance data.

Notes: China includes Manchuria and Guangdong Province. Prewar trade totals include Korea and Taiwan, then Japanese territories.

coking coal, wheat, and other basic commodities (Table 1.8). Paying for dollar-area imports was burdensome because they consumed precious foreign exchange.[13]

Japan's export trade was in even greater disarray. The Pacific and Korean wars closed valuable export markets for Japanese goods (Table 1.9). Yet the opportunity lost because of the division of Asia must not be overstated. Prewar trade patterns were dependent to an enormous extent on the Japanese political and military presence in Korea, Manchuria, China, and Taiwan. After the war Japan's major imports (in terms of value) such as rice, cotton, and petroleum came from the dollar area; the imperative was to penetrate these markets to earn dollars to pay for them. A reorientation of trade westward also promised access to the new technology required to modernize Japanese industry.

The problem was that Japan's export trade was unequal to this task of paying for its imports. During the war almost one-third of industrial capacity was destroyed.[14] The war also arrested the technological development of Japanese industries, thus widening the gap between Japan's level of technology and the best industrial technology available in the West. Changes in markets abroad underscored the need to modernize. The light industries that had propelled Japan forward in the first half of the century were an insufficient foundation for national prosperity in the second. Markets in which Japan had traditionally enjoyed a price advantage, such as textiles, tuna fish packing, and chinaware, had largely matured. Japanese industries faced increasingly strong competition in such markets from newly industrializing nations. Japanese goods in the newer higher-value-added sectors such as steel and chemicals, however, stood at a competitive disadvantage in world markets.[15] Japan's best hope for future export growth was, paradoxically, those industries which were not yet competitive abroad. To have relied on the labor-intensive industries of the prewar era would have condemned the country to being forever an inferior economic power.

If Japan's influence on the United States after the Occupation was imperceptible, and the U.S.-Japanese relationship of primary concern to very few Americans, the power of the Japanese economy that attracted American attention in subsequent decades was an important legacy of the fifties. For it was during that decade that Japan's economic success, and the structure underpinning it, took firm root.

Toward a Liberal Economic Order

In the same way that American policy toward Japan flowed from national security considerations, the effort to promote Japanese economic revival fit into policy on trade and investment. Beginning with the passage of the Reciprocal Trade Agreements Act (RTAA) in 1934, U.S. policy called for reducing barriers to world trade and creating a system of multilateral trade and payments. In what Alfred E. Eckes Jr. calls "Cordell Hull's Tariff Revolution," implementation of the RTAA dismantled the protective walls shielding the U.S. economy from foreign competition.[16] The act's initial duration was three years. It gave the president the authority to negotiate with other countries for mutual reductions (or increases) of up to 50 percent in tariff rates. Subsequent renewals enabled successive presidential administrations

Table 1.8. *Japan's Imports by Area, 1935, 1950, 1955, 1960*

Area[a]	Volume (¥ million)			
	1935	1950	1955	1960
Asia[b]	1,671	113,587	325,421	506,550
China[c]	350	14,158	29,080	7,462
Southeast Asia[d]	—	70,129	189,834	252,647
Europe	351	13,871	62,999	161,442
United Kingdom	82	2,414	13,650	35,689
West Germany	121	2,460	16,648	44,264
USSR[e]	18	266	1,100	30,690
North America	870	166,723	367,588	691,685
United States	810	150,565	278,021	556,334
South America	43	14,172	37,432	52,109
Africa	69	9,454	22,664	59,002
Oceania	249	30,389	73,569	145,955
Special Areas	19	—	42	64
Total	3,272	348,196	889,715	1,616,807

Source: BOJ, *Economic Statistics of Japan*, 1961, 253–54. All figures are based on Ministry of Finance data.
[a] The country specified in these statistics is classified according to the place of origin or manufacture.
[b] Prewar figures for Asia are adjusted to include imports from Korea and Taiwan, which were then Japanese territories. Turkey is included in Asia.

to rewrite American tariff policy, revising rates downward and signaling a U.S. commitment to building an interdependent international economy.[17]

From the birth of the republic forward American statesmen have often championed the ideal of free trade, but not until the 1930s did the free trade become a defining principle of American foreign economic policy.[18] Tariffs fell briefly during the presidency of Woodrow Wilson. Republican Congresses then raised rates again in the Fordney-McCumber (1922) and Smoot-Hawley (1930) tariff acts.[19] The Great Depression transformed the context of U.S. policy. The United States could no longer boost its exports without allowing its trading partners to earn the dollars necessary to pay for American goods. Yet the political consequences of tariff reduction were most appealing to Cordell Hull, the man whose name is synonymous with the quest to reduce trade barriers. A longtime believer in free trade as a Democratic lawmaker from Tennessee, Hull achieved the power to reorient American commercial policy as President Roosevelt's secretary of state (1933–44). The RTAA was his pet project, inseparable from his passionate belief in the need to restore "order under law in international relations."

	Percentage Distribution		
1935	1950	1955	1960
51.1	32.6	36.6	31.3
10.7	4.1	3.3	0.5
NA	20.1	21.3	15.6
10.7	4.0	7.1	10.0
2.5	0.7	1.5	2.2
3.7	0.7	1.9	2.7
0.6	0.1	0.1	1.9
26.6	47.9	41.3	42.8
34.8	43.2	31.2	34.4
1.3	4.1	4.2	3.2
2.1	2.7	2.5	3.6
7.6	8.7	8.3	9.0
0.6	—	0.0	0.0
100.0	100.0	100.0	99.9

  c China includes Manchuria and Guangdong (Kwangtung) Province, but does not include Taiwan.
  d Southeast Asia includes Hong Kong, South Vietnam, Cambodia, Laos, Thailand, Malaya, Singapore, the Philippines, Indonesia, Burma, India, Pakistan, and Ceylon.
  e The Soviet Union includes its Asian area.

Only then, he believed, would peace and the opportunity to promote economic welfare be secure.[20]

The irony of Hull's legacy is that while he was unable to foster the peace he desired, the Second World War and the Cold War combined to make liberal trade a primary goal of American policy. In the Atlantic Charter of 1941 President Roosevelt and British prime minister Winston Churchill expressed the new vision championing equal access to the trade and raw materials necessary for prosperity, economic collaboration among nations, and freedom of the seas.[21] At the Bretton Woods Conference in July 1944 U.S. delegates began to build the institutions necessary to enforce rules in international trade and finance. Along with the International Monetary Fund (IMF) and the World Bank, the Americans proposed a grand new body called the International Trade Organization (ITO). In November 1946, the United States invited twenty-two other nations to a round of multilateral tariff negotiations at Geneva.[22]

The postwar structure assumed concrete form in 1947 and 1948. Since the Republican Party was traditionally the party of protection, the Republi-

Table 1.9. *Japan's Exports by Market, 1935, 1950, 1955, 1960*

Area[a]	Volume (¥ million)			
	1935	1950	1955	1960
Asia[b]	2,085	137,931	303,460	540,325
China[c]	575	7,068	10,277	981
Southeast Asia[d]	NA	102,011	203,270	359,640
Europe	259	35,893	74,086	178,200
United Kingdom	119	9,352	21,876	43,396
West Germany	27	3,692	9,058	23,868
USSR[e]	28	147	748	21,387
North America	580	75,688	191,547	477,977
United States	536	64,547	161,732	389,837
South America	73	11,166	53,533	64,657
Africa	184	26,554	74,009	126,637
Oceania	95	10,789	27,181	71,763
Special Areas	—	—	—	74
Total	3,276	298,021	723,816	1,459,633

Source: BOJ, *Economic Statistics of Japan*, 1961, 251–52. All figures are based on Ministry of Finance data.
[a] The country specified in these statistics is classified according to the place of final destination.
[b] Prewar figures for Asia are adjusted to include imports from Korea and Taiwan, which were then Japanese territories. Turkey is included in Asia.

cans' victory in November 1946 (which gave the party control of Congress) raised the question of the U.S. commitment to multilateralism. But the administration won the support of the Republican leadership by agreeing to establish a governmental mechanism to respond to the applications of domestic industry for relief under an escape clause, an arrangement that President Truman established by executive order on 25 February 1947.[23] By autumn nations participating in the trade negotiations agreed upon a General Agreement on Tariffs and Trade. It consisted of a code of practices and schedules of tariff reductions applying to about one-half of world trade. Approximately 54 percent of American dutiable imports were affected, with a weighted average reduction of 35 percent.[24]

Despite the successful launching of GATT, the ITO never came into being. Although the State Department, which negotiated the comprehensive charter of March 1948, regarded the ITO charter as a pragmatic compromise, the proposal enjoyed little support and drew considerable criticism. Significantly, the opposition did not stem solely (or even primarily) from fear of import penetration. Rather, many American businessmen correctly

	Percentage Distribution		
1935	1950	1955	1960
63.6	46.3	41.9	37.0
17.6	2.4	1.4	0.1
—	34.2	28.1	24.6
7.9	12.0	10.2	12.2
3.6	3.1	3.0	3.0
0.8	1.2	1.3	1.6
0.9	0.1	0.1	1.5
17.7	25.4	26.5	32.7
16.4	21.7	22.3	26.7
2.2	3.8	7.4	4.4
5.6	8.9	10.2	8.7
2.9	3.6	3.8	4.9
—	—	—	0.0
99.9	100.0	100.0	99.9

[c] China includes Manchuria and Guangdong (Kwangtung) Province, but does not include Taiwan.

[d] Southeast Asia includes Hong Kong, South Vietnam, Cambodia, Laos, Thailand, Malaya, Singapore, the Philippines, Indonesia, Burma, India, Pakistan, and Ceylon.

[e] The Soviet Union includes its Asian area.

argued that the ITO charter did not go far enough to remove trade barriers set up by foreign countries. As a compromise arrangement, the charter left the Western European nations considerable room to deploy the heavy hand of the state in pursuit of such goals as full employment and planned development. Concluding that the Republican Senate would reject the ITO, the Truman administration never submitted it for ratification.[25] GATT thus became the principal institution responsible for regulating world trade. Consistent with the Cold War division of Europe, the Soviet bloc remained apart from the emerging multilateral system.

The Truman Doctrine of March 1947 and escalating tension with the Soviet Union put the opponents of internationalism in whatever form on the defensive. When the RTAA came up for renewal in 1948, the Republicans sought slight modification rather than wholesale revision of policy. At Republican insistence, the new law included a "peril-point" clause. It required the U.S. Tariff Commission to determine, before negotiations began, the level that could be agreed upon without jeopardizing domestic industry.[26] "Security became a bipartisan affair," political scientist Daniel

Verdier has explained, "and free trade was laid in the procrustean bed of security. The trade-security linkage, in turn, prepared the ground for the transformation of tariff-making from a partisan process into an executive politics process."[27]

Japan represented a crucial test of the postwar order and benefited from the course of American policy. In 1948, as part of its effort to promote Japanese recovery, the Truman administration pressed for Japanese association with GATT. At the first session in Havana (February–March), U.S. delegates unofficially floated the idea of granting most-favored-nation treatment (MFN) to Japan and other occupied areas under a protocol to GATT. The other delegates were unwilling to go along. Representatives from the United Kingdom later informed the Americans that they would not agree to MFN for Japan. Despite this initial rejection, the Truman administration made MFN for Japan a clear objective of U.S. policy. At the GATT session at Annecy in 1949 the United States placed the matter on the agenda, but later withdrew it in the face of widespread opposition. A working group recommended inviting Western Germany and Korea, but not Japan, to take part in the tariff negotiations at Torquay in 1950.[28] An economic order failing to include Japan was guaranteed to be both incomplete and unstable. Yet meaningful Japanese participation in postwar institutions was far from certain in 1950.

Analysts of economic history have disagreed on the sources of postwar changes, their extent, and the significance of their consequences. American policy makers at the time tended to cast themselves in the heroic role of building a liberal international order that would enable the nations of the world to avoid falling back into the pattern of the 1930s. Scholars have generally reaffirmed such views, in large measure because they have shared the same economic principles. In his detailed study of Eisenhower's foreign economic policy, for example, Burton Kaufman gives the president high marks for securing renewal of the RTAA and bringing Japan into GATT. To the extent that he is critical of Eisenhower, it is for not fighting harder for trade liberalization.[29]

Beginning during the late 1960s, flowering during the next decade, and then returning with a vengeance after the Cold War's end, a popular reaction against both the postwar order and the principles of liberal trade set in. In the face of foreign (and especially Japanese) trade competition, many Americans have come to believe that, in the interest of security, the postwar presidential administrations opened the American market to a flood of foreign manufactures, while permitting unreasonable restrictions abroad against American exports. This view finds expression in revisionist scholarship such as Eckes's book, *Opening America's Market* (1995).

The present study emphasizes the need for a more balanced view of past foreign economic policy. All writing reflects the concerns of its time, and scholarly work is no exception. Without denying the many difficulties that U.S. industries have faced in their competition with foreign rivals, the American economic record is not as grim as it seemed to Eckes and others during the 1980s and early 1990s. U.S. economic vitality in the 1990s, particularly a continuing ability to foster new industries, illustrates the inherent dynamism of an open and competitive system. Although protectionist economies may display impressive strength at certain moments, the anemic performance of Japan and Germany in the 1990s stands as an example that in time governments can get it wrong. Restrictive practices intended to protect the economy can have the contrary effect of stifling the innovation required to maintain a position of economic leadership, thus resulting in stagnation rather than continued growth.[30]

In casting advocates of trade liberalization as ideologues willing to sacrifice American workers on the altar of free-trade theory Eckes risks becoming equally doctrinaire in his criticism. Regarding the early Cold War years, any attempt to lay the blame for the difficulties of American industry on American foreign economic and defense policies is unconvincing. Security considerations were an important source of American policy during that decade. But the evidence from the 1950s shows that Eckes overstates the extent of trade concessions, especially with regard to Japan. Domestic opponents of free trade were actually more vocal and influential during the fifties than during the previous decade. Despite administration enthusiasm for trade liberalization, American policy contained numerous restrictions on most agricultural products, manufactures of labor-intensive industries, and many goods exported by Japan. At least with regard to the 1950s, the evidence does not bear out Eckes's claim that the institutional provisions to protect domestic producers from injurious competition "were largely window dressing."[31] This is not to deny that Japanese competition held the potential to have a disruptive impact on domestic industry. But the United States possessed—and often employed—the ability to protect domestic industry, usually by demanding that Japan voluntarily restrict its exports. The most notable example was the case of cotton textiles.

Consistent with business criticism of the ITO at the time, more significant than concessions to trading partners was U.S. acquiescence in restrictions against American exports and outward foreign investment. This willingness to tolerate discrimination stemmed in part from the mistaken belief that the American economy would remain far ahead of all likely competition. But American protectionism also played a significant role. U.S. representatives could not effectively demand that others open their markets when the United States refused to do the same. With few exceptions, the most important being Senator Eugene Millikin (R.-Colo.), the advocates of protection with whom Eckes sympathizes were far more concerned with protecting the home market than with expanding the nation's export trade.

The contribution of this study is to spell out the dynamics of the interaction betweeen the movement toward trade liberalization and countervailing pressures for reform as they applied to Japan. It is tempting to take Japan's readmission into the international community for granted. But the United Kingdom and other GATT members fought against Japanese accession to the General Agreement. In contrast to their favorable reception to German participation in GATT, several contracting parties sought to attach conditions to Japanese membership—particularly the right to discriminate specifically against Japanese trade—if Japan were admitted. The U.S. executive branch fought hard on Japan's behalf against restrictions abroad and attempted to secure Japanese reciprocity. Progress toward Japanese reintegration into the Western trading bloc was slow and contentious. By pressing successfully to bring Japan into GATT on the basis of equality, however, the Eisenhower administration laid a stable foundation for both the Cold War alliance and Japan's growth in later years.

The Japanese Miracle

The final body of scholarship from which this book draws and on which it builds is the literature on the phenomenal growth of Japan's postwar economy. Over the course of the period 1946–76, Japan's economy grew 55-fold.[32] By the Cold War's end, the identification of Japan with corporate power had become so complete that few could appreciate how bleak the nation's prospects were in the early fifties. How did Japan accomplish this transformation? The technical means of Japan's economic triumph are a matter of record: high rates of savings and capital investment, acquisition and application of new industrial technology, successful penetration of foreign markets, and ever expanding domestic demand. This list is by no means exhaustive. The real debates over Japan's resurgence are less about the main facts of its postwar expansion than the sources of such impressive performance, particularly the miracle years from the mid-fifties through the sixties.

This book does not focus on Japan's internal affairs, but the ongoing scholarly debate over the significance of the state in Japanese development and the matter of Japanese uniqueness are highly relevant. Japanese observers have long insisted that Japan's national character has contributed to the nation's economic success by fostering consensus and cooperation among government, ruling party, leaders of industry, and the people.[33] Specialists in Japanese studies have also long understood that Japan possessed many unique institutions that have fostered postwar economic achievement: consensus-oriented corporate management, the seniority wage system, and enterprise unions, to name only a few.[34] Perhaps it is because Japan is so alien to most westerners that the demand for an all-encompassing theory to explain Japanese economic success has been so strong. Describing Japan as a "system" designed to promote economic growth, rather than being a nation-state like most of its trading partners, the Dutch journalist Karel van Wolferen provided the model that achieved popular acclaim in the late 1980s.[35] Critics of familiar social scientific approaches to the study of Japan like van Wolferen have called themselves revisionists, and their work has sparked a wide-ranging debate. Although the present work may be understood as a critical response to most revisionist literature, the aim is to understand the history of the early postwar years rather than to join in the debate on more recent affairs. Thus, it focuses narrowly on the revisionists' interpretation of Japan's postwar economic development, particularly the role ascribed to what Chalmers Johnson has called "industrial policy."[36]

The inspiration for revisionist thinking was the inescapable fact that, especially during the fifties and sixties, the Japanese government intervened in economic life to an extent wholly inconsistent with the principles of neoclassical economic theory. The pioneering study was Johnson's book, MITI *and the Japanese Miracle* (1982). It is a history of the Ministry of International Trade and Industry as well as a compelling analysis of the relationship between Japanese industrial policy and economic growth from 1925 to 1975. Johnson's thesis is that Japan is a state-guided market system, and that state guidance of economic enterprise has been the crucial element in Japanese success. Taking a broad view of Japan's many institutions, he argues that a commitment to growth is inherent in the nation's postwar structure and organization. The government's economic ministries, particularly MITI, business organizations, enterprise unions, and various other institutions together form an entire system whose reason for being is to promote Japanese growth.

"Industrial policy," as Johnson describes it, is the substance of state guidance of industrial development. Classifying Japan as a "developmental state"—as opposed to a "market-oriented system" (like the United States)—Johnson emphasizes the goal-oriented character of government intervention in the Japanese economy.[37] Ably led by the bureaucrats at the top, particularly in MITI, the system has supposedly avoided the dangers associated with excessive statism on the one hand, and the disadvantages of laissez-faire on the other. The point deserving emphasis is the flexible character of Japan's industrial policy. Like the mercantilism of seventeenth-century Europe, it is an expression of economic nationalism, but it is not so narrowly conceived. Industrial policy may mean trade protection, capital controls, or like measures. But it can also mean participation in free-trade relationships when the national interest suggests it would be advantageous to do so. The criterion is outcome, not procedure.[38]

After the publication of *MITI*, the notion that Japan and other Asian economies have pursued a model of development wholly different from the market economies of the West took on a life of its own. In his comparative study, *Governing the Market* (1990), for example, Robert Wade has emphasized that the governments of other successful industrializers like Taiwan and South Korea have intervened in economic life far beyond behavior consistent with the tenets of liberalism. Their success was due in part to the planners not getting it wrong. The world economy is littered with examples of nations whose governments have failed their economies badly. Japan was fortunate that its planners did not let interventionist policies distort prices, confer special advantages on only a select few, or otherwise interfere with their country's growth.[39]

Since the 1980s the economic and scholarly climate has turned against the state-centered paradigm. The collapse of Japan's so-called bubble economy during the early 1990s and the currency crisis that struck the region in 1997 have tarnished the popular reputation of the economic bureaucrats and raised doubts about the Japanese model of economic development. Academic analysis of previous industrial policy has also forced a reassessment of the bureaucrats' wisdom in the past. An outstanding example of such research is that of Richard Beason and David Weinstein. Comparing thirteen sectors that received support through Japan's various industrial policies from 1955 to 1990, these researchers found that support was haphazard and uncoordinated. Significantly, the most-helped sectors were not the winners (those which experienced the highest rates of growth). Rather, they were the slow-growth industries such as mining and textiles.[40] Other scholars have questioned the existence of any consensus in favor of growth during the early postwar years.[41] Such findings do not deny Japan's economic success, but they suggest that Japan's bureaucrats were not the miracle men of revisionist acclaim.

Michael E. Porter's landmark study, *The Competitive Advantage of Nations* (1990), has reaffirmed the central role of competition in creating national wealth. In its analysis of the export industries of ten countries including Japan, the study's focus is the firm. Competition in the domestic market, a hallmark of Japan's successful export industries such as consumer electronics, forces companies to innovate and to upgrade. A lack of competition, by contrast, encourages complacency and inefficiency, as Japan's highly protected and highly inefficient agricultural sector bears out.[42]

Studies of Japanese policy have also questioned whether the bureaucrats were really the source of government policy. In so doing they effectively reduce the role of the state in leading Japanese economic enterprise. Kent Calder, for example, has studied Japan's credit industry, and the Industrial Bank of Japan in particular. He emphasizes the divisions within the government, and a resulting paralysis in decision making. The government successfully created an environment for Japan's development, but within that environment Calder identifies Japan's large industrial firms as being the distinctive and decisive force in Japanese capitalism. In a survey of American multinationals in Japan that covers the period from 1899 to 1980, Mark Mason has likewise found that Japanese business, rather than the economic planners in Tokyo, initiated and shaped the application and often the removal of postwar capital controls influencing American foreign direct investment in Japan.[43]

With the sweeping claims for industrial policy now scaled down, it is possible to go beyond searching for a single cause of the Japanese miracle. Japan's economic revival was clearly born of a complex configuration of factors, the most obvious of which comprise the domestic context. Gazing inward, however, risks obscuring one of the most recognized and least studied variables: the international context. The Japanese system, however one defines it, cannot be isolated from the world in which it flourished. During the fifties the forces reshaping the world more than any other were the escalating Cold War and the U.S. commitment to rebuilding a thriving world economy.

Chapter Two
TO KEEP THE JAPANESE ON OUR SIDE

In January 1951 Ambassador John Foster Dulles made a last round of calls in Washington before traveling to Tokyo to confer with Japanese leaders about a peace treaty. The atmosphere in the capital was tense. The aftershocks of China's "fall" to communism and the intervention of the Chinese Communists in the Korean War still reverberated. Fighting in Korea dragged on. Vulnerable, President Truman's administration was under fire. Led by Robert A. Taft of Ohio, Senate Republicans launched an attack on the Democrats' foreign policy. Fittingly, Senator Joe McCarthy (R.-Wis.) made the most sensational allegations, charging that a vast international Communist conspiracy had hoodwinked even the war hero General George C. Marshall.[1]

Dulles's conversations with congressional leaders and administration officials, however, seemed untouched by the partisan tension poisoning the air and polarizing the nation's leaders. The purpose of his trip, he informed each group of listeners, was to discover the prospects and price of "a reliable commitment of the Japanese nation to the cause of the free world." Dulles explained that a settlement required making economic and security assurances to Japan. Although Senate Republicans were challenging the president on collective security in Europe and foreign aid, Dulles's comments met with no objection. Rather, each meeting closed with "complete agreement that it was important to keep the Japanese on our side."[2]

For the rest of the year Japan policy remained above the partisan fray at home. As a Republican, Dulles owed his appointment to the administration's desire for a bipartisan Japan policy. In this position between parties he was able to broker a consensus national policy and then negotiate the peace treaty and bilateral security agreement signed at San Francisco in September 1951. As intended, the settlement defined Japan as a U.S. ally in the Cold War. Forty-eight other nations signed the peace treaty, but the agreement was essentially a separate peace between Japan and the nations of the American-led "free world," a point that the U.S.-Japan Security Treaty underscored.

The familiar perspective on the peace with Japan emphasizes Dulles's ability to secure the agreement of so many parties of divergent interests to a liberal settlement.[3] Without detracting from this achievement, viewing the negotiations in the context of Japan's broader postwar resurgence reveals their significance in new ways. As prelude rather than finale, the peace settlement is a window on official attitudes and the divisions among the main actors shaping the course of events after the Occupation. Dulles's peace treaty diplomacy testifies to the American consensus on the need to win Japanese loyalty in the Cold War. In sharp contrast with so many other concerns of diplomacy during the fifties, American debate over policy toward Japan—both within the Truman and Eisenhower administrations and in public—occurred within a very narrow field of possibilities. With few exceptions, all parties agreed upon the overriding priority of strategic cooperation.

Underneath this desire for strategic solidarity, however, lingered anxiety about the future. Despite Japan's pro-American orientation during the Occupation, U.S. leaders worried that the alliance might unravel. A chief source of this anxiety was Japan's fragile economy. From the year 1950 forward, doubts about Japan's reliability and future prospects intertwined ever more tightly with U.S. strategy and foreign economic policy in East Asia. The effect was to reinforce the American commitment to promote Japanese recovery. The same disjuncture between hope and anxiety affected relations between the United States and West Germany, but it applied with much greater force to relations with Japan. Not until 1960, with the revision of the security treaty, was the bilateral axis secure. Even then, American concerns did not disappear.

Competing Strategies of Containment

The logic of the U.S. postwar effort to contain Communist expansion abroad led naturally to closer cooperation with its erstwhile enemies. In Germany the new line confirmed the nation's postwar division and accelerated the creation of a separate West German state (created in 1949, given internal independence in 1952, and recognized as a sovereign state in 1955). In Japan the immediate effect was to prolong the Occupation. Outward differences aside, both Japan and the Federal Republic of Germany were becoming client states of the United States.

By the spring of 1947 the Truman administration heard several calls for an end to the Occupation of Japan. A State Department working group completed a draft treaty. General MacArthur himself called for a peace agreement. Japanese government officials were also discreetly inquiring into the possibility of a settlement.[4] During the summer of 1947 the USSR twice brushed aside American calls for an allied peace conference of Far Eastern Commission nations, suggesting instead that the proper forum was the Council of Foreign Ministers (where the Soviets would enjoy the right of veto). On the American side, George Kennan, then head of the State Department's Policy Planning Staff (PPS), stifled talk of peace. Suspicious of Soviet intentions and convinced that reform had weakened Japan, Kennan and other planners refused to relinquish control of the islands. The Occupation entered a new phase, its goals being Japanese economic revival and a purge of leftist influence in politics.[5]

The collapse of Nationalist rule under Chiang Kai-shek (Jiang Jieshi) on the Chinese mainland the next year reinforced this shift in policy. In response to events in China, President Truman's advisors divided into two hostile factions that advanced competing strategies of containment.[6] The hard-line camp within the administration, centered around the Joint Chiefs of Staff and the Department of Defense, held out for an aggressive anti-Communist policy toward the PRC. This group included defense secretaries James Forrestal (1947–49) and Louis Johnson (1949–50). Influential lawmakers, among them Senators H. Alexander Smith (R.-N.J.) and William Knowland (R.-Calif.), held sympathetic views. Hard-liners supported sending military aid to the Nationalists on the mainland and Taiwan and opposed recognition of the PRC. They also desired an embargo of the mainland economy, both to contain its power and to prevent Japanese dependence upon areas under Communist control. The idea was to maintain the maximum possible pressure on the two bastions of Communist power in Asia, the USSR and the PRC. This strategy depended on indefinite retention of military bases in Japan, or continued occupation if at all possible.

The second group, centered in the Department of State, envisioned a less confrontational strategy. Equally anti-Communist, but more sensitive to the politics in the region, Secretary of State Dean Acheson, and key advisors such as Kennan and W. Walton Butterworth, sought to frustrate Soviet intentions while enhancing American influence by holding out the prospect of cooperation with Beijing. Fearful that open confrontation would drive the Chinese Communist Party (CCP) into Moscow's arms, the State Department opposed prolonging the civil war on the Chinese mainland, although it did support extending economic aid to Taiwan. The hope was that the prospect of American recognition and trade might induce Communist moderation. Permitting Sino-Japanese trade would fuel Japanese recovery. Aware of the Japanese desire to end the Occupation, the Supreme Command for the Allied Powers and the State Department were more willing to permit the reemergence of an independent Japan, tied to the United States for its security. Maintaining allied forces "without continuing Japanese consent," these officials reasoned, "would not only be ineffectual in promoting U.S. security." It threatened to undermine the American position in both Japan and Asia.[7]

President Truman did not resolve this conflict of visions before the outbreak of the Korean War. At the close of the NSC meeting of 29 December 1949, however, he signaled his willingness to move toward a Japanese settlement. He said that he "had no doubt" that the United States and the United Kingdom "could negotiate a peace treaty with Japan whether the USSR participated or not."[8] His announcement undercut the long-standing claim of the military that a treaty had to provide for U.S. military use of Japan and, at the same time, meet with the approval of the PRC and the USSR. The effect, if not the intent, of such mutually exclusive demands had been to prolong indefinitely the Occupation.

As the president's advisors considered a separate peace in the following months, the outline of a consensus began to emerge. Neither department believed that a Soviet attack on Japan was imminent. Both sides believed that limited Japanese rearmament and U.S. retention of military bases in Japan were necessary after the Occupation. They also envisioned guaranteeing Japanese security by means of a bilateral security treaty and the creation of a pact of non-Communist states in the region.[9] Differences nevertheless remained. Whereas the Joint Chiefs of Staff (JCS) viewed Japan as a forward military base in a potential war with the USSR, the diplomats emphasized the defensive character of the U.S. presence in Japan. Defense officials, particularly Army Under Secretary Tracy S. Voorhees, doubted Japanese loyalty and political maturity. They sought to postpone indefinitely the conclusion of a treaty, wishing instead to permit only partial restoration of Japanese sovereignty. Acheson and his advisors also worried about the prospect of Japan opting for neutrality in the Cold War. But in their view a lenient peace treaty was the best guarantee of maintaining a pro-American government and promoting long-term cooperation.[10]

Unfortunately for the secretary of state, controversy over China policy in the spring of 1950 put the State Department on the defensive. In February, the previously undistinguished Senator McCarthy catapulted himself to prominence with wild allegations of Communist subversion in the department. No such conspiracy was found, but the ensuing investigation severely politicized U.S. policy making. The same month Americans learned that the PRC and the USSR had signed a thirty-year treaty of friendship. The extent of the security threat to Japan was unclear, but the pact shocked the department and the nation. Acheson's advisors had mistakenly expected a quick break between the two Communist giants, not Sino-Soviet solidarity. Hard-liners saw in these events an opportunity to shift the direction of policy their way.[11]

Dulles and the Search for a Consensus Policy

In an attempt to deflect partisan criticism of his administration's policies, President Truman invited a leading Republican into the government. At the request of Senator Arthur Vandenberg (R.-Mich.), Truman and Acheson chose John Foster Dulles. Dulles had long been fashioning himself as the party's authority on foreign affairs. Senator Vandenberg was one of his chief sponsors. It is unclear what assignment Secretary Acheson had in mind for his department's new "consultant." On 18 May, following Butterworth's appointment as ambassador to Sweden, Acheson assigned Dulles primary responsibility for negotiation of the Japanese treaty. The matter was not at that time a partisan issue, but Acheson clearly sought to blunt Republican criticism of administration policy. Dean Rusk, then assistant secretary for Far Eastern affairs, had written the previous month about "how we might best use Mr. Dulles": "*First priority* should be given to development of a bipartisan position on the Japanese Peace Settlement."[12]

Despite an outward similarity in the course of their careers, Acheson and Dulles shared little in temperament and manner except for a hearty dislike of each other. Few men symbolized as visibly as Acheson the American establishment of which he was a part. The secretary's neatly trimmed mustache and impeccable attire set him apart in Washington, only the most obvious manifestations of a confidence cultivated in youth and flowing from achievement. An affluent childhood in Connecticut, attendance at Yale University and Harvard Law School, and an apprenticeship as a clerk for Supreme Court Justice Louis D. Brandeis prepared Acheson well for a lucrative legal career and public service at the heights of power. Of President Truman's appointments as president, none was more important than Acheson. Of the members of the cabinet, none was closer to the president or more influential than the secretary of state.[13]

As a distinguished corporate lawyer who moved easily from the position of senior partner at the New York law firm of Sullivan and Cromwell to national politics, Dulles was as imposing a figure as Acheson. But if Acheson was the quintessential diplomat, Dulles is remembered as a partisan and missionary. Both men possessed exceptional minds. In contrast to Acheson's social poise, however, Dulles often displayed the awkwardness of an outsider. In a sense he was. Although born in the house of his grandfather John W. Foster, who served briefly as secretary of state under Benjamin Harrison, Dulles grew up in the small upstate New York community of Watertown, where his father was minister of the First Presbyterian Church. He then attended Princeton Theological Seminary and George Washington Law School. Despite success on Wall Street and a diplomatic career that began in 1907, when he served as his grandfather's secretary at the Second Hague Peace Conference, influence of Dulles's rustic boyhood endured. He was, in the words of one biographer, "a rare blend of Spartan and sophisticate."[14]

History has not been kind to Dulles. His fiery public speeches as a Republican campaigner and secretary of state projected the image of a crusader leading the nation on a holy war against communism. Since Dulles neither lived to write his own memoirs nor recorded his thoughts in a diary, private character and public caricature have merged in the American mind. Recent scholarship has led to a dramatic reestimation of President Eisenhower, but it has not similarly rehabilitated Dulles. Scholars now agree that in private he was pragmatic and appreciated the complexity of problems facing the United States. As a man, however, his image remains dour and forbidding. Few appreciate the "unexpected fun and lack of reserve behind that exterior" which those who worked with him remember. There exists no consensus regarding his impact on U.S. foreign policy.[15]

That Dulles was able to fashion a Japanese settlement sufficiently acceptable to the different branches of his own government and to the other signatories stands as one of the great achievements of his diplomatic career. It also placed him at the center of U.S. decision making regarding Japan for the remainder of the decade. As secretary of state under Eisenhower, Dulles dealt far more regularly with Japanese affairs than the president. Having served in both Democratic and Republican administrations, Dulles enjoyed a profile that transcended his official position. U.S. policy toward Japan during the fifties is also a fundamental part of Dulles's own legacy in foreign affairs.

Dulles's sensitivity to the views of the different actors in the policy arena calls attention to the importance of the context within which he fashioned a working consensus. Despite personal and political differences, Dulles and Acheson shared the conviction that American policy in Asia depended upon the restoration of Japanese political stability and economic power. Together with Assistant Secretary Rusk, the two men cooperated with each other admirably. Rusk was, one career Foreign Service officer later recalled, "an absolute master" at diffusing tension. "You could just feel the air almost electric as we'd go into the meeting, with the hostility around the room," he explained referring to Rusk's handling of a tense moment with allied representatives during the Korean War. "And Dean would start talking; he would talk and talk and talk and talk and talk, and you could sort of feel them relax."[16] Together, Dulles, Acheson, Rusk, and their assistants were a strong team.

Agreement on the terms of peace with Japan flowed from a consensus among American policy makers on Japan's importance to the United States. Everyone accorded a high priority to maintaining close political ties with Japan. Differences abounded on how to preserve the U.S. military position and Japan's pro-Western orientation. But everyone appreciated the potentially disastrous consequences of alienating Japan. The contrast with Sino-American relations reveals the implications of this consensus on Japan. No such agreement, whether within the administration or in Congress, existed on China policy. Open disagreement in America on China obviously complicated the conduct of diplomacy just as it rendered politics increasingly bitter. But to hard-liners that was the point; the PRC was already a hostile power. An open fight over Japan policy, by contrast, would have had immediate repercussions in Japan, jeopardizing transpacific cooperation. Japan was too important to divide over.

Dulles's first concern was to define the U.S. negotiating position. Although relatively unfamiliar with East Asian affairs, he was committed to a liberal settlement with Japan from the beginning. Having served as an expert on reparations during the negotiations after World War I, he believed that a punitive settlement would undermine a lasting peace. Dulles was also doubly conscious of the need to gain Senate approval of any agreement. He owed his appointment to the Truman administration's desire for bipartisanship on the Japan question, and he wished to avoid following in the footsteps of Woodrow Wilson, whose prized Versailles Treaty met with defeat on Capitol Hill.

Dulles's attentiveness to congressional opinion proved to be one of the most immediately visible and distinctive characteristics of his approach to policy. It is worth recalling that Dulles represented New York State in the U.S. Senate for four months in 1949 (Governor Thomas Dewey appointed him when Senator Robert Wagner resigned). Dulles gave his maiden speech in support of NATO within days of arriving in Washington. During his brief tenure he worked closely with his fellow Republicans on both European security and China policy. That experience and the relationships Dulles established with his Senate colleagues prepared him well to conclude a peace with Japan acceptable to the Senate. During his first briefing on Japan at the State Department in April, Dulles was quick to indicate that the Senate would be very reluctant to consent to any Pacific pact resembling NATO—that is, "carrying an *obligation* to used armed force in the event a member were attacked." He suggested that an arrangement along the lines of the Rio Treaty of 1947, in which "no such obligation was automatically brought into force by an attack against one of the parties."[17]

Dulles also brought a deep suspicion of the Soviet Union to the task of peacemaking. Explaining that "[n]eutrality had no meaning for the Russians," he immediately rejected a neutralization arrangement for Japan just as he had previously done for Germany. In the case of "actual Soviet armed aggression" anywhere in the world, the United States "would inevitably have to go to war." "[A]s long as the USSR continued to be so eminently successful in achieving its objectives by means of indirect aggression," however, Dulles did not expect a direct attack.[18] Such concern with Soviet power strengthened his commitment to an early and lenient settlement with Japan.[19]

Once assigned, Dulles worked with his small staff to outline U.S. aims and a general framework of how to proceed. His closest assistant was John M. Allison, then director of the department's Office of Northeast Asian Affairs. A native of Nebraska, Allison was a career Foreign Service officer with long experience in Japan.[20] Dulles ruled out calling a multilateral peace conference to draft a treaty. He rightly saw multilateral negotiations as the road to deadlock or a punitive settlement. The only way to avert either disaster, he believed, was for the United States and Japan to press ahead toward a settlement whether the other powers followed or not. "The U.S. and Japan are the only significant sources of power in the Pacific," he later wrote to General MacArthur during a moment of trial. "If we can work in accord, the lesser Pacific powers will get security and will sooner or later, formally or informally, endorse that accord. If the United States and Japan fall apart, the situation in the West Pacific is grave for a long time."[21]

By early June Dulles had devised a preliminary statement of objectives, problems, and possible solutions. He sought a continued U.S. military presence in Japan, but he envisioned "a phased withdrawal from Japan" except for certain points held by joint agreement. Like Secretary of State Acheson, he saw in trade with China and Southeast Asia a partial solution to Japan's foreign trade requirements.[22] Revealing his pragmatism, Dulles did not seek to secure in writing elaborate rights for the U.S. military "to meet all conceivable contingencies." As he remarked during his first briefing, "bases in a hostile country would be useless." Like the British, the Japanese had "to request that the United States establish bases on Japan." The challenge was to cultivate Japanese goodwill and a spirit of common interest. This commitment to conclude a nonpunitive agreement echoed State Department thinking, but placed him at odds with the military, which zealously guarded its privileges and did not even wish to consider a treaty.[23]

Toward a National Policy

Several developments in June 1950 hastened the move toward an agreement. Dulles and Allison visited Korea and Japan where they met with General MacArthur and Japanese leaders, including Prime Minister Yoshida Shigeru.[24] Underscoring the gulf between the two departments, Secretary of Defense Johnson and General Omar Bradley traveled to Japan on a separate mission and also consulted with the supreme commander. Then on 25 June, while Dulles and Allison were still in Tokyo, North Korean forces attacked South Korea.

In an effort to break the impasse in Washington, General MacArthur proposed a formula for the placement of U.S. military forces in Japan. He recommended that the United States reserve the right to access "the entire area of Japan" as "a potential base for defensive maneuver." To avoid provoking Japanese hostility, however, he called for the U.S. military commander to consult with the Japanese prime minister before making any major changes in the deployment of American forces. By shifting the discussion of troop placement away from individual "predetermined points," MacArthur thought it possible to effect a military presence in Japan required for the "accelerated speed and power of modern war." At the same time it limited controversy accompanying any effort to secure specific "bases."[25] Dulles seized on this formula as a means of reaching a compromise.

The impetus for action was the war in Korea. Dulles wrote that, "the Korean attack makes it more important, rather than less important, to act." He hoped that it would awaken the Japanese from their "postwar stupor," and thereby provide an opportunity to "bring them an insight into the possibilities of the free world and their responsibility as members of it." "[T]heir mood for a long time may be determined by whether we take advantage of this awakening," he added. Letting matters drift because of the war on the other hand, carried the risk of losing more in Japan than could be gained in Korea.[26]

The other nettlesome problem was the question of Japan's own military strength. Dulles himself considered Japanese rearmament vital. Defense of Japan "without any help from the Japanese themselves" was "an almost impossible burden." No country was fully sovereign so long as it was wholly dependent on another for its security. Rearmament was a visible means of enhancing Japan's power, making the nation less dependent upon the United States and more valuable as an ally.[27] The PPS spoke for everyone in stating that, "we are justified in resorting to extraordinary measures to enable Japan to contribute to its own defense."[28] By 1950, a principal U.S. aim was to avoid writing any restrictions on Japan's capacity to rearm into the peace agreement.[29]

After preparing a draft statement in July, Dulles pressed for wider approval. The JCS, however, attempted to postpone the treaty negotiations demanding that the treaty "must not become effective until after favorable resolution" of the war in Korea. Dulles accepted this unacceptable condition in order to continue his planning for the negotiations, and to maintain the momentum building behind them.[30] He and Allison then began consultations with allied representatives in New York, where the General Assembly of the United Nations was in session. Desiring the adherence of as many nations as possible to the final accord, they began lobbying the members of the Far Eastern Commission (FEC).[31] Consisting essentially of the wartime allies, the FEC was nominally responsible for supervising the Occupation of Japan. The precise format for negotiating the peace was not yet decided, but Dulles was already working through bilateral channels. This preference for bilateralism enabled him to maintain the momentum behind the peace process. It also shaped the outcome.

The widening of the Korean War in the fall of 1950 accelerated progress toward a treaty. To Dulles the crisis in Korea reinforced the need for a "prompt effort" to secure a Japanese commitment "to the cause of the free world." Conceding that success was not certain, he insisted that "the only practical procedure" was a mission to Japan to "ascertain what, if any, arrangements were feasible."[32] Fortuitously, the departure of Defense Secretary Johnson in September removed one of the last obstacles. General George Marshall, Johnson's successor, cooperated with Secretary of State Acheson to begin negotiations, just as he and Dulles had earlier pressed for the creation of a separate West German state. On 10 January, President Truman proposed the appointment of Dulles as head of a peace treaty mission carrying the rank of ambassador. After consulting with lawmakers, administration officials, and allied government representatives in Washington, Ambassador Dulles and his staff departed for Tokyo.[33]

Negotiation of the Peace and Security Treaties

In Tokyo, Dulles found Prime Minister Yoshida Shigeru prepared to negotiate. Because agreement on the security relationship was the necessary foundation for any settlement, these talks focused principally on defense issues. In the same way that German chancellor Konrad Adenauer understood that his new West German state depended upon the United States for its security, Prime Minister Yoshida never doubted that Japan needed an American defense commitment. He also recognized that in return Washington would expect Japan's alignment alongside the United States in world affairs. On the specific terms of the American commitment and Japan's obligations in return, however, the particulars of Yoshida's agenda and American expectations were far apart. In early 1951 Dulles and Yoshida reached a provisional agreement after hard bargaining, but both questions remained unresolved for the rest of the decade.

Although the details of the negotiations are beyond the scope of this study, the points of disagreement merit attention because they affected the substance of economic policy on both sides. Dulles was willing to discuss a mutual security pact. Such an agreement had to fall within the bounds of likely congressional approval, reflected in the Vandenberg Resolution of June 1948 (the basis of U.S. participation in NATO). The United States could enter into collective security arrangements to protect vital American interests, but participation had to be based on the principles of self-help and mutual assistance. To Dulles and American lawmakers the most visible demonstration of such commitment was rearmament. In one estimate, the JCS later placed the number of Japanese ground troops required at 300,000.[34] Dulles did not have a specific figure in mind. His purpose was to inquire into the scope of the effort Japan was prepared to make.

The depth of Prime Minister Yoshida's reluctance to rearmament reflected his ability and will to act on conviction. Yoshida sought to restore Japanese sovereignty, to pick up the pieces of the shattered empire, and to succeed in building the nation where the militarists had failed. Yoshida's career before the war did not anticipate his rise to the pinnacle of power, but his life does reveal the paradoxical mix of nationalism and diplomatic sense, of stubbornness and flexibility, of reverence for tradition and modern sensibility that defined his leadership as premier.[35] The adopted son of a wealthy and cultured family, Yoshida had attended Tokyo University before entering the Foreign Ministry. After his marriage to Makino Yukiko, the eldest daughter of Count Makino Nobuaki, Yoshida enjoyed access to the social circle including the imperial family. He regarded the 1902 Anglo-Japanese alliance as the foundation of Japanese foreign policy. Conflict with the Anglo-American powers was suicidal. Hostile to communism and socialism, he was deeply conservative on most social issues. He supported Japan's empire in Manchuria, yet opposed the military's later involvement in North China.

Arrested by the armed forces during the war, Yoshida was suspicious of military power and feared the resurgence of a Japanese military caste. Historically the Japanese armed services had not submitted to civilian control but sought to be masters. Yoshida doubted that they would remain servants of the nation. His first priority was Japan's economic development. Yoshida attempted to explain to an unsympathetic Dulles how the price of rearmament was unbearable for the nation. "The burden of rearmament," he insisted, "would immediately crush our national economy and impoverish our people, breeding social unrest, which is exactly what the Communists want." "Japan's security depends far more upon the stabilization of people's livelihood than on armament."[36] Hyperbole aside, Yoshida's economic logic was questionable. His political calculation, however, was anchored in a profound Japanese anxiety about war. Any security treaty calling for extensive rearmament was bound to be highly unpopular.[37]

Occupation policies exhibit an element of tragedy on this point, which explains why postwar debates over Japanese rearmament have been so difficult to resolve. Each side has interpreted the issue in terms of right versus wrong yet both have been engaged in a psychological struggle pitting one profound truth against another. Faced with the Soviet military threat after the war, Americans were able to shift with relative ease from seeking Japan's disarmament to recasting the nation as a comrade in arms in the Cold War.[38] Even before the Korean War administration officials regarded the notion of a demilitarized Japan as a visionary remnant of a bygone age.

To the Japanese, however, American demands for rearmament exposed a great contradiction in U.S. policy. More Japanese embraced the ideals of demilitarization to a much greater extent than SCAP officials could have imagined in 1945. It was impossible to rebuild any military establishment, much less deploy Japanese forces overseas, without revisiting images of the disastrous war that led to Japan's defeat and occupation. The reverse course was, therefore, deeply unsettling. On rearmament, the reversal was so complete that it called into question the motives behind American policy. Was America merely using Japan? One fear was that the United States wished to use Japanese soldiers as mercenaries for its own foreign wars. Yoshida did not need to mention this concern to Dulles. Opposition politicians voiced such fears in public.

As a clash with roots in the deepest national fears on both sides, the argument over whether to rearm Japan has never been solely a military matter. Compromise has enabled the U.S.-Japanese partnership to endure. But, on the Japanese side, such agreements have never put to rest unspoken fears. The misfortune befalling Dulles (and successive U.S. administrations) was to be in power after SCAP had succeeded as completely in demilitarizing Japan, as the world inspiring such reform had changed.

In Yoshida's view, as long as American forces were present in Japan, the nation was unlikely to experience an external attack. Enjoying this de facto guarantee of security, Yoshida thus downplayed Japan's military obligations. In his proposal to Dulles, the prime minister broke down the problem of Japanese security into two factors: internal security and external defense. He pledged that Japan would "ensure internal security by herself." Regarding external defense, however, Yoshida requested "the cooperation of the

UN, and, especially, of the U.S." by "appropriate means such as the stationing of troops." With each power attending to half of the equation in this fashion, Japan and the United States would be equal partners. He also asked that the security arrangements be concluded separately from the formal peace treaty.[39] On the face of it, Yoshida proposed that Japan receive a guarantee of security without providing anything in return. With the United States at war in a region divided, Japanese leaders hoped that American leaders would see a secure and non-Communist Japan as a vital national interest of their own.

In the Japanese proposals Dulles saw the basis for security cooperation, but he met his match when he attempted to bring Yoshida around to his position on rearmament. Yoshida had resisted rearmament the previous June when the two men first met, and he held his ground the second time around. Dulles hoped that General MacArthur would break the deadlock, but the supreme commander sided with Yoshida.[40] The talks in January and February 1951 nevertheless served as the basis for the security arrangements signed at San Francisco in September. Dulles accepted the suggestion to conclude separate peace and security treaties. The peace treaty contained no prohibition of rearmament, and the terms implementing the security treaty were to be spelled out in an executive agreement not requiring legislative approval. But Dulles refused to agree to either a formal U.S. guarantee of security or to the internal-external formula for Japanese defense. In the middle of Dulles's visit Yoshida promised to initiate a rearmament program (consisting of the creation of a militarily insignificant 50,000-man force) in the future.[41] Dulles then inserted Yoshida's pledge that, "Japan will itself increasingly assume responsibility for the defense of its own homeland" into the preamble of the security treaty. Until Japan made a tangible commitment to its own security, he explained, "the U.S. would want rights rather than obligations." The United States "was not in a position to guarantee indefinitely a totally unarmed country."[42] The only formal obligation appearing in the final text was the U.S. pledge to station its military forces in Japan.[43] This pledge was the main point on which Dulles and Yoshida agreed.

Thus, the security settlement was a shadow of Yoshida's initial design. There was no mutual, cooperative character to the treaty or the administrative agreement to implement it.[44] It was at best a provisional formula to ensure Japan's security. But Yoshida did get the de facto guarantee he sought, separate from the peace treaty and without obligating Japan to rearm extensively or to participate in multilateral schemes for regional defense. Dulles himself recognized that, "the practical consequences of our keeping troops in Japan would be more important than any paper guarantee."[45]

The bilateralism that Dulles espoused from the beginning also manifested itself clearly in the other elements of the San Francisco settlement. Although neither Dulles nor the Truman administration had defined the terms of the Pacific security arrangement they desired, the general goal was to establish a security pact. Likely members included Japan, the Philippines, Australia, New Zealand, and possibly Indonesia. After the talks in Japan, Dulles and his staff traveled to the Philippines, Australia, and New Zealand before returning to Washington. If the Cold War defined the American agenda, the last war loomed much larger in the minds of Japan's neighbors. The essential problem in reaching a security settlement, Dulles recognized, was "to devise some arrangement which would protect Japan from outside aggression and at the same time re-assure to the greatest extent possible Japan's former enemies that Japan would never be a threat to them."[46]

Unlike in Europe, the idea of integration went nowhere. Whereas some sense of a Western European community existed before the last war, it had to be invented in the Pacific. American efforts were simply unequal to the task. Japan had already refused to carry out the requisite rearmament. Public opinion in the Pacific Dominions was not receptive to undertaking any obligation to protect Japan. Limiting a Pacific pact to the United States, Australia, and New Zealand, however, would play badly in an era of decolonization, suggesting that the white powers were forming an alliance against yellow and brown. To include some Southeast Asian nations but not others would engender bad feeling in those areas that were left out. Yet to embrace all of the nations of the region would be to take on too many commitments.

Out of these discussions a solution suggested itself: conclusion of three interlocking pacts. To insure the defense of Japan, the United States and Japan signed a bilateral security treaty. An agreement between the United States and the Philippines formalized defense agreements to protect that archipelago. Finally, in exchange for supporting a liberal peace, Australia and New Zealand received American reassurance, by means of the ANZUS pact, against potential Japanese aggression. Back in the United States, Dulles brought the members of the FEC up to date in March 1951 and prepared a draft treaty for circulation. Momentum had built up after his trip, and the

British were also preparing a draft. Dulles desired that the United Kingdom be a cosponsor of the treaty, and his obvious preference was that the American draft be the basis of discussion.

Just as the peace process was gathering momentum, President Truman's firing of General MacArthur on 11 April dealt it a shock. The move raised grave questions in Japan about the course of U.S. policy in Northeast Asia. Dulles had privately doubted the wisdom of keeping the aging general in command.[47] But in April 1951 he was counting on MacArthur's prestige to commend the final treaty to the American public. President Truman and Secretary of State Acheson insisted that the general's departure signaled no change in policy toward Japan. They encouraged Dulles to return to Tokyo to reassure Japanese leaders of American intentions.[48] Upon departure, Dulles received assurance from MacArthur of continued assistance in the future. In Tokyo he conveyed to the Japanese the Truman administration's intent to continue "pushing ahead vigorously with the Japanese peace treaty." President Truman's announcement on 18 April of the security agreements to be concluded with the Philippines, Australia, and New Zealand "strongly reinforced" the message.[49]

After returning to Washington, Dulles prepared to depart for London and Paris where he hoped to reach agreement with the British and the French on the outstanding details of the draft treaty. Aside from the economic aspects of the settlement, to be treated shortly, the most divisive issue between the United States and the United Kingdom was the question of Chinese participation. The two allies avoided letting the matter stall the negotiations by agreeing to invite neither the PRC nor the Republic of China to participate. On 3 July, Dulles circulated copies of the joint Anglo-American draft to the allies and released it for publication on 12 July. During the following month Dulles and his staff "made no less than thirty additional changes" in the draft. The final text of the treaty, dated 13 August, was released to the press on 15 August.[50]

No event reflected more completely the dynamics of the peace process than the San Francisco conference itself.[51] Owing to the superpowers' inability to agree on any basic framework for a peace settlement, Dulles had proceeded without substantive Soviet participation. (He did meet several times with Soviet representatives.) The United States desired an arrangement for the conference that neither excluded the Soviet Union entirely nor allowed it the opportunity to block approval of the draft accord. With the concurrence of the United Kingdom and other allies, the State Department carefully planned the event. Opponents of the peace could comment on the text of the treaty, but they could not propose revisions. When the Soviet, Polish, and Czechoslovakian representatives suggested amendments intended to nullify the treaty's terms, they were ruled out of order. At the signing ceremony on 8 September, forty-eight nations signed the peace treaty with Japan. At a separate ceremony the same day, American and Japanese representatives signed the security treaty. Just as he had kept congressional leaders informed during the negotiations, Dulles made sure that both Democratic and Republican leaders were represented on the U.S. delegation. Japan ratified both treaties on 19 November. The U.S. Senate ratified the agreements (66-10 and 58-9 respectively) on 20 March 1952.

An Open Question

Having secured Japan for the "free world," the challenges for the United States in the post-Occupation era were not only to strengthen the emerging alliance but also to ensure that it did not weaken. A National Intelligence Estimate (NIE) of 20 April 1951 explained the stakes in a way that was already familiar: "Japan's ultimate political alignment will be a decisive factor in the balance of power in the Far East." Strategic location, industrial capacity, and military potential combined to make a friendly Japan indispensable to American strategy. If the effort to prevent Japan from slipping out of the "free world" camp defined the United States policy toward Japan throughout the decade, the motive behind that policy drew its strength from the difficulty and uncertainty of the enterprise. During the early fifties, members of the U.S. foreign policy establishment were convinced that Japanese loyalty in the Cold War was still an open question.[52]

American analysts did not worry very much about Japan's orientation in the near term. "Assuming a reasonably early end to the occupation and continued faith in U.S. military and economic strength," NIE 19 (1951) concluded, "the Japanese attitude toward the U.S. is likely to remain favorable or at least not so unfavorable as to be a major obstacle to cooperation in the early post-treaty years." The world situation, however, appeared to be worsening. Another estimate warned that the Soviet sphere will likely "continue to increase its military, economic, and political strength over the next two years." Analysts correctly predicted that, "further Soviet initiatives to forestall the rearmament and pro-Western orientation of Germany and Japan are almost certain."[53]

A 1952 report, NIE 52, agreed that the most probable future prospect for Japan was a "generally pro-Western orientation." Within this framework, however, it predicted that Japan would seek to expand its contacts with the Soviet Union and the PRC. The same estimate also expressed concern about Japan's orientation over the long-term. For reasons ranging from "the essential conservatism of Japanese society" to the weakness of the political left, the report did not envision Japan itself becoming a Communist state. The dangers were more subtle and related to the prospects for Japan becoming a less reliable ally. On the one hand stood the "unlikely event" of a coalition government "with strong Socialist representation" coming to power. In such a case Japan would "probably tend toward a 'third force' position in Asia." Further, it would "probably seek to reduce Japan's commitments under the Security Pact with the U.S."[54]

Greater worries flowed from the likely political consequences of economic instability. As NIE 52 explained: "If . . . Japan is unable to solve its economic problems, it will be particularly vulnerable to economic and diplomatic pressures from the Soviet Bloc and will be tempted to seize opportunities for closer economic and political relations with the Bloc. Even in this situation a conservative government would seek to avoid courses of action that would be likely to lead to Japan's absorption into the Bloc. Serious internal pressure in Japan would be more likely to result, at least initially, in a trend toward traditional authoritarian measures rather than the rise of a pro-Communist regime."[55] Either turn of events would have represented a defeat for the United States; each held the potential to cause the unraveling of U.S. policy in Asia.

Shortly before the peace and security treaties entered into force in April 1952, President Truman directed the NSC to review thoroughly U.S. policy toward Japan. The final paper, NSC 125/2, set forth the assumptions, objectives, and courses of American policy until middecade. Approved on 7 August, the document essentially formalized previous plans. Recognizing both American security interests in Japan and the importance of developing Japanese national power, it set codified American plans to preserve Japanese security, strengthen the Pacific alliance, and promote Japanese resurgence along liberal lines.[56]

U.S. strategy was predicated upon a close interconnection between economic and military strength. NSC 125/2 called for promoting Japanese rearmament. Another aim was a Japanese economy that is "self supporting, expanding, capable of maintaining adequate living standards, supporting the defense of Japan, and contributing to the defense of the Pacific area." Because the United States was still at war in Korea, the report also called for securing Japanese compliance in the embargo of the Chinese mainland.

U.S. planners recognized, however, that Japan was no longer an occupied territory, but a sovereign nation. Maintenance of the strategic partnership depended on continuing Japanese goodwill. The report thus emphasized that the United States should "strive to maintain a political relationship of trust and confidence between Japan and the U.S."[57]

Japan's priority in administration eyes is also evident in the work of the Psychological Strategy Board (PSB). Shielded by the opaque walls of the national security state, the PSB is one of the less familiar institutions of the early Cold War years. Established by presidential directive in 1951, it grew out of the desire for an effective mechanism to coordinate the nation's psychological warfare operations abroad. Headed by Gordon Gray, its members included representatives from several executive departments and agencies. It reported to the president and kept the NSC informed of its deliberations. The aim of the PSB was, in the words of Director Gray, "to lift the Board's activities to a strategic plane in point of level and to the longer range problems in point of time."[58] Given its ongoing efforts to reduce Communist influence in France and Italy, Japan was a natural target of PSB attention.

Immediately after the San Francisco conference, Gray raised the question of whether the PSB should take up the task of developing "a long-range plan to prevent Japan's defection from its anti-Communist posture."[59] By September 1952 the board had completed the basic draft of PSB D-27, a paper that outlined a psychological strategy program for Japan. The final paper's aims echoed the list of objectives of earlier NSC policy. It correctly observed that "no keynote of positive national purpose or 'mission' has yet emerged" in Japan. Always searching for a new turn of phase, the board members desired that the "fementitious groping" for security, prosperity, and prestige underway in Japan would "give way" to the "wide marshalling of sentiment" behind a new course for the nation. Their aim was to provide that mission: "the construction of a Pacific system for mutual defense and development among the free, independent, and self-respecting nations of the area." More concretely, the United States had to convince the Japanese that strategic cooperation was the path toward "international prestige along with more pragmatic benefits."[60]

Because implementation of policy was the responsibility of other bodies, the PSB never achieved control over either policy or operations. With few exceptions, recommendations concerning economic and defense policy added up to a reaffirmation of NSC policy, coupled with the suggestion to "capitalize propagandistically" on developments of benefit to Japan. To facilitate popular acceptance of U.S. armed forces stationed in Japan (euphemistically described as "preservation of the security and independence of Japan") for example, the PSB offered such bland advice as using "all means and media" to convey to the public the temporary nature of the security treaty and the various dimensions of Soviet hostility to Japan.[61]

The most brazen calls for action were the recommendations intended to secure the goals of "a Japan allied to the U.S.," and "a politically stable Japan maintaining the principles of representative government." Through overt and covert means, the United States was to encourage those Japanese groups and individuals "who demonstrate sympathy with U.S. aims and objectives," while at the same time combating advocates of Communism and neutralism. Various recommendations spelled out ways to intensify the exchange of government officials, labor leaders, professors, journalists, artists, sportsmen, and other opinion leaders to maximum positive effect. Aware of both Japanese pride in their own tradition and the exposure of educated Japanese to Marxist criticism of the West, the PSB also emphasized the need to "[m]ake arrangements, preferably through private auspices, to confront Japanese intellectuals with outstanding American and European liberals and intellectuals. Most dramatic of all was the recommendation that covert support be extended to "militant anti-communist student and faculty groups," "the anti-communist labor press," and other such organizations.[62]

Although U.S. policy never yielded results approaching the ambitious aims of PSB D-27, psychological warfare was an important, if subterranean, element of postwar U.S. diplomacy. By middecade United States Information Agency (USIA) and other organizations were leading a propaganda campaign in Japan along the lines of PSB D-27.[63] The most sensational revelations about this secret war in Japan concern the CIA's covert financing of the Liberal Democratic Party (to counter the Socialists' gains) from the late fifties forward.[64] The PSB considered similar activities as it was preparing its recommendations regarding Japan. A 1952 paper recommended that priority studies be made by the CIA of the "detailed methods which can be most effectively employed against CPs [communist parties] in France, Italy, India, Japan, Iran, and Guatemala." It also recommended that operatives covertly approach "key individuals" in foreign governments—including that of Japan—so as to "orient favorably to U.S. interests" governments of areas in danger of developing regimes "inimical to U.S. interests."[65]

The work of the PSB reinforced official American concern about Japan and strengthened the commitment within the executive branch to win over

Japan by any means necessary. After all, many of the officials who drafted the NSC 125 papers assisted in preparing PSB D-27. In these deliberations, concern for the future continued to strike an uneasy balance with the cautious optimism inherent in any plan of action. As ever, the great worry was that Communist pressure "could conceivably succeed in confusing and partially paralyzing important segments of Japanese society whose active support is necessary if Japan is to remain fully and effectively aligned with the West."[66]

As soon became apparent, however, U.S. diplomacy was actually aggravating the problem of winning Japanese loyalty in the Cold War. Instead of achieving U.S. objectives, American attempts to strengthen the alliance revealed instead the tension between the various goals spelled out in NSC 125/2. The consensus in Washington held that it was possible to press for Japanese rearmament, promote economic revival, and restrict Japanese ties with the Communist bloc, all the while respecting Japanese sovereignty. In Japan on the other hand the prevailing view was that rearmament was an expense that the nation could ill afford.

Friction over rearmament also strained relations between the United States and the Federal Republic of Germany, but it posed a much greater threat to the alliance with Japan. In part, the difference was that German rearmament provoked more intense controversy abroad than in Germany. The French, for example, rejected the European Defense Community treaty in 1954, even though they had proposed the idea as a means of containing a West German military presence in Europe. When the Korean War sparked American enthusiasm for German rearmament, Chancellor Adenauer saw in the creation of a West German military a way to increase the Federal Republic's stature in Europe (and gain sovereignty). Although the military buildup progressed more gradually than the United States—and Dulles in particular—desired, American leaders reached a closer understanding on the issue with their German counterparts than they did with the Japanese. The threat posed by Communist military forces no doubt concentrated minds. Despite demilitarization and denazification after the war, West Germans never embraced the pacifist ideal to the extent the Japanese did. Nationalistic opponents of the Cold War alliance in West Germany focused instead on the ideal of German unification.[67]

Other controversies particular to Japanese interests added to the powerful undertone of frustration in the U.S.-Japanese relationship. U.S. pressure to restrict trade with the PRC was to most Japanese an infringement on national sovereignty rather than a common cause. Even matters far removed from security affairs assumed strategic significance when they heightened bilateral tension. A plethora of irritants served as ever ready sources of anti-American feeling. Among them were nuclear testing, the fate of the Bonin Islanders, and disputes over land in Okinawa.[68]

Economic recovery in 1955 actually intensified American unease about Japan's future orientation. With revival, both economic and psychological, the popular Japanese desire to pursue a more independent course in the world strengthened. U.S. leaders never had confidence in Prime Minister Hatoyama Ichirō (December 1954 to December 1956), in part because his appeal flowed from his promises to lead Japan on a more independent course in the world. More troubling was the reunification of Japan's two Socialist parties into one in October 1955. Like the West German Social Democrats—who rejected both rearmament and membership in NATO until 1959 because they rendered the task of German unification more difficult—the Japan Socialist Party favored neutrality in the Cold War. Yet in contrast to Adenauer's steady (and pro-American) leadership of the Federal Republic, Japan exhibited a continued absence of strong conservative leadership despite the establishment of the Liberal Democratic Party in November 1955.[69]

Ambassador Douglas MacArthur II addressed the matter of U.S.-Japanese ties in a long letter to Dulles that the secretary circulated among other members of the administration in 1957. MacArthur's concern was how to *"align and, if possible, to knit Japan so thoroughly into the fabric of the free world nations that it will not in the next few years be easily tempted to take an independent course leading either to non-alignment or neutralism (at best of the Swiss-Swedish type or at worst of the Nehru brand) or worst of all some form of accommodation with the Communist bloc."* He compared the fundamental objective in Japan with that in Germany. But whereas in Germany there existed "the same basic Christian religion, culture, and civilization as its European neighbors and the U.S.," Japan had no such common ties with the United States or its neighbors. The ambassador's analysis of economic ties was revealing, for in them he identified the greatest opportunity for success: "Identification in Japanese minds that their future economic viability depends upon the closest cooperation and alignment with the United States will more than anything else serve to tie Japan to the West."[70]

Conclusion

Both American policy toward Japan during the fifties and Japan's own resurgence were inseparable from the broader strategic setting. This is not to reduce either American policy or Japanese history to mere adjuncts of the superpower rivalry. Both American foreign economic policy and Japan's revival had deep roots in experience far removed in place and time from the Cold War. But that conflict brought the two nations together in new ways just as it divided them. The strategic imperative to "keep Japan on our side" intertwined with other issues and long-standing dynamics in the American-Japanese relationship. It provided an overall framework for policy and reinforced bipartisanship in Washington. Most important, the challenge of winning Japanese loyalty in the Cold War highlighted the significance of economic affairs during the fifties. The peace settlement was only the first step toward consolidating the alliance. Economic recovery represented the crucial test of Japan's commitment to the strategic partnership. Hence, the United States set out to reintegrate Japan into the U.S.-led world economy while containing Soviet and Communist Chinese power in Asia.

Chapter Three
THE ECONOMICS OF PEACE

If security arrangements provided the basis for a separate peace between Japan and the West, the creation of an enduring order in the Pacific depended on the resolution of Japan's economic difficulties. Yet precisely that challenge most confounded occupier and occupied before Japan regained its independence. From the reverse course through the peace negotiations, the United States attempted to strengthen Japan's ability to make a living in the world. This policy comprised the economic component of American Cold War strategy in the region. The economics of peace also reaffirmed the familiar ideal of free trade, which was by this time a central element of U.S. foreign economic policy.

The economic settlement reflected both a retreat from reform in Japan, and the pressure that the United States exerted on its allies to accept Japan as member of the international community. Economic matters did not figure prominently in the negotiations between John Foster Dulles and

Prime Minister Yoshida because Japan welcomed a liberal peace settlement. Japan's neighbors and the Western European allies, however, opposed in varying degrees American calls to lighten Japan's reparations burden and to clear away barriers to Japanese trade. Although advocates of Japanese integration into the U.S.-led order prevailed, victory did not seem so certain at the time. American policy heightened interallied tension over reparations, relations with China, and Japanese membership in GATT. Defenders of the new line in some allied nations endured criticism at home. Japan's reentry into international life occurred when the system itself was in flux, and the prospect of Japanese revival added to the sense of instability that defined the period. The story begins before the end of the Pacific War, with the United States' planning for the postwar world.

Planning for the Peace

American planning for peace grew out of Secretary of State Cordell Hull's vision of a cooperative postwar world order and the sense of administrative drift that flowed from President Roosevelt's hesitation to plan for the peace. "The unconditional-surrender formula," the historian Manfred Jonas has observed, "was a war measure and not a peace plan." While President Roosevelt concentrated on carrying the war to its conclusion on all fronts, others contemplated the shape of the postwar world. Hull's enthusiasm for freer trade and an international order based on legal principles, rather than the politics of political power and material interest, gained currency among other officials, particularly his deputies in the Department of State. Such ideas were part and parcel of the popular American hope for a better world expressed in the objectives of the Atlantic Charter of August 1941. The document's political clauses, for example, included such lofty goals as "abandonment of the use of force" and disarmament "pending the establishment of a wider and permanent system of general security."[1]

As secretary, Hull sought allied agreement on overall principles to govern international conduct. The actual terms of the peace were to be disposed of after the war. He described the new day for diplomacy after the Moscow Conference of Foreign Ministers in October 1943: "As the provisions of the Four-Nation Declaration are carried into effect, there will no longer be need for spheres of influence, for alliances, for balance of power, or any other of the special arrangements through which, in the unhappy past, the nations strove to safeguard their security or to promote their interests." Hull's willingness to entrust postwar American security to international agreement and goodwill was not universal, however. Others took such language to mean that that the Soviet Union would acquiesce in American designs for the postwar world. As the historian Melvyn Leffler has described, military planners, including several who later served in President Truman's administration, paid careful heed to the likely balance of power in the world after the war as well as the material requirements of American security.[2]

Within the U.S. government, divergencies in thinking about peace with Japan disrupted the policy-making process far less than was the case with the occupation of Germany. Whereas the allies agreed during the war to carve Germany into zones of occupation, American officials refused to allow the division of Japan. In the absence of clear direction from the president, except in general terms later formalized at the Potsdam Conference of July 1945, German occupation policy was the result of a bureaucratic free-for-all. Proposals ranged from the moderate treatment suggested by military planners to the short-lived "Morgenthau Plan" to pastoralize Germany prepared by the secretary of the treasury. Postponement and public debate added to the ambiguity.[3] Disagreement regarding the treatment of Japan was no less real, but it was more contained, focusing on whether Japan should be permitted to retain the emperor.

From the beginning, the United States maintained control over policy toward occupied Japan. After Secretary Hull retired because of ill health in November 1944, planning moved forward quickly. The most important administrative body was the State-War-Navy-Coordinating Committee (SWNCC), organized in December 1944. Official policy assumed that the details of the peace settlement would be settled later, thus leaving countless issues unresolved. Yet U.S. planners seized the initiative and began planning for an American-dominated occupation of Japan. The work of the Far East subcommittee of SWNCC is striking for its divergence from popular sentiment at the time—expressed in demands that the emperor be tried as a war criminal, for example—as well as the views of officials who called for dealing harshly with Japan.

SWNCC's attitude toward Japan softened markedly during the brief tenure of Secretary Hull's successor, Edward Stettinius (November 1944 to July 1945). The pivotal figure was Joseph Grew, the former ambassador to Japan then serving as undersecretary of state (1944–45). Unaware of the development of the atomic bomb, Grew desired a compromise peace with Japan. Other influential leaders, particularly former U.S. president Herbert Hoover and Secretary of War Henry Stimson, were of a similar mind. Like

Grew, they saw in Japanese diplomacy of the twenties a model for the postwar era.[4]

Although out of step with popular feeling during the war, these figures' vision of a strong partnership between the United States and Japan in defense of capitalism and global stability anticipated the consensus that defined official thinking by the Occupation's end. Grew's most notable legacy was his effort to modify the definition of unconditional surrender to allow for the possibility of retaining the emperor. SWNCC-150/4/A, the statement of the United States initial postsurrender policy for Japan sent to General MacArthur on 6 September 1945, also reflects Grew's influence. SCAP was to exercise power through the Japanese governmental machinery rather than as an independent military government as planners had initially assumed.[5]

The war's sudden end following the atomic bombing of Hiroshima and Nagasaki did not resolve the tension between all of the various strands in U.S. planning for peace with Japan. SWNCC's consideration of economic affairs reveals the uneasy balance. American planners did not seek to be too punitive. The Potsdam declaration of 26 July 1945 specified the terms of Japan's surrender. In it the allies promised that, "Japan shall be permitted to maintain such industries as will sustain her economy and permit the exaction of just reparations in kind, but not those which would enable her to re-arm for war." The proclamation also allowed that "eventual Japanese participation in world trade relations shall be permitted."[6] In 1945 the expectation was that a distinction between the victorious coalition partners and the defeated Axis powers would persist for a long time.

SWNCC planners did not exhibit blanket hostility toward the Japanese, but neither did they show any enthusiasm for helping Japan to rebuild its economy. General MacArthur received instructions "not to assume any responsibility for the economic rehabilitation of Japan or the strengthening of the Japanese economy." American policy did not seek to prevent "the eventual readmission of Japan to the ranks of peaceful trading nations." But such revival was to be contingent upon demilitarization and democratization of Japan's economy.[7] Postwar planners embraced Hull's vision on a systemic level. The purpose of economic reforms was to facilitate the broader aim of democratizing the nation. Except in such abstract consideration, trade liberalization was not a salient issue at all. The reform agenda likewise eclipsed attention to Japan's political relations with its neighbors.

As in the planning for Germany, U.S. policy at the outset of the Occupation of Japan called for sweeping reform of political, economic, and social life under military occupation. Yet the alternative of reconstruction and reintegration into international life was also visible. Immediately after the war, officials in the occupied territories had the initiative. Thus, the reforms in Japan were in a sense the product of an odd marriage between the imperious General Douglas MacArthur and the former New Dealers who staffed many sections of the supreme commander's bureaucracy. Back in the United States, however, influential conservatives and advocates of realpolitik saw the Japanese political establishment as a potential anti-Soviet ally rather than an object of reform. They were not party to the reform agenda. When the effort to remake Japan faltered two years later, they were quick to reorient U.S. policy, all the while using Secretary Hull's language of internationalism.

Reform and Reverse Course

Of the reforms implemented during the Occupation, the most important ones in the economic sphere were land reform, promotion of the labor movement, and the breakup of Japan's large industrial combines (commonly known as zaibatsu).[8] The reparations program was also a prominent concern during the Occupation. The course of zaibatsu dissolution and the short history of the reparations program illustrate the dynamics of the change in U.S. policy before the peace negotiations.

As in the planning for peace, events in Germany often anticipated developments in Japan. Early efforts to lighten Japan's reparations burden in particular echoed the American preference for restoring German economic health over exacting reparations. At the Potsdam Conference the allies agreed on the principle that Germany should be compelled to compensate the allies for the loss and suffering caused by the war. Worried about the desperate state of Germany's postwar economy, General Lucius Clay ordered a halt to the delivery of reparations from the American occupation zone in May 1946. At the war's end, the allies and domestic opinion favored a punitive reparations program for Japan, but American policy makers were divided. The Joint Chiefs of Staff and SCAP held to a relatively soft position because they would be held accountable for conditions on the ground.[9]

The first U.S. initiative was the report of a commission headed by the California oil baron, Edwin W. Pauley. In return for his generous support of the Democratic Party, President Truman appointed Pauley in 1945 to advise him on reparations policy for Germany and Japan. Operating on the dubious assumption that Japan retained "more industrial capacity than she needs or has ever used for her civilian economy," Pauley proposed that surplus Japanese industrial plants be used as war reparations in order to promote economic development elsewhere in Asia. Pauley suggested severe restrictions on Japan's heavy industries, particularly steel, chemicals, and machine tools. The mission allowed Japan to maintain a level of foreign trade providing for a minimum standard of living, namely the same as the nation's preindustrial neighbors.[10]

Fearing the consequences of leveling Japanese industry, neither the JCS nor other Washington planners moved quickly to implement Pauley's recommendations. On 20 January 1946, General MacArthur ordered that four hundred Japanese war plants be taken into SCAP custody to insure their availability for reparations. The directive shocked the Japanese, but the facilities' eventual disposition was actually undecided. Study of the matter dragged on throughout the year. SWNCC proposed the creation of a separate Inter-Allied Reparations Commission to oversee the program, but SCAP and the JCS strongly opposed the proposal. After settling for a reparations committee under the auspices of the Far Eastern Commission, in April and May SWNCC specified the extent of assets to be made available for removal under the reparations program.[11]

As Pauley had lamented on several occasions, the delay proved more significant than the details of the reparations directive. Enthusiasm for an extensive program was evaporating quickly, and the process of earmarking certain assets for delivery focused attention on the narrow question of removals, thus divorcing it from Pauley's larger aim of refashioning East Asia's economic landscape. By this time, U.S. planners and the FEC envisioned a program that limited Japanese reparations to the transfer of existing capital equipment and facilities. The FEC, however, could not agree on the shares of the claimant countries. On 4 April 1947, as a matter of urgency, the JCS issued an interim directive authorizing SCAP to begin delivery. Even then, removal of equipment and facilities was to be distributed such that they did not exceed, in quantity or value, 30 percent of any single category of assets. Recipients included China, the Philippines, Britain (for Burma and Malaya), and the Netherlands (for the Netherlands East Indies). Only in 1948 did transfers begin.[12]

Reform of Japan's industrial structure followed a similar course. As the dominant force in Japan's prewar economy, the huge family-owned and controlled conglomerates (zaibatsu such as Mitsui and Mitsubishi) were a natural target of reform. The monopolistic character of the zaibatsu is familiar and does not bear repeating here. SCAP officials and outside observers alike agreed on the need to break up the holding companies for the ten principal zaibatsu together, which allowed about fifty-six families to dominate nearly every sector of the economy. SCAP thus purged the leadership, ordered the dissolution of the combines, and forced them sell their stock to the general public.[13]

Dissolution of the family holding companies, however, only partially addressed the problem of fostering a more competitive marketplace. Established buying, selling, financing, and trading relationships between the firms that previously made up the zaibatsu remained in place. Many of these companies were themselves large and monopolistic. In early 1946, with the backing of both the State and Justice Departments, the mission of Northwestern University economist Corwin D. Edwards investigated the problem of what to do with the Japanese combines. If Edwards overstated his case for the zaibatsu being "principally responsible for the war," his mission was correct in identifying the combines' dominance of the economy: the zaibatsu enforced "semi-feudal relations between employer and employee, held down wages, and blocked the development of labor unions." Arguing that the initial zaibatsu dissolution failed to establish a solid foundation for competitive capitalism, Edwards pressed for further decentralization (usually called "deconcentration") of Japanese industry on two levels. To break up existing monopolies, the mission called for selling their stock to small holders. To prevent the emergence of new monopolies, it recommended enacting antitrust legislation to prohibit monopolistic practices and to restrict companies' size, scope, and structure of ownership.[14]

Implementation of the Edwards mission recommendations was incomplete and time-consuming. In October 1946, the JCS issued an interim directive to SCAP calling for their implementation. Acutely sensitive to the slightest challenge from the outside, General MacArthur and SCAP moved slowly on deconcentration at first. Motivation aside, any such program seeking the wholesale reorganization of the Japanese economy raised fundamental questions about SCAP's mission in Japan. By definition, pursuit of systemic change on this scale required both extensive allied intervention in the Japanese economy over a period of time and domestic support of the initiative. Reformers were disappointed on both counts. Japanese hostility to the alien program was nearly unanimous. Eleanor Hadley, who was one of the authorities supervising antitrust reform, described reception to the effort: "First an attempt is made to prevent the antimonopoly legislation from getting on the books; secondly, if legislation cannot be avoided, effort is made to emasculate as far as possible its various provisions; thirdly, and as a last resort, comes sabotage of enforcement."[15]

For both political and economic reasons, however, the aim of fostering a competitive economy in Japan was a sufficiently high priority to engage both Washington and SCAP. In mid-1947, the U.S. government forwarded a deconcentration proposal, numbered SWNCC 302/4, based on the Edwards report for consideration to the FEC, where it became FEC 230. By this time General MacArthur had come around to favoring passage of antitrust legislation. Under pressure from SCAP the Diet passed such a law (formally titled the Law Relating to the Prohibition of Private Monopoly and Methods of Preserving Fair Trade) in April 1947. To establish the framework for deconcentration of the subsidiary companies, SCAP pressed the Diet to pass the Law for the Elimination of Excessive Concentration of Economic Power in December 1947. This law empowered the Holding Company Liquidation Commission (HCLC) to designate monopolistic companies and to reorganize them in a manner that ensured reasonable competition and freedom of enterprise. In February the HCLC prepared a list of 325 companies slated for deconcentration.[16]

Unfortunately for the advocates of deconcentration, the political ground in Washington was shifting just as SCAP was making demonstrable progress toward reorganizing the subsidiary companies. In early 1947 the Truman administration was making the containment of Communist power the defining feature of American foreign policy in both Europe and Asia. Because economic reforms figured more prominently in policy toward occupied Japan than in the occupation of Germany (where General Lucius Clay regarded the promotion of economic recovery as a top priority), the political and psychological impact of retreating from reform there was proportionally greater. In contrast with Japan, borrowing institutions, ideas, and technology from the United States had played only a minor role in forging Germany's identity before 1945. As one of four occupying powers in Germany, the United States was also not in a position to press for comprehensive economic legislation.

Still, the proclamation of the Marshall Plan in June 1947 and the ensuing American effort to fashion the Western zones of occupation into a West German state foreshadowed and then reinforced the reverse course in Japan. In Asia, as the Nationalist Chinese regime collapsed in the face of the CCP challenge, Japan's strategic importance grew. John P. Davies Jr. of the State Department's Policy Planning Staff summarized the new ideal: "a stable Japan, integrated into the Pacific economy, friendly to the U.S. and, in case of need, a ready and dependable ally."[17]

Japanese economic instability threatened this vision, and to officials in Washington conditions in Japan appeared to be growing worse, not better. Industrial production remained far below prewar levels. Deflated for population, production in 1948 stood at 47 percent of the 1934–36 average. Japan's export trade also failed to revive after the war. Owing to the nation's dependence upon foreign goods for its very survival, Japan's trade deficit was soaring. The United States covered the gap with foreign aid, but such assistance was merely a stopgap measure. Financial instability added to the uncertainty about the future. Japan had not one but many exchange rates. By 1947, inflation had fallen from the astronomical levels immediately after the war, but that year it was still running at an annual rate of about 195 percent.[18]

Without question, this inattention to price stability ranks as one of the greatest failures of the Occupation, both for its immediate social consequences and for undercutting reform. In such conditions collective bargaining agreements became meaningless as soon as they were signed. Discontent mounted and labor unions turned leftward. On 31 January 1947, General MacArthur intervened personally to prevent a general strike. In this inauspicious setting the Social Democrats captured a plurality of the vote in the national elections held the following April. The next month Katayama Tetsu became Japan's first Socialist prime minister. Although the Katayama government worked closely with SCAP to implement various reforms, the prospect of socialism triumphant in Japan caused alarm in the United States.

After the Soviets' refusal to consider the U.S. proposal in July 1947 for an early peace with Japan, George Kennan, then head of the PPS, took the lead in reevaluating Occupation policies in light of changing conditions. General William H. Draper Jr., who became under secretary of the army in August 1947, was particularly important. In his previous appointment as General Clay's chief economic advisor in occupied Germany, Draper successfully pressed his superior to devote U.S. attention to German economic revival rather than reform. When he became under secretary, Draper brought the same perspective to policy regarding Japan. Although Kennan thought that an early treaty was neither possible nor desirable, he saw that the Occupation and its reforms were "entering on a period of diminishing returns." "The reparations program," he pointedly suggested in October, "should be wound up at the earliest possible date."[19]

Kennan's chief concern was the defense of Japan, but both he and Draper understood that Japan's external security had an internal dimension that was necessarily affected by the reparations and reform programs. In March 1948 Kennan and then Draper traveled to Japan to meet with MacArthur and to impress upon him the need to promote Japanese revival. Kennan's trip to Tokyo confirmed his worst fears. SCAP, he concluded, had rendered Japan vulnerable to Communist infection from within. By displacing the traditional conservative groups that had led Japan, SCAP reforms had torn the nation from its moorings and opened up—but not answered— the question of who was to guide it in the future. Economic anarchy and the attendant unrest thus posed a greater threat than Russian military power. Further reform was out of the question. For Kennan the orders of the day were to restore a stable political system and to promote economic revival.

Kennan also emphasized "the deleterious effect" of the reparations program. "In every category of plant subject to reparations removal," he noted, were "plants now engaged in turning out products which are either vital to the recovery of Japan, or at least completely unrelated to war manufacturing." Taking issue with the claim that reparations were justified on the grounds that they would neutralize Japan as a military threat, he responded that in its postwar condition the nation "cannot be regarded as a potential military threat in the predictable future." It was "absurd," he added, "to suppose that many of the facilities tentatively scheduled for removal from Japan could ever be effectively utilized in other Far Eastern countries or could contribute in this way to the basic recovery of the Far East."[20]

The reverse course that Kennan charted received enthusiastic support from many quarters. Within the administration, Draper, Secretary of Defense James Forrestal, and other high officials joined forces. Fiscal conservatives, alarmed at the Occupation's mounting cost, followed. Influential individuals outside of government, particularly those known as the "Japan Lobby," also rallied against General MacArthur and reform. This group included such men as Joseph Grew, James Lee Kauffman, a lawyer who represented several leading companies doing business in Japan, and Harry F. Kern, the foreign editor for *Newsweek*. Kern did not hesitate to employ his weekly magazine as a forum for criticism of the Occupation. The issues of 23 June and 1 December 1947, for example, featured sharply critical articles on the anti-zaibatsu program. Conservative Japanese leaders were quick to turn this anxiety to advantage by presenting themselves as reliable partners against radicalism at home and abroad. In MacArthur's Japan they did not have easy access to the heights of power in the United States. Japan Lobby members, with their long experience in transpacific relations, stepped in to facilitate communication.[21]

On reparations, the dispatch of two new teams in the spring of 1948 to investigate economic conditions in Japan signaled the new attitude in Washington. Sent by the War Department, the mission led by Clifford Strike was supposed to inquire into the technical condition of industries to be removed under the existing program. From the beginning, however, Strike favored scaling back Japan's reparations burden. The second mission was organized by army under secretary Draper, who named Percy Johnston, then chairman of Chemical Bank and Trust Company, as the committee's head. Draper opposed holding Japan to the standard of living prevailing during the period 1930–34 (the starting point of the FEC program). He argued that certain industries classified as "primary war facilities"—such as civilian aircraft manufacturing plants—had peacetime uses and should be retained by Japan. Strike later agreed on this point. The total transfers the Strike and Johnston missions recommended were ¥1,648 million and ¥662 million respectively. Events soon overtook these revisions. Actual deliveries amounted to ¥160 million, down from the total of about ¥2,466 million recommended by Pauley in 1946.[22]

Draper also gutted the antitrust reform program. During his visit to Japan in early 1948, he met with MacArthur to impress upon him the need to promote Japanese economic recovery. Then, in an effort to circumvent the Holding Company Liquidation Commission, he proposed setting up an alternative Deconcentration Review Board consisting of American businessmen to review the HCLC orders. MacArthur agreed. Draper then announced in April that the United States was abandoning most of the antizaibatsu program. By July the new Deconcentration Review Board had eliminated all but one hundred companies and all banks from the HCLC list. When the program concluded formally in December, its scope had been reduced to a mere nineteen companies.[23]

As examples of the effort to remake Japan into a less threatening and more democratic power, the reparations and zaibatsu dissolution programs were consistent with Secretary Hull's highest hopes for the postwar world. During the translation from war to peace in Japan, however, Hull's vision witnessed a strange bifurcation. In the abstract, law-abiding conduct and prosperity were complementary and mutually reinforcing. Neither the United States nor SCAP, however, wished to assume responsibility for Japan's economic well being in 1945. In practice, reformers pressed for action without paying great heed to the nation's economic prospects. When, after two years, the economy seemed no healthier than before and Japanese recovery became a top priority, the effect was to forestall further reform. This rhythm of policy during the Occupation is now widely understood. But it was no less significant throughout the fifties. Ironically, Japan's economic weakness—and the anxiety that it unleashed in Washington—proved to be a powerful ally of Japanese conservatives and a great obstacle to liberal reform.

Codification of the reverse course came in late 1948. The NSC prepared a new paper on Japan, NSC 13/2, which President Truman approved on 9 October. Citing interallied differences on the timing and procedure for concluding peace with Japan, and "the Soviet Union's policy of aggressive Communist expansion," the paper observed that the United States "should not press for a treaty of peace at this time." It called instead for the United States to concentrate on strengthening Japan for independence under the U.S. security umbrella. Specifically, economic recovery was to be "the primary objective" of U.S. policy for the coming period."[24] In addition to American assistance, this policy translated into "a vigorous and concerted effort . . . to cut away existing obstacles to the revival of Japanese foreign trade, with provision for Japanese merchant shipping, and to facilitate restoration and development of Japan's exports." Although it set the reparations issue aside, the report recommended that SCAP "should be advised not to press upon the Japanese Government any further reform legislation."[25]

Subsequent initiatives confirmed the new direction of U.S. policy. Following the example of the June 1948 currency reform in Western Germany (which established a stable deutsche mark), President Truman approved a stabilization plan for Japan in December. When Joseph Dodge implemented the plan the next year, one of its elements consisted of setting the value of the Japanese yen at 360 to the dollar. In May 1949 the United States announced the termination of the reparations program begun under the auspices of the FEC. The administration simply rescinded the directive to make available assets for transfer and halted further removals, except for those already processed. "So-called primary war facilities" previously slated for removal were to be used instead for "recovery purposes." Henceforth, there was to be "no limitation on Japan's production for peaceful purposes." Finally, during the GATT session at Annecy the United States officially proposed that the contracting parties grant most-favored-nation treatment to Japan and other occupied areas.[26] As the opposition of other GATT members revealed, reorienting American policy was only the first step toward achieving the goals of the reverse course. The greater challenges were to bring the allies around to the same view, and to consolidate the new order in the peace settlement.

Negotiation of the Peace Treaty

If the most divisive issues in the negotiations between the United States and Japan concerned the two nations' security relationship, the economic clauses figured more prominently in talks between the United States and its allies. Ambassador Dulles conveyed the consensus view in Washington when he expressed his desire for a "complete restoration of sovereignty to Japan free of onerous restrictions."[27] To American leaders, post-treaty restrictions were undesirable. The whole point of a peace treaty was to foster an identity of interest between Japan and the "free world," as Dulles explained on numerous occasions. Treaty compulsions would by definition cast doubt on Japanese good faith.[28] Outside of America and Japan, however, Japanese economic revival was not a popular proposition. Even British leaders, who were anxious to maintain Anglo-American solidarity in the Cold War, held out for a more restrictive treaty than Washington desired. Where the United States worried principally about how to provide security for Japan, the allies and Japan's neighbors sought protection or compensation from Japan instead.

Dulles dealt with the economic aspects of the settlement and questions of postwar restrictions on Japan through overlapping bilateral channels, much as he had negotiated security arrangements. To maintain control of the negotiating agenda, Dulles first sought Japanese approval of the American proposals and then secured the support of the Commonwealth nations and sympathetic allies, making adjustments as necessary. During his first substantive discussions with Yoshida, Dulles presented a provisional outline of U.S. aims for the peace. The draft proposed that all parties waive claims arising out of the war, although it did enumerate a few exceptions. Consistent with the U.S. effort to reduce trade barriers around the world, Dulles proposed that Japan and the signatories apply the principles of most-favored-nation and "national treatment" to all trade between them. U.S. terms also envisioned Japan entering promptly into negotiations to conclude new commercial treaties to regulate its foreign trade.

According to the American design, the allies would demand no reparations, either out of industrial assets, current productions, or gold stocks. They would not claim any continuing right to reclaim looted property, nor

The Economics of Peace 65

would there be treaty restrictions on Japan's commercial activity "other than such as Japan may voluntarily adopt in the interest of promoting international goodwill." Likewise, the treaty would not obligate Japan to repay its GARIOA debt (Government and Relief in Occupied Areas aid provided during the Occupation to feed, clothe, and house the Japanese). That obligation, the most pressing claim in American eyes, could be settled separately through what Dulles termed "mutual adjustment." The memo cautioned, however, that there existed considerable differences between the allies on such matters. In person, Dulles suggested to Yoshida that the Japanese government consider voluntary payment of reparations in order "to satisfy public opinion in certain countries and secure their adherence to the treaty."[29]

Winning over the British proved difficult for many reasons. In early 1951 British foreign secretary Ernest Bevin was ill (Herbert Morrison succeeded him in March). The Foreign Office, as one diplomat explained, stood "quite leaderless."[30] Several important differences of interest also placed the American and British governments at odds with each other. Whereas American leaders sought to rebuild Japanese power, the British were unenthusiastic about such plans, much as they had been skeptical of the U.S. reform agenda after the war.[31] The American preference for unilateral action—on display throughout the Occupation—certainly added to a sense of alienation from U.S. policy.

Moreover, a reservoir of bad feeling from the war remained in Britain, rather than dissipating as it did in the United States. The British agreed easily with the Americans on the goal of achieving a "peace-loving Japan with a settled government and viable economy," just as they deemed it necessary to cooperate closely with the United States during the negotiations.[32] But this desire to cosponsor the peace treaty stemmed as much from the fear of being left out as it did from a change of heart about Japan. British officials were more suspicious of Japanese intentions and thus willing to consider imposing post-treaty restrictions. Examples included the proposal that the treaty specifically outlaw certain "undesirable political societies in Japanese territory." Another talking point was the idea of inserting into the preamble of the treaty "a reference to the responsibility of the Japanese militarist régime for having provoked a state of war."[33]

Awareness that Britain's entire postwar foreign policy was predicated upon alliance and cooperation with the United States obscures the extent of postwar Anglo-American rivalry. The historian Lanxin Xiang has made a persuasive case that tension between the United States and the United

Kingdom exerted greater force than the American-Soviet rivalry in shaping relations with China between the defeat of Japan and the triumph of the Chinese Communists.[34] Although Anglo-American differences over Japan were less pronounced, they were no less real. British anxiety about the future stood in the way of freer economic exchange during the peace treaty negotiations and the following decade. British leaders naturally recognized that the United Kingdom would have to go along with whatever the United States decided in the end. But the habit of taking the lead died hard— particularly when it seemed that the Americans were mistaken. The British economy's precarious condition called for making the most of every opportunity. The United States and the United Kingdom thus prepared draft treaties separately, and raced to complete them in early 1951.

The United States finished its provisional draft in March, which it then presented to the FEC countries as well as Indonesia, South Korea, and Ceylon. U.S. officials were familiar with the details of the U.K. outline for peace well before the British draft was completed in April. Trade was a particularly sensitive issue. Japan had been such a disruptive competitor in world markets during the 1930s that no British leader was about to place unqualified trust in a resurgent Japan's pledges to engage in fair play. On 19 March 1951, Harold Wilson, then president of the Board of Trade, publicly expressed the government's commitment to see Japan restored to economic health. "But," he added, "it must be the paramount concern of His Majesty's Government to uphold the United Kingdom's vital economic interests and to maintain full employment." Citing the "quite special characteristics" of prewar Japanese competition, Wilson explained that "it would be unwise for us to tie our hands in any way until the future course of the Japanese economy and Japanese commercial policies have become more clearly established."[35] The Foreign Office explained to the State Department that the United Kingdom did not wish to commit itself to extend MFN to Japan's trade.[36]

Other Commonwealth members were even less enthusiastic toward Japanese revival as the Canberra Conference in August and September 1947 revealed. The conference actually marked a shift toward recognition that "Japan's economic development ought to be encouraged rather than hindered."[37] But the reorientation was far from complete. The communiqué emphasized the members' concern with security from future Japanese aggression. Conceding that restrictions written into a peace treaty "should not go beyond what is demanded by considerations of military security," the group defined "security" broadly. Primary war industries "such as armament and aircraft manufacture" were to be prohibited. Production and capacity in "key industries which could form part of war potential" were also to be "limited to defined levels." Controls on Japanese imports were to supplement the above restrictions. A peace crafted along these lines was bound to stifle Japanese economic opportunity. Some leaders such as Australian prime minister Robert Menzies agreed with the U.S. aim of securing Japanese loyalty in the Cold War by means of a nonrestrictive treaty. But popular sentiment lagged behind.[38]

The gap remained apparent in May 1950, just as Dulles was beginning his work on the peace. Under instructions from the Colombo Conference, members of a Japanese peace treaty working party met that month in London. Several representatives voiced support for restrictions. Others supported more liberal settlement. The delegates wished to draft a treaty "so as not to incur the permanent resentment of the Japanese people." Japan was to be encouraged to join such international organizations as the United Nations, GATT, and ITO, and "to obtain a reasonable standard of living." But they continued to press for restricting industries with "war potential." Similarly, "unfair competition in overseas trade" was not to be permitted. Although the U.K. representative did not approve of the notion, such controls were to "be of a long-range nature."[39] Since the delegates to the London party were unable to rally around a coherent alternative to the U.S. draft, Dulles ignored them. By first securing British agreement, he kept the peace talks moving forward without having to agree to many restrictions.

The most important positive item was foreign trade. Dulles aimed to secure MFN and national treatment for Japanese trade. The United States did not depend on foreign trade to the same extent as the allies. Americans could thus face the prospect of absorbing more Japanese imports without great sacrifice. The allies were far less sanguine, but a U.K. proposal offered the basis for compromise. In March 1951 the Foreign Office suggested that MFN and national treatment be applied in such fashion that each territory that is a separate entity for customs purposes (such as a colony) count as a separate country. The idea was to retain freedom to protect British industries without sacrificing the potential benefits accruing from MFN or national treatment because one colony (such as Jamaica) failed to extend such privileges to Japan.[40]

Reciprocity provided a formula to enable the signatories to retain their freedom of action while expanding Japanese economic opportunity. As late as July, the French government held out for requiring Japan to offer MFN without regard to reciprocity for a period of several years, or excluding mention of MFN altogether. Dulles refused to concede the point. Article 12 of the peace treaty simply provided that during the four years following the treaty's entry into force Japan would extend MFN treatment to trade with each allied power from which it received similar treatment. The treaty placed no restrictions on Japanese industry. The only trace of such concern found expression in the security treaty, where Japan pledged to avoid always "any armament which could be an offensive threat or serve other than to promote peace and security in accordance with the purposes and principles of the United Nations Charter."[41]

Signatories nevertheless remained, as the president of the Board of Trade announced in Parliament, "free to impose quotas, to put on tariffs or to discriminate against Japanese trade."[42] Although the government believed it necessary to be able to make such statements should the need arise, British officials recognized the likely ineffectiveness of restrictions and took pride in the liberal, nonpunitive nature of the treaty. While acknowledging the potential dangers of future Japanese competition, their preference was that Japan compete fairly. The Japanese declaration (attached to the peace treaty) that it would abide by the International Convention for the Protection of Industrial Property and the Berne Copyright Convention, which prohibited copying and other unfair practices, made an impression in Britain and undercut support for a more restrictive settlement.[43]

Although they did not drive British policy during the negotiations, bitterness and anxiety persisted. Japanese imperialism and the Second World War had shattered Britain's empire in Asia, and the extent of the fall reinforced British worries about the future. During the peace negotiations, for example, the Foreign Office proposed several restrictions that led the Americans to question whether the British were trying to "block or obstruct" a settlement. The most gratuitous demand called for the destruction of Japan's excess shipbuilding capacity. Arguing that Japan's "inflated" shipbuilding capacity exceeded "her normal peace time needs," the United Kingdom insisted that "the shearing away of her surplus capacity is therefore justifiable on economic grounds." Dulles rejected the proposal as fatal to the peace treaty. "[N]o government required to carry out such destruction five or six years after the conclusion of hostilities," he explained, "could be expected to survive."[44] The British also demanded that Japan renounce its rights under the Congo Basin Treaties of 1919, withdraw from the board of directors of the Bank for International Settlements, and admit allied shipping to the Japanese coastal trade as part of the national treatment provided for in the treaty. Dulles opposed these demands but eventually conceded some of the latter two points.[45]

Reducing Japan's Reparations Burden and Building Ties with Southeast Asia

Reparations were the source of considerable dissension among the allies. Dulles, who had served as a consultant on reparations issues in Paris in 1919, wished to avoid following the example of the Versailles settlement. He and other U.S. planners recognized that imposing a heavy reparations burden on Japan would depress the nation's economy and alienate it from the West. He doubted that extensive reparations could be collected, yet he was certain that the prospect of such receipts would divide the allies. Thus, his task was to get the allies to acquiesce in lenient treatment of Japan.

This effort required adjustment on all sides. Dulles's September 1950 list of talking points had stated simply that all parties would waive claims arising out of acts of war.[46] The United Kingdom did not comment at the time, but the Philippines, the Republic of China, Burma, Australia, and New Zealand all pressed for reparations. By December the Nationalist Chinese were willing to waive reparations, provided that the other parties did the same. Australia and New Zealand eventually waived their claims, after receiving reassurance on their security in the ANZUS pact, as the trilateral security treaty among the United States, Australia, and New Zealand was called.[47] Recognizing the need to make some concessions, Dulles added provisions on reparations in the first draft of the peace treaty, dated March 1951. The relevant clauses stipulated that Japan lacked the capacity to maintain a viable economy, to repay the United States for aid during the Occupation, and to pay adequate reparations for war damage. Claims for reparations were "deemed to be satisfied" out of Japanese assets within territories of the Allies, administered by the Allies, or renounced by Japan.[48]

Southeast Asian nations were understandably less willing to forgo their claims as revealed in the protests of the Philippines and Burma. Citing the provisions on reparations of a later draft treaty as one reason, Burma eventually decided not to send a representative to the peace conference as part of its broader policy of remaining unallied in the Cold War.[49] The Philippines, by contrast, pressed the United States to provide for the maximum possible reparations in the text of the treaty. President Elpidio Quirino demanded "at least some payment" of the estimated $8 billion in total damage caused by Japan. American exhortations to recognize that fulfillment of such inflated demands was impossible had little effect. Dulles attributed the problem to "the emotional prejudices" of the people coupled with the government having "neither the political stability nor the courage" to rein in popular expectations. In March American officials also learned that Filipino leaders were covertly using their demand for reparations, as the acting foreign secretary expressed the point, "as bargaining lever to pry additional aid from the U.S."[50]

Dulles and Allison were also surprised when the United Kingdom pressed for reparations. In March 1951 the British demanded Japanese gold stocks under SCAP control (valued at $200 million), official and private Japanese assets in the territories of the allied governments, and Japanese assets in neutral and ex-enemy countries. Australia concurred, since such reparations were to compensate former prisoners of war who had suffered ill treatment at Japanese hands as well as the relatives of those who had died.[51]

Caught in this crossfire, Dulles showed his characteristic mixture of firmness and flexibility. He suggested to Yoshida that Japan consider the possibility of reparations from current production. The idea was to concede the point that reparations would be paid, but to circumscribe the treaty obligations so as to prevent them from interfering with Japanese recovery and trade. Yoshida was noncommittal but promised to study the matter. He did, however, suggest that in the case of the Philippines, reparations could take the form of salvage operations of (Japanese) ships sunk in Philippine waters.[52] In June Dulles moved to clinch the details of a joint Anglo-American position. Although unyielding in his opposition to any British seizure of the "gold pot" in Tokyo, he agreed that Japanese assets in neutral countries should be available for reparations.[53]

Dulles moved to meet the form, if not the substance, of the demands of the Philippines by inserting two new provisions in the treaty. The first established the principle that Japan should pay reparations; the second provided that Japan would negotiate with countries that had been occupied and damaged by Japan with a view to rendering them assistance. No amounts were specified and Japanese compensation was to take the form of services such as manufacturing and salvaging. Dulles and Allison kept the Japanese government informed, and the Japanese consented to the changes.[54] Because opinion in the Philippines remained unsatisfied, negotiations continued until the two governments reached agreement on

10 August. This exchange was marked by the gradual retreat of the Philippines and constant tinkering with the language of the clauses in question.

The reparations clause of the peace treaty provided the basis for the reestablishment of relations between Japan and the nations of Southeast Asia. A step down from both the American and Filipino positions, the treaty granted the principle of reparations but qualified significantly the implementation. Actual settlement was to be determined by negotiation between Japan and claimant nations. Ironically, Burma was the first power to conclude such an arrangment.[55] While the Philippines and the other signatories deliberated over whether to ratify the treaty, Burma negotiated a treaty of peace and agreement for reparations. The 5 November 1954 accord paved the way for agreements between Japan and the Philippines, Indonesia, and South Vietnam in the following years.

Although economic ties between Japan and Southeast Asia never developed as American planners hoped at the time of the peace settlement, they figured prominently in U.S. policy during the early postwar years. As part of the reverse course, the United States arranged bilateral trade agreements for Japan, as if to rebuild the Southeast Asian component of the former Greater East Asian Co-Prosperity Sphere in fact if not in name. U.S. efforts to secure markets and sources of raw materials for Japanese industry in Southeast Asia were ultimately most significant for leading to an American commitment to contain Communist revolution in the region. Economic backwardness, political instability, continued struggle against the former European imperial powers (especially in Malaysia, Indochina, and Indonesia), as well as wariness of Japan all impeded the growth of trade with Japan.[56]

Neither Dulles nor other U.S. planners envisioned much more than recreating an essentially colonial relationship between Japan and Southeast Asia, but they were correct in identifying the potential for a complementary economic and political relationship between Japan and the region. By 1960 Japan's exports to Southeast Asia totaled ¥359,640 million. Imports lagged behind at ¥252,647 million the same year.[57] Unlike in Northeast Asia, anti-Japanese feeling in some nations of Southeast Asia was tempered by Japan's role in ending European imperialism there. In wartime Indonesia, for example, Japanese military authorities equipped the nationalists' fighting force. The surge in Japanese trade and investment in the region during the sixties and again since the mid-1980s would have been gratifying to American postwar planners. But it came far too late to meet the ambitious goals of American policy or to alleviate Japan's trade deficit during the fifties.

The China Question

The peace conference at San Francisco heralded the end of the Occupation of Japan, but it restored only partial peace in Asia. The Chinese were conspicuous for their absence, and the Cold War division of East Asia actually widened as a consequence of the peace process. Dulles was by no means the principal force keeping Japan and the PRC apart from each other, but his diplomacy was a reflection of the larger forces that were. In the wake of the Chinese Communists' triumph in 1949 and the PRC's subsequent moves toward solidarity with the USSR, both extremes—the most radical Chinese revolutionaries and the U.S. military establishment—curiously agreed that the PRC was a revolutionary power. No effort to find common ground between the PRC and the West succeeded during the fifties. One result of growing Sino-American hostility was that Japan's economy developed apart from the Chinese mainland after the war, in contrast to the intimate, if imposed and unequal, relationship of only a few years before.

Although policy on all sides was in flux during the period, this outcome represented a clear triumph of American over British designs for the peace. Without great territorial or financial interests in China, the United States was relatively free to take drastic measures against the Chinese Communists. Domestic politics reinforced a hard-line policy. Developments in China resonated with American public opinion in a way that Japanese affairs never did. Decades of missionary reports home and Madame Chiang Kai-shek's triumphal speech-making tour in 1943 had fostered the image that the generalissimo and his wife were "living symbols of a Christian, anti-Communist, anti-fascist, and pro-American China." If the American public knew nothing of actual conditions in postwar China, the sense of "loss" in 1949 nevertheless seemed real.[58]

British weakness and a dread of war, by contrast, inspired caution in dealing with Chinese affairs. Concrete British aims included safeguarding investments in China and the colony of Hong Kong. Because the CCP controlled the vast area and population of China, British leaders regarded it as axiomatic that to deal with China meant to deal with the Chinese Communists. Sir Esler Dening, an expert on Japan and the Foreign Office's leading official on East Asian affairs, expressed the dominant view when he criticized the U.S. hard line toward the Chinese Communists as misguided and dangerous. The high point of British diplomacy came in January 1950, when the United Kingdom recognized the PRC. The Sino-Soviet alliance of

February 1950, the outbreak of war in Korea four months later, and disagreements over trade and investment undercut support for the British line at home and abroad, however. Dening went to Hong Kong in October with the expectation of becoming Britain's first ambassador to the PRC. But the Communists refused him entry and intervened the next month in Korea on behalf of the North.[59]

Despite the failure of negotiations to establish diplomatic relations between the PRC and the United Kingdom, in March 1951 the British proposed inviting the Communist Chinese to the Japanese peace conference. Given the war in Korea and Senate enthusiasm for Nationalist China, Dulles had little patience with Britain's demand. Yet he was also aware of the unpopularity of the Nationalist Chinese, who requested to attend. Because inviting either China promised to wreck the conference, Allison suggested compromising on the point by excluding the Chinese altogether. The political advisor in Tokyo concurred.[60] Dulles and Foreign Secretary Herbert Morrison agreed upon a compromise formula in June. The multilateral treaty would safeguard Chinese interests by Japanese renunciation of special rights and interests there, but no power would sign or ratify the treaty on behalf of China. "Japan's future attitude towards China" was to be determined by Japan itself "in the exercise of the sovereign and independent status contemplated by the treaty." The cabinet had previously rejected this formula, but the ministers backed down after Dulles threatened to end negotiations rather than allow the United Kingdom to have veto power over Japan's option to conclude a bilateral treaty with the ROC.[61]

Allison later wrote that when Dulles concluded the agreement with Morrison he "had an oral understanding" with Yoshida "that gave him confidence the Japanese would not make a deal with the Chinese Communists." Although the documentary record does not yield explicit confirmation of such a deal, Yoshida was clearly aware of U.S. sympathy for the Nationalists. He was not about to jeopardize the success of the treaty by willfully inflaming U.S. hostility toward the PRC. In a 6 August 1951 letter to Dulles, Yoshida gave his personal assurance that the Japanese government "has no intention to conclude a bilateral treaty with the Communist regime." The words "bilateral treaty" themselves represented another maneuver by Dulles. Less comprehensive than the expression "treaty of peace," the phrase "bilateral treaty" did not force Japan to recognize the Nationalist regime as the sole legitimate government of China.[62]

Despite such assurances, Yoshida believed that the American hard line was misguided. Education in the Chinese classics and twenty-two years as a diplomat in China and Korea convinced him that Japan's long-term future depended upon close ties with China. The Communists' rise to power did not shake this conviction. Chinese civilization and tradition, he believed, were essentially incompatible with Marxism. The Chinese would ultimately transform or reject Communism. Chinese and Russian national interests were similarly too divergent for the Sino-Soviet alliance to long endure. Popular Japanese sentiment for restoring ties to the Asian mainland was strong. Some Japanese businesses looked to the Chinese market for deliverance from hard times. The Socialist and Communist parties agitated for actual recognition of the PRC. Yoshida understandably wished to keep his options open.[63]

The prime minister soon learned, however, that Japanese recognition of the Republic of China (ROC) was the price of Senate ratification of the San Francisco treaties. A majority of U.S. senators feared that Japan would recognize the PRC if the United States were to adhere strictly to the Dulles-Morrison agreement. On 12 September, Senator William Knowland (R.-Calif.) sent a letter to President Truman expressing his desire that Japanese policy on China conform to that of the United States. The letter bore the signatures of fifty-five other senators. When Yoshida's interpolations in the National Diet left open the possibility of Japan concluding a peace treaty with the PRC, Dulles moved quickly to contain the damage. In mid-December he traveled to Japan to meet Yoshida face to face. Accompanying him were Senators John Sparkman (D.-Ala.) and Alexander Smith (R.-N.J.), both of whom sat on the Far Eastern subcommittee of the Senate Committee on Foreign Relations.[64]

Within days of the American contingent's departure, Yoshida clarified Japan's policy toward China in a letter to Dulles. Although Dulles was the author of the so-called Yoshida letter, neither side acknowledged the fact. Yoshida pledged that Japan was prepared to conclude a "bilateral treaty" with Nationalist China, and that it had "no intention to conclude a bilateral treaty with the Communist regime of China." On 16 January 1952, before the Senate took up the matter of the Japanese treaties, the Truman administration released the letter to the press. Predictably, the letter drew fire from every direction in Japan, antagonized the British, and provoked the Chinese Communists.[65] Negotiations between Japan and the ROC nevertheless opened in Taipei in February. On 28 April 1952, the same day that Japan regained its sovereignty, Japan and Nationalist China concluded a treaty of peace along the lines of the San Francisco agreement.[66]

Despite the criticism that the Tokyo-Taipei treaty drew, Dulles was justifiably satisfied with his handling of the China question. ROC sympathizers in the Senate rallied around several reservations to the treaty proposed by William Jenner, an Old Guard Republican from Indiana. The most important of these recognized the Nationalist regime as China's sovereign government. The release of the Yoshida letter and progress toward a Sino-Japanese pact in Taipei undercut support for the Jenner reservation. It was defeated 48 to 29, with 19 abstentions. Although the narrow vision of the Republican Old Guard may have horrified him, Dulles's aim was to lock the peace settlement in place. The hallmark of his political style, as the journalist James Reston observed, was "to hold the votes of senators, regardless of what he thought of them." The reservation got twenty-nine votes despite vigorous opposition from Senators Smith and Knowland, both of whom staunchly supported the Nationalist regime. "I know that what we did put an undesirable strain upon our U.K. relations," Dulles later wrote, "but it was not nearly as bad as what seems to me was clearly the alternative."[67]

Toward Japanese Membership in GATT

Peacemaking also placed the United States and the United Kingdom at odds over Japan's relationship with the Western trading bloc. Whereas the landmark events in the integration of West Germany into the international economy were participation in the European Coal and Steel Community and later the European Economic Community, in Japan's case all sides focused on the issue of Japanese membership in GATT. Encouraged by the United States, the Yoshida government naturally sought to rejoin the international community in a visible fashion.[68]

Owing to the memories of Japanese competition in Western markets before the war, the prospect of Japanese membership in GATT was highly sensitive abroad. Powerful interests in the nations of Western Europe, the British Commonwealth, and the United States opposed Japanese accession. As a leading power in GATT (but not in the emerging European Economic Community), the U.K. played a pivotal role. Because there was no countervailing force in East Asia similar to the political momentum in Western Europe underpinning the European Common Market, the effect of opposition to Japanese economic integration was more pronounced than hostility toward German trade recovery. If West Germany's non-Communist neighbors increasingly regarded economic integration as a hedge against future conflict, the opposite held true in East Asia. Political animosity toward Japan tended to reinforce anxiety about Japanese economic competition.

The challenge for the Truman and Eisenhower administrations was to overcome opposition at home and abroad without precipitating a counterproductive backlash against either further liberalization of trade or Japanese revival.

In September 1951 Japan asked to send an observer to the sixth session of GATT then in progress at Geneva. Reaction to the Japanese request varied widely. To the United States the question was purely procedural.[69] Taking the view that the Japanese observer issue had "wider implications," the United Kingdom urged that it be deferred to the next session (effectively shelving it for about nine months). The British government opposed Japanese membership in GATT and was not prepared to soften its policy, adopted in 1950, of refusing to grant most-favored-nation treatment to Japan.[70] In a manner that anticipated their behavior throughout the entire controversy, other opponents left the unpleasant task of stating the case against Japanese accession to the U.K. delegates.

The British government was in fact divided on the issue. The Foreign Office favored bringing Japan into GATT, but the Board of Trade opposed doing so. To the diplomats, inclusion in the institutions of the postwar order would persuade Japan "to co-operate in orderly participation in world trade." The board, by contrast, feared a negative political reaction at home. The timing of the Japanese bid played into the hands of the board. In the run up to the general election of 25 October—an election in which the Conservatives defeated the ruling Labor Party—no one of either party wished to appear soft on the threat of Japanese commercial competition. Thus, the Foreign Office effort to "buy time" represented a middle way between the harsh requirements of domestic politics and the increasing foreign pressure to admit Japan into GATT.[71]

Britain found itself leading a small minority. The contracting parties granted Japan's request and sent an invitation welcoming a Japanese observer.[72] By the end of 1951 Japan was obviously poised to apply for accession to GATT. Although a majority of the contracting parties were reluctant to oppose a Japanese application, the prospect of accepting Japan into GATT on equal terms created immediate political difficulties for all. Hence, the issue was not whether Japan would eventually succeed in becoming a member. The open questions were when and on what terms Japan would accede to GATT.

Recognizing the likelihood of strong opposition to GATT membership for Japan in the United States, officials in the Department of State's Bureau of Economic Affairs looked ahead to meeting the challenge during the early months of 1952 while the Japanese peace treaty was making its way through the U.S. Senate. In a lengthy memo, John Leddy, who had spoken for the United States at the previous GATT session, summarized the bureau's views and the department's position. The United States had to take the lead in finding alternative "free world" markets for Japanese goods. If "the free world close[d] its doors to Japan," Leddy reasoned, "the latter will have no place to turn except to the Communist world." The military establishment similarly supported Japanese integration with the Western trading bloc as compensation for forcing the nation to forgo economic opportunity in its trade with the Asian mainland.[73]

Such expansion of Japanese opportunity was not preordained. Meaningful tariff negotiations required concessions on sensitive commodities, something certain to "stir up vocal domestic interests." The United States and Japan had never before negotiated for reciprocal reductions in tariffs, and in previous negotiations with other countries (under the RTAA) American negotiators had taken care to not to grant concessions that would chiefly benefit Japan. Goods that Japan sold in the United States such as cotton textiles, canned fish, and chinaware were still subject to the high rates of duty set by the Tariff Act of 1930.[74] Further, as the RTAA—the executive branch's source of authority to conduct reciprocal trade negotiations—was due to expire in June 1953, there was little chance of conducting tariff negotiations with Japan before the second half of 1953.

One way out of this bind was to seek specific "bipartisan agreement" in the United States "on bringing Japan into [a] closer trading relationship with the United States and the rest of the free world." John Foster Dulles was the natural figure to approach the nation's lawmakers. On 18 March 1952, the Bureaus of Economic and Far Eastern Affairs prepared a memorandum recommending that Secretary Acheson ask Dulles to request a bipartisan congressional resolution in some form authorizing trade negotiations with Japan.[75] Nothing ever came of the March initiative. Dulles was weary of both Washington and the restrictions that bipartisanship placed upon him. With the Senate's ratification of the peace and security treaties on 20 March, Dulles was already thinking of the Republican presidential campaign.[76] Without a compelling strategic or political interest at stake, the details of economic policy bored him. Ironically, one of the problems requiring Dulles's attention after his appointment as secretary of state was the matter of securing congressional authorization for trade negotiations with Japan.

In the absence of American action, Japan submitted a formal application for accession to GATT in July 1952. By this time the GATT session originally scheduled for June had been postponed until October. Japan's trade deficit was alarmingly high, domestic industries were pressing for opportunity abroad, and the Yoshida government was anxious to bolster its political standing at home.[77] The postal ballot procedure for application under which Japan applied required each contracting party to reply within thirty days whether it had any objections to Japan's entering into negotiations for accession. Unless there were three or more dissenting votes, the application would be accepted.

Neither Japanese nor American officials were very optimistic about securing a favorable vote. Japan even requested U.S. support for two fallback options. Instead of outright rejection, the contracting parties might agree either to extend an invitation to Japan subject to an informal understanding that actual negotiations would not begin until 1953, or to postpone consideration of the application until the 1953 session.[78] The interdepartmental U.S. Trade Agreements Committee (TAC) saw "no real alternative to our supporting the application and agreeing to enter into tariff negotiations with Japan." The TAC qualified its recommendation, however, adding that the United States was not to press the Japanese application "to the point of incurring the risk of outright rejection." President Truman approved the recommendation on 22 August.[79]

Only the United Kingdom, Australia, and New Zealand dissented. Even powers such as France and South Africa—nations that did not intend to undertake tariff negotiations with Japan—were hesitant to oppose Japanese membership. Yet the aim of pressing for Japan's accession to GATT in 1952 was to secure improved treatment of Japanese trade. The issue was not as simple as forcing a vote in the face of favorable numbers. Winning an invitation for Japan by such a vote would be a "Pyrrhic victory," one State Department official explained, "unless the British Commonwealth countries were included among those agreeing to invite Japan."[80] Hence, the department preferred to seek a consensus solution, even if the result was delay.

Such attention to the Commonwealth nations, particularly the United Kingdom, composed a vital thread in the story of Japanese accession to GATT. The State Department was receptive to a British suggestion to postpone formal decision until the next year's GATT session. Nothing was to be gained by forcing the United Kingdom to vote against Japanese accession, and the United States had promised Japan only that it would instruct the

U.S. delegation "to favor postponement of consideration or some other feasible alternative and to oppose outright rejection." Thus, in October 1952 the contracting parties approved a resolution recognizing that "Japan should take her rightful place in the community of trading nations and to that end should be admitted to the appropriate international arrangements." It authorized an intersessional committee to take up the conditions and timing of action on the Japanese application.[81]

Perceptive observers recognized that the GATT resolution represented a play for time. The *Manchester Guardian* correctly identified the resort to an intersessional committee as "a calculated move to delay the accession of Japan to GATT for as long as possible."[82] Failure to decide the question of Japanese accession understandably drew criticism in Japan, particularly from the business community. Although they attempted to put the best public face on developments, Japanese diplomats resented the committee's instructions to consider "conditions" to Japanese entry into GATT. The Japanese hoped for tariff negotiations to commence and a favorable decision to be made in 1953.[83] Despite independence, Japan was still dependent upon American sponsorship and access to Western markets remained elusive.

Conclusion

In its economic provisions, the San Francisco peace settlement was a clear triumph for the United States. The terms of the peace treaty represented the culmination of the policies first implemented in Japan during the reverse course. By reducing Japan's reparations burden, avoiding the imposition of enduring restrictions, and pressing for the normalization of international commerce, the treaty paved the way for Japan's return to the global economy. Although Britain was a cosponsor of the draft treaty unveiled before the peace conference, the substance of the agreement reflected the extent to which the United States had replaced Britain as the leading Western power in East Asia.

Yet if the peace treaty brought the Occupation to a close and ratified U.S. designs for the postwar world, the new order was far from settled. By so visibly excluding the Communist Chinese from the peace settlement, American policy contributed to Japan's isolation from the Chinese mainland and ensured that Sino-Japanese relations would be a source of interallied friction in the future. Similarly, the Truman administration's preliminary support for Japanese accession to GATT aroused the opposition of various nations. The lenient peace settlement and the continuing U.S. effort to find a means for

Japan to balance its trade offered the promise of a more prosperous future. But the precise terms of Japan's relationship with China and Japanese integration with the American-led economy remained open questions.

Both questions were settled by the decade's end. Economic ties between Japan and the West multiplied, while relations between Japan and the Chinese mainland remained distant. The peace treaty diplomacy of John Foster Dulles reflected the extent to which these two developments were connected. But one must look beyond American high-handedness to understand why the settlement endured. Of the wider forces at work reinforcing the Cold War division of East Asia, the most important by far were the Korean War and the economic blockade of the Chinese mainland, as the next chapter explores in detail.

Chapter Four

WAR IN KOREA AND THE
CHINA TRADE EMBARGO

During the spring of 1950, both Japanese leaders and the U.S. foreign policy establishment shared a feeling of unease. Despite efforts to promote recovery, Japan was treading water, not moving forward. Negotiation of the peace treaty promised to be a lengthy process. Lawmakers in Washington balked at spending more money on defense and foreign aid. The European allies displayed a similar reluctance to respond to news of the Sino-Soviet alliance announced in February. A potentially debilitating sense of drift was settling in on both sides of the Pacific.

The North Korean assault across the thirty-eighth parallel on 25 June 1950, provided deliverance. In leading the United Nation's defense of South Korea, the Truman administration was able to implement its ambitious strategy for expanding the struggle against the Communist bloc outlined in the policy paper NSC 68.[1] With Communist armies on the march, congressional opposition to greater defense spending evaporated. European resistance to imposing tight restrictions on strategic trade with the Communist bloc similarly, if temporarily, eased. The war undercut opposition to a continuing American military presence in Japan while U.S. war orders sparked Japanese economic recovery. The price of this windfall was tight control on trade with the Chinese mainland.

Thus, the Korean War's significance extends beyond its role in defining the Cold War confrontation in Asia. It shaped both the Japanese peace settlement and the contours of economic relations across the Pacific for the remainder of the twentieth century. This division of East Asia's economy was highly unpopular in Japan and the allied nations of Western Europe. But the escalating Sino-American polarization that grew out of the Korean War proved stronger than the advocates of cooperation. Until President Richard Nixon's reversal of U.S. China policy two decades later, the Japanese and Chinese economies remained apart. The wall separating them was thus as important a feature of the emerging order as the economic ties binding Japan and the United States.

"Divine Aid": The Korean War Boom

One of the greatest ironies in the vast growth of private trade across the Pacific since 1945 is the preponderant role government has played in its expansion. The U.S. and Japanese governments went far beyond providing a legal framework within which trade and investment could flow. Japan's defeat and occupation by the United States necessarily expanded American influence in Northeast Asia. In 1950, however, American policy was at a crossroads. Coming when it did, the Korean conflict had the effect of pulling the United States more deeply into Asian affairs than anyone had previously imagined possible.

Wartime spending contributed to a reorientation of Japan's trade and investment westward. Congress no longer hesitated to approve the Truman administration's expansionary budgets. U.S. military spending surpassed 10 percent of GNP.[2] American war orders stimulated the depressed world economy, and Japan was the greatest beneficiary. Overnight a market for Japanese industrial production appeared. Japan filled orders for American forces in Korea ranging from construction services to ordnance, automobiles, and textiles. Large Japanese businesses such as Toyota and independent contractors alike reaped unexpected profits. The governor of the Bank of Japan called U.S. spending "divine aid." Scholars have identified in the Korean War's impact on Japan as an equivalent of the Marshall Plan in Europe.[3]

Although the Korean War infused new life into both the Truman administration's global strategy and the Japanese economy, its salutary impact must not be overstated. No boom lasts forever, and leaders of both nations worried about what would happen when it ended. Joseph Dodge warned, the nation had "not yet answered its need and proved its ability to earn its own living with normal exports in increasingly competitive world markets."[4] More recently the historian Roger Dingman has explained how a "dagger" came with the "gift" of the wartime boom. Inflation, shortages of raw materials, production bottlenecks, and increased dependence on the United States all accompanied the windfall profits.[5]

Such pressures are the natural consequence of overstimulating any economy, but they show how there was no easy formula for Japanese recovery. Japanese attention focused on the distortions in the nation's economy and the moment of reckoning that would accompany the war's end.[6] During their conference at Wake Island President Truman and General MacArthur brushed aside optimistic speculation that Japan's dollar gap was a worry of the past. They agreed to implement a "pay-as-you-go" system of financing the costs of the Occupation with dollars (effective in July 1951). Alongside military procurement and the spending of U.S. forces in Japan, these new dollar expenditures implicitly acknowledged that Japan remained unable to balance its trade alone.[7]

The Korean War was nevertheless a primary event in the U.S. foreign policy of containment, and its impact on the course of international relations in East Asia was to establish the political fault lines in the region for the next two decades. The war's most immediate legacy was to institutionalize U.S. military spending in Japan. Postwar aid had been a stopgap measure. Military spending held longer-term potential, because it naturally accompanied any American security commitment to Japan. Spending associated with maintaining a military presence abroad and rearming American allies was more acceptable to the U.S. lawmakers. Whereas congressional critics of both containment and deficit spending fought vigorously to reduce foreign aid expenditures, they were much more hesitant to cut the defense budget.[8]

Japanese receipts from U.S. military expenditures declined after the war, but they remained at a significant level, averaging slightly over $550 million per year from 1950 to 1960 (Table 1.4). The same pattern of spending reappeared during the Vietnam War.[9] Besides the obvious stimulative effect, such spending played a vital role in offsetting Japan's chronic foreign trade deficit during the fifties. The accounting was complex and the nominal figures overstate the actual dollar contribution, but U.S. military expenditures assisted in stabilizing Japan's balance of payments while the nation made the transition from postwar reconstruction to high-speed growth.

In binding Japan and the United States together more tightly, however, the war disrupted Japan's economic relations with the Chinese mainland. Despite the pervasive hope that Asia could avoid becoming divided into two hostile camps, the prospects for cooperation in the region rested on a fragile foundation. Prospects for Japan becoming a viable third force between East and West were particularly illusory. Memories of the last war remained vivid in Chinese minds, further complicating Japan's relationship with China.[10] By locking the United States and the PRC into confrontation, the Korean War polarized East Asian politics. To understand how the war institutionalized controls on trade with China, the place to begin is the unsettled state of U.S. export control policy and economic relations in the region before the fateful events of June 1950.

Export Controls and the China Trade

The executive branch had imposed controls on foreign trade for strategic purposes since 1940, but not until the decade's end did China figure prominently in U.S. policy. Although export controls have comprised a fundamental element of American diplomacy, the technical aspects of policy and a shroud of secrecy have inhibited public inquiry into the subject.[11] During the Second World War the U.S. restricted exports of defense-related materials. With the onset of the Cold War the policy shifted toward curtailing the flow of strategic materials into the Soviet bloc. The Commerce Department administered the program, and the public face of policy was the "Positive List." It listed items restricted either for short supply or for security reasons. Following congressional pressure in 1947 and the Communist coup in Czechoslovakia the next February, the department classified controlled items into two categories: 1A items consisted of materials contributing directly to war potential such as munitions; 1B items such as steel, by contrast, were simply important to a war economy. U.S. policy prohibited the export of 1A items and called for the screening of shipments of 1B items, the aim being to insure that they were for normal peacetime uses.

Truman administration officials recognized that multilateral action was necessary to curtail strategic trade with the Soviet bloc. In 1948 W. Averell Harriman took up the issue with the Marshall Plan countries. The next year the governments agreed on three new international lists: IL/I, fully embargoed items; IL/II, goods subject to quantitative control; and IL/III, items under consideration for control. In November 1949, the participating countries established a multilateral forum in Paris that became known as the Consultative Group. Beginning in January 1950, the group's Coordinating Committee, known as COCOM, attended to the task of coordinating and enforcing controls.[12]

Even as the CCP gained control of the Chinese mainland, the United States refrained from imposing strict controls on the China trade. This difference in policy toward the two Communist giants was the result of both careful deliberation and constant bureaucratic wrangling. Dean Acheson, immediately following his appointment as secretary of state, took the initiative. In early 1949 he asked W. Walton Butterworth, director of the Office of Far Eastern Affairs, to draft a policy paper on Chinese trade for the NSC. Acheson paid careful attention to policy regarding Chinese trade because it was potentially significant to the Japanese economy. Thus, although the overall policy objective of the new policy paper, inherited from NSC 34/1 of January the same year, was "to prevent China from becoming an adjunct of Soviet power," the secretary's concern with promoting Japanese recovery figured prominently throughout.[13]

NSC 41 spelled out two possible alternatives, or what it termed "the least disadvantageous of alternative courses open to us." The hard-line option was "mobilization of the political and economic power of the western world to combat openly, through intimidation or direct pressure, a Chinese Communist regime."[14] The paper rejected this course of heightened confrontation for several reasons. It recognized that "determined and ruthless leadership can survive and even consolidate itself in the face of extreme economic hardships." China was relatively self-sufficient economically, and existing trade served various interests. Severe restrictions would jeopardize Japan's trade with North China and Manchuria, thereby increasing the cost to the United States of supporting the Japanese economy. Confrontation would also "provoke and justify Communist expulsion and seizure of American and business and mission interests and property in China." In short, all-out confrontation promised to be self-defeating. Butterworth conceded, however, that such a policy "might be forced upon us, but should be adopted only after the failure of other courses had been demonstrated."[15]

The other strategy aimed to preserve the opportunity to exploit any rift between Moscow and Beijing while encouraging trade between Japan and China. "[G]erms of friction between a Chinese Communist regime and the Kremlin undoubtedly exist in the Chinese situation," the policy paper's authors proposed. Even if the United States could do little to foster Sino-Soviet conflict, by preserving its influence in China, it could "exploit" any "centrifugal forces as may develop." This course was not to be construed as a "soft" policy, however. American policy was to make clear "the potential power of the United States" to impose "severe restrictions on trade" if the Communist regime demonstrated "its determination to follow policies inimical to United States strategic interests."[16]

In embracing the less confrontational of these two strategies, NSC 41 recommended that trade between Japan and China be "encouraged on a *quid-pro-quo* basis." It warned against "preponderant dependence on Chinese sources for Japan's food and critical raw material requirements," however. The policy paper advised imposing an embargo on all exports of items of direct military utility to China (on the 1A list). It further recommended screening of important industrial, transportation, and communications supplies and equipment (the remaining 1A items and certain 1B items), mostly for the purpose of guarding against their reexport to the USSR or Eastern Europe. All other trade was to be permitted in accordance with normal commercial guidelines. Japanese exports to China were to be made subject to the same considerations. The cooperation of other friendly governments in imposing similar controls was to be sought wherever necessary. Finally, the United States was to seek the cooperation of private American firms operating in areas beyond the jurisdiction of governments imposing controls.[17]

President Truman approved NSC 41 on 3 March 1949. Upon receipt of the policy from the JCS, SCAP acted immediately to apply the new NSC requirements in Japan. Occupation authorities justified the decision on the grounds that responsibility for the security of Japan permitted imposition of controls over exports of strategic materials. Since SCAP licensed all foreign exchange transactions, implementation was a simple matter. Although SCAP transferred this responsibility to the Japanese government in December 1949, the same procedures remained in effect. To ensure compliance, the Department of the Army and SCAP developed surveillance procedures in Japan.[18]

Despite the State Department's pessimistic evaluation of the consequences of heightened confrontation with the Chinese Communists, American policy became progressively more restrictive. In December the administration agreed upon a new statement of Asian policy (NSC 48/2). The relevant paragraph on trade with China deleted the allowances for case-by-case exceptions on export of 1A items (permitted in NSC 41). In addition to being screened, exports of 1B items were to be severely limited.[19] SCAP chafed under the growing restrictions.[20] After the announcement of the Sino-Soviet alliance in February 1950, movement toward greater restrictions quickened. By June even the State Department conceded that, with two minor exceptions, policy on exports to China should follow the same guidelines as that toward the Soviet Union.[21]

The Reluctant Allies

America's Western European allies resisted imposing restrictions on their exports to the Communist bloc, except for items of direct military utility. The allies' economies were in precarious condition, and the United Kingdom especially had a greater economic stake in China than the United States did. Despite Anglo-American differences on East-West trade, the United Kingdom was the closest ally of the United States. The two powers attempted to agree on a common position before beginning multilateral discussions. Interallied negotiations on export control issues thus displayed a mix of cooperation and discord.

The State Department approached the United Kingdom immediately after President Truman approved NSC 41. The United States requested that the British impose controls on exports of 1A and certain 1B commodities to China, from the United Kingdom as well as the nation's dependencies in East Asia.[22] The British moved part way toward meeting the American request, agreeing in July to create a mechanism for controlling exports to China. British participation was contingent upon Belgian, French, and Dutch cooperation.[23]

Following protracted talks, the Foreign Office agreed in October 1949 to control export of 1A items to China, Macao, and Korea, from the United Kingdom, Hong Kong, and Singapore, provided that alternative suppliers such as Japan likewise controlled their trade. The British further agreed to "watch the flow" of 1B items to China and exchange information on such trade. But they refused to restrict 1B items. Finally, they sought to exercise control over exports of petroleum products to China, in cooperation with the Netherlands, the United States, and the major oil companies of the three nations.[24] Then, until April 1950, the two sides addressed the question of timing and sought the cooperation of other governments, particularly Vietnam, Laos, Cambodia, and Indonesia. London also approached the Commonwealth governments with mixed results.[25]

The British refused to limit trade with China as strictly as the United States desired for several reasons. The Labor government was averse to antagonizing the CCP, and the same attitude permeated Britain's foreign policy establishment. British diplomats recognized the anticapitalist, antiimperialist, and antiforeign biases of the PRC leadership. They nevertheless hoped that the Communists would eventually "realize their need for beneficial economic relations with the West." Fear reinforced such thinking. In the Foreign Office view, controlling 1B items would achieve little while drawing a hostile response from the PRC, thus jeopardizing both the position of Hong Kong and the substantial British investments in and trade with China.[26]

The position of British firms in China deserves particular mention because the difficulties they faced reinforced official caution. Although British businessmen recognized that the CCP was not likely to be dislodged from power after 1949, many hoped that they would be able to work out a modus vivendi with the People's government to continue their operations. The Chinese understood more clearly that the decline of British military influence in Asia left foreign merchants virtually defenseless against the new regime. The result was not rapid confiscation of Britain's firms in China, however. "British merchants in China," one scholar concludes, "had become hostages not only to the immovable assets built up in China over the years, but hostages as well to the determination of the People's Government to strictly control the new economic environment in the interests of its own people."[27]

Rather than rapidly liquidate the British firms, Communist authorities used them for their own ends. During the first years of the People's Republic they forced the foreign capitalists to maintain production and employment despite losses, for example. In order to insure that the firms maintained their operations, the Chinese commonly required the continuing presence of a senior European firm executive in China. The Three-Anti Campaign against corruption, waste, and bureaucracy during the winter of 1951–52, along with the Communists' other attempts to socialize the country, soon convinced British capitalists that the best course was to get out of China. In the world of "hostage capitalism," however, closing the doors of a foreign firm required Chinese consent. Hostile pressure promised only to increase the price of a deal.

The ambition of the United Kingdom to exert a moderating influence on the PRC never disappeared entirely, but Britain's China policy was neither static nor inflexible. Early on, the hope for better relations with the PRC defined policy. Anglo-American discord was thus real, but each side also believed that its representations to the other would make a difference. No one in London seriously entertained the prospect of going it alone. Following the outbreak of war in Korea and Chinese intransigence on a number of bilateral issues, British policy—including that on export controls—shifted toward a harder line. Differences between London and Washington remained, but they existed in the context of a close partnership between the two countries.

Despite British unwillingness to accede to all U.S. demands in 1949, the State Department had good reasons to agree to Britain's terms. Further negotiation was unlikely to lead anywhere. Barring the outbreak of war, the low level of trade with China provided a unique opportunity to impose controls. Revival of trade, department officials correctly surmised, would have rendered their imposition more difficult.[28] Because the entire discussion was secret, there was no leverage to be gained by going public. Formal agreements relating to trade were supposed to be registered with the United Nations. The United States thus preferred to propose an "informal memorandum" as the basis for "oral discussion and agreement" among the allies. Each power could then announce its "unilateral decisions" to adopt controls on trade.[29]

During the spring of 1950, however, multilateral talks in Paris were making little progress and American advocates of stricter controls were losing patience. As in the negotiations with the British on China, the disagreement revolved around items on the 1B list. The United States pressed for control; the Europeans resisted. Whereas American cold warriors saw the USSR making use of 1B items to "build up a maximum war machine," the allies saw their obvious peacetime applications.[30] The State Department estimated that about 25 percent of Western European exports to Eastern Europe and some $200 million were at stake. The same report also envisioned the loss of Western Europe's most strategic raw material imports.[31] Given Western European anxiety about economic recovery, U.S. pressure for restrictions was bound to encounter resistance.

At War

Few events could have heightened the Cold War confrontation in Asia more dramatically than the Communist offensive in Korea. The North Korean attack on the South and the PRC's subsequent intervention on the North's behalf vindicated the Western advocates of a hard anti-Communist line and undercut proponents of a less confrontational stance. The economic significance of the military conflict thus stems in part from its role in clearing away, if only temporarily, resistance to U.S. demands for tighter control of trade with the PRC and the Communist bloc.

The Truman administration immediately imposed an embargo on all exports to North Korea and extended the embargo on exports to the PRC to include the entire 1B list. SCAP enforced the same regulations on Japan's trade. The administration nevertheless permitted a continuation of trade in 1B items with Hong Kong, subject to end-use checks by the Hong Kong government. Consumer goods and other nonstrategic items likewise continued to flow into China. The State Department still desired Sino-Japanese trade in order to "reduce Japan's reliance upon the United States for economic assistance."[32]

State Department officials pressed the allies to tighten their controls. The British reaction, however, was "sluggish." Foreign Office representatives voiced several objections and insisted that British compliance was contingent upon France, Belgium, and the Netherlands acting likewise. The State Department pressed for a favorable decision without waiting for the other governments to act, and by 1 July the Continental powers had agreed in any case.[33] Thus prodded into action, the United Kingdom tightened controls on Far Eastern trade. On 4 July cabinet ministers approved a complete embargo on all exports from Britain to North Korea, but refused to impose controls on shipments of strategic materials to China. On 10 July the cabinet reversed itself, deciding to prohibit the export of strategic goods from Britain to the PRC. Ministers left untouched, however, the question of exports from Hong Kong and Singapore, two ports that were exporting strategic materials.[34]

Reluctance at the top contributed to this delay. The ultimate aim of British East Asian policy was to welcome the PRC into the family of nations. Top leaders did not want events in Korea to wreck such designs. As Prime Minister Clement Attlee noted on 30 June, the government "should keep the question of our economic policy toward China separate from that of any embargo on North Korea."[35] Faith that the United Kingdom could serve as a bridge between the PRC and the West was not easily shaken. Finally, on 14 July, the Defence Committee agreed to stop strategic exports from Hong Kong and Singapore, along with measures to deny oil to the PRC. The government did not announce that controls were imposed for security reasons.[36]

A further reason for British delay was the weakness of the administrative structure governing trade policy and the empire. Neither the Foreign Office nor any other body had centralized responsibility for export controls in East Asia. Improvisation was the order of the day. In Hong Kong, for example, legal procedure for enforcement of the cabinet decision to ban exports of IL/I materials required the public announcement of an executive order. Fearful of provoking Communist reprisal, neither London nor Hong Kong wished to issue such a decree. Ministers and the governor of Hong Kong had to piece together justification for action under various other regulations.[37]

American pressure moved the Western allies, but the shift toward more rigid controls that began during the summer of 1950 was not merely a response to U.S. exhortation. The desire "to do all in our power to stifle the North Korean war effort," as one British official expressed the point, arose naturally from participation in the UN action.[38] As the scale of the war revealed itself during the summer months, London began to consider more seriously how to prevent the flow of valuable goods to Communist armies. Hence, while Foreign Office representatives were resisting U.S. demands to extend the embargo to the entire 1B list in August, an interdepartmental working party was charting a course much more in harmony with American demands.

The point of the working party's paper, dated 4 September, was that the most effective means of preventing industrial goods from reaching North Korea was to prevent their export to "all Communist countries." "The only sure way of restricting sales to Communist Asia," it continued, "would be to include the items on List II of the International Security Control Lists." To guard against exports of these items (such as barbed wire) in the interim, the authors recommended informal action. Departments in close touch with traders were "to use whatever powers or influence they possess" to "discourage exports" of items suggesting support of "the forces of aggression."[39]

The working party's paper served as the basis for the official deliberation leading up to the tripartite negotiations among the Americans, the British, and the French on East-West trade that began in September. Washington's stance had hardened since May, and American frustration with Britain was reaching a peak. The numbers spoke for themselves: of the 288 1B items which COCOM had considered for control, the members had rejected 153 of them, accepted 15 for IL/I and 30 for IL/II, and postponed action on the balance of 90 items. "[F]urther progress," a staff paper concluded, "is unlikely unless changes occur in the U.K. position prior to such a review."[40] The State Department pressed accordingly on several different issues all at once. The idea was to settle for a compromise on the methods of control, where compromise was inevitable, in order to secure maximum concessions on the 1B list. To add to the pressure on the Western European nations, the NSC urged that defense officials approach their NATO counterparts so as to formulate "a military viewpoint regarding export controls."[41]

Domestic politics weighed heavily on the administration. Since American soldiers were fighting and dying in Korea, the prospect of allied firms supplying Communist armies provoked discontent at home. Besides contributing to the American war effort, lawmakers understandably wished to turn the issue in their favor during an election year. In September, Senator Kenneth S. Wherry (R.-Neb.) twice proposed an amendment that would have denied U.S. assistance to nations that exported items of war potential (broadly defined) to the Communist bloc. State Department officials saw no use in bludgeoning the Europeans in public and feared that cutting off aid or risking a stoppage of East-West trade might jeopardize allied economic revival. "Utmost efforts" were required to secure withdrawal of the Wherry amendment. As a substitute, Congress approved an amendment proposed by Congressman Clarence Cannon of Missouri. The latter amendment left case-by-case determination of whether trade with the Communist bloc was "contrary to the security interests of the United States" to the NSC.[42]

From the American point of view, the September Foreign Ministers Meeting and subsequent negotiations turned out to be "much more satisfactory than could have been anticipated." Recognizing that the embargo of IL/I items was insufficient to meet the challenges of the day, Secretary of State Acheson, Foreign Minister Bevin, and Foreign Minister Robert Schuman of France agreed in principle to restrict exports to the Soviet bloc of "selected items which are required in key industrial sectors that contribute directly to war potential." Following the U.S. suggestion, they also agreed that strategic—as opposed to economic—considerations should be predominant in selecting items for multilateral export control. The opinion of military and intelligence advisors was to be sought in "assessing the strategic importance of items for control." The three powers further agreed to inform the other countries imposing controls of their decisions and "urge on them the desirability of instituting the same controls."[43]

In November, Charles E. Bohlen, the head of the U.S. delegation, reported that "more progress was made at the London conversations on increasing the number of commodities under international export control ... than had been accomplished in the two years the matter had been under discussion."[44] Of the 318 items discussed, the three governments withdrew only 74 of them. They agreed to embargo 102 items, subject 73 to quantitative control, and exchange information on the remaining 69. The controlled goods fell principally in the sectors of metalworking machinery, chemicals, chemical and petroleum equipment, and precision instruments. For the first time the governments agreed on policies and procedures to implement quantitative control.[45]

"Virtual Embargo"

Before the Western allies could begin to implement the November agreement, Communist Chinese intervention in the Korean War again changed the strategic context. Delegates to London signed the final report on 20 November 1950. Four days later General MacArthur launched a general assault intended to end the Korean War. Contrary to official expectations, Chinese troops came to North Korea's defense. By the end of the year they had driven the UN forces back to the vicinity of the thirty-eighth parallel. Although U.S. officials appreciated how the war cleared away resistance at home and abroad to a foreign policy of confrontation with the Sino-Soviet bloc, the Chinese intervention presented the nation with a crisis of the first order. On the trade front, the imperative was to deny China access to any item that might contribute to the Communist war effort.

Interdepartmental rivalries, however, delayed an American decision on the precise contours of a trade embargo. At issue were two broad questions: whether the U.S. should act unilaterally, and the means of putting an embargo into effect. As an interim measure, the Commerce Department announced that, effective 3 December, a validated export license would be required for all exports shipped to the territories under the PRC control, Hong Kong, and Macao. American economic leverage was in fact slight. U.S. exports to China had declined to about $1 million per month, 85 percent of which consisted of cotton. Imports totaled $8 million per month and did include some valuable materials, particularly tungsten. The United States was also importing some tin and wool.[46]

Given the military picture, JCS insistence on unilateral action carried the day. At its meeting on 14 December, the NSC did not even attempt to patch together a compromise statement of policy when it considered an alternative proposal suggested by the Department of State. That proposal urged that the United States wait until securing multilateral agreement at the United Nations before imposing a complete embargo of its own. Rejecting State's preferred course of action, the NSC decided to go ahead with a freeze on Chinese assets so as to complete the embargo. Since the United Nations was then considering a cease-fire proposal, President Truman authorized the secretaries of state and the treasury to decide on the most opportune time to block Chinese assets.[47] The wait was a mere two days. On 16 December, the administration announced that, effective the next day, the government was placing under its control all Chinese Communist assets in the United States, and prohibiting all vessels of U.S. registry from calling at ports controlled by the PRC. The State Department, however, downplayed the action in notifications sent to overseas diplomatic missions. Messages to the allies avoided using the terms "blocking" and "embargo." They further pledged that the administration would give "proper regard" to "the interests of areas in the Far East under friendly governments."[48]

Japan was the most important of these "areas." At SCAP insistence, the Japanese government suspended exports of goods requiring export licenses to the PRC, North Korea, Hong Kong, and Macao unless the license was approved on or after 6 December. Unaffected items were of little importance in Sino-Japanese trade. During the first eight months of 1950, however, Japanese imports from the PRC amounted to $28.1 million; exports totaled about $7 million. Although less than 5 percent of Japan's total import trade, coking coal, iron ore, soybeans, and salt from China were available elsewhere only at a much higher cost. Hong Kong similarly depended upon foreign trade for survival. In order to assure a continued flow of the commodities necessary for domestic consumption in Hong Kong, SCAP continued to approve licenses on shipments to the colony subject to end-use checks from the Hong Kong government representative in Tokyo. For the time being, Washington left export control decisions in Tokyo to SCAP's discretion.[49]

The escalation of the war placed the United Kingdom in a bind. British officials privately condemned MacArthur's "deplorable campaign in Korea" and lamented that the American public could not see how "bad generalship" was the cause of the "fiasco." When dealing with the Department of State, however, they put the best face on things and calmly requested "immediate relaxation of this virtual embargo." Britain sought to maintain the flow of American nonstrategic materials and semistrategic materials for Hong Kong industries. The Department of State made no secret of its opposition to "this embargo" and urged the Commerce Department to approve shipments of exports to the colony. Commerce complied, but the review process remained lengthy and rigorous.[50] When the British requested automatic approval of up to 75 percent of the 1949 volume of trade in non–Positive List goods along with continued case-by-case consideration of Positive List items, the Department of State offered its qualified support. The Pentagon, however, buried the proposal.[51]

The Chinese Communists themselves did much to strengthen hard-line sentiment abroad. On 11 January the UN Truce Committee proposed a five-point peace program for the Far East. The next week the Chinese government rejected it. The United States then submitted a resolution in the General Assembly urging that China be found guilty of aggression in Korea, and the body approved it on 1 February. The General Assembly formed a committee (composed of the members of the Collective Measures Committee) to consider additional measures to counter the Chinese intervention in Korea.[52]

Impatience with Britain's China policy was surfacing within the Foreign Office, but the prevailing opinion remained unchanged. Robert H. Scott summarized official thinking in the middle of the crisis. Rather than expecting "dividends" from its China policy, the British position was "a long term lock-up investment which may yet justify itself." To the extent that "it has prevented the fire from breaking out just yet it has paid off." Had "we gone the American way, we would not only have had some extremely difficult passages with India, but we would have had a crisis over Hong Kong and possibly have lost it." Neither Scott nor anyone else in the Foreign Office believed that the West could "drive a wedge between Russia and China." But he was confident that "a rift will appear in course of time, spontaneously, and we must then be ready to help in the divorce proceedings, perhaps as co-respondent, or else as mother to whom the sobbing bride flees from her brutal husband." The effect of American pressure on the PRC, according to this view, was "to rivet Russia and China together, so that a rift will take longer to appear and the alliance is more solid than it need have been." Thus, the Foreign Office opposed sanctions, criticizing them as "useless or counter-productive."[53]

Recognizing British unwillingness to enforce a complete embargo and seeking the broadest possible support for UN action, the Department of State pressed for limited sanctions. As an "irreducible minimum," the United States proposed an immediate halt to exports of petroleum, atomic energy materials, arms, ammunition, implements of war, among other items of direct military utility. The department and the administration also hoped to secure an expansion of COCOM controls, particularly an embargo on IL/II items to China. The practical effects of any new measure were actually political rather than economic. According to department estimates, the Western allies already controlled 90 percent of the trade with the PRC that they could control. The purposes of sanctions were to register the world's moral condemnation of Communist aggression and to deter such behavior in other areas.[54]

The British dread of a general war, so pronounced in December and January, subsided somewhat after the completion of an interdepartmental report on the political and strategic implications of sanctions in February. Among the report's many conclusions was the finding that a selective embargo of the sort the United States was considering was unlikely to expose Hong Kong to great risk. Consistent with the Foreign Office line, however, it also regarded such sanctions as having little effect as an instrument against China. The British sought to postpone any recommendation for economic sanctions to the Additional Measures Committee so as to allow the Good Offices Committee time to make progress toward a peace settlement in Korea. As the U.K. representative on the Additional Measures Committee aptly summarized his mission, the committee's work "should be delayed as long as possible."[55]

The cumulative force of events, however, was working against Britain. U.K. policy depended upon Chinese goodwill for its success. Beijing's every move, however, suggested only continuing hostility. The Chinese Communists' refusal to establish diplomatic relations with the United Kingdom alienated British opinion.[56] The Communists' spring offensives, coupled with the rejection of General MacArthur's 29 March offer of peace, played badly overseas. Most important, by mid-April the Good Offices Committee was unable to report any progress toward a cease-fire after months of effort. The UN General Assembly approved the U.S.-sponsored embargo in May. Fearing that additional delay would encourage the Chinese Communists in their defiance of the United Nations Secretary Acheson pressed forward at the beginning of the month. After assuring the United Kingdom that a selective embargo was not merely an "opening wedge" for a complete blockade, the department gained British support. Other nations followed. On 18 May the General Assembly approved the final draft by a roll-call vote of 47 to 0, with 8 abstentions and 5 (Communist) powers not participating.[57] Beyond isolating the PRC, the effect of the embargo was to consolidate the structure of controls on trade with China.

The Chinese Communists' failure to play effectively on allied hopes for peace by refraining from provocative action in 1951 clinched the unity of the anti-Communist coalition rallied against it. In that sense, the Chinese military offensives early in the year represented an opportunity lost. Available Chinese sources, however, suggest that Western diplomacy did not figure prominently in Chinese decision making. One of the enduring characteristics of Chinese diplomacy is the unusual degree to which it is a function of internal considerations. Intervention in Korea, the historian Jian Chen has shown, was inseparable from—indeed it reinforced—the Chinese Communist Party's revolutionary nationalism, its dedication to Asian-wide revolution, and its determination to maintain the inner dynamics of the Communist revolution at home.[58]

Although vitally affected by events unfolding in Korea, Japan had virtually no part in the UN General Assembly's decision. Japan's restrictions on trade were already greater than those of the Western European allies. Final decision on export controls rested with SCAP, and Occupation authorities were careful to protect their authority over Japan's trade and to discourage public discussion of the matter. SCAP specifically sought to avoid inviting any autonomous Japanese decision against FEC directives. Raising the question of controls, officials in Tokyo rightly concluded, "could precipitate serious and unnecessary domestic political crisis."[59]

Congressional Initiatives

Just as the Korean War fueled the "Red Scare" at home, it led naturally to calls for economic war against the Communist bloc. As required by the Cannon amendment, the NSC studied trade between friendly nations and the bloc. Recognizing that many recipients of U.S. assistance also depended upon some trade with Communist powers, the council did not call for retaliation. The NSC also reviewed American policy in the spring of 1951, and its findings ratified the administration's present course.[60] With the firm support of public opinion, various lawmakers called for a tougher policy. Senator James P. Kem (R.-Mo.) advanced the most significant initiative

Senator Kem's amendment to an appropriation bill (passed on 21 May) was identical to the Wherry resolution. It called for denying economic aid to any country sending military-related items to the Soviet bloc while U.S. forces were engaged in hostilities. The act allowed the president to make exceptions upon the advice of the NSC, but it imposed a limit of fifteen days for compliance with its terms. On 2 June President Truman signed the appropriations act, but he criticized the Kem amendment. He said that the NSC would need to make broad use of the provision for exceptions. On

14 June the NSC approved a general interim exception that temporarily exempted all nations from the provisions of the amendment pending further study of the situation.[61]

The Department of State led the administration's effort to regain the initiative. The department sought to persuade the COCOM powers to add all items on the residual American 1A list (about 10 percent of the original) to International List I, and to tighten quantitative controls on items of secondary strategic significance. In August the COCOM member nations accepted thirty-four out of the fifty-three items proposed by the United States, and referred the remaining ones (mostly in the fields of rail transport, heavy construction, and mining) for further discussion. They also accepted the U.S. proposals regarding IL/II intended to tighten quantitative controls.[62] Since the allies resented what they regarded as unilateral American attempts to force a policy of economic warfare upon them, the State Department attempted to avoid drawing public attention on the matter.[63]

The department also lobbied the Congress to obtain passage of "intelligent legislation." The result was the addition of the final layer of regulations on East-West trade. Rep. Laurie C. Battle (D.-Ala.), who headed a special subcommittee of the Foreign Affairs Committee, sponsored the new bill. Early in March 1951, Battle's subcommittee began holding hearings in executive session on East-West trade. Battle shared the department's basic premise that although certain goods should be completely embargoed, there were economic and political advantages to be derived from allowing some trade in nonstrategic items. Even before the Kem amendment took effect, the department reached out to Battle and other likely supporters of substitute legislation. In June Battle provided the department with a confidential draft of his bill. After securing interdepartmental agreement on an administration position, the department then recommended various changes.[64]

President Truman signed the Mutual Defense Assistance Control Act of 1951 (Public Law 213), more commonly known as the Battle Act, on 26 October. The law, which went into full effect the following January, declared it to be the policy of the United States to embargo the shipments of items of strategic significance (broadly defined) to the Communist bloc. It specified that U.S. aid should only be given to countries that cooperated in administering a regime of export controls. The act enumerated two lists of goods subject to control. The Title I List consisted of items of "primary strategic significance." Category A enumerated 21 listings of items such as arms and atomic energy materials. Category B contained 264 listings covering items such as transportation materials of strategic significance. The Title II List concerned items of "secondary strategic significance," large quantities of which would contribute significantly to the war potential of the bloc. Shipment of either Category A or Category B items required the termination of all U.S. aid, regardless of whether the United States was engaged in hostilities overseas. Only the president was authorized to make exceptions.[65]

Although the Battle Act lists were generally less restrictive than the ever changing lists the administration maintained, the message to the recipients of U.S. aid was clear. East-West trade was to be held to a bare minimum. Pressure for greater restrictions did not end with the passage of the new law. Even Congressman Battle, who traveled overseas on separate occasions to survey his handiwork firsthand, was unhappy with what seemed to be a large volume of goods flowing eastward.[66] In the absence of the Korean War, the United States could never have imposed, and then maintained, as extensive a regime of controls on the trade of its free-world partners.

The Occupation's End

As an occupied power when the Korean War broke out, Japan was not in a position to influence the basic contours of U.S. policy. The broad system of economic controls imposed during the war, however, was a doubly restrictive arrangement that had a proportionally greater effect on Japan than on the other allies. The target of the most extensive controls—the PRC—was in principal the one Communist power that had the potential to become a major Japanese trading partner. The restrictions Japan inherited from the Occupation were so extensive that subsequent negotiations for their relaxation unfolded within very narrow boundaries.

The limits of Japanese opportunity were not fully apparent during the early months of 1952. The entry into force of the Battle Act and the gradual transfer (to the Japanese government) of responsibility for implementing export control regulations overshadowed the question of future prospects. SCAP transferred responsibility for implementing the sanctions with care. The Economic and Scientific Section (ESS) instructed Japanese officials at MITI and the Foreign Ministry in the procedures for issuing and validating export licenses. The United States also shared the Battle Act lists with the Japanese government. On 4 February, ESS transferred authority over less strategic items to MITI. By 17 March transfer was complete. Until the end of the Occupation, however, ESS required prior consultation in the case of licenses for export of strategic materials to sensitive areas.[67]

The controls in place at the Occupation's end were much more extensive than Japan's formal obligations. Those commitments included Prime Minister Yoshida's pledge to the UN secretary-general that Japan would honor the General Assembly's selective embargo of the Chinese mainland and the restrictions imposed on recipients of U.S. aid by the Battle Act.[68] Both MITI and the Foreign Ministry assured ESS that, "Japan will make no attempt to modify the present control system." The Americans nevertheless worried that after the resumption of sovereignty Japanese agencies would seek to revise the controls in place, particularly those on trade with the Chinese mainland.[69]

For this reason, a principal object of U.S. diplomacy in the post-treaty period was to obtain a formal Japanese commitment to maintain a high level of controls. On 28 March 1952, one month before independence, SCAP presented an aide-mémoire to the Japanese government expressing an understanding that Japan would maintain its controls "as long as there is Communist aggression in the Far East and while the United Nations is taking action against such aggression." It also urged that the two countries work out arrangements for "the post-aggression period."[70]

Following the resumption of sovereignty, Japan sought to define the scope of permissible trade and to establish the nation as an independent power on a par with the European allies. In May 1952, Yukawa Morio, the head of the Foreign Ministry's Bureau of Economic Affairs, requested that the United States formally allow Japan to permit the export of dyestuffs, wool yarn and knit goods, textile machinery, and galvanized iron sheets to China. In return, Japan hoped to obtain coking coal, iron ore, and soybeans, among other needed commodities. The items were not on the Battle Act Title II list, and easing restrictions was unlikely to expand greatly Sino-Japanese trade. On 2 June MITI issued a revised interpretation of the list of commodities requiring export licenses and specified a number of non-strategic items that no longer required a license.[71]

More striking than the fact of such pressure to expand trade with the PRC is the limited character of Japan's formal demands. Whereas MITI favored some growth in trade with China, the Foreign Ministry sought to hold the line. Yukawa's memorandum was silent on the many items that business interests wished to export, but which appeared on the Battle Act lists. The principal motive in requesting relaxation, as Japanese officials themselves conceded in private, was to counter domestic criticism rather than to expand trade with the Chinese mainland. Despite unhappiness with American restrictions, in the short term, the Yoshida government did not expect or plan to pursue closer ties with the Chinese Communists. Indeed the government's public position echoed the rhetoric one might have expected to hear in Washington. The same day that Yukawa delivered his request to embassy officials, for example, Foreign Minister Okazaki Katsuo defended existing policy in response to a question in the Diet, declaring that "Japan should avoid any relaxation of the present restrictions placed on her trade with Communist China in view of the spirit of the United States' Battle Act and her cooperation with the United Nations."[72] The distance between the U.S. and Japanese governments—as opposed to popular opinion in the two countries—was clearly much less than the heated public discussion might suggest.

The Japanese government's export controls were unpopular at home for many reasons. Many Japanese business leaders were aware that the controls exercised by other trading nations such as the United Kingdom were less extensive than those maintained by Japan, and this point resonated with government officials and parliamentarians alike. Enthusiasm for trade with China among hard-pressed small- and medium-sized manufacturing enterprises was particularly strong, eager as they were for any available market and cheaper raw materials. The catalyst that brought the issue into sharp public focus after independence was a "peace offensive" launched by the Soviet Union and the Communist Chinese. Several members of the Communist-led Sino-Japanese Trade Promotion Association and three Japanese parliamentarians attended the international Moscow Economic Conference, which opened in April. The politicians then signed what they called a "trade agreement" with the PRC in Beijing. The agreement carried no legal obligation, since the Japanese negotiators had not even consulted their own government. The Foreign Ministry criticized the accord as a political maneuver, "to isolate Japan by severing her relations with the free world, especially those with the U.S."[73]

Advocacy of expanding trade with the PRC was not the exclusive domain of the left. Even among conservatives the issue of relations with China was intertwined with the political issue of Japan's independence from the United States. Some conservatives, for example, saw in ties with China a means of securing a more independent role in the world for Japan. Prince Takamatsu, the brother of the emperor, for example, suggested in 1952 that by cultivating trade and political relations with the Communist bloc Japan could serve as a bridge between East and West.[74] Closely tied to the questions of Japan's relationship with the United States and the nation's alienation from China as they were, trade controls were never a strictly economic matter. Despite all of the advantages of maintaining close ties with the United States, following the American lead on export controls was bound to inflame public opinion at home.

To equate actual public sentiment with the most vocal protest is nevertheless misleading. The movement to expand trade with China did reflect widespread popular feeling, but the government was not alone. Prime Minister Yoshida may have exaggerated the point when he told Ambassador Murphy that "no important Japanese businessman entertains illusions about trade with the Chinese mainland under current conditions." But the prime minister's characteristic bluster was rooted in shrewd analysis of the political landscape. Organizations such as the powerful Keidanren (Federation of Economic Organizations) equivocated. Even as popular pressure mounted after the conclusion of an armistice in Korea, large companies were wary of increasing such trade for fear that it would provoke both the Chinese Nationalists (with whom they were by this time conducting substantial trade) and the U.S. Congress. It was the Chinese Nationalists' policy to suspend trade with firms that dealt with the PRC. Businessmen worried that anti-Japan lobbyists might use Japanese trade with the PRC to urge the denial of tariff concessions to Japan. Some businessmen and China experts also warned of practical difficulties in conducting trade with the mainland, including the problem of arranging payment and the limits imposed by the PRC's own trade controls.[75]

Japanese Membership in COCOM

From the time of independence forward, the Yoshida government sought to blunt criticism of the nation's trade restrictions by portraying them as part of a multilateral effort to control trade with the Soviet bloc. Entry into the Paris Consultative Group and its Coordinating Committee was, therefore, a high priority of the Japanese government. Admission to CG-COCOM (usually called simply COCOM) in September 1952 was also consistent with Japan's pursuit of membership in international organizations as an affirmation of national prestige. Because Japan's aim was to rejoin the international community on a par with Western European allies, however, the terms of Japanese membership in COCOM proved disappointing. The nation's freedom of action remained severely constrained, and the profound asymmetry in the relationship between Japan and the United States persisted. The support of the Western Europeans and Canadians nevertheless enabled Japan to come closer to realizing its objectives than it could have achieved alone.

Although the existence of a Paris-based organization to coordinate NATO members' trade relations with the Soviet bloc was known to the public in 1952, the details of CG-COCOM's operations (including its name) remained a secret. Japan's Foreign Ministry was familiar with the work of the organization well before independence. During the winter of 1951–52 Vice-Minister Iguchi Sadao learned of its existence from the Italian Mission in Tokyo. Haguiwara Tōru, then representing Japan in Paris, inquired further into COCOM operations from an official of one of the participating governments (Japanese records shield the contact's identity). Although Haguiwara found it odd that the committee's office was in the former Japanese Embassy building (which France still held), Foreign Ministry officials were more concerned about the potential for close cooperation between COCOM and NATO. Such obligations were not in fact inherent in COCOM membership. On learning that all of the members except the United States favored admitting Japan, the Yoshida government set out to join. On 30 May the government informed the U.S. Embassy of its desire to become a member.[76]

The U.S. response to Japan's requests for relaxation of controls and membership in COCOM reveal just how complex the task of administering the burgeoning system of trade sanctions had become. Each item under consideration was part of a vast web of controls. Galvanized iron sheets, for example, appeared on the U.K. embargo list as part of an embargo on "all iron and steel products." Since the State Department was pressing for their international control, it did not wish Japan to ease its restrictions. Two years later, when the issue came up again, the worry was that the Germans would point to Japanese exports of galvanized iron sheets to justify export of similar goods, thus causing the embargo on iron and steel to unravel completely.[77] The United States refused accordingly to approve of any relaxation on the export of these sheets in 1952.

The State Department also urged that Japan maintain controls on the other items Yukawa listed. "[A]t a time when we are bringing pressure on all other Governments to tighten their export controls against the Communist bloc," the department explained, "we could not formally agree to a relaxation of controls on even such non-strategic goods as the last four items [dyestuffs, wool yarn and knit goods, textile machinery, and galvanized iron sheets]." Recognizing the possible need for some action to placate Japanese opinion, the secretary of state nevertheless cautioned that the United States could not "formally concur" in easing sanctions. He also asked that the publicity be kept to a minimum. The Japanese finally decided to defer action on the items in question pending the results of its request to join COCOM.[78]

Because the Truman administration was divided on the question of Japan and COCOM, the State Department played for time by deferring the matter to a special conference with representatives of the United Kingdom, France, and Canada in late July.[79] Robert Murphy, the ambassador in Japan, supported Japan's bid to join COCOM. The Departments of Defense and Commerce, supported by Congressman Battle and others, were opposed. They favored the creation of a special new trade control organization (to include Japan) for East Asia. This body was to maintain "sterner controls" than COCOM. The State Department's own Bureau of European Affairs opposed Japanese membership in COCOM in the expectation of closer cooperation between COCOM and NATO. It saw no place for Japan in such a partnership. Opinion in the Bureau of Far Eastern Affairs was divided. Some officials (concentrated especially in the Office of Chinese Affairs) urged maintaining the tightest possible restrictions on trade; others doubted the efficacy of a separate Pacific organization and understood the political difficulty of justifying Japan's exclusion from the Paris group.[80]

The various agencies agreed to split their differences. The compromise position opposed bringing Japan into COCOM but favored the creation of a Far East Consultative Group, parallel to the existing Consultative Group. Both organizations were to have representation at the ministerial level. There would be a Far East-COCOM on a level equivalent to the existing COCOM. Both the FE-CG and FE-COCOM were to include the countries having an important interest in Far Eastern economic security problems, including at least Japan, the United States, Britain, Canada, and France.[81]

American officials attempted to put the best face on the administration position in advance of the conference. The U.S. proposal left open the possibility for closer partnership between COCOM and NATO. The Far East policy could be brought into a broader regional security organization, should one emerge in the future. A separate Far East group would obviously be able to focus on Far Eastern problems, particularly trade with the PRC, in a way that was impossible under the existing Paris organization.[82]

In its messages to allied governments, the department did not mention two other "pertinent" concerns. The proposed organization would prevent countries having little direct economic interest "from imposing delay in reaching agreement on [the] level [of] controls" in Asia. There was also strong feeling that the proposal would "minimize the tendency to drop [Japanese] controls to [the] COCOM level RE China, and would aid materially [in] raising the level [of] COCOM controls RE [the] Far East."[83]

The stakes were higher than these particulars suggest. Japan was at a turning point in its development, and the policies of the Western powers too were in flux. Neither Japanese policy nor American strategy hinged on whether Japan was admitted to COCOM, yet the participants saw in the decision a precedent for the future. Whereas Japan and the Western allies desired relaxation of controls, the United States sought to tighten restrictions on trade. Within the U.S. government debate over the matter affected the terms of the policy paper on Japan then under consideration by the NSC. The Department of Defense seized the initiative in drafting NSC 125/1. The first draft proposed that Japan "maintain substantially its present export controls," and that "those controls will be maintained as long as there is Communist aggression in the Far East and while the United Nations is taking action against such aggression." The policy paper also called for the United States to establish a separate multilateral organization to carry out economic defense measures in East Asia. To the State Department, attempting to maintain the existing embargo promised to be counterproductive. State officials preferred to press for an embargo on strategic items (broadly defined) while allowing some trade in nonstrategic items.[84]

The negotiations at the conference in Washington, which lasted from 28 July to 2 August, defined the substance of the State Department's position. As department officials expected, the U.S. proposal for a separate Far Eastern economic defense group went nowhere. The United Kingdom, France, and Canada all flatly opposed it. Japan too was unhappy with the proposal, but it was not in a position to enforce its will.[85] State's achievement was to fashion a compromise that was acceptable to all.

The Japanese aim was to restore Japan to a position of equality in the world. The Yoshida government desired membership in COCOM; and it did not wish to be party to a separate group intended to retain the inequality between European and Japanese trade controls. Ambassador Murphy recognized, however, that Japan would probably agree to the creation of a separate Far Eastern operations group if it were a subcommittee of COCOM.[86] Japan could not force its way into COCOM, but the sheer volume of attention the Japanese press devoted to the question of trade with China during the summer of 1952 made the membership issue more sensitive by the day. Newspaper coverage of Japan's efforts to relax controls was surprisingly accurate and detailed. The Foreign Ministry denied leaking any information, insisting instead that the press reports were based on "speculation and shrewd analysis."[87]

The British and the French supported Japan's bid to join COCOM. The British opposed any arrangement likely to maintain higher controls in one area for more than a short time. Because a separate organization was unlikely to include the major Southeast Asian powers, the French thought that it "would appear to be exclusively a white man's organ" with a "slight color tint" from Japan. They were also concerned about the prospect of discrepancies between the policies of two separate organizations. The other COCOM members supported Japan's bid, in part out of the misplaced fear that Japan might enjoy more favorable treatment in a separate group.[88]

A British proposal, which Eric Berthoud of the Foreign Office floated in London before the conference, provided the basis for a compromise. It proposed admitting Japan into COCOM and creating a separate Far East committee within the COCOM structure. The compromise suggested by the British was satisfactory to the Japanese Foreign Ministry. The conferees agreed to invite Japan to join the Consultative Group and its Coordinating Committee "immediately." They also decided to establish a new China Committee (CHINCOM) under COCOM, and to invite Japan to take part in its work.[89]

NSC 125/2, the final version of the U.S. policy paper on Japan, reflected this outcome. The Pentagon withdrew its demand for a separate Far Eastern economic defense committee on 1 August. The revised paper called simply for the United States to continue the understanding with the Japanese government that it retain under control "substantially the same list of commodities" that it then restricted. NSC 125/2 further specified that Japan "maintain its embargo on the U.S. security lists," and "those items which after careful review are judged to be of security significance to Communist China and North Korea." In practice, "careful review" meant that Japanese controls were to be decided by means of bilateral negotiations.[90]

During the five-power conference the State Department moved to secure Japanese agreement to these terms in separate bilateral talks. Upon arrival, the Japanese desired that the five powers also take up the question of trade with China. Japan also sought American approval of expanded trade in nonstrategic items with China as a prelude to eventual reduction of Japan's restrictions to the level set by COCOM.[91] The Japanese delegate was extremely unhappy to learn that the other powers did not wish to discuss the status of particular items at the conference. The British delegate's instructions were explicit on this point. Because the United States wished to reach an understanding with Japan on trade with China, a Japanese request to discuss the level of controls provided the opportunity for the two sides to reach a separate bilateral agreement.[92]

On 31 July, Harold Linder, acting assistant secretary for economic affairs, met with Takeuchi Ryūji, the Japanese delegate. Linder explained the U.S. position and added that the other agencies were "greatly disappointed" with their inability to obtain a separate Far Eastern organization. They believed it necessary to obtain a "side commitment" confirming that Japan would "maintain substantially its existing level of controls on trade with Communist China." Such agreement was to take the form of an exchange of letters that Linder could then show to the other agencies. According to Takeuchi's letter to Linder, dated 2 August, Japan agreed to retain its controls on all items appearing on U.S. security lists. Japan also agreed to cooperate in a bilateral review of all other items of potential strategic value with a view to determine "by mutual agreement those on which an embargo should be maintained." A separate agreement set down in detail how Japan would continue to impose controls and how the two nations would conduct the review.[93]

The two sides divided the commodities not on U.S. security lists into three groups: items of high-strategic value on which embargo was generally justified (paragraph 3(A) items); goods of some strategic value that Japan was to be allowed to export in order to obtain vital commodities from the PRC (3(B) items); and nonstrategic items on which Japan was free to exercise administrative discretion (3(C) items). According to the terms of the letters exchanged, the Japanese government was to maintain its controls while a technical group reviewed the 3(A) goods in question. In August the Department of State prepared a list of four hundred items. Understanding the force of public pressure, the department consented to an immediate easing of controls on wool knit goods, textile machinery, dyestuffs, and paper, to the extent that they were not on U.S. security lists.[94] Thus, the State Department was in fact pursuing the courses of action outlined in NSC 125/2 when the president approved the final document.

Immediately after the U.S.-Japan bilateral talks, however, differences arose. Takeuchi had been reluctant to agree to Linder's terms because his instructions did not provide for such a contingency.[95] Pressing for maximum freedom of maneuver, Yukawa signaled in mid-August that the Japanese government interpreted the bilateral agreement to be temporary, pending formulation of the COCOM list (in practice a "few months"). The Japanese insisted that they should be free to make their own decision on paragraph 3(A) items not agreed upon by COCOM, or if COCOM were to delay on a decision beyond a reasonable period. Yukawa also pressed for an amendment to the interpretive notes specifying that Japan was not bound to take action in cases where COCOM has made determinations more permissive than those tentatively agreed upon by the United States and Japan. Yukawa made clear that the Japanese government "fully intends" to retain controls on some commodities in view of the war in progress. But he emphasized that Foreign Minister Okazaki could defend controls above the COCOM level in the Diet only if such restrictions were understood to represent an independent Japanese government decision, rather than the result of a bilateral commitment. As Takeuchi explained to Linder on 18 August, "his government could in fact restrict exports to Communist China more tightly than it could commit itself to do in a formal agreement."[96]

News of Yukawa's moves caused alarm in Washington. The Pentagon protested against allowing Japanese restrictions to fall to COCOM levels and insisted that the bilateral agreement was not temporary.[97] The State Department concurred. Linder moved quickly to reaffirm the original understanding, which allowed the United States to take part in the review of 3(A) items considered for decontrol. Yukawa would have welcomed U.S. concurrence in a relaxation of Japanese controls, but the Foreign Ministry did not expect great change. He was thus willing to concede the substance of the U.S. demand that Japan not act against American wishes on 3(A) items. But in case the ministry officials needed to go before the Diet, he wanted the bilateral agreement to allow Japan the maximum possible freedom of action. In Tokyo the two sides agreed upon a new text.[98]

Linder and Takeuchi signed the final agreement on 5 September.[99] According to this understanding Japan granted the substance of the U.S. demands. As before, the agreement allowed Japanese export of a considerable number of items in exchange for essential commodities. Yet Japanese controls on trade with China were stricter than those of any other nation except for the United States, Nationalist China, Canada, and the Republic of Korea.

In September Japan joined COCOM and the China Committee began its work. While Japan hoped that the bilateral agreement represented the first step toward lifting some of the restrictions on trade, for the remainder of 1952 the Truman administration moved in the opposite direction. At the first substantive meeting of CHINCOM in December, Raymond Ludden, the U.S. representative, sounded a note that he correctly predicted would "ruffle some feathers." Going beyond the draft statement given to him, Ludden explained that the United States was "interested in trade controls to China as a rather long term matter," not "merely during the period of Korean hostilities." He then suggested various new endeavors—cracking down on smuggling into China, for example—on which the committee could begin work.[100] In the interim the U.S. government conducted its painstaking item-by-item review of the four hundred commodities submitted to the Japanese for embargo under paragraph 3(A) of the bilateral understanding. Despite Japan's accession to COCOM, very little changed.

Conclusion

To an extent greater than any other single event in the Cold War, the Korean conflict transformed the content, structure, and flow of economic relations in East Asia. War enabled the Truman administration to export dollars to Japan in the same way that the Marshall Plan had funneled capital to Western Europe. The North Korean offensive and the Chinese Communists' intervention in the war contributed immeasurably to the polarization of politics in the region. Communist aggression put advocates of cooperation with the PRC on the defensive and cleared the way for the triumph of hard-line strategists within the Truman administration. In the atmosphere of war, the United States was able to win the support of its allies for a blockade of the Chinese mainland. Sanctions institutionalized the UN embargo of North Korea and the PRC, consolidation of multilateral controls on trade with the Communist bloc under the Paris Consultative Group, and bilateral agreements with Japan.

Restrictions on Sino-Japanese trade proved to be a source of friction between Japan and the United States for the remainder of the decade. Continuing anxiety about the health of the economy and prospects for foreign trade concentrated Japanese attention on the prospect of the China market. The Yoshida government's close cooperation with the United States in restricting trade also raised the question of whether Japan was truly independent. To an extent long forgotten in the United States, American leaders spent considerable political capital on maintaining Japanese compliance in controlling trade with the PRC.

In the absence of much actual trade between Japan and the PRC, however, the Yoshida government and the Japanese business community relied on its growing commerce with the "free-world" economies to provide for Japan's economic needs. U.S. pressure on Japan to restrict its trade with the Chinese mainland offered the Japanese the perfect lever to press for greater opportunity in the American market. Independent of any Japanese action, the commitment within the American executive branch to maintaining the blockade of the Chinese mainland also reinforced the U.S. policy of promoting Japanese integration with the Western trading bloc. Thus, as the war in Korea wore on and Dwight Eisenhower assumed the presidency in early 1953, attention on both sides of the Pacific focused increasingly on Japan's trade relations with the West.

Chapter Five

THE FIGHT OVER TRADE POLICY, 1953

The Truman administration defined American policy toward independent Japan, but the task of implementation fell to President Eisenhower. Despite the bitter 1952 campaign, this transition from a Democratic to the first Republican administration in twenty years exhibited striking continuity in vision and personnel regarding relations with Japan. Like Truman, Eisenhower was a committed cold warrior. He was hostile to communism and he believed strongly in collective security. Unlike most Republicans, Eisenhower favored free trade. Although Japan was not his first concern, Eisenhower instinctively recognized the nation's strategic importance to the United States.

Consistent with NSC 125/2, the new administration sought to consolidate the Cold War alliance and to stimulate Japanese economic revival. The Eisenhower team attempted to maintain defense spending in Japan, to reaffirm the U.S. commitment to reciprocal trade, to facilitate Japanese access to the American market, and bring Japan into GATT. A backlash against trade liberalization—and Japanese integration with the Western trading bloc in particular—at home and abroad threatened to frustrate the administration on each course of action. Staying the course as the Eisenhower administration did deserves praise. The bipartisan consensus on Japan held, but Eisenhower's first year was a time of great uncertainty. Without a chief executive committed to free trade, U.S. policy would certainly have been less encouraging of Japanese revival and the success of the emerging multilateral trading system than it was.

Setting the Course

Eisenhower was an active chief executive who possessed a much stronger grasp on both his administration and the issues of the day than was apparent at the time.[1] Yet he generally preferred to remain above politics in public and not get too deeply entwined in the implementation of policy. The same pattern is evident in U.S.-Japanese relations. The president played a vital role in fashioning the U.S. response to the two great challenges in American-Japanese relations during his presidency: Japan's ballooning foreign trade imbalance during his first term, and revision of the security treaty during his second.

Behind the scenes, the president often worked hard to see that his policies were carried out. Those close to him never doubted that he was in charge. As Vice President Richard Nixon later recalled, "an Eisenhower characteristic was never to take direct action requiring his personal participation where indirect methods would accomplish the same result."[2] Eisenhower's decisiveness and sense of restraint served the United States well during the major crises of the fifties such as those over Korea, Suez, and the Taiwan Straits.[3] But in foreign economic policy what Fred I. Greenstein has called "hidden-hand" leadership proved less effective.[4] Implementation of economic policies required sustained attention and depended on getting outside parties to act. Eisenhower's deep reluctance to risk his personal popularity to win lawmakers' support of lower tariffs and fewer import quotas therefore limited his power.[5]

Although Eisenhower took greater interest in foreign policy than Truman did, executive officials still made most of the decisions regarding Japan. Secretary of State Dulles and Budget Director Joseph M. Dodge had served under Truman and were more familiar with Japanese affairs than the president. Dulles appointed John M. Allison, his assistant during the peace treaty negotiations, to the post of ambassador to Japan. In Tokyo a similar continuity in U.S. Embassy personnel was evident. J. Graham Parsons and Frank Waring served under both administrations. Some of the State Department's China hands suffered terribly as scapegoats for the Chinese Communists' victory in 1949. Officials attending to Northeast Asian affairs— including Allison, Robert J. McClurkin, Noel Hemmendinger, Kenneth T. Young, and C. Thayer White—remained invisible to the public and on the job. In the Bureau of Economic Affairs John B. Leddy, Leonard Weiss, and Carl D. Corse remained important officials. Continuity in policy flowed in part from continuity in personnel.[6]

Eisenhower set the course for his administration's foreign economic policy early on. In his first State of the Union Address he advanced several proposals to promote trade liberalization. He urged Congress to revise customs and to renew the Reciprocal Trade Agreements Act (due to expire in June). He promised to "encourage the flow of private American investment abroad." He also defended the U.S. military's many purchases oversesas.[7] Although Eisenhower believed that the reduction of trade barriers contributed to American economic opportunity, he did not see trade liberalization strictly in terms of U.S. economic interests. Similarly, he did not emphasize, as economists usually do, that imports were desirable because they facilitated greater consumption. Rather, the president explained how trade was fundamental to global prosperity and stability. He pointed especially to the role of imports in international exchange: "The United States cannot live in a world where it must, for the disposal of its products, export vast portions of its industrial and agricultural products unless it also imports a sufficiently great amount of foreign products to allow countries to pay for the surpluses they receive from us."[8] Reducing trade barriers made it easier for people around the world to make a decent living, thus enabling them to resist pressure to embrace Communism.[9]

Japan's plight was not a pressing concern until later in the year, but Eisenhower recognized that the challenge of securing Japan's—or any nation's—loyalty in the Cold War was as much an economic problem as a political matter. "Communism inspires and enables its militant preachers to exploit injustices and inequality among men," he wrote after the Second World War. "Whenever popular discontent is founded on group oppression or mass poverty or the hunger of children, there Communism may stage an offensive which arms cannot counter."[10] As he made the point in mid-1954:

"Japan cannot live, and Japan cannot remain in the free world unless something is done to allow her to make a living." All of the military power in the Pacific would be useless in the face of Japanese economic chaos.[11]

Although he shared the Democrats' faith in collective security and their commitment to more liberal trade, Eisenhower differed from his predecessors in one crucial respect. He was equally committed to fiscal conservatism. In Eisenhower's view, the deficit spending required to finance the Truman administration's foreign policy of "containment" posed a great danger to the nation's well-being. He recognized that economic health was the ultimate source of American power in the world. Having seen the garrison states of Europe he feared that fighting communism by military means alone would exhaust the United States financially and destroy the nation politically.[12] Eisenhower intended to reduce expenditures for defense and foreign aid and the taxes imposed to finance them. Other factors reinforced this impulse: the winding down of the Korean War, disillusionment with high taxes and deficit spending, Republican fiscal conservatism, and the party's preference for relying upon the private sector.

Eisenhower nevertheless believed that the transition had to be gradual. He was under strong pressure from his party to eliminate the deficit, but he refused to slash spending indiscriminately. "This administration does not and cannot begin its task with a clean slate," he cautioned. At issue were the Truman administration's defense and foreign aid budgets, which amounted to 70 percent of the entire federal budget, and which contributed to a projected $9.9 billion deficit. On foreign aid, Eisenhower supported helping other nations "in the measure they strive earnestly to do their full share of the common task." He favored tax cuts only after "we show we can succeed in bringing the budget under control."[13] In 1953 such moderation placed Eisenhower at odds with the leadership of his own party.

Republican Insurgency at Home

The Republicans' sweeping victory in 1952 did not translate into strong congressional support for the Eisenhower administration. Despite GOP majorities in both the House and the Senate, the party was deeply divided between a nationalistic Old Guard and more internationalist members. Only the latter wing of the party stood firmly behind the president. For precisely that reason, the split in the party was bound to cause problems for him. "As far as his own party was concerned," one perceptive observer has explained, "Eisenhower never had a honeymoon."[14]

Many conservative Republicans had been isolationists before the war. They preferred unilateral action to formal alliances in foreign affairs. Their most prominent leader was Senator Robert Taft of Ohio. Speaking primarily for farmers and small-business owners, Taft and his followers opposed both the creation of the Cold War national security state and the pursuit of a liberal economic order abroad. Internationalist Republicans, by contrast, represented a wider constituency and had generally supported the foreign policies of the Truman administration. The Taft wing of the party was strongest in Congress, and the internationalist wing, led by Thomas E. Dewey of New York, dominated the presidential nominating process. Dewey and his supporters backed Eisenhower over Taft in 1952.

Old Guard Republicans composed a distinct minority of the party. But because they dominated the leadership of the Eighty-third Congress, their influence was far greater than their numbers. Taft was Senate majority leader. Illness forced him to retire in June 1953, but his successor, Senator William Knowland (R.-Calif.), was another staunch nationalist.[15] Eugene Millikin (R.-Colo.), the chairman of the Senate Finance Committee, was a towering figure. Other Republican senators who became prominent critics of the president included John Bricker (R.-Ohio), Joe McCarthy (R.-Wis.), and William Jenner (R.-Ind.). Speaker Joseph Martin (R.-Mass.), generally supported the administration. Chairman Daniel A. Reed (R.-N.Y.) and Richard Simpson (R.-Penn.), however, dominated the Ways and Means Committee. Simpson was the chamber's leading opponent of free trade, and Reed stood close behind. As he remarked candidly during an earlier hearing on a trade matter, "Whenever there is a broadening of protection, I am for it."[16]

Anti-Communist hysteria at home complicated the task of governing during the Eisenhower years. Republicans had long attempted to use the Communist advance in China and stalemate in Korea to embarrass the Democrats. John Foster Dulles, the architect of the Republican Party's platform on foreign policy in 1952, bears some of the responsibility for the decline of bipartisanship on foreign policy. His call for the "liberation" of "captive peoples" was a naked attempt to win over Eastern European ethnic groups who normally voted Democratic, just as it served to rally the right wing of the party behind his bid to become secretary.[17]

Dean Acheson later described the Red Scare of the early 1950s as the "attack of the primitives." The anti-Communist crusade was indeed a political assault on a foreign policy establishment of which the former secretary and the salons of Georgetown were the most visible symbols.[18] Whether

Senator McCarthy or others less brazen made the charge, the tendency to blame the problems of the day on treachery at the highest levels often had a more immediately political aim. Purging the federal government—particularly the State Department—of every "com-symp," "dupe," or other "security risk," offered the chance to root out the "middle-aged New Dealers" who had established themselves in government during the Democrats long tenure in office.[19]

Unfortunately for Eisenhower, the responsibility that comes with power did not inspire moderation among Republican lawmakers. As he confided to his diary on 7 February 1953, "Republican Senators are having a hard time getting through their heads that they now belong to a team that includes rather than opposes the White House."[20] Senator Bricker proposed— and sixty-two other senators supported—a constitutional amendment to limit the president's treaty-making power. Owing to the popular worry that the United Nations represented a threat to American sovereignty and the belief that the presidency had become too powerful, Bricker's proposal was immensely popular. Had it become law it would have jeopardized the president's ability to fashion foreign policy.[21]

If the Old Guard's political excesses reveal an underside to American politics during the fifties that has been an embarrassment to later generations, conservatives' economic grievances deserve to be taken more seriously. On trade especially, the opponents of the administration had an agenda based on principle. Unfortunately, journalistic and scholarly attention lavished on Senator McCarthy has had the effect of obscuring from view the lawmakers who actually dominated Capitol Hill. The men who left the greatest mark on the legislative record regarding trade were Representatives Reed and Simpson, and Senator Millikin.[22]

On fiscal policy, Reed attempted to seize the initiative even before Eisenhower assumed office. The white-maned chairman of the Ways and Means Committee brought to politics the same fighter's instinct and sense of fair play that he had exhibited as a football coach at Cornell University. A devout fiscal conservative, Reed intended to force the administration to cut federal expenditures by reducing revenue. In January 1953 he introduced a bill to reduce income taxes. To show the measure's importance, he entitled it House Resolution 1. It proposed to advance from 1 January 1954 to 1 July 1953 a scheduled elimination of increases in personal income taxes adopted to finance the Korean War. Reed also announced his intention to let the Korean War excess-profits tax expire as scheduled on 30 June 1953. To Eisenhower, these two measures risked costing the federal government over

$2 billion in revenue.²³ The prospect of a smaller budget also raised the specter of greatly reduced American military spending in Japan.

Nationalist Republicans were also hostile to free trade. Old Guard views on the subject echoed the sentiment of the GOP in 1930, when the Congress passed the Smoot-Hawley Tariff. That act wrote into law one of the highest levels of customs duties in American history. The expiration of the RTAA posed an opportunity to reverse the downward course of U.S. tariffs since 1934. Simpson led the crusade to preserve the U.S. market for American producers. He introduced House Resolution (H.R.) 4294, a highly protectionist measure that provided for a rise in existing tariff levels, import quotas, and expansion of the U.S. Tariff Commission by one member. During the years 1948–52, the commission had recommended invocation of the escape clause only when an increase in imports was responsible to a significant degree for the deterioration of the industry's sales and profits. A protectionist minority, however, saw the clause as a means to increase the level of protection afforded to industry, thus nullifying the effect of trade agreements in reducing trade barriers.²⁴ Simpson's aim was to strengthen this protectionist faction.

H.R. 4294 further required that the president heed the Tariff Commission's advice in "peril-point" cases. The peril-point clause required the commission to determine the lowest duties that could be set without threatening serious harm to a domestic industry. As the law stood, presidential approval was necessary for such decisions to go into effect. The purpose of the peril-point provision was to forestall injury before concessions were granted in trade negotiations. The obvious intent of Simpson's proposal was to make it difficult for the administration to offer concessions in the future. As Eisenhower rightly concluded, it would have made the president "a messenger boy, and hamstrung him in his negotiation of reciprocal trade agreements with other countries."²⁵ Simpson's bill enjoyed enthusiastic support among the nation's light industries, and Reed chose to hold hearings on the proposal, ignoring completely the administration's trade bill, sponsored by Representative Kenneth Keating (R.-N.Y.). The committee hearings provided a forum for a parade of interests— from lace makers to fish canneries—all demanding protection in one form or another.²⁶

The most formidable opponent of trade liberalization in the Senate was Eugene Millikin. Although he eschewed the public eye, Millikin enjoyed a stature in the upper chamber during the forties and fifties as imposing as his name is forgotten today. His bald dome sheathed an acute mind and an instinct for the art of the possible. A devout protectionist and fiscal conservative, Millikin disliked the reciprocal trade program. Having risen quickly in the legal profession as an authority on irrigation, oil, and mining issues before entering the Senate in 1941, Millikin brought the same energy to politics. He took the time to learn the details of major policies, and zealously attended to the concerns of his constituents. He did not regard the Senate as a springboard to the presidency and he avoided public crusades. Millikin focused instead on Senate business, particularly the work of the Finance Committee, which he headed during the Eighty-third Congress. As George Reedy has written, "Nothing *could* go through the committee against his opposition and anything reasonable *could* go through with his support."[27]

Millikin's power in the Senate extended far beyond his formal authority as a committee chairman. He owed this influence to his natural talent as a conciliator. Despite his firm principles, Millikin was not a bitter-ender. In Taft's words, "Gene doesn't make people angry." Together, Taft, Millikin, and Arthur Vandenberg constituted the triumvirate that dominated Republican Senate affairs beginning in the mid-1940s.[28] On the substance of policy, however, Millikin's relations with the executive branch were often uneasy. In 1948, he forced President Truman to accept the peril-point and escape clause provisions as the price of congressional renewal of the reciprocal trade program. Millikin also frequently voiced his displeasure that the Senate had never had the opportunity to review the General Agreement on Tariffs and Trade.[29] During the 1952 campaign Eisenhower attempted to reach out to the legislative leadership by building a working relationship with Senator Taft. After Taft's death in mid-1953, the administration had to rely on Millikin.

The rebellion of the Old Guard against the Eisenhower administration's position on reciprocal trade compared with the great debate over collective security during the Truman years. However anachronistic Reed, Simpson, Millikin, and other economic nationalists may have seemed to their critics, they correctly identified the fundamental character of the changes in American foreign economic policy under the RTAA since 1934. Inherent in the administration of the program was a shift in power from Congress to the executive branch, and the rise of trade liberalization as a principal goal of U.S. policy. These changes compared with the end of isolation in the strategic sphere.

Whereas the nation engaged in a debate over collective security before committing to NATO, there was not the same broad public appreciation of either the problems or the stakes in economic affairs.[30] Parties with an interest in the economic debate naturally followed developments closely. But the ironic result of such wide participation in policy making was a blurring of the issues. The stakes were never reducible to the vital question of war or peace. Opponents of the new regime never had the same opportunity to challenge it that the critics of collective security had in the debate over NATO. The Truman administration never submitted the ITO or GATT to the Congress for approval. Hence the bitterness and frequent resort to subterfuge on both sides. Since the discontent was strongest among Republicans, one of the first challenges for President Eisenhower was to rally his own party behind him.

The Fight over the Budget and Trade Policy, 1953

Eisenhower's strategy to accomplish his legislative agenda was to conciliate the right wing of his party with high profile gestures of symbolic value, while standing firm on most substantive issues. Day to day, Eisenhower went out of his way to keep Republican lawmakers informed of administration policy.[31] The president also relied on Senate Majority Leader Taft, who reciprocated. The first major test—and impressive victory—for the administration came on fiscal policy.

Taft agreed not to demand a tax cut until the budget deficit was under control. Eisenhower unveiled his budget for the coming fiscal year in a meeting with the legislative leadership on 30 April. The projected deficit was less than $4 billion. Taft exploded when he learned that Eisenhower had not balanced the budget. "With a program like this," the senator shouted, "we'll never elect a Republican Congress in 1954. You're taking us down the same road Truman traveled. It's a repudiation of everything we promised in the campaign." Eisenhower handled Taft with care. He calmly reviewed the nation's foreign policy, emphasizing how additional cuts would compromise security. He also stressed the need to reduce the deficit before cutting taxes. The president's commitment to reducing the deficit, his language of economy, and his nonconfrontational approach won over the majority leader.[32] With Taft, Speaker Martin, and House Floor Leader Charles Halleck of Indiana on his side, Congress fell into line. Eisenhower appreciated the effort of his "model teammate," and was "deeply grieved" when Taft succumbed to cancer in July.[33]

Budget issues affected relations with Japan. U.S. military purchases were so important to the Japanese economy that business leaders feared the economic fallout of an armistice in Korea. The Japanese Embassy in Washington pressed the Department of State for some assurance on the point. The boom in U.S. military purchases was over, but Eisenhower's budget provided for a substantial level of procurement in Japan. Reductions in defense spending would be gradual rather than precipitous. Equally important, Eisenhower's budget preserved the Mutual Security Program (MSP), which provided for continued military purchases abroad. Negotiations to include Japan opened at Tokyo in July, culminating in Japan's full participation in the lucrative program two years later.[34]

Continued U.S. military spending was of course not certain in April 1953. The Department of State pondered how to reassure opinion in Japanese industrial circles. Complicating matters was a national election in Japan. Prime Minister Yoshida had provoked a vote of no confidence in his government when he called a Socialist representative a "stupid fool" during a Diet session. As Japanese voters went to the polls that month, State Department officials opposed "any overt effort by the United States to influence the outcome of the elections."[35] Any government was likely to be pro-American. No one wished to tie the United States to Yoshida's declining political fortunes. The department finally decided to issue a statement in order to offer a "general reassurance" that total U.S. expenditures in Japan would "remain at [a] relatively high level" for at least the next two years. Spokesman Michael J. McDermott made the announcement at a press briefing on 15 April.[36] Four days later Yoshida's Liberal Party won the election, but it failed to regain a majority in the lower house of the Diet.

Eisenhower was less successful at reaffirming the U.S. commitment to liberal trade. Republican leaders simply ignored his call to renew the Reciprocal Trade Act for two years. During the Ways and Means Committee hearings on trade policy, cabinet officials were forced to testify against Simpson's proposal (H.R. 4294) rather than for the administration's own bill. On 7 April, Eisenhower backed down and asked for a one-year extension. Such "temporary continuation" of existing policy was to allow time for "completion of a thorough and comprehensive examination" of foreign economic policy.[37] Although Dulles listed Japan's need for foreign markets as a reason for opposing H.R. 4294 in his testimony before the Ways and Means Committee, he promised a "standstill" in tariff-lifting action for the coming year so that the study could begin.[38]

Neither Eisenhower nor Dulles really needed instruction on trade policy. Both men strongly supported the reciprocal trade program, and abundant evidence confirmed the need to reduce trade barriers. In March the Public Advisory Board for Mutual Security, commissioned by President

Truman and headed by Daniel W. Bell, presented a 119-page report to President Eisenhower on U.S. trade and tariff policy. The report warned that unless this country is prepared to increase its imports, the other nations of the free world will regard it as futile to take the measures they should to establish better balance in their payments and in their national economies. United States exports will decline and American industry and agriculture will be seriously affected.[39] The Bell Commission's ten steps to promote freer trade were a mirror image of Simpson's H.R. 4294. Predictably, they carried little weight in the eyes of most Republicans. Thus, the challenge was to marshal a consensus behind a more liberal trade policy.

Congressman Simpson continued to press ahead with HR 4294. But by summer it was in trouble, having become the target of a vigorous public relations campaign sponsored by the Venezuelan business community and several large oil companies. The prospect of higher-priced fuel oil prompted New England legislators to oppose it. Eisenhower himself also came out publicly against the Simpson bill.[40]

With victory beyond the reach of either side, they compromised rather than let the system break down entirely. Congress renewed the existing act for one year. Eisenhower named a protectionist to the Tariff Commission, where there was a vacancy each year. A commission was formed to study American foreign economic policy and draft a set of policy recommendations. The president named Clarence B. Randall, a free trader and retired chairman of Inland Steel, to head the group.[41] Thus, in 1953 future trade policy remained undefined. Each side had another year to rally its forces.

Faced with a party hostile to reciprocal trade, the creation of the Randall Commission represented a clear attempt by the president to seize the initiative on trade policy. Paul Hoffmann, President Truman's director of the Marshall Plan, made the suggestion to Eisenhower shortly before his inauguration. Harold Stassen, then director for mutual security, also favored establishing some form of Foreign Economic Policy Council. As Eisenhower explained to Dulles in January, a study group offered a means of "providing a reason—or an excuse—for urging postponement of unwise legislation pending the receipt of the committee's findings."[42] In March Eisenhower distributed a paper by Allan B. Kline proposing the idea to the secretaries of the treasury, commerce, and agriculture, as well as the mutual security director. Thus, the idea had momentum behind it before Eisenhower suggested it in public on 2 May.[43]

George Humphrey, Eisenhower's conservative secretary of the treasury, immediately identified the possibilities and problems inherent in such a panel. Humphrey thought that a foreign trade commission might be useful, provided that, "you can be sure that you appoint or control the appointment of the majority of the Commission."[44] The president placed his faith in Randall to guide the commission to assemble a set of recommendations to serve as the basis for administration policy. But in neglecting to heed more completely Humphrey's advice Eisenhower guaranteed that Randall's assignment would become an exercise in frustration. Reed, Simpson, and Millikin all secured appointments to the panel.[45]

The unsettled state of U.S. policy aroused concern overseas, particularly in Japan, because the RTAA provided the legal basis for American participation in tariff negotiations. Having applied to become a member of GATT, the Japanese government was highly anxious. On 27 April, the Japanese Embassy conveyed its well-founded concern that asking for only a one-year renewal of the RTAA effectively postponed Japan's entry into GATT. The United States would be unable to engage in the major tariff negotiations that ordinarily preceded a nation's entry into the organization. The Japanese were also worried about a Tariff Commission decision recommending that the duty on silk scarves be raised to 65 percent.[46] Access to the U.S. market appeared as uncertain as ever.

As on the issue of U.S. military purchases in Japan, the Department of State paid careful attention to the effect of American actions on Japanese opinion. One sign of the administration's continuing commitment to expanding trade across the Pacific was the Treaty of Friendship, Commerce, and Navigation signed in April.[47] The treaty restored commercial relations on a normal bilateral basis for the first time since 1940. The president's decision to pursue a one-year renewal of the RTAA, however, did result in the delay of major tariff negotiations for at least a year.[48] President Eisenhower thus paid careful attention to the escape clause cases that reached his desk. Regarding his decisions as "establishing the administration's attitude and future policy," Eisenhower defended open trade.[49] In April the Tariff Commission recommended doubling the duty on imported screen-printed scarves. About $7 million of trade was at stake. Eisenhower did not approve the increase.

Japanese interests and their allies appealed to the president not to increase the duty, but Eisenhower justified his decision on strictly economic grounds. The line between domestic industry and imports was unclear. Many businesses claiming to represent "domestic industry" in fact consisted of American entrepreneurs using Japanese labor at piece rates for printing and finishing before exporting the scarves to the United States. It was also uncertain whether increasing the tariff would actually benefit any segment of the apparel industry or simply increase the cost to the consumer. Owing to disparities in quality and price, Eisenhower was not convinced that imported silk scarves were actually competing for the same market as domestic silk scarves. They seemed instead to be creating additional markets for themselves.[50]

The Intersessional Committee on Japan and GATT

The other major question relating to Japan's economy that the Eisenhower administration faced during its first year was the matter of Japanese accession to GATT. The State Department was principally responsible for attending to GATT affairs. Like Truman and Acheson before them, Eisenhower and Dulles left the details of policy to the department bureaus concerned. In January 1953 the contracting parties were preparing for the intersessional discussion of Japan's application. One of the Truman administration's last actions was to define the U.S. objective for the intersessional committee: to secure the contracting parties' agreement to allow Japan to negotiate for accession on the basis of complete equality. The Eisenhower administration maintained this stand, and the same officials attended to the matter during the transition.[51]

The success of both the preparations for the meeting and the February intersessional discussion itself hinged on reaching an Anglo-American consensus on Japanese accession. In the months leading up to the intersessional meeting, American and British officials attempted to resolve their differences in a fair-minded way. Representatives from both sides were well versed in the issues involved, and relative secrecy made possible a constructive exchange of opinions. The Japanese diplomats, for their part, went out of their way to provide information and to be available in case questions arose.

Japanese accession to GATT presented the British government with a dilemma of the first order. On the one hand, for sound economic and political reasons, the United Kingdom desired "to see Japan associated with the world community of trading nations in accepting the only existing international code of commercial behavior." Yet, for understandable political reasons, the government desired "adequate safeguards" against possible repetition of "Japanese malpractices and unfair competition" before the war.[52]

Neither trade liberalization nor GATT was popular at home, and the prospect of increased Japanese imports was a particularly explosive issue.

The most important interest opposing concessions to Japan was the depressed cotton textiles industry. Because the mention of Japanese trade sparked memories of Japan's export offensive during the 1930s, discussion of Japanese trade was inseparable from the pervasive fear of unfair or disruptive economic competition. "The real bogey," the British ambassador to Japan mused, "is the thought of shut-down weaving sheds and queues outside the Labor Exchanges in Lancashire at a time when Japanese shirts and socks and dresses are to be seen in the draper's round the corner."[53]

Specific concerns at issue included "sweated labour," Japanese price slashing and dumping, misleading trade names, and protection of patents trademarks, and copyrights.[54] Because British opposition to Japanese textile imports was highly concentrated, however, the real problem which Japanese accession to GATT posed was political. As one official noted after months of grappling with the problem, "it is not the real economic consequences of acceptance of GATT obligations towards Japan which are feared so much as Lancashire's fears of what those consequences may be."[55]

The British government began to grapple with the problem in earnest during the winter of 1952–53. The Board of Trade prepared a detailed paper that provided the basis for a new policy. The board was prepared to agree to Japanese accession (and thus concede a contractual right to MFN), but only on terms that allowed Britain "freedom to take *discriminatory* action against Japan." Because the vital issue was retention of the freedom to act in case of injury, Japanese adherence to international fair labor standards or other conventions on commercial practice were insufficient insurance to the board, which preferred an extension of the emergency escape clause in Article 19. It authorized the suspension, withdrawal, or modification of a tariff concession (or other obligation) in the case of serious injury to domestic industry producing like or competitive products. Specifically, the board insisted on writing into the Japanese protocol of accession a provision allowing escape clause relief in the event imports from Japan caused or threatened to cause serious injury to domestic industry, or if they caused or threatened to cause serious injury to the exports of one contracting party to another contracting party.[56]

Although the Foreign Office favored Japanese entry into GATT, officials there saw in the Board of Trade proposal the basis for a national policy. As restrictive as it was, the new paper represented a shift away from prior noncooperation. Foreign Office opinion preferred attaching conditions to Japanese accession over invocation of Article 35, the general escape clause.[57] Invoking Article 35 allowed a contracting party to deny GATT privileges to another. But invocation was possible only once, here before formal acceptance of Japan into GATT. Besides being offensive to Japan, it would also place the United Kingdom at odds with the United States. A member nation that did not invoke Article 35 would be obligated to treat Japanese trade in the same manner as it treated the commerce of the other contracting parties.

The ministers agreed in January 1953 to sound out the governments of the United States and other powers represented on the intersessional committee, but their initiative fell flat. Ambassador Sir Esler Dening conveyed the Tokyo Embassy's opposition to such open discrimination against Japan.[58] Canada, Australia, and New Zealand offered only qualified support in advance of the meeting. No power was willing to join with the United Kingdom in putting forward the proposal at the February meeting.[59] U.S. opposition, however, was decisive.

Despite the many questions about the future, U.S. policy remained consistent. The U.S. Embassy in Tokyo worried that the contracting parties overemphasized Japan's economic threat to them and underemphasized Japan's deteriorating foreign trade position.[60] Winthrop Brown of the U.S. Embassy in London told the British even before consulting with Washington that he was "profoundly disturbed by the idea of discriminating against Japan even in an emergency." He specifically emphasized that it would provide a "handle" for congressional opponents of MFN commitments. "Once the principle of discrimination against an individual country was admitted," Brown reasoned, he could "see no defense against those Congressmen . . . who would argue that United States legislation should similarly permit discrimination," perhaps against the United Kingdom.[61]

The economic principle at stake was the most compelling issue. Acceptance of the principle of discrimination against a particular country was a precedent that other countries were bound sooner or later to follow.[62] Department of State officials were loath to approve of any further extension of escape clause activity under the General Agreement, and Article 19 in particular, because the department was then reviewing the escape clause provisions of the existing RTAA. The department's aim was to reduce the number of applications to the Tariff Commission for relief by making the standards for such appeals more demanding.[63]

At this juncture the Executive Secretariat volunteered a compromise formula based on the "nullification and impairment" provision of the General Agreement (Article 23). The idea was to allow a contracting party, under circumstances of serious injury, to suspend the appropriate concession pending a decision of the contracting parties.[64] State's Bureau of Economic Affairs opposed the idea. The Bureau of Far Eastern Affairs supported it because it did not single out Japan and it seemed to do less violence to the principles of GATT. Haguiwara Tōru, the Japanese representative in Geneva, signaled Japan's approval of any formula that would be applicable to all.[65] The British government was divided. U.K. representatives continued to participate in the committee's work on a noncommittal basis. Not wishing to commit the new administration, the United States delegation did likewise.[66]

Thus, the committee submitted its report *ad referendum*. The report suggested modifying Article 23 to allow a contracting party to take protective action against the threat of injury, but it retained the principle of equal treatment. The report did not make any suggestions on the timing of future tariff negotiations, but it did affirm that "a substantial majority" of the committee endorsed further liberalization of trade.[67]

The report's reception in the United Kingdom predictably echoed the debate over Japanese accession to GATT. Except for the *Daily Express*, the press did not make predictions of disaster for Britain. The *Times* accepted "without hesitation" the principle that any safeguards introduced before Japanese accession should not be aimed solely at Japan. The *Economist* also affirmed that suggestions of such discriminatory treatment were "very properly turned down." U.S. officials were nevertheless justifiably concerned that GATT's detractors enjoyed sympathy among government back benchers.[68] The Foreign Office and the Exchequer favored accepting the intersessional report, while the Board of Trade and the Commonwealth Relations Office were opposed. Unable to agree, the cabinet resorted to deferral once again.[69]

Since the Yoshida government sought to undertake tariff negotiations with the United States, Japanese frustration with the slow progress focused on the United States rather than Britain. Although Japan desired British support for Japanese accession to GATT, tariff negotiations with the United Kingdom were comparatively unimportant to Japan.[70] Thus, the U.S. decision not to begin negotiations for another year proved particularly disappointing. The State Department insisted, however, that negotiations would be inconsistent with a review of U.S. policy. Department officials also feared that announcing "major" tariff negotiations risked "arousing protectionist pressure," thus jeopardizing one-year renewal of the RTAA without "damaging amendments."[71]

Provisional Japanese Membership in GATT, 1953

Upon recognizing that a major tariff conference was not on the horizon in 1953, the Japanese government pressed for action in some other form before the year's end. In April the Japanese sounded out department opinion on several proposals. One called for an Annecy-type round of negotiations. That is, the present contracting parties would negotiate only with Japan and any other country wishing to accede. An alternative approach called for bilateral negotiations between the United States and Japan to bind existing tariff rates.

Walter Robertson, the newly appointed assistant secretary of state for Far Eastern affairs, brought the matter to Secretary Dulles's attention in April. Dulles relied on Robertson. A courtly investment banker from Virginia, Robertson had served with the State Department in China late in the Second World War. After General Patrick Hurley resigned as ambassador in 1945 he assumed charge of the U.S. Embassy there. If Robertson's strident anti-Communism appealed to Dulles, it put him at odds with many career China hands. On most issues concerning Japan, however, Robertson and the career officials cooperated smoothly. Robertson recommended that Secretary Dulles avoid making any reply to a question during the hearings on the Simpson bill precluding American agreement with the Japanese proposal. Before Congress, Dulles affirmed that the administration did not envision concluding any reciprocal trade agreement, but he did suggest that the United States and Japan could always negotiate a separate treaty and submit it to the Senate for approval.[72]

Without any sign of tangible gain, the Japanese became increasingly impatient. Owing to the public feeling in Japan that the United States now bore primary responsibility for the delay in Japan's accession to GATT, Ambassador Allison pressed for interim action.[73] The problem for the department was to find a way to do something meaningful without engaging in actual trade negotiations. With a bold gesture, the Japanese finally forced the issue. In early July the Yoshida government informed the department that it planned to ask the contracting parties to permit Japan to accede to GATT on a temporary basis.[74]

Although neither Dulles nor his subordinates communicated their views to the Japanese, they strongly favored the initiative. Noting that Japan saw accession to GATT, even on a temporary basis, as being "of the utmost political importance," U. Alexis Johnson urged that the secretary support the Japanese proposal. With Dulles's approval, Japanese accession became a concern at the highest levels.[75] Provisional membership was a step down from the State Department's initial design. But it provided a way to accommodate Japan's aspirations, to assuage the anxiety of contracting parties such as the United Kingdom, and to circumvent the domestic constraints on U.S. policy. In mid-August the Trade Agreements Committee unanimously approved supporting temporary membership for Japan.[76]

Yet the State Department neither went public nor informed the Japanese. Administration officials wished to secure President Eisenhower's support in advance of any announcement and thus preempt any protest. Because Dulles had promised lawmakers that the administration would not engage in major tariff negotiations, there was a great risk of embarrassment. On 26 August Eisenhower agreed.[77] One month later, he approved the TAC recommendation on temporary Japanese accession and extension of GATT tariff concessions to Japan.[78]

The State Department then began lobbying the other contracting parties as the eighth session of GATT (scheduled for September) approached. Confirmed opponents of Japanese accession were a small minority, but there was little enthusiasm for provisional membership. On 3 September, Dulles informed Sir Roger Makins, the British ambassador in Washington, that the United States would support the Japanese proposal.[79] Other GATT members such as France were on record as supporting Japanese accession only after tariff negotiations. That position was actually a formula for delay. State thus pressed its position where possible. In the case of Australia and New Zealand, the Bureau of Far Eastern Affairs urged the secretary to raise the matter at an ANZUS meeting. Both powers held to their position of not entering into GATT commitments toward Japan, however.[80]

At the eighth session, the Japanese attempted—with U.S. support—to reassure the hesitant members. Japanese participation in GATT would not cause the disruption of the trade of other countries. Japan would accept the safeguard proposed by the intersessional committee. Japan would bind over 90 percent of the nation's customs tariff involving 85 percent of the value of all imports.[81] Despite lobbying by Matsumoto Shun'ichi, ambassador to the United Kingdom and the leader of the Japanese delegation, the British promised to abstain.[82]

At the session, the American delegation enjoyed considerable freedom to define the terms of provisional Japanese accession. Eisenhower's instructions asked that the United States seek agreement on three items: GATT treatment (including extension of MFN) for Japan's trade, extension of tariff concessions incorporated into GATT for Japan, and Japanese acceptance of GATT obligations, including a satisfactory tariff commitment (such as binding a substantial portion of existing tariff rates). The United States was also prepared to agree to the Article 23 safeguard proposed by the intersessional committee.[83]

A simple majority vote was sufficient, but the American delegation desired at least a two-thirds majority because the U.S. goal was to make a political and psychological impression as much as to secure economic benefits for Japan. Initial attempts to secure approval of Japanese accession in one stage by this margin failed. The idea was to allow Japanese participation in GATT on a provisional basis, until the conclusion of major tariff negotiations. Then Japan would become a full member.[84] Unable to win over wavering nations such as Burma, Indonesia, and Peru, the United States backed a compromise proposal suggested by Eric Wyndham-White, the executive secretary.[85] The Secretariat's initiative called for a "unanimous or virtually unanimous decision" to invite the Japanese to participate in GATT. The price of this unanimity, however, was a "separate protocol" providing for the mutual application of GATT terms on trade with Japan.[86] Thus, the contracting parties were able to approve of provisional membership for Japan, yet refrain from extending GATT treatment to Japanese trade.[87]

On 24 October, Winthrop Brown, the head of the U.S. delegation finally reported "mission accomplished." In a vote on the compromise resolution, twenty-seven members invited Japan to participate without formal voting rights in the work of the organization until 30 June 1955. During this period the contracting parties could agree to apply GATT rules to their trade with Japan. The United Kingdom, Australia, New Zealand, South Africa, South Rhodesia, and Czechoslovakia abstained. More memorable than the abstentions was the "quite dramatic moment" after the vote when the chairman asked the Japanese representative to take his seat at the table. "Ambassador Matsumoto rose from the observers' table in the middle of the room and walked to a place which was then prepared for him at the regular conference table," Brown recorded. "There was a sense that this small action symbolized an event in history."[88] By the end of the year eighteen countries, including the United States, signed agreements to extend GATT privileges to Japanese trade. The United Kingdom maintained its system of import quotas and refrained from any formal commitment. Britain nevertheless granted equal tariff treatment on certain items on its direct trade with Japan.[89]

Preparation of the Randall Report

In the United States the fight over trade policy continued. Difficulties began with the very idea of assembling a group such as the Randall Commission. Rather than merely give a seal of approval to a policy defined in advance, the task of the commission was to study the many facets of U.S. foreign economic policy and to draft recommendations for action. Political differences between the various members compromised the body's usefulness from the start.

Randall was a strong personality who maintained tight control over the group, but he was unable to control all of the centrifugal forces at work. He managed the schedule in a way to minimize expression of differences and the delay that such debate would cause. He rationed the time for the commission's hearings according to a strict schedule during the autumn months, and then pressed for completion of the final report by January 1954 in time for the Congress to consider its recommendations that year. Randall believed that reducing trade barriers was in the U.S. interest, but he was willing to compromise for the sake of reaching agreement.[90] He recognized immediately that the members of the group could never agree on a statement of economic philosophy. Randall was of strong opinions himself. He thought Dan Reed was "as stubborn as it is possible for a human being to be."[91] Rather than pose divisive philosophical questions about the purposes and basic character of American policy, Randall sought to focus the commission's energy on the more practical problem of reducing the huge U.S. commercial trade surplus, the so-called dollar gap.

Stubborn or not, Reed correctly identified the debate within the Republican Party on trade to be over the fundamentals of policy and economic philosophy rather than differences over means toward the same end. The dollar gap was an obvious indicator of imbalance in international economic life, but it was more the symptom of disequilibrium than its cause. Reed, Simpson, Millikin, and other economic nationalists were unconvinced that the benefits of liberalizing trade were consistent with either economic health or American tradition.

Advocates of liberal trade rightly emphasized the connection between the economic health of other nations and American economic opportunity. The reduction of trade barriers abroad depended upon the United States taking the lead in clearing away restrictive measures, such as the Buy American Act. To committed free traders, even reciprocal trade had outlived its utility. Since low-tariff countries and the United States had exhausted their capacity to grant tariff concessions during the initial rounds of GATT negotiations, insistence on strict reciprocity promised diminishing returns in the future. Winthrop Aldrich, the U.S. ambassador to the United Kingdom, identified the stakes. Failure to act would "allow existing restrictions to become crystallized," and the world would "be less able to resist the innumerable pressures of particular vested interests for added restrictionism" in the future.[92] Economic liberals desired an interdependent world economy based on a system of multilateral trade and payments pegged to the dollar. They were willing to tolerate some unemployment and economic readjustment in declining industries at home.

Economic nationalists, by contrast, believed that "foreign economic policy should be considered primarily in relation to the domestic economy."[93] In trade liberalization since 1934 they accurately identified a radical break with the U.S. tradition of protection. U.S. policy no longer sought primarily to maximize commercial advantage at home in the same manner as before. American tariff walls remained high, particularly in the case of Japan, but the new priority was to reduce rather than to fortify them. In opposing this trend, conservatives like Reed spoke for those industries and their workers most at risk in a more open economy. They also criticized tariff concessions and economic aid programs as rewards for fiscal irresponsibility abroad. Such commercial nationalism was the economic counterpart of "fortress-America" thinking in the strategic arena. Conservatives were alarmed over the transfer of power accompanying and facilitating liberalization. They recognized that authority over the details of trade policy was slipping from the Congress to trade negotiators in the executive branch and international organizations such as GATT. By pressing for import quotas and expansion of the Tariff Commission, they attempted to reverse this trend and to expand institutional support for protective policies.

Both sides viewed events through the experience of the 1930s. Liberal internationalists correctly understood that one cause of the Second World War was the economic instability that undercut democratic governments and paved the way for aggressive nationalist regimes in Germany, Japan, and elsewhere. Unless the United States took responsibility for bringing order to the world economy, the vicious cycle of mercantilism, depression, political instability, and war seemed likely to repeat itself. In laying stress on the danger of not changing, however, the internationalists downplayed the price of changing course.

Although economic nationalists overstated the constructive role of the tariff in promoting economic growth in U.S. history, they saw clearly that its revision downward had important consequences in various segments of industry and agriculture, the employees working in them, and their communities. Free traders' descriptions of heightened competition in declining light industries as a natural structural transition toward higher-value-added production often failed to include the negative effects of economic change. In seeking to protect the U.S. market from a renewed Japanese export offensive, however, economic nationalists skewed public debate on the issue of trade friction with Japan. By focusing on the threat posed by Japanese imports, they neglected the problem of restrictions on U.S. exports to Japan. Pressure on the administration to retain as many restrictions on Japanese imports as possible actually compounded the problem by making it difficult for U.S. negotiators to make inroads into the Japanese market as it was taking shape during the fifties.

As he compiled the final report, Randall found "endemic in this Commission a vortex of differences which no power on earth can change or assuage." At one low moment, he recorded in his diary that he was "afraid that the whole concept of the Commission thus appointed is mad, and if we come out with any report at all, let alone one that makes sense, it will be a miracle."[94] Although Randall met his deadline, the commission's report did not chart a bold course of action. Its contents were testimony to how Randall tried and failed to reach a consensus on a set of recommendations to close the dollar gap. Despite his flexibility on several points, Reed and Simpson filed their own dissenting *Minority Report*. Millikin also submitted a separate statement qualifying his support for the commission's report.

Even as a statement on the imbalance in world trade, the report fell far short of a free-trade agenda and the needs of the day. It timidly advised that the president's authority to reduce tariffs be limited to 5 percent of existing rates for the first three years. It also recommended retaining the peril-point and escape clauses of the existing act. The report advised renewal of the RTAA for three years as well as the further study of tariff schedules, rate structures, and customs administration (the idea being to simplify procedures). It recommended revision of the Buy American Act to enable foreign firms greater opportunity to bid on U.S. government contracts. It criticized the use of offshore procurement for foreign aid purposes, and recommended that economic aid in grant form should be terminated as soon as possible. Finally, the report recommended allowing trade in peaceful goods with the Eastern bloc, but not the PRC or North Korea. In short, the report inspired no one. In Japan, the reception ranged from "qualified welcome to downright dissatisfaction."[95]

Conclusion

Successful integration of Japan into the Western trading bloc was hardly foreordained. The prospect of closer economic relations with Japan aroused opposition on its own merits, and it was intertwined in the broader controversy over trade liberalization. Eisenhower and his advisors favored the reciprocal trade program and expanded economic ties with Japan for economic reasons, but the priority of both issues owed more to their salience in the Cold War. To a greater extent than most security issues, however, trade liberalization depended on congressional approval at home and international agreement abroad. In 1953 both the Republican leadership in Congress and the non-Asian members of the Commonwealth resisted offering such approval.

The American and British governments were both divided over the issues of trade and Japan. The executive organs principally responsible for foreign policy strongly favored integrating Japan into the new commercial order on the basis of equality. The U.K. Board of Trade and conservative elements in the American Congress, however, pursued their own protectionist agendas. The Eisenhower administration (and the U.K. Foreign Office) thus proceeded cautiously. In so doing, the president was able to avoid defeat. But a one-year renewal of the Reciprocal Trade Agreements Act and temporary Japanese accession to GATT represented only partial accomplishment of the administration's agenda.

At the end of Eisenhower's first year, the fight over trade remained alive. In the same way the members of the Randall Commission disagreed over the policies to recommend to the president and the Congress in 1954, GATT members were still at odds over how to handle Japan's application for accession. Not until middecade, after another round of fighting, and further escalation of the Cold War in Asia, did the reciprocal trade program rest on more secure footing and Japan become a full member of GATT.

Chapter Six

JAPANESE INTEGRATION WITH THE WESTERN TRADING BLOC, 1954-1956

The institutions underpinning Japan's high-speed growth after World War II—often called the "1955 system"—took shape over many years.[1] This incremental pace of change holds particularly true for the structure of international trade supporting the Japanese economic advance. If the eventuality of Japanese accession to GATT was fully apparent by 1953, the terms regulating Japan's foreign trade were not clearly established until middecade. Despite a sense of inevitability in hindsight, much remained in doubt. The sense of contingency at the time reflects how gradually the new order emerged.

Japan's problem was that expanded access to foreign markets required the cooperation of other powers, particularly the United States. In one sense President Eisenhower's commitment to move forward on tariff negotiations and his ability to secure a second one-year renewal of the reciprocal trade program in 1954 testified to the momentum behind Japanese integration with the Western trading bloc. Yet the slow pace of change heightened awareness of the obstacles to progress. American support for Japanese access to Western markets also exacted a price of its own: continued acquiescence in the virtual embargo on trade with the People's Republic of China. Japanese admission to GATT in 1955 visibly confirmed the opportunity available in the emerging order. But the persistence of discrimination against Japanese trade and the slight results of the now forgotten "fourth round" of tariff negotiations in 1956 showed the limits of change.

The Trade Fight in Congress Renewed, 1954

The Eisenhower administration began the second round of the fight over reciprocal trade in Congress at a strategic disadvantage. The problems began with the Randall Commission's report. Its tepid recommendations surrendered all room for bargaining from the start. President Eisenhower nevertheless uncritically endorsed the report and made it the basis of the administration's foreign economic policy.[2] The administration hoped that the whole package would command wide legislative support, but the Republican leadership again refused to cooperate. Only Robert W. Kean (R.-N.J.), fourth-ranking Republican on the Ways and Means Committee, was willing to introduce the administration's bill to renew the RTAA for three years. When he did so shortly before the Easter recess, he got no help from either his fellow Republicans or the Democrats.

A proviso in the Kean bill (H.R. 8860) showed the priority the administration assigned to negotiations with Japan. Because the Randall Commission's recommendations severely limited the tariff concessions the United States could offer, the proviso made an exception for Japan. The president could make reductions in tariffs of up to 50 percent from the 1 January 1945 level. From the Department of State's position, however, even this provision was inferior to simple extension of the existing RTAA.[3]

Eisenhower's tendency to let the control of trade policy slip from his grasp played into the hands of protectionists. By simply accepting the Randall Commission's recommendations, he passed up an opportunity to come down more firmly in support of trade liberalization. The amount of pulling and hauling involved in securing passage of trade legislation seems to have surprised both Eisenhower and Randall. A conversation with Ambassador Henry Cabot Lodge in February 1954 left Randall with "a very unhappy impression." "He told me," Randall recorded in his diary, "that whatever I may have thought about the rough time I have had within the Commission, it was as nothing to what would happen to me when I got to the Hill with this program, where they would simply tear me to pieces." Lodge added that "there is a certain group of senators who will pay no attention whatsoever to what the Administration wants, and who will block every move I make, unless they are bought off. He said that the only thing to do was to be practicable and buy them off." Although Lodge's understanding of the legislative process represented the voice of experience, Randall resisted, preferring to fight for the administration's program on its merits. "I don't live in that kind of an atmosphere," he recorded.[4]

In sharp contrast with decision making on security issues and the budget, President Eisenhower also had no taste for the constant maneuvering required in foreign economic policy. In the absence of sustained attention, no administration can secure congressional approval of very many items on its agenda. In fairness to Eisenhower, he did not wish to sacrifice party unity over the matter. The result was unusual White House deference to the legislative leadership, especially Senator Millikin.

Fortuitously for the administration, crisis abroad forced the issue. Japan's record trade deficit in 1953 prompted the sustained high-level attention necessary for action in Congress. On 10 May Eisenhower backed down and asked for a simple one-year extension of the RTAA. He consulted extensively with Reed and spoke out in public on the need to expand Japan's foreign trade. Most dramatically, Secretary Dulles suddenly took up the issues of reciprocal trade and Japanese tariff negotiations and pressed the Congress with his characteristic vigor. He met many times with Reed and other Republicans on the Ways and Means Committee to impress upon them the need to allow Japan to make a living in order to secure the nation's loyalty in the Cold War.[5]

French defeat at Dienbienphu in May made lawmakers wary of appearing to undermine the administration's policies in Asia. Even Reed and Simpson put aside temporarily their differences with the administration. Reed conceded: "There is a great reservoir of people out of work [in Japan] and the Communists are working to the best of their ability among these people. We need Japan on our side in this troubled world, and we are not going to gain their support by starving them to death. We have to do at least this much for them, at least give them a chance to be heard through trade negotiations. I am not willing . . . to take the responsibility under present conditions of the world of killing this bill and shutting the door to such negotiations."[6] Japan's economic crisis was real, but the actual likelihood of Japan falling to communism was small. Appealing to the Communist threat prompted lawmakers to act. Reed introduced a bill to extend the RTAA for another year. Both houses of Congress passed the measure, and the president signed it into law. All sides understood that the administration planned to go ahead with Japanese tariff negotiations.

Trade Promotion: Revision of the "Buy American" Policy and PL 480

If the Eisenhower administration achieved only the mandatory minimum in the fight over reciprocal trade, 1954 saw considerable progress on the other points of the president's foreign economic policy agenda. Congress and the executive branch took important steps to facilitate increased imports. The Customs Simplification Act of 1954 directed the Tariff Commission to study U.S. customs laws and procedures and then submit to Congress its recommendations for consolidation, simplification, and rational organization of the tariff schedules and classifications. The act also amended the antidumping laws. It transferred authority to determine injury from the Department of the Treasury to the Tariff Commission and provided that dumping duties would not be levied against imports made more than 120 days before the issue was raised. The purpose was to help reduce the interference with trade during investigation of suspected dumping.[7] The Bureau of Customs moved to speed clearance of goods and persons through customs. For example, the bureau's new guidelines exempted all imports not exceeding $500 in value from the requirement to have the invoice certified before the nearest U.S. consul.[8]

The most significant change concerned the Buy American Act. Enacted in 1933 and signed by President Herbert Hoover on his way out of office, this Depression-era measure sought to remedy unemployment by requiring that supplies for government-assisted public works be domestically produced. Government agencies were required to award contracts to American firms unless their bids exceeded that of a foreign competitor by an "unreasonable" amount. As applied, "unreasonable" was defined as exceeding the price of a foreign article, after figuring duty, by more than 25 percent. Because the cycle of trade restriction and retaliation of which the law was a part actually increased economic distress in the world, the Buy American Act was of questionable economic utility from the start.[9]

The act's restrictive and discriminatory provisions conflicted with the postwar policy of reducing unnecessary trade barriers. It also impeded efforts to reduce the cost of government operations. Inclusion of a "Buy

American" requirement in appropriation legislation for the Defense Department for 1953 (the "Berry amendment") affected military purchases from Japan. Its effect was to prohibit procurement of Japanese cotton and woolen textiles ($35 million in fiscal year 1952) as well as materials for the construction of military bases in Alaska.[10] Estimating the total effect of "Buy American" practices is very difficult because of their tendency to deter foreign competitors from submitting bids at all. The few contracts awarded to Japanese companies—such as Nippon Gaisha Kaisha, Ltd. of Nagoya (for porcelain electrical insulators)—drew immediate criticism from American industry.[11] The few successful Japanese firms exhibited unusual drive.[12]

Pressure for revision of "Buy American" policies was mounting in the executive departments and agencies even before Eisenhower assumed the presidency. Mindful of the economic impact abroad, Secretary Dulles was a particularly strong advocate of revision. On 10 July a cabinet committee recommended revising the 25 percent differential down to a 5 percent margin of preference for American business. Secretaries Humphrey and Weeks, however, opposed making any change without consulting the legislative leadership, or before the completion of the Randall Commission report. The Department of the Interior was the sole opponent of change. The president agreed not to announce any policy change while the commission completed its work.[13] News of the draft proposal then leaked to the press, and government agencies were reluctant to make any changes without a clear directive to which they could refer in public.[14]

Although he supported a low differential, Eisenhower did not issue any directive until the next year. He desired a consensus of opinion before taking action. The Randall Commission recommended eliminating "Buy American" preferences on a reciprocal basis. At a meeting on 18 August 1954, the cabinet again divided. Pointing to the need for action, Dulles pressed for an immediate decision. In his view the level of preference was a secondary concern. It was an election year, however, and Commerce Secretary Weeks feared a political backlash from an early announcement. Eisenhower too suddenly hesitated to support a differential as low as 5 percent. The president attempted to forge a compromise by suggesting a couple of alternate formulas: a 10 percent differential at the point of entry, or 6 percent on the delivered price. After the 1954 elections the cabinet considered the final draft, and Eisenhower issued the directive as Executive Order 10582 on 17 December 1954.[15]

Domestic politics figured even more prominently in efforts to promote American agricultural trade. The landmark measure was PL 480 of 1954, the Agricultural Trade and Development Assistance Act (more commonly known as the Agricultural Surplus Disposal Program). PL 480 sought to lessen the burden of agricultural surpluses held by the federal government while providing some aid to foreign nations in need of farm products. In part as a consequence of the Truman administration's abolition of acreage requirements for the 1952 and 1953 harvests, the federal government had accumulated $5.5 billion of surplus agricultural commodities at a cost of $1 million per day.[16]

Owing to this expense and the legislative clout of lawmakers from the farm states, congressional pressure for disposing of the surpluses was strong. In 1953 Senator Hubert H. Humphrey (D.-Minn.) pressed for an expansive program. But Congress adjourned before the House could consider such legislation. This delay afforded the administration an opportunity to consider the matter. Despite some misgivings in the Departments of Agriculture and State, President Eisenhower decided to support the measure in 1954. The administration was desperate to get rid of its surplus commodities. The proposal also offered a means to assist needy countries while expanding the market for American farm exports. The terms of PL 480, which became law in July 1954, consisted of three titles. Title I provided for the sale of U.S. commodities to friendly governments in exchange for local currencies. These funds were to be used for various purposes including economic development abroad. Title II authorized donations of food in case of famine or emergency. Under Title III, the barter program allowed the United States to exchange surplus agricultural products for nonperishable strategic materials.

Although the PL 480 program was the target of much well deserved criticism from the start, it contributed significantly to consolidating the postwar economic partnership between the United States and Japan. As the historian William Borden has concluded, the program "disposed of the American farm glut and locked industrial competitors into the American economic orbit."[17] In the abstract, the postwar American and Japanese economies complemented each other much as they had in fact before the war. Japan depended upon foreign sources of supply for food and raw materials; American farmers produced an abundance of agricultural commodities. But the United States was not the only producer of such farm products, and during the fifties every dollar purchase constituted a demand on Japan's meager foreign exchange holdings. The Agricultural Surplus Disposal Program and other agricultural export promotion initiatives forged the links between American producers and Japanese buyers of farm commodities during the period when Japan was rebuilding its economic ties with the world and making the transition from recovery to high-speed growth.

The PL 480 program for Japan was modest. In late 1954 the Eisenhower administration decided on the amount: $85 million worth of commodities. Not until 31 May 1955, however, did the two nations agreed upon the terms of the program.[18] The Japanese were less enthusiastic about the program than their American benefactors were. Fundamentally, PL 480 was an economic development program grafted onto a scheme for unloading American agricultural surpluses abroad. According to the terms of the program, 30 percent of the yen generated by the agricultural sales in Japan was to be devoted to procurement of military equipment, purchase of goods and services for other countries, efforts to develop new markets for U.S. agricultural commodities, the financing of international educational exchange activities, and payment of U.S. obligations in Japan. The other 70 percent was to be credited to Japan as a development loan through the Export-Import Bank of Washington to the government of Japan for a period of forty years (at 3 percent per annum, the first three years exempted).

Since PL 480 disposed of U.S. surpluses overseas, it was unpopular in Canada, Australia, and other nations that exported agricultural commodities. In the planning of the 1955 program for Japan, the most sensitive item was rice. Dulles and the State Department were concerned about the negative effect of rice sales on the export opportunities of Burma, Thailand, and Taiwan.[19] The 1955 package nevertheless included $15 million of rice. The amount scheduled for 1956 was about $14 million, after which time it dwindled to zero. In the mid-1960s, Japan again imported American rice for a brief period.[20]

PL 480 sales, primarily during the period 1955–56, facilitated greater agricultural trade between Japan and the United States. Title I sales in Japan for those years totaled $213 million, and barter transactions amounted to about $207 million. By the decade's end Japan's consumption of American agricultural commodities was escalating rapidly: $485 million in 1960, $750 million in 1965, and over $1 billion by 1970. From 1955 to 1973, Export-Import Bank loans to Japan totaled slightly more than $1.3 billion. Commodity Credit Corporation sales amounted to over $424 million.[21] Although Japan's booming economy was the engine that created the demand for American agricultural products, the U.S. government actively promoted such exports.[22]

The Persistence of Controls on Trade with China

Although Japanese attention focused increasingly on expanding trade with the West, the China market remained an ever present object of desire. When Eisenhower took office in January 1953, American policy on East-West trade called for intensifying controls on exports to the Communist bloc.[23] The Western European allies and Japan chafed under these restrictions. Several of the Western powers had long depended upon sources of raw materials in the East. Allied governments had never accepted the Truman administration's broad definition of "strategic" goods. Because one result of postwar recovery was to create a buyers' market in several industries, Western European manufacturers were anxious to find new outlets for their goods.[24]

Domestic pressure on the Japanese government to relax controls on trade with the PRC escalated in 1953. The armistice in Korea, Prime Minister Yoshida's weakening hold on power, and the nation's ballooning commercial trade deficit contributed to the change. The Yoshida government spoke with many voices on the issue. Foreign Minister Okazaki defended a restrictive policy "in concert with other free nations." MITI Minister Okano Kiyohide, however, openly advocated expanded trade with the PRC.[25] MITI was gradually permitting many items previously embargoed to be exported to China on a barter basis.[26] Yet, as before, Japanese policy was conservative. The main aim of the Japanese government was not to reorient the nation's export trade toward the Asian mainland, but to achieve a position of equality with the Western members of the Paris group while securing whatever economic advantage was available.[27]

Japanese public opinion was more anxious for change. Many different organizations and interests joined in the call for increased trade with China. Socialist politicians naturally championed closer economic ties with the mainland. A group of Diet members who traveled to Beijing in 1952 concluded the first unofficial Sino-Japanese Trade Agreement. A second agreement, concluded the next year, kept the issue in the public eye.[28] Left-leaning organizations such as the Sino-Japanese Trade Promotion Association (Nitchū Bōeki Sokushin Kaigi) also pressed for more trade. Such bodies, however, were often divided. Small businesses were unhappy that the goods the PRC desired (e.g., steel and machinery) were more easily supplied by big business than light industry.[29] Intellectuals were another prominent force for change.[30]

Advocacy of greater Sino-Japanese trade was not confined to the political left. *Tōyō Keizai Shinpō* (Oriental Economist) and other national publications regularly featured articles and interviews with business leaders advocating trade with the Communist Chinese.[31] Among the most vocal constituencies for increased Sino-Japanese trade was the Osaka business community, which was particularly hard hit by recession in 1952. Big business, however, generally maintained a tactical silence in 1953. Some analysts pointed to other barriers impeding trade, such as Chinese import restrictions and the stark fact that Japan's trade deficit with the dollar area was several times the potential of the China market.[32] As public opinion became more excited, Prime Minister Yoshida attempted unconvincingly to downplay the issue altogether. In August the National Diet nevertheless approved unanimously a resolution demanding liberalization of trade with the PRC. The Yoshida government then stepped up its pressure on the United States to permit more trade in the items still restricted under the September 1952 bilateral agreement.

President Eisenhower was sympathetic to the Japanese position. The United States could not both refuse to accept Japanese goods and at the same time deny Japan access to China's materials and markets. Eisenhower's preference was to allow some trade in goods between Japan and the Asian mainland to ease Japan's commercial trade deficit with the dollar area.[33] If the president was critical of the expansive nature of the Truman administration's export control policy, his advisors generally defended the system of controls. Two exceptions were Secretary of the Treasury Humphrey and Under Secretary of State Walter B. Smith. Visceral anti-Communist officials such as Assistant Secretary Walter Robertson, however, delighted in pointing to "the pinch in Red China caused by the trade embargo." Powerful Republican lawmakers such as Senator H. Alexander Smith (R.-N.J.) made clear that they saw "almost any article today" to be "of some strategic value." Senator McCarthy further politicized the issue by conducting televised hearings on allied trade with the Communist Chinese.[34]

Significantly, Dulles was more hesitant to permit relaxation of controls than President Eisenhower. While he conceded that an increase in Sino-Japanese trade was likely and beneficial over the long term, he did not wish to hasten the process. When Senator McCarthy inquired about the Department of State's attitude, Dulles protected his right flank. "Our policy," he affirmed, "is to do all that we can by measures short of war to weaken Red China economically while she is an open aggressor in Korea."[35]

In the face of this bureaucratic inertia, shifting American policy proved very difficult. Eisenhower pursued a consensus policy, and the result was very gradual change until British pressure moved events forward. In February 1954 Premier Winston Churchill called for "a substantial relaxation" of controls on trade in the House of Commons.[36] The eventual result was multilateral agreement on a shorter COCOM list, at least for trade with the European Soviet bloc, effective 16 August 1954. By consenting to relax various controls, the Eisenhower administration was able to preserve the COCOM structure and secure agreement on policy for what the American representative called the "long haul" ahead.[37]

Friction over the embargo of the PRC mounted more gradually, but owing to its longer duration the effect on interallied relations was more corrosive. As long as the war in Korea continued, the United States was able to secure allied compliance in enforcing existing controls on trade with the PRC and North Korea. Even after the conclusion of the Korean armistice at Panmunjom in July 1953, the Western allies heeded American calls for refraining from easing restrictions before the achievement of a wider peace in the region. Although Prime Minister Churchill did propose relaxing controls on trade with the PRC to President Eisenhower at Bermuda in December 1953, the United States and the European allies maintained a common front on the issue until after the conclusion of the Geneva Conference in July 1954. During the Geneva Conference, the Communist Chinese delegation, which included several officials specializing in foreign trade and economic matters, approached representatives of the Western European nations in an attempt to expand East-West trade, but to little effect.[38]

Having imposed greater restrictions on trade than the Europeans, the Japanese government grew impatient after the Korean truce. Although MITI was gradually relaxing controls on a variety of goods, the press renewed agitation for additional releases in the fall of 1953. Reports that Japan's controls were still stricter than the other COCOM members caused the greatest uproar. Attention focused, for example, on a *Mainichi Shimbun* report (of 14 October) that Japan still retained an embargo on items such as serum and blood plasma—goods that European countries were reportedly exporting to the PRC.[39]

In response, the Eisenhower administration reduced its demands of the Japanese government. In early August 1953 the president said he desired greater Sino-Japanese trade in nonstrategic goods. Secretary of State Dulles even softened his public objections to Japanese trade in strategic items.[40] But change came slowly. The State Department wished to concede as little as possible in its review of the four hundred items covered by the 1952 bilateral agreement. As one official in the Office of Northeast Asian Affairs summarized official thinking: "as long as the Japanese Government can continue to show progress toward reaching the multilateral level of controls it can and will resist the internal political pressures to reach the multilateral level quickly."[41] Such opinion reflected American officials' shrewd understanding of the political pressure that they could bring to bear on the Japanese government. It is also testimony to the amount of political capital the administration was willing to spend to maintain a tight blockade of the Chinese mainland.[42]

Japan's growing commercial trade deficit and rising domestic criticism finally led the Eisenhower administration to cancel the 1952 bilateral understanding. On 11 March 1954 the NSC approved of allowing Japan to reduce its controls on trade with the PRC to the level set by the Paris group's China Committee. Cancellation was not contingent upon special action by Japan. The Government of Japan did, however, comply with a departmental request to avoid sudden and extensive decontrol.[43] The Japanese were gratified to be treated in the same way as the other nations of the Consultative Group. But the "China differential" still rankled. Given the geographical proximity between Japan and China, the effect if not the intent of continuing restrictions on trade with the PRC discriminated against Japan. With some justice, the Japanese feared that European traders were able to tap into the China market by selling goods to the European Soviet bloc. The U.S. administration took note of Japanese opinion but held to the hardline policy of NSC 152/3.[44]

The promise of peace following the conclusion of the Geneva Conference brought a sharp increase in pressure on the Yoshida government for expanded Sino-Japanese trade. Taking advantage of the opportunity to drive a wedge between the United States and its allies, representatives of the PRC and the USSR issued a joint declaration in October proposing the restoration of diplomatic relations and an increase in trade with Japan. Given the U.S.-Japanese alliance, Tokyo had little choice but to rebuff the Sino-Soviet bid.[45] Such episodes never jeopardized the alliance, but they did contribute to a strong undercurrent of friction in bilateral relations.

Less obvious at the time was the effect of the China trade embargo on Japan's commercial ties with the West. Given the paltry amount of Sino-Japanese trade Japanese businesses and political leaders alike looked to Western markets with unprecedented vigor. During his visit to the United States in November 1954, Prime Minister Yoshida called for relaxed trade barriers and normal trade treaties with the United Kingdom, France, and Italy, among other nations.[46] The same imperatives moved the Eisenhower administration to accelerate the effort to expand Japanese economic opportunity in Western markets. The president's advisors varied considerably in their enthusiasm for promotion of Japanese imports, but they all recognized that without access to the markets of the United States and the other nations of the Western trading bloc, Japan's economy—and the alliance—would remain unstable.

Preparing for Tariff Negotiations with Japan

Despite President Eisenhower's inability to win Congressional support for a more ambitious foreign economic policy in 1954, his administration made visible progress toward bringing Japan into GATT that year. At home, the primary concern was to lay the groundwork for tariff negotiations in 1955. The high priority of expanding Japanese foreign trade flowed from Japan's record trade deficit of $1.3 billion in 1953. Abroad, the administration pressed the other GATT members to conduct tariff negotiations with Japan.

In discussing the long-delayed Japanese trade negotiations, administration members focused on how to "sell the necessary program to the American people." Since authorization to negotiate expired in June 1955, the timetable for negotiations was shorter than usual by a period of several months. The ordinary procedure was for the president to announce the list of possible articles of concession and then to transmit the list to the Tariff Commission for study of the peril-point levels and related issues. Following this procedure in 1954 would have given opponents of Japanese trade time to organize against the administration's effort, and delayed the start of negotiations until well into 1955.[47]

On 6 August, the president and the cabinet considered the problem of Japanese trade in detail. Secretary Dulles emphasized the urgency of negotiating international trade agreements to expand Japan's foreign trade. Although pessimistic about the prospects for Japanese goods in the American market (he believed that Japan's best trading opportunities were in underdeveloped areas such as Southeast Asia), Dulles emphasized that the United States bore "the major responsibility" to develop markets abroad for Japan. Japan's dependence on the United States, American Cold War strategy, and Japan's "extremely dangerous current economic position" all reinforced the need for action.[48]

Japan's plight preempted certain objections to conducting tariff negotiations, but the administration was not entirely united. Assistant Secretary of Commerce Samuel Anderson conceded the need to include Japan in GATT and to provide various forms of assistance. But he emphasized that economic revival depended upon "greater austerity within Japan," expansion of shipping, modernization of Japanese industry, and elimination of certain unfair trading practices. Commerce Secretary Weeks and Treasury Secretary Humphrey were likewise unenthusiastic about opening further the American market to Japanese goods. Humphrey called attention to the unemployment and dislocation already resulting from the import of Japanese electrical equipment and put the case in perspective: "1954," he explained, "was the first year since the beginning of operation of reciprocal trade practices in which there had been a competitive world economy." Hence, the problems of adjustment were bound to "become much more acute" as competition increased. Rather than "having the U.S. carry the burden of buying Japanese goods," Humphrey urged that "the emphasis should be put on spreading Japanese exports throughout the world."[49] Eisenhower, however, did not let these objections derail American policy. Acknowledging the various points of view aired at the meeting, the president insisted on the need to attack the problem "on a broad front."[50]

Controversy over tariff negotiations with Japan coincided with considerable protest against GATT itself. The General Agreement was up for review at the ninth session (which opened on 28 October 1954). In both the United States and the United Kingdom the organization's detractors made their case throughout the year. In August Senator Millikin sent a fifteen-page critique of GATT—in which he argued that the agreement was unconstitutional—to the Department of State rather than follow the lead of Secretary Dulles (who was trying to rally support for Japanese accession). If critics tended to overstate the power of the contracting parties, they were justified in claiming that the conduct of foreign economic policy through executive agreement enabled successive administrations to move much further in the direction of trade liberalization than the Congress would have allowed on its own. The two sides never really achieved a meeting of minds.[51]

The many views on trade policy aired during Eisenhower's first two years as the president did not bring about a consensus of opinion. Since both sides got to voice their opinions, however, public commentary was the closest approximation of a national debate on the topic that the country saw during the fifties. There were many influential figures who favored moderate tariff reduction. Political commentators such as Joseph Alsop tended to see conflict over foreign economic matters as another battle in the Cold

War. Associations such as the Committee for Economic Development (CED) focused more on the economic issues. The CED's board of trustees read like a who's who of American industry and banking. It also included several high government officials and university administrators. The organization's Research and Policy Committee regularly published studies relating to public policy.

The CED focused on tariff policy in 1954. Although its report did not discuss Japanese imports, it did unequivocally support the "gradual and selective" tariff reduction recommended by the president. A more coherent document than the Randall report, "United States Tariff Policy" affirmed that U.S. tariff policy was inseparable from the task of strengthening the nation's Cold War allies. "Trade among nations can be a powerful force making for unity," it reasoned. Because Western Europe and Japan had not yet recovered their economic strength, the role of the United States was decisive: "Whether their strength increases or declines depends in part on whether they are able to expand their trade with the United States and other countries."[52]

Administration officials maintained tight control over the details of American preparation for the 1955 tariff negotiations with Japan. In order to delay public announcement of the list of goods under consideration for tariff concessions, the president and the cabinet agreed in August to have the TAC (rather than the president) send it to the Tariff Commission immediately. The idea was to allow the commission to begin its work before the list was made public.[53] Formal announcement came on 6 November.[54] By then the ninth GATT session was in progress. On 12 November, during Prime Minister Yoshida's visit to the United States, the Department of State announced that the United States intended to conduct tariff negotiations with Japan beginning in February 1955.[55]

The Struggle to Expand Japanese Access to Western Markets

By 1954 administration hopes focused on GATT much more than they had before. For both strategic and economic reasons, the China market was not a solution to Japan's trade deficit. Similarly, it was finally apparent that the markets of Southeast Asia were unequal to Japan's economic needs. Even Secretary Dulles recognized that the most promising short-term solution to the problem of the dollar gap was greater Japanese access to the markets of the United States and Western Europe.[56] While the Eisenhower administration was justifiably pleased with the success in moving forward with the Japanese tariff negotiations, the reluctance of the other contracting parties to accept Japan as an equal threatened to compromise Japanese accession to GATT.

British opinion was not any more enthusiastic about admitting Japan to GATT than it had been the previous year. Controversy over Japanese copying of British designs that year actually heightened popular sensitivity to increased trade with Japan.[57] Secretary of State Dulles, the American Embassy in London, and the Japanese all lobbied U.K. officials.[58] Besides the emotional element in British opposition, the principal barrier to U.K. acceptance of Japan into GATT was the conflict between the British system of imperial preferences and the requirements of trade liberalization. Competition in third markets rather than in the home market posed the main problem. Neither Article 35 nor the other escape clauses offered a means of protection from Japanese competition in the markets of the Commonwealth nations, because no question of serious injury to *domestic* producers arose. Suspension of trade agreement concessions under GATT had to be on a nondiscriminatory basis, thereby affecting all other contracting parties.[59]

In advance of the GATT session of October 1954, the United Kingdom solicited support for a set of proposals to allow discrimination against Japanese trade. The choice of means was an amendment to GATT allowing "an old member" to subject "a new entrant" to a separate bilateral agreement as the price of admission. The Foreign Office understood that the U.K. initiative depended on American and Japanese approval, and that it had only a "long chance" of success.[60] Assistant Secretary for Economic Affairs Samuel C. Waugh immediately blasted the compromise proposal for introducing the principal of discrimination.[61] Australia, New Zealand, South Africa, and Rhodesia expressed willingness to go along, but Canada opposed treating Japan as a second-class member. Asian nations criticized the discriminatory character of the proposal yet still wished to safeguard their trade. France expressed some interest but did not wish to make a definite statement.[62]

Japan dealt the final blow to the British scheme. Even before formal receipt of the proposal, someone in the Japanese government leaked its contents to a hostile press. The main Japanese objection was that any bilateral agreement with Britain "provided an opening for many other members of G.A.T.T. to demand the same or even greater concessions." Ambassador Haguiwara Tōru explained that Japan preferred Britain to invoke Article 35 and then to negotiate a proper bilateral commercial treaty with Japan.[63] Haguiwara's suggestion was no doubt calculated to force the

British government's hand. Yet he was also optimistic. In conversation with American officials, he said that most of the contracting parties would likely grant Japan full GATT rights; only about five or six would refuse to do so.[64] State Department officials, however, did not wish to see Britain invoke Article 35.[65]

By mid-December the president of the Board of Trade conceded that the British proposal was dead, but he wished to postpone any decision to invoke Article 35. The Foreign Office briefly considered an American counterproposal to write into the protocol of Japanese accession a provision that countries could invoke Article 35 "at any time if the Japanese engaged in disruptive competition."[66] Ambassador Dening suggested securing Japanese agreement to voluntary export restraints on sensitive items. None of these options, however, offered the degree of protection that the Board of Trade and the ministers wished to show to voters at home. The cabinet approved invocation of Article 35 on 30 January 1955. There was some hope that the ministers would also promise to extend GATT obligations to Japan at a fixed time and subject to modest conditions. But as one Foreign Office recorded, "considerations of domestic policy prevailed, as it was always probable that they would."[67]

The problems of the timing and wording of the announcement remained. Viewed from the perspective of Anglo-Japanese relations, early disclosure was desirable but not before the general election in Japan (scheduled for 27 February). Since GATT was up for review in Parliament in late March, the government could not postpone indefinitely its announcement. The Eisenhower administration, however, saw difficulty in both an early public statement and any formal suggestion that Japan was an unsatisfactory trading partner. Britain acquiesced in the administration's request for delay until April and softened the language of the announcement.[68]

Although the volume of Anglo-Japanese trade was relatively small, other European nations often followed the British lead. The United Kingdom did not undertake tariff negotiations with Japan. France followed, and in February the Benelux nations even reversed an earlier decision to participate. U.S. officials revised downward their initial estimate that twenty countries would participate. They pressured others—particularly Burma, Norway, Finland, Sweden, Greece, and Peru—to offer meaningful concessions to Japan and to draft requests for concessions in return.[69] This effort yielded fewer gains than either the Americans or the Japanese desired. But without such pressure on Japan's behalf, Japanese accession to GATT would certainly have been more halting and circumscribed than it was.

The Trade Agreements Extension Act of 1955

Before the negotiations with Japan, the Eisenhower administration sought congressional renewal of the reciprocal trade act yet again. In the November 1954 elections the Democrats recaptured control of the Congress, and the Democratic leadership was enthusiastic about the reciprocal trade program. In the House, Reed lost his chairmanship to Jere Cooper (D.-Tenn.), a longtime advocate of lower tariffs. His assistant and third-ranking Democratic member of the same committee was Wilbur Mills of Arkansas. Harry Byrd (D.-Va.) assumed the chairmanship of the Senate Finance Committee. Speaker of the House Sam Rayburn and Senate Majority Leader Lyndon Johnson, both of Texas, firmly supported reciprocal trade.

When the Eighty-fourth Congress convened, Speaker Rayburn labeled the reciprocal trade renewal bill H.R. 1. Chairman Cooper held lengthy hearings on the bill, which extended the RTAA for three years. In scheduling witnesses to appear before the committee, he featured administration spokesmen, including Secretary Dulles and other cabinet officials.[70] Despite the commitment of the Democratic leadership to renewal, the fight over reciprocal trade in 1955 was just as close as the previous rounds. The prospect of tariff negotiations with Japan and trade friction over textiles led many Democrats to back away from the position of the leadership. Congressmen Simpson and Reed teamed up with other Republicans to propose a flood of protectionist amendments. After great effort Cooper and Mills reported the bill unamended in any substantive way. House Democrats, however, proved less sympathetic toward the measure than their party's tradition of supporting lower tariffs.

One reason was a national campaign launched by textile interests. Soon after Prime Minister Yoshida's November 1954 U.S. visit, textile manufacturers and unions protested against lowering tariffs on Japanese goods. They argued that Japan's performance before the war showed that Japan could compete effectively in the American market without lower duties. They also contended that lowering tariffs to keep Japan in the non-Communist camp was costly and impractical. On 7 December 1954, the *New York Times* carried a feature story on the issue. In 1955 the leading American trade associations representing textiles took their case to the Congress and appeared as witnesses in the reciprocal trade hearings.[71]

Japanese imports had long been anathema to Republicans. But in 1955 Democrats from depressed regions—in the Appalachian Mountains, Oklahoma, and Rhode Island—and the industrializing South also exhibited protectionist sentiment. With great effort Speaker Rayburn got the House to pass the measure. If there had been another speaker, a weaker leader, or one less devoted to reciprocal trade, the original bill would not have survived.[72]

Progress was equally difficult in the upper chamber. Senator Millikin and others proposed numerous amendments, of which two survived. One gave the president the authority to fix quotas on imports if in his opinion they harmed domestic industries crucial to national security. The other modified the escape clause provision to enable the Tariff Commission to consider relief for the makers of any one product suffering from foreign competition, even if the industry as a whole was prospering. Dependent upon Senator Millikin and the other Republican leaders in Congress as he was, Eisenhower did not oppose these amendments.

Eisenhower called the 1955 renewal act "an important milestone" in the development of U.S. foreign economic policy. The measure was actually more restrictive than the one it replaced.[73] Although the new law renewed the act for three years, the administration's authority to reduce tariffs was limited to 15 percent (implemented in three annual stages of up to 5 percent per year). The basis for these reductions was the schedule of rates existing on 1 January 1955. The only exception was the act's "fifty percent" authority, which permitted the president to reduce rates over 50 percent to that level.

From the standpoint of American-Japanese trade negotiations, the most important aspect of the new law was the January 1955 baseline. H.R. 1 originally provided that the schedule of tariff rates existing on 1 July 1955 serve as the basis of negotiations. In theory, then, a 1956 round of negotiations could have provided the opportunity for reductions beyond those achieved during the 1955 negotiations, then in progress in Geneva. For precisely this reason textile interests opposed the bill. When the Senate Finance Committee considered H.R. 1 in April 1955, Senator Walter George (D.-Ga.) proposed an amendment to move the baseline back from 1 July to 1 January 1955. As a long-standing internationalist, Senator George was an unexpected protectionist. But the senator faced an uphill reelection battle against Herman Talmadge, a challenger who was turning George's internationalist record against him. George was forced to stand up for local industries. That the George amendment was directed against Japan was clear to all: the principal tariff negotiations scheduled for the period between January and July were those with Japan. When adopted by the Finance Committee and approved by the Senate, the Trade Agreements Extension Act

(TAEA) automatically excluded from the 1956 round all items on which the United States granted a concession of 15 percent or more the previous year.

Bad timing accentuated the negative impression that the George amendment made in Japan. At the State Department's request, the Board of Trade put off its announcement that the United Kingdom would invoke Article 35 until 19 April in order to avoid jeopardizing congressional consideration of HR 1.[74] The unfortunate result was that the Japanese learned of Britain's resort to the escape clause and the Senate Finance Committee's adoption of the George amendment within a span of two days. The change of the schedule dates drew the most severe criticism in Japan. The *Nihon Keizai Shimbun* of 6 May 1955 claimed, like other commentary, that "Japan was robbed of one of the important results of the GATT negotiations," namely a new starting point for tariff negotiations.[75]

The White House and the Department of State did not miss the significance of the George amendment. But they did not oppose it. Administration opinion held that opposing the amendment, which was popular, would put the entire trade bill at risk. Compared with losing the bill, a few protectionist amendments seemed a tolerable price to pay. But there was another, less reported provision of the George amendment: if the United States and Japan were unable to conclude a trade agreement by 12 June 1955 (when authorization to negotiate under the 1954 renewal expired), the act would extend the president's authority to cut tariff rates (existing 1 January 1945) up to 50 percent in negotiations with Japan only. Senator George thus allowed everyone room for maneuver. The negotiations then in progress in Geneva were not going well. Administration officials considered inclusion of this provision a "real victory."[76]

The 1955 Tariff Negotiations and Japanese Accession to GATT

Japan conducted bilateral negotiations with sixteen countries besides the United States, but the negotiations with the Americans were from the start of greatest interest to the Japanese just as they yielded the greatest expansion of Japanese economic opportunity. The United States and Japan also conducted triangular negotiations in which the United States offered concessions to third countries in exchange for compensatory concessions from Japan. The negotiations were a political success. Accession to GATT promised improved tariff treatment on 40 percent of Japan's 1953 export trade.

By promoting economic exchange across the Pacific, the United States strengthened the actual links between the American and Japanese economies and reinforced the feeling among Japanese that the partnership with the United States in the Cold War was in Japan's interest.

The economic content of the 1955 negotiations has drawn more criticism. In *Opening America's Market*, the historian Alfred E. Eckes Jr. criticizes the State Department for being too eager to conclude an agreement, any agreement, even if its terms were not in America's economic interest. The result, he argues, was that the United States negotiated an unbalanced agreement that opened U.S. borders to imports of labor-intensive manufactures without any compensating gains in return. Eckes attacks the State Department's aggregate figures of the total volume of trade affected. On first glance, the numbers suggest that American gains in the negotiations surpassed Japanese gains by over three to one: Japan made concessions affecting $395 million of imports from the United States; American concessions affected only $131 million of imports from Japan.[77] Eckes claims with some justice that basing these calculations on 1953 trade figures understates the extent of Japan's gains. In 1953 Japan supplied only 2.4 percent of all U.S. imports for consumption, whereas the average Japanese share for the 1934–36 period was 7.2 percent of all U.S. imports.[78]

If Eckes is correct to note the low Japanese export volume of 1953, he ignores the extent to which that low volume was not just unusual but dangerous. Japan was negotiating from a position of desperation rather than advantage. In 1953 the nation ran an overall commercial trade deficit of over $1.1 billion. On paper the U.S. surplus in trade with Japan was $424 million (Table 1.3). In reality, U.S. military spending was subsidizing Japan's deficit. The Eisenhower administration's attempt to allow Japan greater access to the U.S. market was hardly popular. But the alternatives of continuing to subsidize Japan's deficit with tax dollars or allowing expanded Japanese trade with the Communist Chinese commanded far less public support.

The heart of Eckes's case is that in the 1955 negotiations the United States gained few meaningful reductions in Japanese duties. By his account, the minutes of the negotiations show "eager U.S. participants pressing the Japanese for concessions on leaf tobacco, soft drinks, lubricating oils, automobiles, synthetic fibers, and many other products important to political supporters of the administration." According to the final terms of the agreement, 84 percent of Japanese concessions were bindings of existing rates, "not real tariff reductions." He is particularly critical of the U.S. failure to win "major tariff reductions" (over 35 percent) on only $6.4

million of trade in 1953 figures, or 1.6 percent of the trade in all tariff concessions. By contrast, 45 percent of U.S. tariff concessions were tariff reductions affecting $72 million in 1953 trade. And of these reductions, those of 35 percent or more affected $37.2 million in trade. The clear implication is that except for items of concern to certain powerful interests back home, American negotiators failed to press the Japanese hard enough.[79]

Such a portrayal misrepresents the character of the talks. It is true that the initial U.S. offers represented its best offers. This strategy was in fact standard practice in GATT negotiations. The aim was to obtain greater concessions from the other side by forcing them to match the American offers. In response, the Japanese displayed an unusual combination of shrewdness and naiveté, simply refusing to believe that the United States would not improve its offers over the course of the negotiations. The head of the American delegation rejected the initial Japanese list of proposed concessions as offering "no basis for negotiations."[80] Thus, the bilateral talks consisted principally of repeated American demands for additional offers from the reluctant Japanese delegation. Particularly sensitive items included canned tuna fish (in oil), on which the Japanese desired an additional reduction in duty, and automobiles, on which they were equally reluctant to grant any duty reduction.

In April Ambassador Haguiwara assumed personal responsibility for the negotiations, after the Japanese side presented its third list of offers. Concluding the negotiations proved difficult, however. Following the passage of the George amendment to H.R. 1, the Japanese stalled in the vain hope that President Eisenhower would oppose it. The 12 June deadline for completion of the tariff negotiations was fast approaching, and Congress had not yet renewed the reciprocal trade act, with or without the George amendment. On 25 April Assistant Secretary Waugh attempted to spur the Japanese to action. He cautioned the Japanese ambassador that H.R. 1 might not be passed by 12 June at all. Thus, he urged the ambassador "to use his influence with Tokyo and the delegation at Geneva to conclude the agreement as soon as possible." After agreeing to split their differences on tuna fish and automobiles (the new rate of duty for each was to be 35 percent) the two sides initialed the final lists on 5 May.[81]

Eckes similarly fails to mention that the baseline for the negotiations on the Japanese side was the revised tariff of 1951, which had been enacted in accordance with the advice of SCAP. In place of the former rates of duty, most of which were 100 percent, the 1951 tariff rates ranged mostly between 10 and 40 percent. The baseline for the American concessions, however,

Table 6.1. *Reductions in Japanese Rates of Duty on Leading Items, 1955*

Commodity Description	Duty (%) Before 1955	Duty (%) Under Agreement	Imports from the United States in 1953 ($1,000)
Automotive passenger cars over 254 cm	40	35	24,383
Lubricating oils	30	22.5	3,901
Bourbon and rye whiskies	50	45	3,446
Tetraethyl lead	20	10	3,050
Airplanes, four-engine or more	15	10	3,000
Aureomycin [chlortetracycline]	20	17.5	2,715
Tomato paste and puree	25	Duty free	1,209
Measuring and testing instruments	20	10	1,210
Statistical card system			
Punching machines	15	10	1,682
Other machines	15	10	1,590
Television receivers with cathode tubes			
of 23 inches and over	30	25	1,017
Cash registers	20	15	708
Radio receivers	20	18	140
Fountain pens [& like instruments]	50	40	28

Source: U.S. Department of State, *General Agreement on Tariffs and Trade*, 32–111.

was the high rates of duty prevailing at the end of the war, some of them unchanged since the 1930s. In previous negotiations, the State Department had been careful not to grant concessions on items of primary interest to Japan, particularly textiles.[82] Thus, application of the GATT principle that a binding of, or a small reduction in, a low rate of duty was equivalent to a deep reduction in a high rate of duty tended naturally to result in more bindings on the Japanese side.

Japanese concessions reflected the moderately protective character of the 1951 baseline. Reductions in Japanese rates of duty on items of interest to the United States were modest (Table 6.1). Reductions in duty affected items such as bourbon and rye whiskies, lubricating oils, television receivers, large and medium-sized passenger automobiles, and airplanes. Few ranked as major decreases. But the Japanese rate structure, even on manufactured items, did not constitute an impenetrable tariff wall.[83]

Japanese bindings affected numerous high-volume items that figured prominently in the U.S. export trade (Table 6.2). These included soybeans, antibiotics other than penicillin, raw cotton, raw petroleum coke, and large airplanes.[84] Statistics confirm that the share of agricultural commodities

Table 6.2. *Bindings of Japanese Rates of Duty on Leading Items, 1955*

Commodity Description	Duty (%) Before 1955	Duty (%) Under Agreement	Imports from the United States in 1953 ($1,000)
Raw cotton, ginned	Free	Free	122,009
Bituminous coal (for coking)	Free	Free	57,437
Soybeans	10	10	49,933
Beef tallow	5	5	14,719
Corn, unmilled, for feedstuffs	10	10	11,549
Bituminous coal (other than for coking)	Free	Free	8,274
Airplanes less than four-engine	15	15	4,513
Raw petroleum coke	5	5	4,441
Steel plates	15	15	4,221
Antibiotics other than penicillin, streptomycin, and aureomycin	20	20	3,177
Chassis, with engines mounted, passenger road motor vehicles, over 254 cm	30	30	2,241
Trucks, over 254 cm wheelbase	30	30	1,908
Rosin	5	5	1,807
Radar	15	15	1,783
Magnesia clinker	Free	Free	1,737
Wool dresses, suits, and overcoats	25	25	1,500
Books and pamphlets	Free	Free	1,482
Evaporated and condensed milk	30	30	1,447
Synthetic rubber	Free	Free	1,407
Television receivers, with cathode tubes of less than 23 inches	30	30	1,016
Polyethylene glycol	20	20	1,010
Metalworking grinding machines	15	15	1,043
Agricultural machinery	15	15	86
Engines, automobile	30	30	68

Source: U.S. Department of State, *General Agreement on Tariffs and Trade*, 32–111.

and other raw materials in American exports to Japan was high. Yet to suggest, as Eckes does, that exports of such commodities are somehow less important than manufactures is illegitimate. Producers of farm products, for example, were not merely "supporters of the administration's tariff reduction program." They composed a vital part of the American economy and U.S. export trade.

A large share of American concessions counted as major tariff reduc-

Table 6.3. *Reductions in U.S. Rates of Duty on Leading Items, 1955*

Commodity Description	Duty (%) Before 1955	Duty (%) Under Agreement	Imports from Japan in 1954 ($1,000)
Cotton table damask, over $.075/lb.	$0.225/lb.	$0.175/lb	5,572
Cotton cloth, unbleached[a]	41.5%	27.5%	4,890
Cotton cloth, bleached[a]	13%	10%	59
Cotton cloth, printed[a]	16%	12%	87
Cotton fabrics, velveteens (plain)	31.5%	25%	41
Cotton fabrics, velveteens (twill)	$0.25/sq. yd. (22.5% min. to 44% max.)	$0.25/sq. yd. (22.5% min. to 30% max.)	96
Cotton rugs	35%	17.5%	42
Cotton towels	25%	20%	695
Cotton sheets and pillowcases	20%	12.5%	239
Cotton gloves and mittens	60%	30%	1,928
Knit cotton outerwear	35%	25%	863
Cotton ornamental fabrics	90%	50%	107
Pearls and parts	10%	5%	4,334
Parts of toys	50%	35%	202
Artificial or ornamental fruits, yarn	60%	50%	2,962
Methanol	$0.40/lb.	$0.35/lb.	1,903
Table and kitchen earthenware	45%	40% or 20% dep. on value	1,118
China, porcelain plates, decorated	70%	60%	3,912 (est.)
Prism binoculars	30%	20%	1,605
Opera or field glasses	20%	17.5%	699
Manufactures of rattan	45%	25%	1,310
Baskets and bags of bamboo	50%	25%	854
Frog legs and whole frogs (dead)	10%	5%	1,077
Ajinomoto (MSG)	25%	20%	732

Source: U.S. Department of State, *General Agreement on Tariffs and Trade*, 32–111.
[a] Duties varied according to yarn count. In the aggregate, the reduction in rates of duty on cotton cloth was 25%. The items affected composed 10% of U.S. cloth imports.

tions, but the rates of U.S. duty remained significant (Table 6.3). Reductions affected ajinomoto (monosodium glutamate), low-grade porcelain china, prism binoculars, miniature Christmas tree lamps, rattan and bamboo manufactures, and pearls.[85] The most important U.S. concessions were on textiles, particularly low-priced cotton cloth, velveteens, and cotton outerwear. High tariffs blocked the large-scale import of Japanese textiles before 1955. The 1955 concessions were intended to open the American mar-

Table 6.4. *Bindings of U.S. Rates of Duty on Leading Items, 1955*

Commodity Description	Duty (%) Before 1955	Duty (%) Under Agreement	Imports from Japan in 1954 ($1,000)
Silk, raw	Free	Free	30,662
Sewing machines	10	10	17,621
Canned tuna in brine	12.5	12.5	13,473
Tuna fish, fresh or frozen	Free	Free	11,161
Jewelry and parts, valued at not over $5 per dozen	55	55	7,671
Crab meat, canned	22.5	22.5	2,916
Parts of sewing machines	10	10	1,591

Source: U.S. Department of State, *General Agreement on Tariffs and Trade*, 32–111.

ket to some Japanese competition. Bindings of U.S. duties were fewer (Table 6.4). But they affected significant items, including sewing machines, tuna, crabmeat, and raw silk.[86]

The limits of these concessions must be emphasized. American negotiators in 1955 did not sacrifice the interests of light manufactures on the altar of the interests of producers of primary products. As State Department officials prepared for the negotiations in Geneva, they received a flurry of last-minute appeals on behalf of the producers of various goods likely to be affected: crabmeat, dried egg albumen, tuna fish, tableware, thermos bottles, monosodium glutamate, and especially textiles.[87] At Geneva, in the face of blunt Japanese demands, the U.S. side offered concessions below the maximum extent allowed by law (50 percent in many cases applying to trade with Japan). Items in question included monosodium glutamate, Christmas tree ornaments, prism binoculars, microscopes and parts, hypodermic syringes, bamboo articles, cotton towels, rubber balls, fireworks (the United States offered no concession), and artificial flowers. U.S. officials devised concessions on earthenware, chinaware, crab meat, cotton velveteens, and other textiles to limit the import of goods which competed directly with American products. Significantly, Eckes fails to note that no U.S. concession breached a peril point set by the Tariff Commission, a body whose advice he usually identifies with the interests of American industry.[88]

Of the problems with the American-Japanese agreement of 1955 that Eckes describes, the most significant by far concerned the Japanese rather than the U.S. market. Owing to Japan's precarious balance-of-payments position, the United States permitted the Japanese to retain controls on foreign exchange, including the freedom to impose quantitative restrictions on imports. While Japan indeed experienced balance of payments crises in 1953 and 1957 (Table 1.1), the Japanese government also restricted imports competing with domestic manufactures. As events turned, Japan employed exchange controls as nontariff barriers for decades after the Geneva negotiations.[89]

Eckes's criticism of the triangular negotiations for yielding little of value to the United States carries more weight. Italy, for example, reduced its barriers on agar and camphor, of which Japan was the principal supplier. The United States reduced its duties on leather goods from Italy, and in return Japan reduced its duty on tape recorders and bound the rate on parts for tape recorders. Since Japan retained nontariff barriers on the same products, the American gain was illusory. In aggregate terms, however, the volume of trade affected was small: about $2 million of added export trade coverage was obtained for Japan, against U.S. concessions covering a trade of about $3 million.[90]

American negotiators were surprised at the depth of Japanese economic nationalism. The Japanese negotiators rejected the principle of comparative advantage as well as American demands for concessions on manufactured items. The Americans lectured their counterparts on "the folly of attempting to diversify their economy by building up inefficient industries behind a tariff wall" to little effect. The Japanese team replied with a case for protection. Japan did not wish to remain a producer of light manufactures, one diplomat explained. A proper role for government is to encourage and protect those industries which it believes are important for national policy.[91] Until Japan developed its higher-value-added industries, however, the less glamorous sectors in which the nation enjoyed a comparative advantage continued to earn valuable foreign exchange.

Had Japan's mercantilist policies not enabled the nation to make the transition from postwar recovery to world-class competitor, the nature of Japanese protectionism and the details of the Geneva negotiations would be of little interest after the fact. The composition of Japan's foreign trade shows that the nation was clearly increasing its competitiveness in manufacturing. U.S. exports to Japan rose from $684 million to $1.33 billion from 1954 to 1960. During the same period, imports from Japan rose from $279 million to $1.12 billion. But while the United States increased its share of Japan's imports, the growth largely took the form of shipments of raw materials and agricultural commodities. Japan, by contrast, more than doubled its share of America's manufactured imports, from 7.6 percent in 1955 to 15.4 percent in 1960.[92]

Equating the production of manufactures with economic success, however, misrepresents the nature of the problems associated with trade liberalization. Rather than a defeat, absorption of more manufactured imports was necessary to close the persistent dollar gap. The early postwar years were highly unusual. Historically the United States has not enjoyed a comparative advantage in its light-manufacturing and labor-intensive industries. Eckes criticizes Eisenhower for leading the Republican Party "from protectionism to Cobdenism." His preference is for Eisenhower to have continued "to protect the home market, using tariff and nontariff barriers, while encouraging the export of U.S. goods and private capital."[93] Such a policy may have preserved light-manufacturing jobs, but the system could not have long endured if the United States had continued to maintain the burgeoning trade surpluses of the early fifties. Drained of foreign exchange and unable to gain access to the American market, other countries would have had to turn elsewhere.

Protection of the home market also conflicted with opening markets abroad. Agricultural policy demonstrates the point. During the fifties U.S. agricultural policy required that the U.S. delegation to GATT demand a "blanket waiver" permitting whatever actions were necessary under Section 22 of the Agricultural Adjustment Act. In practice this act required the imposition of tariffs or quotas on any agricultural imports that threatened to compete with domestic production. Forcing the other contracting parties to accept its restrictive policies undercut U.S. efforts to seek strengthening of GATT rules, or to get other countries to accept more American goods. Other contracting parties could always counter, "You are not willing to accept any obligation with respect to imports of agricultural products, which might perhaps someday come under one of your agricultural programs. Why should we?"[94]

Japan did pose a fundamental challenge to the designs of free traders and the postwar trading system itself. In focusing so narrowly on tariff policy, however, Eckes follows in the footsteps of the American officials who failed to grasp the nature of the Japanese challenge to the system. The fundamental problem was not that U.S. trade negotiators failed to secure adequate Japanese tariff concessions in return for the ones they granted. Instead Japanese nontariff barriers reduced the importance of the tariff altogether.

Japanese negotiators also had real ability to turn American security interests to Japan's commercial advantage. In 1955 Joseph A. Camelio, the Commerce Department representative at the Geneva talks, described how the Japanese were "shrewd negotiators." "They knew very well that the United States considered a trade agreement with Japan to be extremely important to the United States as well as to Japan," he reported. Reasoning that the United States "cannot risk to lose an agreement because of the importance which we attach to Japan," the Japanese "played their hand well being certain that we would not permit the negotiations to fail."[95] Although Camelio's portrayal of the 1955 negotiations is overdrawn, the dynamic he described summarizes the great dilemma for the United States in dealing with Japan throughout the postwar era.

At middecade, however, the contingency of Japan's access to GATT overshadowed thoughts of future Japanese success. The contracting parties had until 11 August to vote. Given prior agreement on the two-stage track for Japanese accession, Japan seemed assured of receiving the necessary two-thirds majority in favor. As one country after another—fourteen in all—resorted to Article 35, the possibility emerged that Japan might be denied admission to GATT altogether. The usually unflappable Haguiwara even confided to the U.S. delegation that he was "in a quandary" as to what he should recommend to his government.[96] In April the United Kingdom called for a new Anglo-Japanese commercial treaty when announcing its decision on Article 35, but in truth the cabinet had not yet made a decision on its vote. Hoping to make a decision only after Japan was assured of a favorable vote, the ministers procrastinated through June and July.[97] The other contracting parties invoking Article 35 eventually voted for Japanese accession, and the United Kingdom joined them in August.[98] The final decision was unanimous, and Japan became a contracting party on 10 September.

The "Fourth Round" of Tariff Negotiations and Japan's Article 35 Problem

The results of the obscure "fourth round" of trade negotiations in 1956 reveal how uninspiring reciprocal trade appeared to the world at middecade. Since any tariff reduction negotiated under the Trade Agreements Expansion Act of 1955 was to be implemented in three yearly stages, negotiations had to be completed within one year not to lose one-third of the authority. The Department of State began preparations immediately. Negotiations opened at Geneva in January 1956 and concluded the following

May. The Japanese again attempted to pressure the United States by offering little at the outset. When that tactic failed, they requested special treatment for "political" reasons, namely the health of the bilateral relationship. The State Department refused to budge, explaining to the Japanese that a "one-sided" agreement" would not be in the interest of either country.[99]

The result was a relatively balanced set of agreements, although the concessions varied widely in depth and significance. Twenty-two governments participated. The other twenty-one granted concessions to the United States applying to $400 million of U.S. exports to them in 1954. The United States granted concessions on $653 million worth of imports in 1954. No concession granted breached a peril point set by the Tariff Commission. U.S. negotiators employed the "fifty percent" authority sparingly.[100]

As before, cotton textiles figured heavily in tariff negotiations with Japan. Because Japanese imports were so heavily concentrated in a few segments of the market, the administration attempted to encourage diversification. Among the most important items on which the United States granted concessions were cotton yarn, embroidered hose and half hose, certain lace, rugs, quilts, and bedspreads. Compared with domestic production, imports of these items were insignificant (less than 1 percent). In several categories, such as the laces in question and ornamented wearing apparel, no comparable products were produced in the United States.[101] Announcement of the results of the tariff negotiations drew little response at the time, and scholars have ignored the round. The reason, as the *Times* of London correctly observed, is that agreements reached were "inevitably slight in substance."[102] GATT seemed to be losing momentum.

The question of whether the movement toward freer trade under GATT was stalling had immediate relevance to Japan. Japanese trade with countries refusing to extend complete MFN treatment amounted to over 40 percent of that with GATT nations.[103] Japan's "perplexing dilemma" was "whether (1) to insist upon MFN treatment prescribed by GATT, thus forgoing for the foreseeable future limited trade benefits otherwise probably available, or (2) [to] accept less favorable treatment, thus gaining immediate benefits, but postponing, perhaps indefinitely, MFN treatment as [then] prescribed by GATT."[104] The Japanese government itself was undecided upon how to proceed. In September 1955, Ambassador Haguiwara floated the idea of permitting a contracting party to resort to the protective measures permitted by Article 23. At the tenth session of GATT the next month, the contracting parties examined the problem officially and unofficially, but to no effect.[105] Bilateral commercial treaty negotiations offered another forum for addressing the matter, but talks between Japan and the United Kingdom went nowhere.[106]

Facing growing political pressure to provide protection for the domestic cotton textile industry during the spring of 1956, the Eisenhower administration renewed its effort to assist Japan solve the Article 35 problem.[107] Japanese officials agreed that of the fourteen countries, France, Cuba, Haiti, Australia, New Zealand, South Africa, and the Federation of Rhodesia/Nyasaland were unlikely to reverse their position. India was a special case, since its intransigence on Article 35 was a bargaining ploy in its discussions with Japan about settlement of war indemnity claims. Many officials thought that the United Kingdom and the Benelux countries would "have a controlling influence on eventual decisions of most other countries."[108] Ambassador Haguiwara believed that no single formula could solve the problem with all fourteen countries. By focusing on the United Kingdom, he aimed to hold the British restrictive treatment of Japanese goods to temporary and limited measures, to be applied only under "exceptional, well-defined circumstances." Japan could accept such restrictions "*provided other* CP's will acquiesce."[109]

Haguiwara's views, however, did not necessarily represent government policy as other officials made clear to the American Embassy. The Finance Ministry, MITI, and even some Ministry of Foreign Affairs officials were of the view that Japan should persist in demanding full GATT treatment from the United Kingdom. Some of these officials also believed that negotiations with the Benelux countries were likely to be more promising than those underway with the United Kingdom. Others hoped to secure more immediate benefits from Australia and New Zealand, even if it meant forgoing full GATT treatment. No one disagreed with Haguiwara's assessment that "adoption of American import quotas such as those proposed for cotton textiles would immediately terminate any chance Japan might have to obtain full GATT treatment by any of the fourteen countries."[110]

Japanese hopes eventually focused on Brazil and Austria. Brazil's invocation of the escape clause was a response to Japan's refusal to grant unilateral tariff concessions on coffee (from 35 to 25 percent), cocoa (from 20 to 10 percent), and carnauba wax (from 10 to 5 percent). Austria was already extending MFN to Japanese trade on a de facto basis. Austria's foreign exchange position was precarious and its government wished to promote foreign trade. Evidently drawing upon their own experience, the Japanese figured that Austria could protect its market from Japanese products by resorting to quantitative restrictions for balance-of-payments reasons.[111]

The U.S. Embassy in Tokyo agreed that these two nations were more likely than the others to abandon their resort to Article 35.[112] Department officials pressed Vienna and Rio de Janeiro. Austria refused to reverse its position, but in August 1957 Brazil withdrew its invocation of the escape clause. Ironically, Japan also improved its commercial relations with Australia. The Australian government, prodded by the wool producers and wheat growers, overcame its reluctance to conclude a commercial treaty with Japan in July 1957. Australia did not withdraw its invocation of the escape clause, but the new treaty did extend MFN status to Japanese trade. Not until the sixties was Japan successful in securing full GATT treatment from all of the other parties.[113]

Conclusion

The Eisenhower administration's record on integrating Japan into the Western trading bloc ranks as a qualified success. In 1954, the administration made concrete progress toward reaffirming the U.S. commitment to reciprocal trade and securing Japanese access to GATT. By the year's end, tariff negotiations were finally on the immediate horizon. The conclusion of those negotiations and approval of Japanese membership in GATT completed the task of laying the institutional foundation for Japanese integration with the Western economies. The growth of Japan's foreign trade from 1955 forward depended to an unusual degree on the expansion of world trade made possible by GATT and other efforts to remove institutional trade barriers.[114] Passage of the Trade Agreements Extension Act of 1955 anchored the reciprocal trade program more firmly in place, and made possible another round of tariff negotiations.

But by the end of 1955 the limits of both reciprocal trade and the new order were apparent to all. Japan still faced discrimination and its own commitment to the principles of liberal trade was highly suspect. The disappointing 1956 round of tariff negotiations suggested that both reciprocal trade and GATT had exhausted themselves. Owing to the continued imposition of restrictions on trade with the PRC, Japanese opinion remained sensitive to any limits placed on Japanese opportunity in Western markets.

A profound change was nevertheless underway. Japan's foreign trade was in the process of being reoriented westward (as shown in Tables 1.8 and 1.9).

The bilateral axis between Japan and the United States was also becoming more, not less, important. However unexpected, Japan seemed to be on its way to making a living, and that perception had profound implications for both American strategy in the Cold War and bilateral economic relations. But in solving old problems, greater economic integration created new ones, most notably friction over trade and investment. During the second half of the decade, American and Japanese leaders confronted such problems in the atmosphere of the escalating and expanding Cold War.

Chapter Seven

THE LIMITS OF INTEGRATION: FOREIGN DIRECT INVESTMENT IN JAPAN

A defining feature of Japan's economic development during the years of high-speed growth was an extremely low amount of inward foreign direct investment (FDI). Even in the 1960s and 1970s FDI contributed only one-tenth of 1 percent to the gross fixed capital formation of Japan, the lowest figure among all industrialized countries.[1] Although Japan's controls on foreign capital and technology transfer have attracted comparatively little public attention, they were more restrictive than its trade policies. Government policy rendered Japan, relative to Western Europe, largely impervious to American FDI for a generation after the Second World War.

Mark Mason has likened the postwar regime of Japanese capital controls to a "screen door." Policy was designed to *discourage*, or filter out, most inflows of FDI, but to *encourage* inflows of foreign technology." Although a few exceptional companies such as Coca-Cola were able to establish a direct presence in Japan, government controls had precisely their intended effect. The result was that Japanese companies were able to acquire a wealth of new technology while enjoying protection from competition by foreign multinational firms in the vast domestic market as they developed into multinational companies themselves.[2]

If the nationalistic motives of the economic bureaucrats in Tokyo and Japanese businesses are readily apparent, the reasons for American acquiescence in this restrictive order are not. Mason correctly observes that Japanese restrictions on investment "were largely unchallenged by U.S. government officials." "As in the prewar decade," he adds, "so too during the decades following war and occupation the U.S. government largely subjugated concerns over Japanese economic protectionism to bilateral security issues."[3]

This chapter investigates why the U.S. government tolerated Japanese restrictions. It shows how the priority the Americans placed on Cold War security partnership played itself out in the specific context of investment relations. U.S. decisions did not reflect a simple trade-off between security and American commercial interest. Differences in the government-business relationship between the two nations were at least as important. Just as the full significance of the decisions of the 1950s was not apparent until later, the process of balancing priorities on the American side consisted of several steps, each a response to circumstances at the time. Conditioning attitudes and policies on both sides was the sharp contrast in the two nations' historical traditions.

The Historical Background to 1945

Japanese policy flowed from a long-standing and pervasive suspicion of foreign capital. Japan's first experience as a host of foreign investment in the industrial era followed Commodore Matthew Perry's opening of Japan. In 1858 Townsend Harris, the U.S. consul, negotiated the first commercial treaty with Japan. The difficult negotiations culminating in that agreement revealed that if the Japanese looked outward with trepidation, the Americans were impatient to open wide the gates.[4] The other European trading nations soon concluded similar treaties, and these agreements allowed their business enterprises to establish themselves in specified port areas known as "treaty settlements." The British soon came to dominate trade with Japan. Fear of following the examples of India and China—particularly the cycle of Western investment, default, and foreign military intervention—led the leaders of the Meiji government to ensure that every major industry (except foreign trade and finance) was in Japanese hands. Thus, despite granting extraterritorial rights in these so-called unequal treaties, Japanese leaders generally prohibited foreign investment beyond the treaty settlements.[5]

With the revision of the so-called unequal treaties in 1899, Japan liberalized its policy toward foreign capital. An accord with the United States provided for protection of patents and trademarks and granted U.S. citizens rights to trade, invest, and lease land. Revised again in 1911, the new treaties reflected a Japanese desire for Western technology and capital. Concurrent increases in tariffs on trade offered multinational firms such as General Electric, B. F. Goodrich, and Singer Sewing Machine an additional incentive to establish operations in Japan (behind the tariff wall). Besides being the largest export market for American goods in Asia, Japan became the safest place for U.S. investments in the region. Yet Japanese leaders remained wary of foreign capital. From 1899 to 1930 policy was significantly more liberal than before. But government authorities imposed various restrictions on foreign investment in industries such as banking and transportation, and they preferred portfolio rather than direct investment.[6]

During the 1930s the foreign investment climate in Japan turned highly unfavorable. Despite recovery from the depression of the early 1930s, the government reversed direction and imposed increasingly severe controls on foreign capital. This shift reflected the rising power of the militaristic armed services and nationalistic bureaucrats, reinforced by pressure from certain sectors of Japanese industry. The National Diet enacted a round of industry laws intended to limit foreign influence in Japan. The Automobile Manufacturing Industry Law of 1936, for example, required firms to obtain a government license to produce more than a designated number of cars per year in Japan. Government authorities further limited the market share of Ford and General Motors in Japan by imposing tight restrictions on the foreign exchange and import licenses both enterprises needed to conduct their businesses. Such regulations reduced the two American companies to mere shells. Total stocks of U.S. direct investment in Japan, which had risen to $61.4 million in 1930, declined to $37.7 million a decade later.[7]

The war brought the greatest disruption. Following U.S. abrogation of the bilateral commercial treaty (effective in 1940), American investors in Japan no longer received the benefit of international legal protection. In July 1941 the two governments froze each other's assets. Japanese authorities then attempted to mobilize enemy investments to military and political advantage. Two weeks after the attack on Peal Harbor the military ordered the nationalization of Ford Japan and General Motors Japan assets. By expropriating patents held by foreign companies and transferring the technology to Japanese firms, the government also sought to promote economic development. Although the militarists' rise to power led to catastrophe, prewar and postwar industrial policy alike allowed extensive state intervention into the economy. During the war, however, no institution acquired the power necessary to guide that intervention. Policy was the result of a chaotic struggle among the military leadership, the zaibatsu, and competing government agencies.[8]

The Occupation and the Consolidation of Administrative Power

After the war the economic bureaucrats consolidated their control over policy. Whereas the military services were dismantled and the zaibatsu dissolved, the imperial ministries responsible for economic affairs survived the war largely intact.[9] The U.S. decision to conduct an indirect occupation added another layer of state control and created a natural opportunity for the trade and industry bureaucrats to expand their reach over policy. Indeed, from a foreign investor's point of view, Occupation-era capital controls were hardly less severe than those of the wartime period. Authority to regulate the introduction of foreign capital rested with SCAP. American officials initially restricted FDI largely out of the desire to focus on the reforms then underway. Even when Japanese economic recovery became a top priority of U.S. policy, SCAP maintained controls in order to prevent foreign interests from buying up Japanese companies' undervalued assets or otherwise exploiting Japanese weakness.[10]

Specific SCAP orders included the prohibition of foreign acquisition of Japanese assets, including the purchase of stock in Japanese corporations. SCAP even barred the entry of foreign business representatives, a policy that drew the protest of several U.S. firms with substantial prewar operations in Japan. The exception to these restrictions was the permission SCAP granted to companies such as Coca-Cola and International Business Machines to provide goods or services to support Occupation operations. These firms were permitted to serve the Japanese civilian market only with the express permission of Japanese officials, however, and such permission was usually denied.

As U.S. interest in Japanese economic recovery grew, SCAP released some controls on international transactions such as those on travel by prewar investors. As they shifted the primary authority over policy to the Japanese government, officials in SCAP's Economic and Scientific Section sought "the encouragement of a legal atmosphere friendly to foreign investment." They also desired to find sources of capital to replace the voluminous economic aid that the United States was then extending to Japan. In January 1949 SCAP instructed the Japanese to begin establishing the regulations under which foreign nationals and foreign-controlled firms could engage in business in Japan.[11]

In 1950 the National Diet enacted the Law Concerning Foreign Investment, a landmark statute usually called the Foreign Investment Law (FIL). Because it was not a cabinet order issued after receipt of instructions from SCAP, the FIL set forth basic Japanese government policy much like the Banking Law. Ostensibly intended to encourage foreign investment, the FIL was actually a highly restrictive measure. As Article 1 states, the purpose of the law was "to create a sound basis for foreign investment in Japan, by limiting the induction of foreign investment to that which will contribute to the self-support and sound development of the Japanese economy and to the improvement of the international balance of payments, by providing for remittances arising from foreign investment, and by providing for adequate protection for such investments."[12]

Although not entirely at odds, the three objectives of the law—to encourage foreign investment, to limit and regulate investments to ensure the maximum benefit to the Japanese economy as a whole, and to protect the foreign investor—coexisted uneasily with each other. The principal effect was to establish a centralized process, including an appeal system, for screening inward foreign investment. One official worry, shared by the Keidanren and other business associations, was that alien investors could, with a very modest investment, acquire controlling interests in the country's leading enterprises. The Japanese government was also concerned that allowing repatriation of foreign capital from equity investments would cause a drain of valuable foreign exchange in the future.[13]

Of the activities that the FIL regulated, technology transfer and acquisition of stock or a proprietary interest in a Japanese company were the most sensitive. To implement the law, a Foreign Investment Commission reviewed applications for foreign investment. The main criterion for approving technology transfer agreements was whether the technological know-how was desirable, as determined by the various ministries concerned. Stock purchases were more complex.[14] The FIL initially prohibited purchase of outstanding stock. Acquisition of stock was permitted only in cases where it expanded the capital assets of a company. Aliens who had previously acquired shares in connection with technological assistance or like contracts could purchase newly issued stock (resulting in increased assets for the company issuing it) on a limited basis.

In 1952 the National Diet enacted several amendments to the FIL. One made possible the purchase of outstanding stock, bonds, and investment trust certificates, but in foreign exchange only (as opposed to with yen not converted from foreign exchange). Such investments were subject to validation. Such validation—hardly a formality—guaranteed remittance of dividends in full and the principal, not in excess of 20 percent annually beginning two years after the acquisition. Validation depended largely on the industry involved and the percentage of foreign control. The effect, as the U.S. Embassy noted, was "to prevent the acquisition of old stocks by aliens to any significant degree." Purchase of new stock in yen was possible without validation, but no remittance guarantee was granted. Purchase of new stock with foreign currency was similarly permitted, but guarantee of remittance was only given in conjunction with validation.[15]

U.S. policy contributed to the consolidation of administrative power over foreign capital in other ways. In 1949 SCAP ordered the creation of a Foreign Exchange Control Board to regulate the investment of all foreign exchange accruing from international trade, the idea being to ensure that the funds were invested in industries essential to economic recovery. SCAP also encouraged the National Diet to enact the Foreign Exchange and Foreign Trade Control Law. It required that any person acquiring foreign exchange from trade had to turn it over to a government account, and it placed the Foreign Exchange Control Board in charge of the use of these funds. The Economic Stabilization Board (created in 1946) also drew up regular foreign exchange budgets.[16]

American officials regarded restrictions imposed on foreign capital during the Occupation as temporary measures. Yet sometimes nothing proves more enduring than the provisional. In the hands of talented career bureaucrats these temporary powers became what Chalmers Johnson has called "weapons of industrial management and control that rivaled anything [their] predecessors had ever known during the prewar and wartime periods."[17] The Foreign Exchange Control Board and the Economic Stabilization Board were both abolished in August 1952. Japanese officials, however, transferred the powers to decide the foreign exchange budget as well as the Economic Stabilization Board's authority to supervise joint ventures and imports of technology to MITI. The Ministry of Finance acquired jurisdiction over the Foreign Investment Commission, which was renamed the Foreign Investment Council. The Japanese government also enforced strict controls on outward foreign investment.[18]

The only sector of the Japanese economy in which foreign firms established a major presence was the petroleum industry. During the early postwar years, the nation's desperate need for energy, the initiative of Japanese petroleum companies, and various other factors gradually pressed Japan to rely upon foreign oil for energy. Japanese industry leaders led the way and the government acquiesced in joint ventures between the international oil companies and Japanese firms. Standard-Vacuum, Caltex, and other firms guaranteed Japanese access to vital supplies of crude oil and investment capital, and in return they acquired direct stakes in the Japanese economy. Outside of the energy sector, the ironic legacy of the Occupation was to reinforce bureaucratic control and to discourage foreign investment. Together the war and the Occupation brought a decline in American FDI, from $37.7 million in 1940 to just $19 million a decade later.[19]

Negotiation of the Treaty of Friendship, Commerce, and Navigation, 1953

The bilateral Treaty of Friendship, Commerce, and Navigation, concluded in April 1953, ratified Japan's restrictive legal framework affecting foreign investment. Such was not its intent, at least on the American side. The purposes were instead to restore commercial bilateral relations on a normal basis for the first time since 1940, and to set a precedent before other nations set to the task. FCN agreements were a principal means by which the U.S. government sought to promote trade and investment.[20]

Exploratory talks began in December 1951 based on the State Department's standard draft of an FCN treaty. Final agreement was reached in March 1953, after lengthy negotiations.[21] Long-standing sources of controversy such as immigration, land ownership, and labeling of manufactures arose. The negotiations thus reflected the actual mix of hope and tension in bilateral relations. Both governments paid careful attention to the talks and kept their respective business communities informed. The U.S. mission in Tokyo, for example, requested that the American Chamber of Commerce in Japan review the provisions of the State Department's own standard draft treaty.[22] The Japanese press paid close attention to the negotiations.[23] The asymmetry in power between the United States and Japan naturally heightened its sensitivity. The State Department did not desire to force an agreement upon an unwilling partner or make it "appear as a condition precedent to peace."[24]

From the beginning, Japanese officials were more wary of foreign investment than they were eager to encourage it.[25] The bureaucrats, however, were not the only important actors. Private sector organizations such as the Keidanren and individual companies could and did exert pressure on government officials on issues affecting them. After independence Japanese private sector opinion was generally hostile to foreign equity investment as well as agreements that promised to weaken safeguards then in place.[26] Individual firms often supported specific investment proposals from foreign companies, but the general preference of both government and business was for long-term loans or license agreements.

The heart of the FCN treaty was Article VII (see the Appendix). That provision guaranteed companies of either party "national treatment" with respect to engaging in business activities within the territories of the other. It specifically guaranteed the ability "to establish and maintain" business establishments of various forms, "to organize companies," and "to control and manage enterprises" so established or acquired. On this point the United States made a significant concession, namely acceptance of Japan's process of screening foreign investments as prescribed by law. Rather than simply bowing to Japanese pressure, the Americans recognized that Japan's precarious balance-of-payments position did not permit the free flow of capital across national borders. A protocol to the treaty specifically allowed Japan to impose restrictions on the introduction of foreign capital "as may be necessary to protect its monetary reserves." Paradoxically, economic vulnerability provided Japanese negotiators a winning argument in support of demands for tolerance of controls on trade and investment.[27]

Once the United States granted the principle of allowing Japan to restrict international transactions on balance-of-payments grounds, it accepted the apparatus to put such decisions into effect. The matter of stock purchases, particularly the freedom to reinvest local proceeds in yen, was only one issue on the table, but it illustrates well how the United States attempted to secure national treatment for U.S. capital within the very narrow framework of the FIL. The law then provided for Japanese control over foreign capital even after its initial approval. For example, since it did not permit local reinvestment without the approval of the Ministry of Finance, yen holdings of foreigners were practically frozen. Such approval was very difficult to obtain for purchases of new issues of stock and was not granted in the case of outstanding issues.[28] Because the United States sought to secure national treatment for American capital after the initial screening, the obvious solution was revision of the FIL.

Finance Minister Mukai Tadaharu, himself a successful businessman and recent cabinet appointee, initially expressed sympathy for the American position.[29] The Keidanren, Nisshō (the Japan Chamber of Commerce and Industry), and other business associations, however, opposed any change. Arguing that outstanding shares were undervalued, they urged the retention of the FIL provision requiring government approval (essentially prohibition in practice) for at least five years. Mukai then shifted his position and pressed for U.S. acquiescence in retention for three years. The American Embassy accepted this compromise as a necessary step toward concluding an agreement, aware that few, if any, U.S. investors would be interested in purchasing outstanding shares in the short term as the likely return was low. In theory, the principle was assured even though the specific privilege was postponed.[30]

Despite its restrictive terms, the FCN treaty is not an example of American diplomats eagerly sacrificing the substance of the matter in exchange for an agreement, any agreement. The Eisenhower administration approved of the treaty and the Senate ratified it. Embassy officials kept Washington informed of the progress of the negotiations and carried out their instructions even when the result was sharp disagreement with the Japanese side.[31] Even after the negotiation of the treaty, official U.S. opinion held that it was "probably desirable" for Japan to continue screening foreign investments out of consideration for the nation's balance-of-payments position.[32] The investment climate in Japan was clear to observers. W. W. Diehl, the U.S. financial attaché in Tokyo, explained: "Japan has progressively relaxed restrictions on foreign investment as the economy has strengthened; however, there is no intent to invite foreign capital into Japan without limitation. Such capital is desired for constructive purposes in limited fields on a long-term basis and preferably in the form of loans rather than in equities—and if in equities, on a minority basis if possible."[33] The question was whether the return of prosperity would lead to change in the future.

As events turned, Japanese restrictions grew in their significance. Even before the FCN treaty entered into force, various U.S. companies complained to the Department of State of barriers to investment in Japan. Among them were Parke-Davis, General Foods, and Parker Pen. Parke-Davis, for example, negotiated an investment agreement with the Sankyo Company, Ltd., under which Parke-Davis was to organize a wholly owned subsidiary in Japan to manufacture and sell selected Parke-Davis products. The board of directors of the Japanese corporation was to include one or more Japanese nationals, and Sankyo was to enjoy exclusive sales rights of Parke-Davis products in Japan for a ten-year period. The Ministry of Health and Welfare rejected the application, reportedly because the agreement provided for Japanese control of less than 50 percent.[34]

Official representations on behalf of U.S. firms achieved little. In October 1953, Frank A. Waring, counselor at the embassy for economic affairs, brought the Japanese government's failure to validate proposals for foreign investment to the attention of the Foreign Ministry. In a letter to Okumura Katsuo, vice minister for foreign affairs, Waring specifically mentioned Parke-Davis and the experience of the Celanese Corporation. The latter firm had concluded an agreement with Mitsubishi Rayon providing for 51 percent majority Celanese participation in management. Beyond urging favorable consideration of the cases in question, Waring made the case for the various benefits to Japan of a less restrictive technology. Okumura promised simply to inquire into the matter. Separate conversations the following December with Ikeda Hayato and Ichimada Naoto, then governor of the Bank of Japan, left U.S. officials feeling optimistic. Those talks focused mostly on Japanese law, but they also covered cases involving Coca-Cola and General Foods. Ikeda and Ichimada promised to press for relaxation in the administrative attitude toward foreign investment. As the U.S. Embassy soon learned, however, the Foreign Ministry had little clout in decisions on industrial policy and Japanese politicians were unlikely to risk much for the sake of foreign investors.[35]

In retrospect, the timing of American acquiescence in Japan's screening of foreign investment proved to be as significant as the substance of Japanese policy. Wider developments soon combined to reduce the leverage of the U.S. government in economic disputes with Japan and to enhance the relative importance of Japanese restrictions. Starting at middecade, as U.S. companies came to appreciate the difficulty of investing in Japan, the Eisenhower administration was expanding the scope of its economic policy to meet competition with the Soviet Union for influence in the Third World and the promotion of economic development there. The growing European market and the return of currency convertibility in 1958 then unleashed an unexpected burst of FDI and multinational enterprise, rendering the free flow of private capital far more important than anyone recognized when concluding the FCN treaty in 1953.[36]

The Growth of Multinational Enterprise

The efforts of companies like Parke-Davis and General Foods to invest in the Japanese market were part of a vast expansion of American business activity abroad during the fifties that ultimately transformed both the companies themselves and the structure of the global economy. Instead of attempting to grow and establish a presence in foreign markets by simply expanding production for export, leading manufacturing firms such as Ford, General Electric, and Proctor and Gamble turned to investment, production, advertising, marketing, and research and development overseas. This trend was most pronounced in the technology- and capital-intensive sectors of the economy.[37]

Multinationals such as the Chrysler Corporation and Minnesota Mining and Manufacturing Company bore familiar names and tended to occupy oligopolistic positions in the domestic American market. Since investment overseas required extensive financial capital, managerial skill, and technological sophistication, relatively few firms engaged in extensive foreign investment.[38] Yet by the 1960s overseas operations of those that did were earning a significant share of company profits.[39] Foreign subsidiaries became vital to the operation of the entire firm rather than being establishments of secondary importance. Following the lead of General Motors in the early 1960s, U.S. multinationals began to integrate foreign subsidiaries into their overall management structure, thus creating truly global organizations.

The proliferation of overseas operations by U.S. multinationals changed the structure of the world economy. In several sectors of the economy, exports and imports declined in significance relative to globalized production. By the mid-1960s, markets in chemicals, automobiles, computer technology, and like sectors were internationalized. Growth in the flow of investment actually exceeded that of international trade throughout that decade. Foreign direct investment also fostered the growth of trade in goods and services within the same company but across national lines. Multinational corporations became the agents of change overseas by encouraging greater transfers of capital, technology, and managerial skill between nations. In short, whereas international business had traditionally meant imports and exports, by the end of the 1950s international production, trade, and investment in many vital sectors of the U.S. economy at home and abroad were concentrated in the hands of vast multinational corporations.[40]

Table 7.1. *Book Value and Percentage Distribution: U.S. Foreign Direct Investments (by Area, Selected Years)*

Area	Book Value ($ million)				
	1950	1955	1960	1965	1970
Total[a]	11,788	19,313	31,865	49,474	75,456
Canada	3,579	6,494	11,179	15,319	21,015
Latin America	4,445	6,233	7,481	9,440	11,104
Western Hemisphere dependencies	131	179	884	1,445	1,858
United Kingdom	847	1,426	3,234	5,123	8,016
Other Europe	886	1,591	3,457	8,862	17,239
Japan	19	129	254	675	1,482
Africa[b]	287	572	639	1,390	2,427
Oceania[c]	256	596	1,195	2,334	4,067
Middle East	692	1,014	1,139	1,536	1,521
East Asia (−Japan)	290	483	984	1,366	2,260
Other	356	596	1,417	1,985	4,469

Source: U.S. Department of Commerce, *Statistical Abstract of the United States*, 1950–1972.
[a] Total figures may differ slightly from the sum of the rounded figures listed here.

Neither multinational enterprise nor foreign direct investment was new to the United States after the Second World War. But American FDI was traditionally concentrated in the petroleum and extractive industries. At a mere $19 million, U.S. direct investments in Japan represented only 0.2 percent of the global total in 1950 (Table 7.1). No one expected significant growth in American FDI in manufacturing industries. Postwar recovery of the U.S. economy and the desperate conditions overseas made domestic investment seem more attractive. The greater volume of public debate over the ITO shows how protectionists and free traders alike regarded merchandise trade as the real stuff of international economic exchange.

In defiance of such expectations, twenty-five years after the war the book value of American FDI stood at $78.18 billion, a rise equivalent to a 10 percent increase per year.[41] Investment by manufacturing companies fueled this growth. By the 1960s chemicals, transportation equipment, electrical machinery and like industries accounted for roughly two-thirds of all U.S. direct investment abroad. Accompanying this sectoral shift was a change in the geographical destination of overseas investment. By 1970 manufacturing enterprises overtook petroleum and extractive industries as

Percentage Distribution		
1950	1960	1970
100.0	100.0	100.0
30.4	35.1	27.9
37.8	23.5	14.7
1.1	2.8	2.5
7.2	10.1	10.6
7.5	10.8	22.8
.2	.8	2.0
2.4	2.0	3.2
2.2	3.8	5.4
5.9	3.6	2.0
2.5	3.1	3.0
3.0	4.4	5.9

[b] Does not include figures for South Africa in 1960, 1965, or 1970.
[c] Includes figures for South Africa in 1960, 1965, and 1970.

the leading direct investors, and nearly half of their investment went to Western Europe.[42]

This spread of multinational enterprise was the result of many factors. Advances in transportation and communication facilitated the conduct of business across national lines. Cold War strategists in Washington viewed the economic recovery of American allies with favor. U.S. companies were eager to surmount high tariff walls abroad by establishing subsidiaries on the other side. European governments, particularly the United Kingdom and Italy, encouraged U.S. investment in their technologically deficient industries. The formation of the European Economic Community in 1957 and the return of currency convertibility the next year made it possible to speak of Western Europe as a vast common market. But the engine driving U.S. investment overseas was the economic opportunity in markets abroad. U.S. multinationals manufactured the products—from automobiles to refrigerators to cosmetics—that European consumers desired. By the sixties, American executives regarded Western Europe as part of the vast "consumer market stretching from California to the Iron Curtain."[43]

Japan's economy developed apart from this trend toward international

Table 7.2. *Validated Establishments of Joint Business Ventures in Japan, 1950–1965*

Fiscal Year	\<Percentages of Stock Holdings of Foreign Investors\>						
	100%	99–51%	50%	49–30%	29–15%	Below 15%	Total
1950	1	9	6	2	1	3	22
1951	1	6	3	3	2	8	23
1952	1	2	4	1	3	5	16
1953	1	0	1	3	2	2	9
1954	1	0	1	2	1	1	6
1955	0	0	0	1	0	1	2
1956	0	1	0	1	2	1	5
1957	0	0	1	2	2	2	7
1958	0	0	0	0	1	0	1
1959	0	1	1	3	3	2	10
1960	1	0	3	6	2	0	12
1961	0	0	3	13	3	0	19
1962	0	0	1	15	3	3	22
1963	2	0	10	33	9	1	55
1964	6	6	16	39	9	0	76
1965	14	4	17	32	1	1	69
Total	28	29	67	156	44	30	354

Sources: Jūkagaku Kōgyō Tsūshinsha, *Gaikoku Gijutsu Dōnyū Yōran*, 1965, [Handbook of imports of foreign technology], 63, 471–96; *Gaikoku Gijutsu Dōnyū Yōran*, 1966, 118–24.

Note: Because figures for 1965 are for the calendar year, they understate slightly the trend toward a greater number of joint ventures.

integration in important ways.[44] Japanese industry enjoyed both access to new technology and protection from foreign domination. Since Japan's economy was under the jurisdiction of one government, Japanese authorities were able to exercise proportionally greater control over the activities of foreign investors than was the case in Western Europe. Even in industries where they permitted FDI, the Japanese preferred joint ventures rather than acquisitions, with the Japanese partner controlling a majority of the shares if at all possible (Table 7.2). As the arbiter of technology transfer agreements, MITI wielded the vast power of the bureaucracy on behalf of Japanese enterprises. Japanese companies exerted considerable pressure on the bureaucrats, thus affecting the timing and the substance of government policy. As shown in Table 7.1, American FDI in Japan thus rose slowly, reaching only $254 million in 1960.

As Japan's manufacturing companies became competitive abroad, and Japan's share of global manufacturing and manufacturing exports rose, Japanese firms eventually followed in the path of the American and European firms that invested overseas. Early on IBM and Dow Chemical became familiar beyond American shores, just as British Petroleum and Volkswagen became household words in the United States. By the 1970s, Americans and Europeans alike were familiar with Sony electronics, Toyota automobiles, and Mitsubishi equipment. In time, American, European, and Japanese manufacturing companies sought new opportunities in industrializing nations with a growing middle-class population, such as Brazil, Mexico, and Indonesia.

U.S. Policy on Outward Foreign Investment

Surprising as it may seem, the postwar boom in American foreign direct investment was not an object of government policy. Some American business executives even doubted whether U.S. government policies, particularly foreign aid programs, promoted private investment abroad at all. In retrospect it is clear that they did. Marshall Plan administrators encouraged American direct investment in Europe. Concerned as they were with recovery abroad, U.S. officials saw FDI as a way to funnel badly needed dollars to Europe, to facilitate the technological modernization of European industry, and to spark the confidence that was necessary for economic revival. U.S. antitrust policies also encouraged foreign investment. For large firms unable to expand further at home without risking antitrust investigation, the natural alternatives were to diversify into new products or expand their existing product lines by investing overseas. Many companies, of course, did both.[45]

The primary role of the private sector in the growth of U.S. multinational enterprise requires emphasis because it highlights the differences between American and Japanese business cultures during the postwar period. Government regulation and involvement in the U.S. economy has increased since the industrial revolution, but the authority to make basic decisions about investment, production, and the other aspects of business has rested with corporate management. Government has, often unintentionally, created incentives that skew those decisions, but the state has not guided investment choices according to any proactive industrial policy in the same manner as in Japan. American U.S. firms have traditionally opposed government intrusion in such decision making just as they have jealously protected their freedom to seek out profitable opportunity. Those companies which have turned to the government for support in international trade have almost invariably been those faring badly in the face of one challenge or another. The archives of the Departments of Commerce and State from the 1950s contain voluminous documentation on the problems besetting the textile industry and comparatively little material on the overseas expansion of automotive and electronics firms.

The failure of the Eisenhower administration's efforts to modify the tax code in 1954 and 1955 illustrates the relatively passive role of the federal government in expanding U.S. corporate activities abroad. At issue were the conditions under which foreign income taxes could be credited against U.S. tax liabilities. Existing law allowed U.S. corporations with subsidiaries abroad (that is, operations organized and operated under the laws of the host country) to defer U.S. income tax on profits earned overseas until the time of repatriation to the United States. By allowing corporations to defer taxes in this manner, the law potentially biased corporate choices toward foreign rather than domestic investment. But to limit the revenue losses of the foreign tax credit, the tax code also included limits on allowable tax credits.[46]

Eisenhower proposed broadening the types of foreign taxes that U.S. firms could credit against U.S. income tax liabilities, and abrogating the overall limit then in place. When he took office, U.S. corporations with branches (as opposed to subsidiaries) abroad were not allowed to defer the income of those branches. The president recommended that these branches be permitted to defer taxes on their income. Finally, he proposed a tax reduction of 14 percent on foreign investments anywhere in the world. These initiatives, which Eisenhower presented to Congress on 30 March 1954, were essentially a restatement of the Randall Commission's recommendations, made two months earlier.[47]

Although their popular political salience was negligible, Eisenhower's initiatives enjoyed considerable support. The Council of Economic Advisors, the Foreign Operations Administration, and the Departments of State and Defense favored them. The Randall report actually drew their criticism for not advocating more extensive action (such as technical assistance to foreign countries) to improve the "climate" for foreign investment.[48] Multinational and other business interests, which tended to be well represented in the administration, also favored legislation to expand private foreign investment. Eisenhower's goals of freer markets overseas and economy in government at home naturally resonated well in business circles. Tax incentives and the encouragement of private investment abroad were part and parcel of the administration's effort to scale back foreign aid programs at the outset of Eisenhower's presidency.[49]

Despite this enthusiasm, the president's tax proposals foundered on the opposition of the Treasury Department and Senator Millikin's Finance Committee. The point of friction was the definition of what kinds of business activities would qualify for the 14 percent tax break. Treasury insisted that the only foreign income eligible was that derived from "the active conduct of a trade or business abroad, *with the exception of the export trade.*" The department further specified that "production of goods intended for our home market" would disqualify a company for special tax treatment. As applied in this manner, the tax breaks were to be denied to companies that earned less than 95 percent of their income outside of the United States. In part the U.S. Treasury was concerned with losing $700 to $800 million in revenue if the 14 percent tax reduction were broadly applied. Secretary Humphrey was also unenthusiastic about FDI. He thought that it would undermine the nation's competitive position abroad by placing a strain on the balance of payments and by strengthening the economies of Western Europe and Japan.[50]

Corporate opinion was highly critical of the Treasury proposals. From a multinational company's point of view, separating trade and investment abroad was both artificial and unworkable. As Richard E. Caves has explained, "Often the foreign subsidiary does not just produce the parent's goods for the local market; it processes semi-finished units of that good, or it packages or assembles them according to local specifications."[51] Confronted with such criticism from the business community, the Senate Finance Committee understandably voted against the administration's proposals. In 1955 the same initiatives again met the same fate.

As Joanne Gowa has concluded in her study of the matter, President Eisenhower and his top advisors took little interest in private foreign investment and did not deploy the power at their disposal to win approval of tax credits. The president neither resolved the conflict within the administration nor made the passage of legislation a visible priority. Exports accounted for 3 percent of GNP, but private investment overseas totaled a mere 0.3 percent. Subsequent initiatives by the Commerce Department's Business Advisory Council, the State Department, and Representative Hale Boggs (D.-La. and chairman of the Ways and Means Subcommittee on Foreign Trade) also met with opposition from the Treasury and presidential indifference. Late in his second term, when Eisenhower dealt with the issue again, capital exports seemed to be contributing to the growing U.S. balance-of-payments problem. One of his final acts in office was to endorse a proposal to curb tax abuses by American multinational corporations abroad.[52]

If official interest in FDI was negligible, the political salience of public aid to the Third World was unmistakable at middecade. The depth of the Eisenhower administration's engagement is reflected in its turnaround on the highly visible issue of foreign aid. The expanding Cold War and the growing pressure to attend to the needs of less developed regions were largely responsible for the administration's growing interest in the Third World. As the European powers retreated from empires around the globe, both the Soviet Union and the United States became more deeply involved in the affairs of the developing world. Because many of these nations rejected close alignment with either superpower, the Americans and the Soviets competed intensely for the hearts and minds of the newly independent peoples in Asia, Africa, and the Middle East.

Soviet leaders after Stalin sought to reduce superpower tension, but their appeals for "peaceful coexistence" included vigorous expansion of Communist influence in neutralist nations and the Third World. The principal means toward this end were foreign trade, technical assistance, and the extension of credits. Launched in 1954, the new policy became official at the Twentieth Congress of the Soviet Communist Party in 1956. Soviet trade with the developing world expanded rapidly, reaching $1.4 billion in 1956. During the first eight months of the same year the Soviet bloc countries extended $600 million in foreign credits to various nations including Egypt, Syria, India, Afghanistan, Indonesia, and Yugoslavia.[53]

Although small in total value compared with that of the U.S. aid program, the Soviet economic offensive alarmed the Eisenhower administration. While President Eisenhower's greatest hope was to promote peace between the superpowers, both he and his advisors recognized the political challenge in the new initiatives from Moscow. Many voices contributed to the debate over how to respond to this "Soviet economic penetration" of the Third World. Secretary of the Treasury Humphrey, Chairman Dodge of the Council on Foreign Economic Policy, and other fiscal conservatives downplayed the significance of the Soviet threat and—by extension—the need to spend more money on foreign assistance programs. But the political sensitivity of the Soviet economic offensive and a range of other factors, not least the apparent inadequacy of existing programs to foster development in the Third World, led to expanded public assistance programs for the Third World rather than the retrenchment Eisenhower intended when he assumed the presidency.[54]

The merits of the various programs aside, by the late fifties economic development in the Third World ranked high on the agenda of the Eisenhower administration. The administration pressed for continued renewal of the Mutual Security Program, establishment of the Development Loan Fund, and extension of the PL 480 Program. The president also backed the establishment of the International Development Association (as an affiliate of the World Bank), creation of the Inter-American Development Bank, and lawmakers' efforts to place greater emphasis on economic (as opposed to military) assistance. To the extent that the State Department considered private investment abroad, the principal concern was to increase the flow of private capital to the developing countries of Asia, Africa, and Latin America. This concern with the problems of the Third World and the American-Soviet rivalry there deflected American attention away from private foreign investment in industrialized nations and Japan in particular.[55]

Technology Transfer

In the same manner that Cold War imperatives highlighted the significance of the Third World, strategic considerations shaped American policy on technology transfer. The effort of successive administrations to curtail the flow of technological know-how to the Communist bloc is familiar. The same basic policy also provided for encouraging the transfer of technology necessary for economic advance to Cold War allies. Both NSC 125/2 (1952) and NSC 5516/1 (1955) called for facilitating the "expansion, rehabilitation, and modernization of Japan's industries." The latter policy paper explicitly recommended the improvement of "the productive, managerial, and marketing efficiency and labor relations of Japanese industry, especially through technical assistance."[56]

U.S. policy on technology transfer is not usually viewed in connection with the issue of private investment abroad. But the U.S. government's enthusiasm for technology transfer and its "hands-off" policy on foreign direct investment must be viewed in conjunction with one another because the Japanese authorities saw the two issues as being connected. Japanese interest in foreign technology during the years after the Second World War is legendary. The warm reception that the Japanese accorded to the American quality control expert, W. Edwards Deming, is a famous example.[57] In fact, Japan acquired new technology after the war through a variety of means. A less familiar but instructive example is the story of the Productivity Program in Japan. Since it was jointly sponsored by the American and Japanese governments, it reveals the depth of official involvement in technology transfer during the fifties.[58]

Aware that Japanese industrial efficiency lagged behind that of the United States, Japanese government officials and business shared enthusiasm for a technical assistance program. Various economists were also important, particularly for their influence in drawing attention to the need to borrow modern management techniques from overseas. Leading industrial organizations including the Keidanren, Nisshō, and Nikkeiren (the Japan Federation of Employers Association) understandably supported the idea of establishing an official program, if possible. In March 1954, they established the Japanese-American Productivity Enhancement Committee, a private organization. MITI welcomed these efforts, but wished to establish an official presence in the committee's activities, something the U.S. government likewise desired. For their part, American officials were considering a technical assistance program for Japan resembling the one comprising part of the Marshall Plan aid program in Europe.

In March 1955 the Japan Productivity Center, an organization composed of representatives of management, labor, and the academic research community, was established. The next month the American and Japanese governments launched a joint Productivity Program (under the authority of an exchange of notes on 7 April). The U.S. Operations Mission to Japan sent productivity teams to the United States and brought technical consultants to Japan. Although the range of fields studied included industry, agriculture, labor, and the peaceful applications of atomic energy, the emphasis of the program was on innovations in industry. In the program's first year, 246 of the 305 participants studied improvements in industry. Similarly, the U.S. experts brought to Japan conducted seminars for business leaders in industrial management, cost control, human relations, marketing techniques, and industrial engineering.[59] The United States eventually terminated its financial support in 1961, but by that time the program had developed a momentum of its own. It continued to sponsor study tours and established eight regional centers. In 1961 Japan invited eight Asian countries to a conference in Manila and established the Asian Productivity Organization, a body that expanded to include eighteen countries by the 1980s.

More important than any official technical cooperation program was the private initiative exhibited by private Japanese firms in the international marketplace. As Kobayashi Kōji, chairman of NEC Corporation, recalled in 1982, "whenever we found out about new technology, we could not rest until we went out and bought it." Estimates vary, but they agree on the basic contours of the transfer. Between 1950 and 1972 Japanese concerns concluded 12,000 technical assistance contracts at a cost of $3.3 billion. Because the government classified all technology transfer arrangements as a form of foreign direct investment falling under the purview of the Foreign Investment Law, Japanese economic planners were able to monitor them. If, as Kobayashi has claimed, that "the winner in almost any technology-purchase relationship is the buyer," then these purchases represent one of the greatest successes of Japan's postwar industrial policy.[60]

Until the capital liberalization of the sixties, government (especially MITI) supervision of technology purchases conferred an unusual advantage to Japan in such transactions. As Chalmers Johnson has explained, "no joint venture was ever agreed to without MITI's scrutiny and frequent alteration of the terms"; and "no patent rights were ever bought without MITI's pressuring the seller to lower the royalties or to make other changes advantageous to Japanese industry." Significantly, Japanese economic planners also withheld approval of the import of foreign technology until "MITI and its various advisory committees had agreed that the time was right and the industry involved was scheduled for 'nurturing' (*ikusei*)."[61] One must not overstate the role of the government or ignore the vibrancy of Japanese business, however. Neither these technology imports nor the bureaucrats' intervention in the market would have been very significant unless Japanese companies were able to assimilate foreign technological know-how. As Terutomo Ozawa has concluded, "technological progress was the backbone of Japan's extraordinary performance in manufactured goods in the postwar period."[62]

It is fair to ask why foreign firms—and their governments—tolerated such restrictions. The most obvious possibility is that foreign companies did not attempt to buy into the Japanese market for the simple reason that they did not believe Japan would amount to much. Such thinking came naturally after the war, reflected, for example in the decisions of Ford and General Motors not to reenter the Japanese market during the Occupation. A 1978 report prepared for the U.S. Treasury Department later concluded that a great many companies were in fact "indifferent" to Japan: "The market seemed small and remote. Technology seemed inexpensive. The income from written-off R&D investment was attractive." More than two decades of such sales, the report concluded, nurtured "competitors who now enter or threaten U.S. markets." In retrospect, American industry did underestimate Japan, and the report's conclusion correctly identified the consequences.[63]

But the American private sector does not deserve all of the blame. For some companies, entry into the Japanese market was a high priority. In the same manner that they were entering the Western European market, forward-looking multinationals attempted to buy into the Japanese market with some cooperative enterprise in which American capital would dominate. But during the negotiations, as Herman Kahn has explained, "They found that in almost all cases . . . they could not do it. They finally turned to a straight sales arrangement in which they collected royalties for the new technology. Then they found that the agreement went to MITI for approval—an approval that did not come. Rather the agreement was disallowed on the grounds that it was unfair to the Japanese firm concerned, and there was a whole new round of negotiations in which the entire agreement was written downward."[64] The capital controls put in place after the war were an imposing barrier that effectively shielded Japanese industry from foreign competition. Against the entire Japanese system, the lone foreign firm stood at a distinct disadvantage. Some companies succeeded in establishing a presence in Japan, but many failed. It is not surprising that others did not even bother to try. Thus, from the perspective of Japanese economic advantage, the individualistic business culture of the United States was the perfect, if unwitting, complement to Japan's corporatist order and nationalistic industrial policy.

Dialogue without End

By 1954, the pattern of Japanese resistance to foreign equity investment was unmistakable. The Japanese government rejected Parke-Davis's proposal and delayed on others. A pending application filed by the Studebaker Corporation was particularly revealing because the American company did not even request majority ownership or control in its agreement with the Daihatsu Company to make Studebaker autos in Japan. It would nevertheless have shaken up the Japanese automobile industry. Repeated representations by the U.S. Embassy for favorable consideration of these and other proposals fell upon "deaf ears," Waring reported. Japanese officials reiterated "the same clichés," he continued, all of which appeared to be "intellectual rationalizations for a fundamentally emotional attitude which manifests itself in fear and suspicion of foreign equity capital investment."[65]

High-level political appeals had little effect. Following a meeting between Ambassador Allison and Prime Minister Yoshida in May 1954, Foreign Minister Okazaki attempted to clarify Japanese policy. His letter explained that the Japanese government would encourage investments "which contribute to the development of our essential industries" even if they "compete to a certain extent with the domestic industries." Okazaki added, however, that the government "must give careful study to any investment which would result in the increase of luxury items or purely nonessential commodities in the domestic market."[66] After careful review, the Department of State instructed the U.S. Embassy to convey to the Japanese Government that, under the FCN treaty, the sole grounds for denying national treatment to American capital was the protection of the nation's monetary reserves. Allison's letter to this effect, however, drew no response from the Foreign Ministry.[67]

As events turned, official U.S. policy on the question of foreign investment in Japan became intertwined with a specific dispute involving the Singer Sewing Machine Company.[68] Having qualified to do business in Japan in 1901, Singer was one of the few American companies with a longtime presence in Japan. With the exception of the war years, the company had continuously carried on an extensive business in the sale and servicing of Singer sewing machines, parts, and accessories. Since the firm acquired all of its supplies of such merchandise from factories overseas, the Japanese government's imposition of restrictions on the import of supplies after the war interfered with the restoration of a profitable trade. During the early fifties the company found it impossible to import the household type of sewing machine from any source, and import licenses for industrial sewing equipment were becoming increasingly difficult to obtain. The Singer Company thus inquired into the possibility of developing a source of supply in Japan.

In 1953 Singer surveyed the prospects of investing in Japan, and in the course of this preliminary investigation the firm's representatives held discussions with most of the principal Japanese sewing machine manufacturers. Singer was advised that the Japanese government would not likely approve any investment that did not take the form of a joint venture with Japanese capital, even though the commercial treaty between the two nations did not appear to require such an arrangement. In the interest of securing official approval, Singer examined the feasibility of entering into a joint enterprise with one of the more established Japanese sewing machine manufacturing companies. Singer records indicate that, as it did so, the company "was approached by nearly all of the major Japanese sewing machine companies with requests that the Singer Company consider tying up with them." Of these Japanese firms, several presented detailed requests that compared with the agreement that Singer concluded on 9 July 1954 with Pine Sewing Machine Manufacturing Company. Pine was a wholly owned subsidiary of Japan Steel Works, Ltd., which then manufactured about five thousand sewing machines per month in Japan.

According to the terms of the 1954 agreement, the capital stock of Pine was to be doubled. Singer was to subscribe to the new shares and thus enjoy 50 percent participation in management. Singer would make a long-term loan of $320,000 to Pine, and license Pine to use its patents, trademarks, and methods and processes of manufacture. The license agreement provided that Pine would pay Singer a royalty of $2.00 per machine on one model and $2.50 on another. According to Singer, these royalty rates were substantially below those the company charged in other foreign countries for similar licenses. They amounted to about 5 percent of the anticipated selling price of the sewing machines.

Japan Steel, Pine, and Singer submitted their application for Japanese government validation of the joint venture in July 1954 (in order to secure the right of remittance of foreign exchange), but approval was not forthcoming. As Singer vice president Donald P. Kircher informed the State Department in Washington, the Singer-Pine joint venture provoked a storm in the Japanese business community. Obviously desiring to prevent any competition from Singer, Japanese sewing machine manufacturing companies, including those that had previously solicited a link with Singer, brought a great deal of pressure to bear on the Japanese government agencies concerned to disapprove the application. Arguments against the joint venture included the implausible claims that the Japanese sewing machine industry had advanced to the point that technical assistance from Singer would be of little value, that production of Singer machines in Japan would "oppress" the Japanese sewing machine industry, and that the arrangement would be harmful to Japan's foreign exchange position. As a result of this "vociferous opposition," MITI summoned representatives of Japan Steel and advised them to withdraw the application. Failing withdrawal, the application would be rejected. Singer informed the Japanese that it had had no intention of withdrawing the application and then appealed to the U.S. government for support. In presenting its case, Singer made clear that its technical assistance would be of value to Pine, but that the company's production would represent no more than 5 percent of the industry's output. Singer also projected that the export of Singer machines would in fact improve Japan's foreign exchange position.

The publicity surrounding the Singer case attracted the American Embassy's attention. Press coverage of the matter quoted the MITI and finance ministers to the effect that the government was unable to approve the Singer-Pine link. A local Singer representative informed the U.S. Embassy of MITI's advice to withdraw the proposal. In a second letter to Foreign Minister Okazaki, dated 16 September, Ambassador Allison expressed the U.S. Embassy's dissatisfaction with the Japanese government's failure to approve recent proposals for investment by U.S. firms. Although the letter focused on the Singer-Pine case as the most important example, it also mentioned the proposals of Studebaker Corporation, Parke-Davis and Company, and the Coca-Cola Company. Noting that rejection of these applications "is clearly a violation of the Friendship, Commerce, and Navigation Treaty," Allison expressed the concern that such action could "have an adverse effect on the continued support by the United States Government for Japan's participation as an equal member of the international economic bodies such as GATT."[69]

Unsurprisingly, Allison's charge that Japanese policy violated the FCN treaty provoked a negative response. Citing Japan's "acute shortage of dollars," Finance Commissioner Suzuki Gengo denied the charge. He added that the Japanese government guarantee of remittance was a "privilege" and not a "right." As an alternative, Suzuki suggested that Singer could follow the example of General Foods, which had just tentatively agreed to a conditional guarantee of remittance on a venture to produce an orange beverage under the Bireley's label in Japan. Under this "reporting system," the Japanese government would consider allowing remittances based on the actual foreign exchange earnings of the investment. Two days later, Suzuki again voiced Japanese officials' irritation with Allison's letter, reiterated that Japan's foreign exchange position (rather than political pressure from domestic sewing machine producers) was the reason for the government's position, and referred to the General Foods case. Formal arrangements for a conditional guarantee would require amendment of the Foreign Investment Law, he explained, suggesting that the United States propose such revisions to his government.[70]

After consulting with Singer representatives and considering the matter, the State Department urged that the U.S. Embassy quietly drop the question of treaty violation. Although administration of the FIL clearly frustrated investment, the question of treaty violation hinged on whether the entry of foreign investment was permitted (with or without a guarantee).[71] Conversations in Tokyo were more revealing, but they pointed in the same direction. Despite the many differences between their two countries. Ambassador Allison and Foreign Minister Okazaki were actually good friends who often got together. On 24 September the foreign minister admitted confidentially that industry pressure was the real basis of opposition to the investment in the Singer case. The Foreign Ministry representative on the Foreign Investment Council was the only figure to vote in favor of the proposal. Because the sewing machine manufacturers were strong financial backers of the Liberal Party, Okazaki explained, the government was unwilling to go against their wishes. He had discussed the matter with Ikeda who agreed that the proposal was fair, but that the government could not risk alienating its financial supporters. The foreign minister said that as long as the decision was not formally announced, the matter could be considered unsettled in order that some compromise might be worked out.[72]

From the beginning, Singer Company representatives and their legal advisors were reluctant to adopt an overly confrontational approach in dealing with the Japanese government. In consultation with the State Department, they explored the possibilities of investing in Japan with only a conditional guarantee of remittance. Prime Minister Yoshida's fall from power toward the year's end and the instability of the subsequent government under Prime Minister Hatoyama Ichiro, however, caused the company to wait until after elections and the formation of a new government.[73] In the interim, Vice President Kircher filed a statement with the Committee for Reciprocity Information when it held hearings on Japanese accession to GATT. Japan's policies toward foreign investment were so discriminatory, Kircher observed, that they should be liberalized before Japan "is to become a member of GATT and is to be given the increased trading opportunities" expected to follow from the 1955 trade negotiations.[74]

The dialogue between the two governments lapsed into a pattern of exchange between the embassy in Tokyo and Japanese officials that kept the issue alive. But it did not lead to change. Secretary Dulles and other top officials concentrated on securing Japan's accession to GATT. They predictably decided that the Japanese trade negotiations in 1955 were not the appropriate forum for discussing questions of investment.[75] Because the expanding Cold War and the various crises of the day were Secretary Dulles's first concerns, he paid little attention to the various aspects of foreign economic policy except to the extent that they impinged upon broader political issues. In Tokyo Embassy officials believed that additional pressure on Japanese officials was "worth continuing," but they could not fail to notice that restrictions on equity investment were becoming more pronounced. In December 1955 the U.S. Embassy reported that the number of applications for foreign investment with technical assistance was declining.[76]

The initiative in these circumstances rested with the private sector. Singer decided to go ahead with production of sewing machines at Singer-Pine by importing the necessary equipment into Japan. In dealing with the Japanese government, the company's aim shifted from securing approval of the Singer-Pine venture to simply preventing an announcement of its disapproval. Company officials did not want the exchange to descend to the point of threatening retaliation. The State Department agreed and pressed the Japanese government accordingly.[77]

Although the Japanese government complied with the request not to announce an unfavorable decision on the Singer-Pine proposal, MITI refused to allow Singer to import the equipment necessary to produce Singer machines. Hence, the company arranged for the domestic Japanese production of the machinery to manufacture sewing machines. In 1956 Pine produced a new product under Singer's direction, the Merritt machine, thus earning the American company "grudging admiration" in government and industrial circles for its persistence. In addition to the meeting domestic demand, the company exported these machines to markets in Southeast Asia.[78] Singer's desire was to manufacture a product of sufficiently high quality to be sold under the Singer trademark. Finally, in January 1957 it announced that it would do so beginning the next month.[79]

Japanese industry was becoming resigned to Singer's presence in the domestic market, but Japan's balance-of-payments crisis in 1957 (see Table 1.1) allowed the government to maintain its policy of withholding a guarantee of remittance for equity investments well into 1958. Singer-Pine was only the most high profile case. Significantly, executives of the Singer Company refrained from advocating restrictions on imports of Japanese goods (including sewing machines) to the United States.[80] In 1958 Singer amended its application to the Japanese government for validation of the joint venture, allowing remittances to be limited to 50 percent of earnings (dividends and royalties) on the company's investment.[81]

By 1959 Japan's return to economic health was undeniable, and the nation's booming export trade that year undercut the long-standing argument that the government needed to screen foreign investments for balance-of-payments reasons. In July the Japanese government announced a new program to ease the introduction of foreign investment capital.[82] Once Japan's economy showed clear signs of strength, top-level officials in the Eisenhower administration inquired into Japanese capital liberalization more seriously than before. After Dulles succumbed to cancer in 1959 (he resigned in April), the State Department generally paid greater heed to economic affairs under the leadership of Secretary Christian A. Herter (who succeeded Dulles) and Under Secretary C. Douglas Dillon. Since the essence of any capital liberalization program is in the implementation, administration officials regularly pressed on the issue, urging the approval of the many investment proposals then gathering dust in various Japanese ministries.[83] In October 1959, the Foreign Investment Council finally approved, in principle, Singer's proposal for remittance privileges (not to exceed 50 percent of earnings). Ambassador MacArthur reported that the decision fit into "a pattern of limited, tentative but nevertheless positive steps toward liberalization."[84]

If the dialogue leading to a break in the system had finally begun, U.S. officials learned that it was still going to be a lengthy affair. Japanese authorities responsible for carrying out liberalization were the same bureaucrats who had resisted it so strongly in previous years, and American leverage was limited. The glacial pace of Japan's capital liberalization during the 1960s confirmed the economic bureaucrats' reluctance to ease controls and underscored the limits of Japan's integration into the global economy.[85]

More important than the fact of change in Japanese industrial policy was its timing. On their own, shifts in policy often appeared to be more significant than they really were. The success of a given policy did not depend on its enduring forever. There was always an economic end in view, possibly several. The aim in the Singer-Pine case was not necessarily to lock Singer out of the market. The point was to buy the domestic industry time (and technology, if possible) to develop to the point that it could withstand competition from foreign multinationals such as Singer. By that standard, as Hayashi Shintarō, who was in charge of light machinery in the Japan External Trade Association, later recalled, the bureaucrats' handling of the Singer-Pine proposal was a success.[86]

As the Singer-Pine case illustrates, official U.S. pressure was not very effective at securing change once the system of Japanese capital controls was firmly in place. In order to succeed, a company had to maintain the effort for the long haul. The most effective strategy for penetrating the market proved to be linking up with a strong ally in the Japanese private sector. As Mason has shown, Coca-Cola faced resistance similar to that experienced by Singer during the fifties. The turning point was when the company secured the assistance of Shin-Mitsubishi Heavy Industries (which was interested in making the equipment necessary to produce Coca-Cola beverages). Only after Mitsubishi lined up a beverage company for a joint venture and pressured the government for approval in 1960 did Coca-Cola prosper in Japan.[87] Although Japan's market was not closed to foreign capital investment, the barriers to entry were formidable.

Conclusion

Japan's failure to welcome private investment capital during the 1950s is not very surprising. The clash between the American and Japanese national traditions of economic development was probably sharpest on matters of investment. But the extent and the significance of Japan's capital controls during the era of high-speed growth derived from an unusual convergence of developments that also undercut American ability to press for liberalization.

Occupation era controls were supposed to be temporary, but their effect was to consolidate Japanese administrative authority over foreign investment. Fortuitously for the economic bureaucracy, Japan's precarious balance-of-payments position not only provided the government a justification for imposing restrictions on the movement of foreign capital, it prevented the United States from pressing the matter harder through 1958, the period during which Japan's industries made the transition from recovery to high-speed growth.

Although Japanese government representatives and business leaders could not see the future, their suspicion of foreign capital served them better than they could have expected. The surge of growth in multinational enterprise during the fifties expanded American influence around the globe, but not very greatly in Japan. Rather than opening the gates to the flow of foreign direct investment, the U.S.-Japanese FCN treaty of 1953 ratified Japan's restrictive policies before Americans grasped the extent to which the emerging order would shield Japanese industry from foreign competition.

It is tempting to ascribe all to government policies. But differences in the business-government relationship between the two countries and the asymmetry in their power were at least as important. Whereas American attention was necessarily divided, the Japanese government and business were usually able to present a common front on policy. That front occasionally broke apart, as the experience of some companies reveals. Japan's market was not impossible to break into. But, by any standard, it was unusually difficult to crack.

Chapter Eight
HIGH-SPEED GROWTH
AND TRADE FRICTION,
1955-1960

The economic consequences of expanded trade with Japan became apparent in the United States in 1955. The Geneva tariff negotiations and Japan's domestic recovery that year contributed to a surge in Japanese exports to the United States, inaugurating the era of Japanese high-speed growth (about 10 percent per year) that lasted until the early 1970s. The inevitable result was trade friction.[1] Unlike investment, merchandise trade is immediately visible even to casual observers. Touching innumerable individuals and interests as it did, the political salience of trade friction was high. Particular disputes, most notably that over cotton textiles, could and did develop into political problems far out of proportion to their economic significance. Such friction became a fundamental element of the bilateral relationship during the second half of the fifties.

Access to the Japanese market was not a great issue until the decade's end. Owing to Japan's persistent balance-of-payments difficulties, the U.S.

government tolerated governmental restrictions on the use of foreign exchange at odds with free trade. The Japanese government shielded its fledgling higher-value-added industries from foreign competition. By the late fifties, however, when the United States was clearly becoming Japan's best foreign market, pressure for Japanese import liberalization added another element of friction to the relationship.

If the alliance between the two countries set the stage for such disputes, the U.S. government's desire to keep Japan at its side in the Cold War also created pressure to solve them. For the United States the requirements of alliance management dictated the amicable resolution of disagreements. The continuing effort to blockade the People's Republic of China militated against imposing severe restrictions on Japanese access to the American market. The Japanese government similarly desired stable political relations and did not wish to jeopardize access to the U.S. market. Both governments intervened in the market in ways inconsistent with the principles of free trade.

Thus, developments during the late fifties contributed to an enduring legacy of Japanese economic strength and political management of trade relations across the Pacific. Despite recurrent friction and growing pressure for liberalization, the postwar order worked to Japan's economic advantage. When foreign manufacturers recognized Japan's potential during the 1960s, they faced both a web of protective restrictions and competitive Japanese rivals. Japan's distinctive brand of capitalism thrived, its achievements confirmed each year by the nation's growing trade surplus. The story of how Japan turned its position of weakness to advantage began with the unsettled state of the Cold War alliance in the mid-1950s.

The Changing Cold War and U.S.-Japanese Relations

Indirection and mutual frustration troubled American-Japanese relations at middecade. With the Yoshida government's imposition of austerity measures to keep the budget and inflation in line, American worries about Japanese financial instability dissipated. On defense and economic assistance, both sides lowered their expectations. The United States recognized that Japan was unwilling to pursue more than modest rearmament, and the Japanese understood that a Marshall Plan for Asia was not forthcoming. Although visibly unenthusiastic, Japan followed the U.S. lead on China policy and maintained restrictions on trade with the Communist bloc. Accession to GATT was gratifying to Japan, but the widespread invocation of

Article 35 demonstrated that access to foreign markets required extended effort. Despite American hopes that Japanese accession to GATT would lessen Japan's dependence on the U.S. market, Japan's foreign trade revolved around the bilateral economic axis as much as ever.

Eisenhower approved a new NSC paper on Japan in April 1955. It updated many details of policy, but the aim was familiar: to build Japan into a loyal and more powerful ally. The United States was to "consult with the Japanese Government as an equal partner on matters of mutual interest," but its unimaginative recommendations amounted to maintaining pressure on Japan to contribute more to the Cold War partnership.[2]

As the Occupation faded from memory, Japanese leaders sought greater autonomy from the United States. Prime Minister Hatoyama Ichirō attempted to resume diplomatic relations with the USSR in 1955. His government also requested revision of the U.S.-Japan Security Treaty. From every direction calls for expanded trade with the PRC grew more insistent.[3] Such initiatives provoked growing American unease. The U.S. government welcomed a stronger Japan following in American footsteps. But elected leaders and appointed officials in the United States were alarmed by Japanese assertiveness when the result was disagreement with the United States. U.S. policy still called for maintaining a tight a blockade of the PRC. If the Eisenhower administration justifiably dismissed the Hatoyama government's bid for treaty revision as premature, delay in attending to bilateral disputes (over the parole of Japanese war criminals, for example) incurred considerable ill will for little or nothing in return.[4]

American habits of treating Japan as a junior partner and the revival of national feeling in Japan were both natural developments. But the combination was guaranteed to generate frustration, particularly on the Japanese side. From the beginning, the alliance was a top-down affair. Ties at the popular level were not merely weak; greater involvement of the public in foreign policy often magnified mutual misperception and mistrust. Thus, strain at the top posed a serious challenge to both sides.

American officials responsible for Japanese affairs and private observers both recognized and reported on Japan's discontent at middecade.[5] The U.S. Embassy in Tokyo compiled the most comprehensive analysis of the problem. "The signs of Japan's discontent are subtle as yet," Ambassador Allison warned, but "when they become striking it will be too late to retrieve the situation." He explained: "The Japanese feel, for example, that we tend to take them for granted, and even to expect more from them than from our other friends—in trade matters for example—while in basic decisions affecting Japan we treat her as no more important than the minor countries in this area. On our side there has been disappointment over deficiencies stemming from Japan's persistent political weakness—notably her reluctance to assume reasonable defense responsibilities. There is accordingly no justification for placing all the responsibility on the U.S. for shortcomings in present relationships. Both sides have contributed, and both must contribute to the remedy if one is obtained."[6] Cultivating the sense of mutuality upon which the alliance was predicated required additional work.

The criticism that the United States took Japan for granted has a ring of truth to it. During the second half of the fifties, American attention to Japan was episodic and reactive. When Japanese imports made inroads into the U.S. market or an incident involving U.S. military forces such as the Girard case made for dramatic news copy, the spotlight's glare could be intense.[7] But the moment usually passed quickly. Business interest in Japan was negligible. Except for exporters of agricultural products and a few export-oriented or multinational firms, the Japanese market seemed unimportant.

Crisis elsewhere ensured that the Eisenhower administration did not focus its energy on a positive program for Japan (much less Japanese trade). The lengthy crisis in the Taiwan Straits, simultaneous crises over Suez and Hungary, decolonization, and the growing competition between the United States and the USSR in the Third World all drew official attention away from Japan. Even officials who dealt with economic policy paid less attention to Japan than before. The formation of the European Economic Community in 1957, the return of currency convertibility in Western Europe the next year, and the weakening U.S. balance-of-payments position late in the decade all commanded more attention from the Eisenhower administration.[8] Japan's recovery simply pushed Japanese affairs out of the administration's field of vision. Compared with crisis, stabilization and growth are humdrum affairs.

The Eisenhower administration viewed bilateral trade disputes in terms of their effect on the alliance and, to a lesser extent, the reciprocal trade program. Although administration officials attempted to avoid making concessions that harmed U.S. commercial interests, their first concerns were to maintain an orderly bilateral relationship and to preserve reciprocal trade. The Japanese government also appreciated the political dimension of trade friction, especially with regard to exports destined for the United States. On the question of liberalizing Japan's import trade, however, the economic bureaucrats had greater freedom to give priority to commercial interests.

One must not overstate the conflict between strategic and commercial priorities. Even if Americans had paid closer attention to Japan, they would still have encountered difficulty entering the Japanese market. Japan's economic planners used their control of foreign exchange allocations to promote favored industries and to limit imports to essential items.[9] The nation's unsteady foreign exchange position justified such restriction, and until 1959 such worries appeared fully warranted. The only industries sufficiently competitive in world markets to earn foreign exchange were the nation's light industries, and their products faced many protectionist barriers abroad. High-speed growth actually appeared to upset the balance. The balance-of-payments crisis of 1957 suggested that rapid expansion of the domestic economy caused an even faster rise in imports.[10] For very good economic and political reasons, then, neither the Japanese nor the U.S. government favored rapid liberalization of Japan's import trade.

The terribly unsettled condition of Japanese politics reduced American leverage in bilateral disputes over economic issues. After Prime Minister Yoshida's fall from power in 1954, conservative and socialist politicians gravitated toward two parties, the Japan Socialist Party (JSP) and the Liberal Democratic Party (LDP). The result was not a normal two-party system, however. The Socialists, who reunified in October 1955, rejected the American alliance and advocated neutrality in foreign affairs. Socialist politicians had opposed the security treaty in 1951, and various irritants in bilateral relations provided an ever renewable source of objections to the alliance. Among them were continued U.S. possession and administration of Okinawa, base "incidents" affecting the population near American military bases, and restrictions on trade with the PRC.[11] The LDP, formed in November 1955, held a parliamentary majority, but it was a party in name only, created to block the Socialists from gaining power. Factionalism and division within the new party simply replaced the debilitating factionalism among the conservative parties before the conservative merger.[12] The Eisenhower administration placed a high priority on revising the Security Treaty, and that was possible only if the LDP stayed in power.

The value U.S. leaders placed on the Cold War alliance and their fear of the Socialist alternative offered Japan's conservatives the perfect opportunity to extract maximum concessions, or to stand firm in the face of American demands if need be. Hatoyama, Ishibashi Tanzan, and especially Kishi Nobusuke all portrayed themselves as reliable partners of the United States who faced irresponsible opponents at home. They also did not hesitate to remind the Americans of the political upheaval likely to result if

Japan failed to sustain its economy.[13] Dulles summarized well American thinking when he told Prime Minister Hatoyama in 1956 that the United States "had made both a material and a moral investment in Japan."[14] It could not afford to let that investment fail.

The administration's greatest desire was to find a strong Japanese leader on whom it could rely, and whom it could support in an effort to create a strong pro-American government in Tokyo. Owing to their assertiveness vis-à-vis the United States and their apparently casual attitude toward balancing the budget, neither Hatoyama nor Ishibashi elicited enthusiasm in Washington. Kishi, by contrast, stood up strongly for the alliance. As a leading conservative politician who actively cultivated his own ties with U.S. officials, Kishi was bound to attract favorable American attention. Even before becoming prime minister, he impressed both Ambassador Douglas MacArthur II and Washington. The administration placed its bet on Kishi in February 1957, when he replaced Ishibashi (who retired because of ill health).

Despite the prime minister's high profile in government circles, there was no "Kishi boom" in Japan, as embassy officials noted with some concern.[15] Kishi's political base was shaky from the start because to many Japanese he was forever tainted by militarism. As a leading bureaucrat in the prewar Ministry of Commerce and Industry, he had served as an administrator in occupied Manchuria during the 1930s and rose to head the Ministry of Munitions, as the ministry was called during the war. Following Japan's defeat, Kishi was indicted (but never tried) as a Class A war criminal and purged from politics.

Kishi's political vulnerability and the United States' desire that he stay in power (at least until the two powers concluded a new security agreement) caused the United States to refrain from pressing as hard in economic disputes as it might have. Had Kishi been an advocate of liberalizing Japan's economy, this reluctance may not have made much difference. But Kishi was among the foremost advocates of the state-guided system that enabled the economic planners in Tokyo to wield the power they did.[16] These opposing currents in relations across the Pacific played themselves out most visibly in the wrangle over Japan's textile exports to the United States.

Competition in Cotton Textiles

The irony in the postwar conflict between the United States and Japan over cotton textiles is that it occurred when the industry in both countries was fast declining. Textile industries flourished in the initial stage of industrial development in both countries.[17] Although still important after the Second World War, the American textile industry as a whole had long since ceased to be a leading sector of the economy. The rise of heavy industries during the late nineteenth century and the higher-value-added manufacturing industries during the early twentieth produced new leaders. By the 1950s the rate of earnings of the textile industry was below the average for all manufacturing. As the Council on Foreign Economic Policy concluded in 1956, "This profit record is part of a long term decline in earnings which began in 1907 and has been reversed only in the two World War periods."[18] Producers of cotton and wool textile products faced a difficult future. Makers of man-made fibers such as rayon and nylon, however, were thriving.

Japan's cotton textile industry, by contrast, rose to its peak during the first half of the twentieth century. The ensuing competition between the United States and Japan, particularly during the 1930s, then, was the lens through which the American industry viewed Japan's reentry into the U.S. market during the fifties. At the beginning of World War I, the Japanese industry shifted toward the export of finished goods. The depressed conditions of Japan's economy during the 1920s weakened the industry, but grim prospects for the future served as a spur to action. The government launched a countrywide rationalization campaign consisting of worker training, upgrading of technology, and consolidation. By the early 1930s Japan was able to compete more effectively abroad, and it increased its share of the world market. The devaluation of the yen (in terms of the dollar) in 1931 further stimulated Japanese exports.[19]

The collapse of the export market for silk during the Great Depression caused a reversal in Japan's favorable trade balance with the United States. Japan's exports of cotton manufactures to the American market expanded dramatically: from $3 million in 1929 to $17 million in 1937. Cotton textiles represented less than 1 percent of all U.S. imports from Japan in the late twenties. In 1937 they amounted to 8.5 percent. Of total cotton manufactures imported, Japan's share rose accordingly to 29.8 percent. Total cotton textile imports still represented less than 3 percent of the quantity produced in the United States. Throughout the decade, the United States exported more cotton textiles than it imported. Thus, while Japanese cotton textile exports to the United States increased, there was no overwhelming export offensive.[20]

The U.S. textile industry nevertheless appealed to the Tariff Commission for protection. Japanese market presence was slight in aggregate terms. But it was highly concentrated. Japanese products did not compete in the market for high-quality goods. But they were very competitive at the lower end of the market. Japanese plain cotton cloth, cotton floor coverings, cotton hosiery, and velveteen and corduroy products all threatened to capture those segments of the market. This concentration, coupled with the psychological effect of the steep increase in Japanese imports from 1933 to 1935, provoked a stronger response than the aggregate statistics first suggest is warranted. In separate investigations the Tariff Commission recommended (or was about to recommend) duty increases or quotas on these products to prevent serious injury to domestic industry. Facing the prospect of severe or permanent retaliatory action, Japanese manufacturers agreed to restrict exports voluntarily.[21]

Whereas world war reversed temporarily the declining fortunes of America's textile industry, it devastated Japan's. Following the outbreak of war with China in 1937, Japan developed heavy industry at the expense of its light industries. Government administrators converted plants and equipment of industries in disfavor to other uses, or raided them for scrap.[22] The war also arrested the modernization of Japanese industries. Japan's postwar industry thus faced the twin challenge of rebuilding its production capacity at home and recapturing its markets abroad. Although SCAP encouraged the revival of textile production and Korean War spending temporarily expanded the dollar market for such manufactures, the industry never recovered its commanding prewar position. As in the United States, the leading sectors of Japan's postwar economy were in the higher-value-added industries.

Although in decline, Japan's light industries were still important in international trade. During the 1950s the products of Japan's leading industries were not competitive abroad. Because the products of light industry were competitive overseas, they earned the foreign exchange to buy the raw materials required by the steel, automotive, and other rising industries. In 1955 the Japanese government sought tariff concessions on textiles during the tariff negotiations with the United States.

The Department of State similarly favored opening markets for Japanese textiles. The Eisenhower administration was fully aware of how sensitive Americans were to the issue of Japanese imports. But expansion of Japan's foreign trade was impossible without making some concessions on textile items. In order to shore up support for the reciprocal trade act then under consideration, President Eisenhower intervened. In a letter to Republican congressman Joseph W. Martin, which Martin read to the House, Eisenhower assured the nation that no American industry would be placed in jeopardy by his administration of the reciprocal trade program.[23] The United States then granted tariff concessions on low-priced cotton cloth of low yarn count, cotton velveteens, cotton towels, gloves and mittens, and knit or crocheted cotton outerwear (polo, T, tennis, and sweat shirts).[24] No concession breached a peril point set by the Tariff Commission.

The resulting increase in Japanese fabric imports provoked a massive outcry from American textile mill owners and workers. Industrial associations had begun mobilizing the previous year to oppose renewal of the RTAA, GATT, and tariff negotiations with Japan. This high degree of political organization and the wide geographical distribution of the industry (across both the northeastern and southeastern states) made for unusually extensive protest. Again, the sudden increase in a few imported items rather than the total market presence of Japanese goods fueled the alarm. Cotton manufactures imported from Japan rose steeply at middecade: from $12 million in 1952, to $60 million in 1955, and then $84 million in 1956. After falling to $66 million in 1957, they stabilized at slightly over $70 million for the remainder of the decade.[25] The volume of domestic production of cotton manufactures was increasing, but imports were increasing slightly faster.[26]

The Tariff Commission and the State Department expected that expansion of the domestic market would allow all producers to continue to expand their sales. Japan's textile exports were concentrated in a few segments of the market. U.S. makers of plain cloth, women's blouses, cotton pillowcases, and velveteens were hard hit. Imports of Japanese-made cotton blouses, for example, jumped from 189,000 in 1954 to 2.8 million dozens in 1955.[27] Domestic producers had reason to seek protection from continued increases, and they applied for a duty increase under the RTAA escape clause.[28]

The protest against Japanese imports, however, went far beyond such limited appeals. Japan got the blame for the myriad difficulties plaguing the industry in the mid-1950s. Lester Martin, president of the Consolidated Textile Company, echoed a pervasive feeling when he said, "Japanese goods are cancer and they will kill the entire textile industry. They should be kept out of the U.S. market entirely."[29] The most sensitive and misunderstood issue concerned Japanese wage scales. Although it ignores the connection between wages and worker productivity, the argument that low wages abroad give foreign manufacturers an unfair advantage resonates with the public during hard times. In a January 1955 letter to Secretary of State Dulles, for example, the entire congressional delegation from the State of Maine urged that the department not grant any tariff concession on textiles to Japan.[30] The liquidation of eighty-four cotton and rayon plants in 1954 and 1955—closings that were associated with layoffs—seemed to confirm such claims.[31]

Members of Congress were quick to propose that the Tariff Commission investigate the danger Japanese goods posed to the industry.[32] In 1956 Congress considered two proposals to impose quotas on imports of cotton textiles from Japan.[33] Given other GATT members' invocation of Article 35, it seemed to lawmakers that the United States was doing more than its fair share to expand Japan's foreign trade.[34] The most extreme expressions of protest actually found their way into law. In early 1956 the states of South Carolina and Alabama both enacted statutes requiring stores selling Japanese goods to display the sign, "Japanese Textiles Sold Here."[35]

Japan's Voluntary Export Restrictions on Cotton Textiles

Well before Japanese cotton textile imports peaked in 1956, the Eisenhower administration understood the political sensitivity of liberalizing trade in textiles, however slightly. The executive decision to absorb more Japanese goods was firm, grounded in both the requirements of the alliance and the liberal economic order abroad that the administration was attempting to build. Retaliation against Japanese competition threatened far more than trade across the Pacific. The administration thus saw the protest of the cotton textile industry as a political problem requiring a political solution. This evaluation was very accurate. The eventual answer, namely voluntary export restriction by Japan, echoed the diplomacy of the 1930s and served as a prototype for many more such restrictions in future years.

Secretary of State Dulles's pragmatic attitude toward the Japanese textiles issue typified his sensitivity to the politics of foreign trade as well as his tactical flexibility.[36] If the cause of trade liberalization never inspired Dulles in the same manner as it did Cordell Hull, the secretary strongly supported reciprocal trade. He also opposed Tariff Commission recommendations and visibly protective measures that signaled closure of the American market. Although the details bored him, Dulles paid close attention to foreign economic policy when trade matters affected broader political or security concerns. In the row over cotton textiles he recognized that the twin challenge was to enable Japan to make a living while at the same time reassuring the domestic industry. He never seems to have doubted that a solution could be found.[37]

Anticipating outcry against imports from Japan, Dulles urged that Japanese exporters show restraint. Foreign producers had to be content with "reasonable access to the American market," he explained to Foreign Minister Shigemitsu Mamoru in late 1955. Although U.S. antitrust laws prohibited explicit agreements between representatives of industry, Dulles emphasized that "voluntary self-restraint is not illegal and can be very helpful." He added that "there will always be an imbalance in Japan's direct trade with the United States which would be made up by invisible earnings and earnings from three-cornered transactions." Although few predictions have been farther from the mark, the secretary's views reflected the conventional wisdom at the time.[38]

The fact of Japanese action to prevent flooding of the American market was more important to Dulles than the precise level of control. The steep rise in shipments of Japanese-made cotton cloth and women's blouses to the United States during the second half of 1955 provoked calls for restrictions. Fearing that persistence of the existing situation "might have disastrous results," the Japanese government restricted exports unilaterally in November. The Japanese government informed the State Department of these restrictions and explained that it was considering quotas on exports for 1956.[39]

In a long letter to Senator Margaret Chase Smith (R.-Maine), which she released to the press in early December, Dulles recounted his advice to the Japanese, and explained that Japan was in fact imposing quantitative controls on cotton textile exports to "allay the fears of our domestic producers." The secretary also reviewed the safeguards available to industry under the reciprocal trade program. He cautioned that legislatively imposed quotas would be "a serious blow" to the administration's trade program, to the U.S. effort to get other nations to lift their restrictions against American goods, to Japan's economy, and to American producers of cotton, wheat, rice, and other products purchased by Japan.[40] A few days later, Ambassador Iguchi Sadao expressed the Japanese government's appreciation for Secretary Dulles's letter and reassured the department that Japan had no desire "to kill the United States textile industry."[41]

The calls to restrict imports of Japanese textiles in 1956 surprised no one. But the depth and the extent of anti-Japanese sentiment clearly frustrated the Eisenhower administration, because the basic challenges facing the domestic industry had little to do with Japanese imports.[42] U.S. exports were four times greater than imports. Even the Tariff Commission, not known for being insensitive to the problems of domestic industry, concluded that

Japanese goods did not threaten most segments of the U.S. textile industry. The industry as a whole was in the process of adjusting to the return of a normal global economy. In addition, the New England industry continued to face competition from newer textile mills in the American South.

Although the Japanese often got the blame for the wave of mergers, plant closures, and layoffs within the textile industry, the causes were closer to home. There were over five thousand textile producing firms in the industry as a whole. Even the largest accounted for only 3 or 4 percent of the industry's total business. Consolidation was a sign that the industry was becoming more efficient and its mills more productive. Expenditures on new plant and equipment in the textile industry in 1955 totaled $331 million. The flip side of enhanced worker productivity, however, is displacement. As *U.S. News and World Report* noted, "[p]art of the reduction in textile jobs and many of the mill closings were due to the construction of new mills with more efficient equipment." The *Wall Street Journal* was less charitable, but no less accurate, when it reported that, "many mills are using the Japanese as whipping boys just because of poor business."[43] Tax considerations also encouraged the liquidation of aging plants.[44]

These explanations of the cotton textile industry's difficulties did little to silence the calls to restrict Japanese imports. The administration had to take the initiative or Congress would have retaliated. A more stringent Japanese voluntary export restraint (VER) recommended itself for several reasons, among them the unpalatability of the alternatives. A government-to-government agreement would also have set a dangerous precedent: "other industries which consider themselves injured by imports would reasonably expect to receive similar treatment."[45] A restrictive arrangement between American industry and Japanese industry was also a nonstarter: it would violate U.S. antitrust laws. A Japanese VER was the perfect solution. The United States could, as one advisor expressed the point, "acknowledge a Japanese note which unilaterally, as a matter of Japanese internal policy, stated that such export quotas were being established, such exchange not representing any agreement on our side."[46]

The sense that events could reel out of control pervaded official thinking. The passage of the discriminatory laws in South Carolina and Alabama put the administration on the defensive. Japan protested immediately, rightly arguing that the laws represented a clear violation of the FCN treaty of 1953. The prospect that Connecticut, Georgia, and Louisiana might enact similar statutes heightened official unease.[47] Secretary Dulles protested to the governors of the states in question, but repeal proved difficult. Insisting on the supremacy of federal over state law risked making a bad situation even worse. "States' rights" was a burning political issue in the South, intertwined as it was in the debate then raging over civil rights and the Supreme Court's recent rulings against racial segregation. The administration attempted to put the best face on things by promising action later and pointing to the fact that the laws were not being enforced.[48]

In April 1956 the Council on Foreign Economic Policy (CFEP) addressed the cotton textiles issue in detail. Council members agreed that, except for certain segments of the market, increased imports were not the cause of the U.S. industry's problems, and that no government action was likely to be of assistance. The council advised continuing to resist pressures for import restrictions. On the question of Japanese imports, CFEP endorsed Japanese voluntary export restraint.[49] The Department of State suggested informally to Minister Shima Shigenobu that public Japanese assurance of voluntary export control would assist the administration to head off more restrictive legislation in Congress. On 16 May the Japanese replied that their textile industry had placed limitations on cotton textile exports of 150 million yards of cotton cloth plus 2.5 million dozen blouses. Harold C. McClellan, assistant secretary of commerce for international affairs, then advised cotton textile industry leaders, Representative Joseph Martin, and several senators of the Japanese action. The story of the administration's approach soon leaked to the American press. Significantly, industry leaders were not satisfied with the levels of control proposed by the Japanese.[50]

Japanese patience wore thin in the face of U.S. pressure, particularly the state laws aimed at Japanese textiles. Discriminatory treaties and laws have always provoked a strong reaction in Japan, and the nation's greatest hope during the fifties was to rejoin the international community on the basis of equality. Japanese leaders thus raised the matter of the discriminatory laws at most high-level meetings.[51]

Several pending escape clause cases added to the unsettled atmosphere. Following an appeal, the commission began an investigation of velveteen fabrics in January 1956. It then took up investigations of cotton pillow cases and gingham in March and June respectively.[52] In an August meeting with department officials, Japanese representatives remarked that they had come to view the United States as gradually becoming a more protectionist country. Perhaps it was only a talking point, but they did drop Ambassador Haguiwara's name.[53] The president's imposition of a quota on certain woolen fabrics the next month lent plausibility to the claim. Japanese officials "did not fail to express wonder and disillusion," the U.S. Embassy reported in August, over a "trend in the world's richest and most prosperous market toward the belief that five per cent is the maximum amount of competition from foreign sources which can be tolerated."[54]

Japan's VER for 1957 took shape in this atmosphere. As Ambassador MacArthur later recalled, "it was about as voluntary as your doing something if you've got a pistol pointed at your head."[55] On 27 September the Japanese government announced plans to impose "adjustment measures" for exports to the United States in 1957 and beyond. The government promised to determine an "overall ceiling" on exports of cotton manufactures based on the level of trade in 1955. Ceilings on individual items would avoid "excessive concentration" in certain segments of the market.[56] Unacknowledged in the Japanese statement was the U.S. government's role in these negotiations. Administration attention to the matter was exhaustive. "More time of top-policy officials in the Departments of State, Commerce, and Agriculture, as well as members of the President's staff," one official recorded, "has been devoted to the cotton textiles situation than to almost any other recent economic matter."[57]

The administration held to a much stronger line in 1956 than the year before. It was under greater pressure, and more departments participated. Whereas Dulles and the Department of State tended to regard the peril-point and escape clauses as providing sufficient relief for industry, Commerce officials were closer to the industry and believed that it deserved more protection than it was receiving.[58]

The distance between the two nations' negotiating positions guaranteed that talks would be difficult. Japan proposed an overall ceiling of 270 million square yards (up significantly from the previous year) whereas the United States pressed for a limit of 220 million (the approximate level of trade). The subceilings to apply to specific types of finished goods and to forty-one categories of cloth proved to be equally difficult. Some American demands were severe (particularly the one on velveteens). Various subquotas were in markets where Japanese industry was not competitive. In the Japanese view, the United States was offering "a large number of fishing ponds in which there is no fish."[59]

Commerce officials were also unhappy. "In their plan for diversification," McClellan explained, "the Japanese have taken into account only those items exported to the United States in the past. Their idea of diversification has been to distribute within that list of categories only. From our viewpoint, this does not constitute true diversification." On 24 October the Tariff Commission submitted a unanimous finding that escape clause relief was warranted for producers of cotton velveteen fabrics. As a remedy, the commissioners recommended a duty increase on imports. The Japanese government had not accepted the U.S. terms in the negotiations, and McClellan (among others) favored approving the recommended increase unless a compromise could be found. The American Embassy in Tokyo, however, warned that Yukawa and other officials made clear that if the president were to accept the Tariff Commission recommendation on velveteens, the Japanese would terminate the negotiations on voluntary limitations.[60]

President Eisenhower delayed action on the Tariff Commission decision in order to buy time for the two sides to agree. The final arrangement was far more restrictive than the original Japanese offer. The two governments agreed on a compromise ceiling of 235 million square yards of cotton manufactures. The five-year Japanese program, announced on 16 January 1957, also restricted exports of sensitive items and provided for diversification across a wide range of products. Within a week President Eisenhower announced that in view of Japan's voluntary program to control its export of textiles, he had decided not to accept the Tariff Commission's recommendation with regard to cotton velveteens. Shortly afterward, the companies requesting investigation of ginghams requested that their application for escape clause relief be withdrawn.[61]

In one sense, Japan's export program calmed anxiety on both sides of the Pacific. By assuring the Japanese of continued access to the American market without sudden reprisal and guarding against the flood of imports that U.S. producers feared, the Japanese VER was a political success. It prevented the controversy from upsetting the consolidation of the emerging U.S.-led global economy. Yet the agreement carried a price. The protracted negotiations frayed nerves in government and business on both sides. Most important for the domestic textile industry, the Japanese VER did not provide significant relief. It did not fundamentally improve the industry's competitiveness. If the VER deflected Japanese exports to Southeast Asia, it nevertheless allowed newly industrializing economies such as Hong Kong to sell in the U.S. market and to acquire the share of the market that the Japanese would likely have gained. Japanese frustration with such an arrangement was understandable.[62]

Ending the "China Differential"

Despite resolution of the controversy over textiles, trade friction remained a troubling constant in the U.S.-Japanese relationship. In 1957 the most divisive issue was the question of trade with the PRC. Public sentiment in Japan was overwhelmingly critical of the U.S. insistence on restricting trade with the PRC, especially after relaxation of some controls on trade with the European Soviet bloc. Japan felt what Prime Minister Ishibashi Tanzan called "the squeeze" more acutely than the other allies.[63] President Eisenhower favored relaxing controls. But anti-Communist fever among the American people, the Congress, and the president's advisors pushed in the opposite direction.

The stakes seem unexpectedly small for an issue that consumed far more institutional energy over a longer period of time than even the textile controversy. A National Intelligence Estimate (NIE) of January 1955 estimated the annual loss to the PRC was $200 million, or an amount that would enable the Communist Chinese to increase their imports of capital goods by 50 percent without controls. It also doubted that maintaining existing controls "would produce any significant changes in the basic patterns of Sino-Soviet relationships or of Chinese foreign policy." The report concluded that "Sino-Japanese trade during the next few years will not in itself cause Japan to alter significantly its present orientation to the West barring a serious depression in the Free World accompanied by a drastic curtailment of Japanese trading opportunities."[64]

Trade with the PRC was such a sensitive domestic political issue, however, that the Eisenhower administration was unwilling to consent to eliminating the China differential. Eisenhower personally favored relaxation.[65] He wished to obtain agreement among the various departments concerned before embarking upon a new policy. Yet he did not expend the energy necessary to forge a new interdepartmental consensus. The China trade simply never ranked very high on the president's concerns.

Most of the executive branch was hostile to any relaxation of controls. State Department diplomats were sensitive to allied criticism of U.S. efforts to impose tighter controls on trade with the PRC. Majority opinion in the department nevertheless favored the unilateral U.S. embargo of the PRC.[66] Since the American embargo of the PRC closed the Chinese market to American firms, the Commerce Department argued consistently for holding the allies to the strictest controls possible. As chairman of CFEP, Joseph Dodge strongly supported maintaining the system, as did Harold Stassen, director of the Foreign Operations Administration, and Admiral Arthur W. Radford, chairman of the JCS. The attitude of the defense community as a whole had changed little since the Korean War. "Any delay in Soviet industrial expansion is important and valuable to U.S. security," one official wrote. "In fact, we feel that the situation is such to justify intensified, rather than relaxed, efforts along these lines." Although Senator McCarthy's influence had faded since 1954, congressional opinion also remained hostile to change.[67]

As the voice of American policy to allied governments and the most prominent figure in the Eisenhower administration besides the president himself, Secretary Dulles played a pivotal role in policy on trade with China. By inclination, Dulles was unsympathetic to making unilateral concession to the Communist bloc. He could not help but notice domestic pressures on the department to maintain the China differential. Yet the secretary was also aware of allied opinion.[68]

Dulles responded to these conflicting pressures with an elaborate balancing act. He played for time while talking down the likely benefit of eliminating the China differential. Trade with China, he explained to Shigemitsu in 1955, "was more of a psychological than an economic factor" in Japan's foreign relations. Japan had never enjoyed extensive trade with China proper, and "in the main China is a poor area and does not have much to export." Other countries that had tried to trade with the Chinese Communists simply did not get much in return, even for strategic goods. He doubted that a change in the control lists "would have great economic results." "Sooner or later some revision of the export list is inevitable," he conceded, "but the time has not yet come."[69]

Without denying the accuracy of the secretary's prediction, the policy's bitter harvest reveals it to have been one of his—and the administration's—least impressive performances. To the Japanese, particularly the public, the American position was self-contradictory. It failed to explain why, if relaxing controls was unlikely to have great effect, the United States should not eliminate the China differential. American calls to maintain the pressure on the Communist Chinese for their aggressive intentions and for its support of revolutionaries in the region did not persuade the unconvinced.

Whereas the American public embraced the logic of withholding concessions to the Communist Chinese so as not to reward aggression, the Japanese did not fear the Chinese as they did the Soviets. In one sense China represented a great Asian nation, to which Japanese civilization owed a great cultural debt. Yet since the mainland economy was essentially preindustrial, Japanese romanticism for China was mixed with disdain. Earlier optimism in Japanese business circles about the prospect for trade with the mainland was fading somewhat. But American pressure on Japan reinforced the political sensitivity of the issue. Precisely because the United

States opposed a relaxation of controls, the issue seemed a test of whether Japan had really regained its independence.[70]

U.S. reluctance to compromise on the China trade issue reveals the depth of official anxiety about the fragility of the anti-Communist front in Asia. If the public and the Congress were unaware of the complete picture, the administration had information that should have provided the basis for more confidence. Dulles was right when he said not to expect much increase in trade if controls were lifted. Part of the reason why the European allies were pressing so hard on the issue of the China differential in 1957 was their failure to expand trade with the autarkic European Soviet bloc. In consenting to the relaxation of controls on trade with the USSR and its European satellites in 1954, the Eisenhower administration was able to ease interallied friction without losing the substance of the strategic issue. In holding firm on trade with the PRC, however, the administration made the United States the target of allied frustration and criticism.[71]

To an extent badly underestimated at the time, the Chinese Communists' economic policy undermined any prospect of flourishing external trade. Applying the logic of popular political revolution to economic development (as Mao Zedong's Great Leap Forward did) isolated the Chinese economy from the world. Contrary to expectations, attempting to industrialize the economy in a single bound squandered the gains of previous years, destabilized the nation's foreign trade, and sacrificed thirty million Chinese lives or more in perhaps the greatest man-made famine in history.[72]

Although both Hatoyama and Ishibashi raised the issue of trade with China, the climax came during Kishi's first year as prime minister. Rather than defy the United States alone, Prime Minister Kishi followed the lead of the United Kingdom. Parliamentary criticism of the China differential in Britain was intense. Prime Minister Harold Macmillan's preference was to work out a compromise with the Eisenhower administration regarding controls on about three hundred items. The British wished to trade in certain potentially high volume items including locomotives, diesel engines, and surveying instruments.[73]

Neither Eisenhower nor Dulles was willing to spend the political capital necessary to win bureaucratic approval of a compromise.[74] After several unsuccessful attempts to reach bilateral agreement, Prime Minister Macmillan announced Britain's unilateral decision to abolish the China differential on 29 May.[75] Shortly before the announcement, Dulles wrote to Eisenhower that, "from the standpoint of our Congressional relations and probably from the standpoint of our relations with such anti-Communist allies" as Taiwan and South Korea, the best course would be to allow the British and the Japanese to "go it alone." He was concerned, however, that if the allies started "going it alone" on that issue, "we cannot be sure that they will stop with the present measures."[76]

The fear was misplaced. Indeed, the outcome of this interallied conflict proved unexpectedly disappointing for the advocates of closer Sino-Japanese ties. Prime Minister Kishi was scheduled to visit Washington in June. He held off making any move before this state visit, but he did raise the subject in his talks with President Eisenhower. Although Eisenhower cautioned against expecting any overall gain in trade, he was very conciliatory. "We understand," he said, that "Japan must keep its competitive position vis-à-vis England. We appreciate Japan's sticking with us . . . and we recognize her needs now."[77] Effective 30 July, Japan aligned its controls with those for the other countries in the Communist bloc. The third Sino-Japanese trade agreement had expired in May 1957, but Japanese representatives and the PRC did not reach a new accord until March 1958. At the urging of interests in both countries, Sino-Japanese trade for the first quarter of 1958 rose dramatically. Japanese exports reached $27.2 million and imports were $22.5 million (4.5 and 3.5 percent of Japan's total world trade respectively).[78]

The politics of diplomatic recognition, however, wrecked commercial relations. A memorandum attached to the fourth Sino-Japanese trade agreement allowed the PRC to fly its flag over trade mission buildings, which seemed to observers to imply de facto recognition. The memo did not in fact enjoy the approval of either Prime Minister Kishi or the National Diet. Taiwan's reaction was immediate. In the words of Chiang Kai-shek, "If their flag goes up, mine comes down." Financial and industrial leaders were reluctant to abandon Japan's lucrative trade with Taiwan (about $85 million annually). At the same time Secretary Dulles anxiously attempted to restrain Chiang from severing ties with Japan.[79] Given Kishi's desire to maintain close relations with the United States, his effort to maintain Japan's policy of separating trade and politics in dealing with Beijing was unsurprising. Ambassador MacArthur reported that Kishi and his government could not upset the fourth private trade agreement without leading to "very substantial gains for [the] Socialists [in the upcoming elections] which would, they believe, spell [the] end of [the] Kishi Government."[80] No law could be invoked, however, to prevent the Communist Chinese in

Japan from actually hoisting their flag. Kishi also made clear to the United States that he was in communication with the Republic of China with an eye to reach a compromise of some sort.[81]

Taipei's insistence on the flag issue was consuming sufficient energy during the spring of 1958 to strain relations between the United States, Japan, and the Republic of China when Chinese Communist intransigence came to the rescue. The PRC simply rejected the policy of the Kishi government in April. The next month, following an incident in Nagasaki, where a Japanese demonstrator tore town the Chinese Communist flag at an exhibit of international postage stamps, the PRC government abrogated the trade agreement and suspended all trade with Japan. This blatant attempt to force political concessions out of the Kishi government failed. Japanese pressure groups and public opinion continued to favor opening relations with the PRC, but the American Embassy correctly reported that the whole affair "strengthened the hand of opponents of trade with the mainland and instilled the business and trading world with a new spirit of caution and hesitation."[82] The standoff continued through the crisis over revision of the security treaty with the United States in 1960. Not until the early sixties did Japan and the PRC resume trade in considerable volume.

The American Market: Growing Access and Continued Friction

Japan's exports to the United States expanded rapidly during the years 1957–60, as the nation's industries vigorously pushed sales to the American market. Spectacular growth in 1959, a rise of 52 percent over the previous year, confirmed the reorientation of Japan's foreign trade begun earlier in the decade. Whereas the share of Japan's exports to Western countries stood at 31 percent in 1954, it reached 56 percent in 1959.[83] This expanding commerce consolidated the bilateral axis across the Pacific as the Eisenhower administration intended. But it also heightened trade friction. American producers sometimes felt the effect of Japanese competition quite suddenly, and they were quick to protest. Cold warriors did not simply open the American market to Japanese goods. Japanese exporters continued to face trade barriers and the threat of retaliation. The VER remained an integral part of Japanese foreign economic policy.[84]

Making possible Japan's growing presence in the American market was the Eisenhower administration's success at redeeming the U.S. commitment to reciprocal trade. The duration of the 1958 trade act was for four years, the longest period of renewal to date in the history of the program. Steering the legislation through Congress required a concerted effort on the part of the Eisenhower administration and the Democratic leadership, particularly Senate Majority Leader Johnson (Tex.) and House Ways and Means Committee Chairman Wilbur Mills (Ark.).[85] Since the trade negotiations with Japan were not pending in the same way as during the three previous renewals, Japanese trade did not figure directly in the politics of renewal in 1958.

Having barely survived the previous fights over reciprocal trade in Congress, the administration prepared more carefully than before to sell the program on Capitol Hill. In the course of the administration's unsuccessful effort to win support for the Organization for Trade Cooperation in 1957, both Secretary of State Dulles and Secretary of Commerce Weeks learned firsthand just how unpopular the administration's trade policy was among lawmakers. Representative Simpson spoke for many when he said the State Department had "too large a voice" in the program, and that the president took the advice of the Tariff Commission too lightly. Dulles was "deeply disappointed" that exporters (whose total volume of trade reached four times the proportion of dutiable imports) "were not more vocal in supporting the RTAA."[86]

Consultation with lawmakers encouraged both willingness to compromise on some points of the protectionists' agenda, and reinforced the executive branch's commitment to organizing for victory in 1958. Momentum behind the administration's effort flowed from many quarters. In January Henry Cabot Lodge, U.S. Representative to the United Nations, urged that the president appoint a manager having "overall authority" for the effort.[87] The administration was already moving forward. A trade policy committee under the Department of Commerce took responsibility for advising the president on the Trade Agreements Act. Neither Eisenhower nor the Department of State wished to grant Commerce blanket authority over trade policy, however. Secretary Weeks enjoyed little clout on Capitol Hill. Dulles advocated renewal with vigor, both before Congress and in his public addresses. But he left the day-to-day management to his subordinates. Thus, Assistant Secretary of Commerce Henry Kearns, Under Secretary of State Christian Herter, and Deputy Under Secretary of State for Economic Affairs C. Douglas Dillon attended to most of the consultations with lawmakers.[88]

In his State of the Union Address, President Eisenhower proposed extending the Trade Agreements Act with broader negotiating authority for five years. He asked for authority to reduce tariffs 25 percent over that

Growth and Friction 219

period.[89] Congress delivered renewal for four years with authority to cut tariffs 20 percent, effective no later than four years after the bill expired in 1962. The powers of the Tariff Commission figured prominently in congressional debate. The most controversial proposal was an amendment sponsored by Senator Robert Kerr (D.-Okla.). Proposed earlier by Senator Strom Thurmond (D.-S.C.), the measure provided that the president would have only thirty days to accept a Tariff Commission recommendation to take protective action. In case the president refused to accept a recommendation to raise duties or to impose import quotas, it would take effect automatically after ninety days unless the president secured a majority vote in both houses of Congress. Another proposal in the House provided more simply for a congressional override of a presidential decision to disregard Tariff Commission recommendations.

The White House and the Democratic leadership predictably opposed both amendments. Owing to the legislative skill of Lyndon Johnson, the Kerr-Thurmond amendment failed, but several restrictions did find their way into the 1958 law. Among these were the proposal allowing Congress to override presidential action on Tariff Commission recommendations, an increase in the time allowed for the commission to investigate peril-point cases (from 120 days to 180 days), a reduction in the duration of escape clause reviews (from nine months to six months), and authorization for the president to restrict imports deemed to be threatening national security.[90]

Although the U.S. recession in 1958 dampened expectations on both sides of the Pacific that year, the Department of State recognized that with recovery in 1959 a firm foundation for expanded Japanese-U.S. trade was in place. Speaking before the American Chamber of Commerce of Japan in Tokyo, Ben H. Thibodeaux, Waring's successor as the U.S. Embassy's Minister for Economic Affairs, expressed the "economic optimism" with which both nations entered the new year. He outlined the possibilities for expanded cooperation between the two governments and business communities in trade, tourism, technology, and investment. Pointing to the upward movement of most sectors of the economy, Thibodeaux confidently predicted that 1959 would be "significantly better than last year." The Japanese press reported Thibodeaux's address widely and favorably.[91]

Leading Japanese industrialists also called attention to the importance of the bilateral relationship. Keidanren President Ishizaka Taizō, an outspoken advocate of rearmament and the American alliance, echoed Thibodeaux's call for expanded trade with the United States. Pointing to the limited prospects for growth in trade with Southeast Asia, he suggested that, "Japan must turn more and more to the export of high quality products for the American and European markets to support her economy." Nisshō president Adachi Tadashi also urged that Japanese manufacturers concentrate on the American market. "From the viewpoints of price and quality," he explained, "it is hardly possible for Japan to switch for her raw materials needs from the United States to another area of supply." Japan's trade with the United States, however, remained badly unbalanced. Like Ishizaka, Adachi identified exports to the U.S. market as the solution to this problem.[92]

Simply increasing exports as much as possible was a formula for irritating the competing industries in the United States, particularly if the price dropped below a "reasonable level." Adachi's analysis of this problem summarizes well the emerging conventional wisdom: "In the face of this situation, Japanese trade and industry circles must try to develop new markets in the United States by studying closely American market trends, and by creating new products. They must also raise the quality and improve the design of their conventional export goods. Through cooperation among themselves and with the collaboration of American importers they must try to achieve a gradual and steady increase in their exports to the United States."[93] Far more than the advantages derived from cheap labor or individual tariff concessions, innovation and high product quality enabled Japan to succeed in the American market.

Such calls for improving the quality of Japan's exports were not new in 1959. Later generations of Americans and Japanese may cringe when they read of Secretary Dulles's blunt comments to Prime Minister Yoshida that Japanese manufacturers "don't make the things we want." On one occasion in 1954, Dulles even showed Yoshida a "brightly patterned flannel shirt of cheap material made in Japan" copying better-quality American-made cloth. Adding that "an influential senator" had discussed the matter with him, the secretary pointedly remarked that it was "one of the reasons Japanese have difficulty expanding their trade."[94] However uncharitable, Dulles's assessment at the time was in large measure correct. During lengthy talks with top Eisenhower administration officials in 1953, Ikeda Hayato admitted as much. One of the chief merits of the prewar China market, he explained, was that it absorbed the low-quality manufactures that Japan could not export to the West.[95] Given the terribly limited opportunity for trade with the PRC after the war, Japanese industry faced the challenge of bringing the quality of its products up to international standards, or not competing at all. Japanese industrialists took seriously the issue of product quality. The shipment of only a few shoddy goods was sufficient to tarnish the image of all Japanese manufactures.

In 1957 the Japanese National Diet enacted the Export Inspection Law. It provided the standards to be met before government approval was to be granted to an inspection firm. It specified clearly what constituted "inspection approval" of a product, imposing penalties for violation of the law. It created the administrative apparatus (the Export Inspection Council within MITI). In passing and enforcing the law, the Japanese government took a major step toward what one observer called "a really effective export inspection system." The law shifted responsibility for inspection from manufacturers to independent authorities at various phases of the production process, and institutionalized the principle that the purpose of inspection was to protect the buyer (as opposed to facilitating the export of substandard goods). Another consequence of the law was to reinforce the power of the Tokyo bureaucrats responsible for industrial policy.[96]

Japan's export growth in 1959 bore out Thibodeaux's optimistic prediction at the beginning of the year. Exports of consumer goods registered the most dramatic growth that year. Products catering chiefly to the U.S. market such as garments, sewing machines, and toys accounted for most of the overall increase. Exports of transistor radio sets in 1959, officially classified as machinery, rose even more precipitously ($100 million, at 2.06 million sets up from 640,000 in 1957). The sectoral shift in the economy from labor-intensive to higher-value-added industries was also evident in the dynamism of the export trade of Japan's metal goods, chemicals, and other heavy industries.[97] Numerous sectors remained inefficient by international standards, but recent advances exceeded all expectations and provided the foundation for continued high-speed growth.

If American consumers welcomed Japan's growing presence in the U.S. market, certain industries voiced their protest. The result was a persistent undercurrent of friction in commercial relations. As before, attention on both sides of the Pacific focused on the Tariff Commission's investigations. In 1957 the Stainless Steel Flatware Manufacturers Association of Englishtown, New Jersey, appealed to the commission for escape clause relief. The same year associations representing the manufacturers of umbrella frames and clinical thermometers also filed escape clause applications. The Tariff Commission completed all three investigations the following year.[98]

The immediate cause of the American industry's discontent was a sudden and precipitous increase in Japanese shipments. Again the Japanese government moved to restrict the exports in question before the Tariff Commission completed its investigation. The most sensitive item was cutlery. Japanese exports of stainless steel flatware to the United States expanded at an annual rate of 200 percent from 1952 to 1956, rising from about $555,000 to $5.6 million (approximately 5.5 million dozens). Although consumption in 1958 dipped slightly, to 22.8 million dozens, the high U.S. birthrate and the shift away from silver-plate tableware promised to fuel continued high demand in the future.[99] The same pattern was even more pronounced in the case of umbrella frames.[100]

On 10 January 1958 the Tariff Commission submitted its report on flatware, finding unanimously that flatware imports were causing injury to the domestic industry. Three commissioners urged the president to withdraw the tariff concessions (granted in GATT negotiations) on flatware valued at less than three dollars per dozen pieces. The other three commissioners urged withdrawal of the concessions on all such items regardless of value. Neither recommendation was to apply to cutlery over ten inches in length, however. Four days later the commission released its report on umbrella frames, finding (with two commissioners dissenting) that the domestic industry deserved escape clause relief. The next month the commission found (with two commissioners dissenting) that escape clause relief was warranted for domestic makers of clinical thermometers.[101]

The geographical concentration of the Japanese industry magnified the political concern over these Tariff Commission recommendations far beyond their actual economic significance. The makers of umbrella frames for the U.S. market were located almost exclusively in Osaka, and producers of stainless steel flatware were concentrated in the city of Tsubame, Niigata Prefecture. Although the Osaka economy was highly diversified, the population in and around Tsubame was dependent upon the export-oriented cutlery industry (about fifty thousand people were affected). For this reason, community and industry leaders were able to rally national attention to their cause, and developments relating to the Tariff Commission's investigation of the matter were headline news in Japan. Even before the commission submitted its report, the government of Japan both informed the Department of State that it began restricting exports in October and proposed to limit exports of flatware for 1958 to the 1957 level (approximately 5.9 million dozens). Once the commission's recommendations were released, representatives from the Japanese industry, political leaders in Tsubame City and Niigata Prefecture, and Diet members took Japan's case to the U.S. Embassy. The mayor of Tsubame even led a ten-member delegation to Washington. Representatives emphasized Japanese willingness to unilaterally impose quotas.[102]

Owing to the simultaneous spread of Japanese protest against the American alliance, this trade friction alarmed political officials who did not normally deal with economic affairs. Ambassador MacArthur stated the argument most clearly. Starting from the premise that "Japan must trade or die," he explained that "disillusion as to U.S. trade policy resulting from its restrictive action will certainly start many people in Japan, including pro-American elements, quietly to start taking a really hard new look at whether close association with us pays off in terms of Japan's own vital self-interest. Restrictions will also give aid and comfort to those forces pressing for indiscriminate trade with Communist China and [the] Soviet Union. [The] ability of our friends in Japan (whom we will most certainly lose over [a] period of time if we start down the restrictionist path) to defend close association with us will diminish with every instance of new restrictions on Japanese imports."[103] Presidents do not always hear, or take seriously when they do hear, the opinions of their ambassadors. One of the qualities that recommended MacArthur to the Japanese, however, was his access to the upper reaches of the Eisenhower administration.[104]

Word of the U.S. Embassy's concern carried weight in Washington. The United States Information Agency director warned Gabriel Hauge, for example, that implementing the Tariff Commission recommendations on flatware would "change the political complexion of Niigata Prefecture from Conservative to socialist overnight." Echoing MacArthur's words, the director emphasized that "U.S. restrictions on Japanese trade will lead many Japanese leaders, even our best friends, to begin looking elsewhere than to the U.S. for Japan's best interest. No amount of exhortation and explanation by U.S. representatives in Japan will be able to reverse this trend in the face of actual restrictions imposed by the U.S."[105]

Japanese officials played on this anxiety. Ambassador Asakai Koichirō drew Under Secretary Dillon's attention to the "cumulative adverse political effect in Japan" of trade restrictions. He emphasized that the items under investigation by the Tariff Commission "were the products of small business in Japan and in each case the industry was dramatically affected." He added that "the owners and workers of small businesses were among those who strongly supported a conservative Japanese government and . . . not Leftists as was the case of some of the workers in large industries in Japan."[106]

Eisenhower pursued a middle course between the options before him.

The administration's highest priority in the trade field in 1958 was renewal of the reciprocal trade act. Given his record on escape clause cases, Eisenhower could not have easily rejected all three on political grounds alone. The Department of State pressed the Japanese government to restrict further flatware exports, lowering them from the 1957 level of 5.9 million dozens to the 1956 level of 5.5 million dozens.[107] On 7 March Eisenhower announced that, in view of Japan's decision in February to limit exports, he was deferring action on the report. Serious questions existed about the statistics used by the commission, and the president asked for a supplemental investigation of the experience of the industry in 1958. The next month Eisenhower accepted the commission recommendation on clinical thermometers, even though the Japanese had put the item under an export licensing system to control exports.[108]

The case for relief for makers of umbrella frames was the weakest of the three. Eisenhower asked for a supplemental report on the industry's experience through 31 March 1958, which the commission completed in August. This request conveniently bought time while Congress considered the reciprocal trade bill. On 30 September, he rejected the commission recommendation on umbrella frames without event.[109]

American concern over Japanese imports did not dissipate completely in 1958. The flatware case continued to resonate. The Tariff Commission's supplemental report in 1959 on flatware imports again found unanimously that, despite the Japanese VER on cutlery exports, the domestic industry was sustaining serious injury. On 20 October the president established a tariff quota on stainless steel flatware.[110] Flatware, however, was the exception that proved the rule. By employing quantitative restrictions in various forms, the Eisenhower administration successfully deflected most of the pressure for restrictions on Japanese imports. As Japan's foreign trade boomed toward the end of Eisenhower's second term, the greatest trade friction concerned the Japanese market.

Japan's Import Trade: Expansion and Restrictions

If the Japanese government and the nation's industries sought out foreign markets with vigor, they protected the home market with equal zeal. Because Japan ran a trade deficit until the end of the decade, the U.S. government acquiesced in Japan's many import restrictions. The most important method consisted of reserving allocations of foreign exchange for imports of raw materials, foodstuffs, and other commodities considered essential to the economy. American exporters rightly suspected that the economic planners were using these controls to protect various sectors of the economy (by not allocating foreign exchange for purchase of competing foreign goods).[111]

As long as Japan's balance-of-payments position remained unstable, however, U.S. officials had few levers at their disposal to force a change in policy. The primary options, namely consultation and exhortation, yielded little. Recognizing the discriminatory effect of restricting "luxury" items, department officials took up the matter during the eleventh session of GATT in Geneva (October–November 1956). The problem of dollar-area import restriction was actually widespread. During the session U.S. delegates carried out bilateral consultations with delegates from thirteen countries, including Japan.

Specific items at issue included Japanese restrictions on imports of fountain pens and television receivers. The U.S. participants reported that the meetings with the Japanese "were held in an informal, friendly, and cooperative manner," and both countries agreed to follow up on the issues discussed. In reality, the talks were more significant for revealing the gulf between the two sides. Japanese import statistics revealed a steady decline in the import of both items, even though the nation's balance-of-payments position was improving. The inescapable conclusion was that the government was using the foreign exchange allocation system for protective purposes. Japanese delegates contended that the items were "luxuries" and that domestic industry was able to supply the market. Hence, there was no need to allocate foreign exchange for their purchase.[112]

In July 1957, the U.S. Embassy in Tokyo compiled a detailed study of Japan's balance-of-payments position and import restrictions. It laid stress on the "incidental protective aspects" of Japanese import restrictions. Items from U.S. suppliers experiencing such discriminatory treatment included passenger automobiles, television sets, writing implements, and lemons. The study noted that the Japanese government had been unresponsive to repeated representations for liberalization but cautioned that change was not likely in the near future owing to Japan's deteriorating foreign exchange position that year.[113]

Two developments in 1958 combined to intensify demands on Japan to remove its discriminatory import restrictions. The most obvious was the remarkable growth of Japan's export trade—and corresponding amelioration of the nation's balance of payments—that year. It was finally possible to press forcefully without jeopardizing Japan's solvency. In Japanese eyes, the return of currency convertibility in Western Europe late in the year was probably more significant. The European nations' move drew attention to Japan's restrictions and placed the government under pressure to respond.

The Japanese government announced a series of countermeasures in early 1959. Neither the economic planners nor industrial circles were enthusiastic about actually liberalizing the nation's import trade. The most telling proof of resistance was the government's failure to expand significantly the scope of its automatic approval system. The government issued import licenses under two formulas: the foreign fund allocation system and the automatic approval system. Under the former system the government made foreign exchange allocations individually by item and currency in the compilation of the import currency budget. The opportunities this process afforded to protect favored sectors of the economy were legion. The total amount of foreign currency for imports by automatic approval was set in the budget. Imports were approved automatically upon application by the government within the frame of this total allocation. The test of whether the Japanese government was following through on promises to liberalize its import trade was whether it would move items from the foreign fund allocation system to the automatic approval system. During the first half of 1959, such transfers were limited to items having virtually no repercussions on domestic industries.

In July the Eisenhower administration began to press hard for the relaxation of restrictions. Ambassador MacArthur took the U.S. case to MITI Minister Ikeda, Finance Minister Satō Eisaku, and Foreign Minister Fujiyama Aiichirō. Although these conversations did address some individual problems, they mostly revolved around the theme that trade is a two-way street. MacArthur cautioned that Japan must not expand its exports to the United States too precipitously, that orderly growth over the long term was Japan's best guarantee of prosperity. Similarly, he made clear how Japanese import restrictions gave ammunition to the forces in the United States most eager to retaliate against Japanese goods. MacArthur emphasized that the two countries could not let friction over the little things interfere with cooperation on the big things.[114]

The Department of State planned to address the problem in detail at the fifteenth GATT session in the fall of 1959. The American Embassy in Tokyo urged that the United States give priority to pressing for an end to Japanese discrimination against ten commodities. Among them were beef tallow, soybeans, and copper alloy scrap. Embassy officials documented additional discrimination in the import of goods under the fund allocation system. They also took up the familiar cases of discriminatory treatment on certain items, the effect being to exclude them or reduce their share of the Japanese market. This list also included motorcycles, cotton, and motion picture films. In the period since 1957, Japan's bureaucrats had not been completely unresponsive to American demands. But liberalization was greatest on primary products such as raisins, lemons, and cheese.[115]

On the eve of the GATT session the Eisenhower administration impressed upon the Japanese government the need to act. In September, Finance Minister Satō traveled to Washington and met with Secretary of State Herter. The following month Under Secretary Dillon discussed the issue in separate meetings with Kishi and Satō. The administration's first concerns were understandably the conclusion of a new security treaty and completion of the many related arrangements. Kishi's plan to travel to the United States to sign the treaty and the possibility of Eisenhower visiting Japan underscored the attention each government was paying to the matter of strengthening bilateral ties.[116]

Unusually, this attention to security relations accentuated the pressure on the Japanese government to make concessions on trade. Because Kishi faced both an opposition hostile to concluding a treaty at all and opportunistic elements within his own party, he could not afford needless disagreements with the United States. The recent surge in Japanese exports, however, invited attention to Japan's import restrictions. During their October meeting with Kishi, Dillon and MacArthur made unmistakably clear that unless Japan made visible progress toward removing restrictions on dollar trade by the spring of 1960, the U.S. Congress was certain to retaliate. "Once restrictions are imposed," MacArthur emphasized, "they are difficult to modify." Dillon asked Kishi to have his people attend to the matter. He added that such action was in fact part of the broader U.S. effort to liberalize trade. One of the items the United States intended to take up at the GATT session was the removal of Article 35 restrictions on Japanese trade.[117]

Japan inadvertently intensified both foreign and domestic attention on its web of import restrictions by hosting the fifteenth session of GATT in the fall of 1959.[118] The Japanese government hoped that bringing the other delegates to Tokyo would impress upon them Japan's special economic problems and allay fears of low-wage competition from Japan. The larger goal was of course the removal of the trade barriers created by GATT members' resort to Article 35. The immediate effect, however, was to heighten domestic interest in GATT issues. Extensive press coverage made the session a headline item. Analysis of the history of GATT and its objectives of expanding world trade placed Japan's own restrictions in an unfavorable light. The Japanese government's call for a cautious and partial liberalization attracted little support and drew widespread criticism. Among the critics were most influential business groups. Although the enthusiasm for relaxation of restrictions varied, calls for liberalization dominated public discussion of the issue. Of the business organizations, the most forceful advocate for change was the Japan Management Association. Not least among the concerns of business interests was the role of import controls in elevating the power of central government bureaucrats.[119]

Rather than being able to assume the offensive in pressing for repeal of Article 35, Japan found itself the target of criticism demanding import liberalization.[120] The United States pressed for abolition of discrimination against imports from the dollar area. U.S. officials criticized Japan specifically for discrimination against the ten items on the automatic approval list. Finally, U.S. and Western European representatives pressed for a special committee to study the problem of "market disruption." The aim was to find a means of alleviating the effects of sharp increases in imports over a brief period of time in established markets while continuing to provide for a steady expansion of trade. Specific discussion drew attention to Japan.[121]

The Kishi government moved to liberalize Japan's import trade on 11 November. The first announcement detailed several changes. Of the restrictions affecting the ten "discriminated imports" on the automatic approval list, those on lauan, copper alloy scrap, gypsum, and abaca were lifted. Further, eighty goods were added to the automatic approval list, and a separate automatic allocation system was established for the import of parts of machinery (forty-eight items) and consumer goods (thirty-four items). The government expanded global allocation (as opposed to procurement by means of bilateral agreement) of items such as raisins. New import frames for items previously unrecognized (such as fountain pens) were to be established. Subsequent moves expanded on these measures and removed the remaining restrictions on the ten "discriminated items."[122]

The liberalization rate for Japan's import trade rose from 41 percent in April 1960 to 65 percent by July 1961. Restrictions on items competing with favored industries (such as automobiles) remained in place. Yet Japan's import of manufactured items rose considerably during the period. Imports of machinery rose 25 percent from fiscal year 1959 to 1960. The 69 percent increase over two years in imports of consumer goods such as textiles, pharmaceuticals, and sundries was even greater.[123] Foreign pressure on the Japanese government had its greatest effect when powerful forces within Japan desired similar action. Domestic enthusiasm for liberalization reached a peak in late 1959 and early 1960. The return of currency convertibility in Europe provoked concern that, if Japan did not follow along, the nation risked being left behind. Later, as Japan's economy continued to boom, Japanese confidence in its own distinctive system was visibly stronger. If Japan's import market was fast opening, the scope of the liberalization demonstrated that the Japanese economy was not simply becoming more like that of the United States. Liberalization reflected instead the mercantilistic priorities of Japan's economic planners and business leaders.

Conclusion

The years from 1955 to 1960 represent a more significant period in the history of U.S.-Japanese trade relations than is usually recognized. Defining features of the bilateral economic relationship became firmly established. The U.S. desire to consolidate the Cold War alliance provided Japan the opportunity to crack the lucrative American market, and Japanese industries seized the moment. As a result of the growth in U.S.-Japanese trade, the differences between the American and Japanese varieties of capitalism became more visible. Although this clash represents an important element in the bilateral relationship, the growing interdependence between Japan and the United States militated against the outbreak of uncontained rivalry.

Because Japanese goods were directly competitive with American manufactures, an immediate consequence of Japan's growing presence in the U.S. market was trade friction. Japanese imports created controversy in part because they awakened protectionist sentiment in the United States. Yet Japan also bears a measure of responsibility for this friction. The tendency to target certain segments of the American market provided an obvious focus for economic grievances and political protest, both against Japanese goods and against liberal trade in general.

Their motives differed, but both governments intervened in the market to manage bilateral trade. They preempted significant retaliation against Japan. The resort to "voluntary" export restrictions arose as a pragmatic solution to highly visible political problems like the dispute over textiles, and it set an important precedent for the future. If such arrangements restored political calm in times of trade friction, they were less effective at alleviating the difficulties of domestic industry, in part because those difficulties were often the result of other factors.

Japan was hardly a passive victim of trade discrimination. To a much greater degree than U.S. officials expected when Japan regained its independence, Japanese economic planners zealously protected favored industries from import competition. The nation's precarious balance-of-payments position afforded the perfect cover for such policies until the decade's end. As in disputes over investment, American leverage was limited. The higher visibility of trade issues and the pressures within Japan itself for liberalization nevertheless led to change. Yet liberalization of the nation's import trade did not fundamentally alter the character of Japan's postwar economy. Japanese officials and business interests remained committed to developing favored industries such as automobiles and consumer electronics as they geared up to compete in foreign markets.

EPILOGUE

The crisis sparked by the massive protests against the Kishi government and the revised security treaty in 1960 marked a turning point in Japan's postwar history that was not as evident at the time as it is in retrospect. Because the U.S.-Japan Security Treaty of 1951 was so unequal, during the fifties the political left held on to the hope of charting a different course for Japan in the world. Diet ratification of the revised security treaty in the face of immense popular outcry not only dashed these hopes and reduced the salience of the alliance in politics, it also diminished the significance of politics itself. Ikeda, Kishi's successor as prime minister, trained Japanese attention on economic achievement by announcing his famous "Income Doubling Plan" in 1960. As Japan's economy flourished and the nation prepared to host the Olympics in 1964, the political debates and economic anxiety of the 1950s receded quickly into the past.

Few observers expected such a soft landing. Although much of the protest in 1960 targeted Kishi himself, particularly his previous association with militarism and his high-handed style in politics, the demonstrations were too large to be explained away by one man's record. Many Japanese regarded the Cold War alliance with the United States as necessary, but it was not popular. Furthermore, Japanese political leaders had rarely emphasized the strategic importance of the alliance when recommending it to the public. More often they had stressed the economic advantages accruing to Japan. Kishi was thus a convenient lightning rod for Japanese anxiety about American military power. More positively, Ikeda, the former Finance Ministry bureaucrat, was the perfect figure to distance both the government and the alliance from the acrimonious debates about militarism and war.

Beneath the frothy surface of alliance politics, a profound change was underway. By binding the United States and its allies more closely together, the proliferation of economic ties accompanying strategic partnership was transforming the character of international relations. Despite the unpopularity of the military aspects of the Cold War alliance, the base of support in Japan for the partnership with the United States remained strong. The alliance endured and the substance of relations expanded to encompass both issues and participants far removed from matters of high politics. Owing to the vast cultural differences between Americans and Japanese and the different political agendas of the two governments, economic ties between Japan and the United States were particularly important in counteracting bilateral tension. The Soviet Union and its allies, by contrast, were unable to maintain mutually beneficial relationships over the course of several decades. To the extent that trade and investment contributed to the resiliency of the alliance and contained American-Japanese political rivalry, they had precisely the effect that America's Cold War strategists during the 1950s intended.

From the perspective of Japan's conservative leadership, close association with the United States served the nation well. The American desire for allies in East Asia afforded Japan an opportunity to secure assistance in providing for both the nation's defense and facilitating economic revival. In the absence of the Cold War, it is unimaginable that the United States would have worked as actively to provide economic assistance, sponsor Japan's accession to GATT, open its domestic market to Japanese goods, or tolerate Japan's many restrictions on trade and investment. There was no simple trade-off between American national security and commercial interest. But the priority that U.S. leaders attached to the alliance and their desire to establish a liberal international economic order fostered official interest in Japanese economic health, and occasionally enabled Japan to drive an unusually hard bargain in negotiations over economic issues.

Viewed from the long perspective, the great achievement of the postwar era was to provide an answer to the question of how Japan was to make a living and live in peace with its neighbors. Leaders on all sides certainly hoped that a solution could be found. The history of the first half of the century underscored the fragility of international order in East Asia. Perhaps because everyone had just witnessed the devastating consequences of getting it wrong, the new order got the chance it needed to take shape.

If the political contours of the postwar order bore a close resemblance to the aims of its architects, the dynamics of the global economy that took shape defied everyone's expectations. Ultimately American and allied prosperity, fueled by expanding global trade and cross-investment, contributed to victory in the Cold War.[1] It also led to the emergence of an interdependent world economy that has outlasted the Cold War. What began as a few tentative rounds of trade negotiations between the United States and its main trading partners gathered a momentum of its own: the Kennedy Round of GATT (1963–67), the Tokyo Round (1973–79), the Uruguay Round (1986–94), and finally the replacement of GATT itself with the World Trade Organization. The makers of such ordinary products as beverages and sewing machines who invested abroad and began manufacturing operations overseas redefined the nature of international business.

Yet the shape and workings of the global economy proved to be quite different than politicians, business leaders, or the public anticipated during the first decade or so after 1945. This gap between expectations and reality became apparent even before the new order was completely formed, and it was especially severe with regard to Japan. The Truman administration's failure to secure approval for the International Trade Organization revealed that government planners did not have the same free hand in the economic arena that they did in security affairs. President Eisenhower likewise underestimated the difficulty of rallying domestic support for a policy of liberal trade.

In voicing his opinion that Japan would not likely amount to much, Secretary of State Dulles probably made the most conspicuous error. But he was not alone. No one was expecting Japan or Western Europe to revive as they did. During the fifties, economists in the Department of State believed that protection was self-defeating, and in large measure they were right. But Japanese industrial policy was more complex and effective than programs of import substitution that had failed so conspicuously elsewhere before the war. Outward-looking American companies investigated the opportunities in Japan, but (outside of agriculture) few businesses regarded the Japanese market as being very important. Protectionists in the United States likewise focused on safeguarding the American market from Japanese competition rather than on eliminating the barriers to entering Japan's market. In short, Americans did not envision the United States slipping from its preeminent position after the war. By the 1970s, when the economies of the Western Europe and Japan had surged ahead to the point that various sectors were competitive with U.S. industries, Americans were not only surprised but also alarmed.[2]

Differences between expectation and reality were more gratifying to the Japanese. But for them too economic trends did not necessarily accord with previous plans. The reorientation of Japan's trade westward was not the original object of Japan's leadership during the years Yoshida, Hatoyama, and Ishibashi were in power. Up until the late fifties, even Japan's conservative leaders envisioned restoring a profitable trade with the Chinese mainland at some point to complement a growing presence in Southeast Asia. American pressure to limit such exchange, and the disruptive influence of the Cold War itself, combined to frustrate such designs. As Sino-American tension escalated, the economies of Japan and the People's Republic continued to develop separately. The significance of this development is not yet fully apparent. What is clear is that after the Cold War's end the economies of the two greatest powers in Northeast Asia stand largely apart from each other, as likely to reinforce political differences as to facilitate greater cooperation between them.[3]

The success of Japan's industrial policy probably ranks as the greatest surprise of the era. Acting at odds with conventional economic theory as they were, bureaucrats in Tokyo were the target of considerable criticism during the fifties.[4] If the planners themselves had confidence in the state guidance of economic enterprise, not until the early 1960s was the success of their approach self-evident. As Japan proved capable of adapting to such shocks as the collapse of the Bretton Woods monetary system and the energy crisis of the 1970s, the nation's economic system earned the ultimate compliment: recognition as a distinctive model of capitalist development.[5]

The problems of the 1970s in fact highlighted the extent to which the global economy was following a different course than the architects of the main postwar economic institutions imagined events would turn. The boom in foreign direct investment and the growth of multinational enterprise had far reaching effects on the structure of international trade and investment, particularly in manufacturing industries. International exchange was no longer simply a matter of trade and payments, and investment led to enduring ties between the parent and host economies.

Imports and exports remained important, however, and the growing U.S. trade deficit made the traditional commercial trade balance a political issue once American growth slowed. Discovery that Western European and Japanese businesses seemed to be playing by a different set of rules—that their systems of capitalism differed considerably from the norms of the U.S. economy—came as an unwelcome surprise to many Americans. The strain on the assumptions and institutions of the postwar years was also evident in the growing U.S. balance-of-payments deficits, culminating in President Richard Nixon's decision to close the "gold window."[6] Even the rise of environmentalism, which gathered unusual momentum in Japan, represented part and parcel of the crisis of the established global economic order.[7]

Despite the shocks to it, the system survived even if the adjustments required were painful. GATT had never been adequately equipped to deal with the charges of unfairness arising from the structural differences between national economies. As friction over subsidies, dumping, and other examples of industrial policy mounted, GATT took up the matter (along side of tariff liberalization) during the Tokyo Round. Many in the U.S. Congress, however, had well founded doubts about GATT's ability to deal with such nontariff measures. The 1974 Trade Act gave voice to such concerns. Section 301 gave the president authority to deal with "unreasonable" and "unjustifiable" trade practices abroad.[8] Although the main concern in the 1970s was protection of the U.S. market, trade protectionism was becoming export-oriented. Japan was becoming increasingly visible during the 1970s, but American concerns that decade focused mostly on competition from Western Europe.

During the 1980s attention shifted to Japan as the economies of Western Europe slowed or stagnated while Japan surged forward. The clash between Japan's industrial policy and the export-oriented "new protectionism" of the United States placed the two nations sharply at odds even as their economies were becoming more closely integrated with each other. Since the actual power of the economic bureaucrats was far weaker during the 1980s than it had been decades earlier, the appropriate focus when analyzing the trade wars of that decade is the contrasting structures of the two economies.[9]

Beyond the competitive position of Japan's firms, prior government policies contributed to the intensity of the trade friction over such items as automobiles and semiconductors. One legacy of Japan's inhibiting inward

Epilogue 237

foreign investment was to exacerbate the adversarial atmosphere. Limitations on cross-investment denied each side a voice in the other's economic affairs. The ties accompanying cross-investment had played an important role in alleviating the stress accompanying previous trade friction between the United States and the nations of Western Europe. During the 1980s Japanese companies seemed starkly alien, outside of the American system, even as Japan's trade surplus grew larger each year. Japanese multinationals have since invested in the United States, which has contributed to a decline in such trade friction. In the same way that American multinational companies became part of the economies of other nations, Japanese direct investment in the United States—the Honda plant in Marysville, Ohio, for example—gave Americans a stake in the welfare of Japanese firms.[10]

The U.S. economic revival and Japan's lackluster economic performance during the 1990s has also lessened, but not eliminated, the level of trade friction just as they have revealed the limits of the Japanese economic model. To outsiders, Japan has tended to appear unusually impressive, even threatening. The most successful Japanese companies have long been world-class competitors. But this achievement has masked the profound imbalance in Japan's economic development. The less visible—and usually more protected—sectors reveal the limits of Japan's economic advance. Agriculture, the financial system, and industries such as food processing have never been competitive. Indeed, the collapse of Japan's so-called bubble economy of the late 1980s revealed the extent to which failures in such sectors (in this case the financial system) can jeopardize the health of the economy as a whole.[11]

The experience of the 1990s has also revealed the limits of state guidance of economic enterprise. Fundamentally, the Japanese industrial policy described in this study facilitated the acquisition of new technology as much as its development. Japanese manufacturers have proved capable of building on what they acquired during the years of high-speed growth. But state guidance brought impressive results only as long as the goals were clear. Governmental leadership has magnified errors once Japan became a leading economic power, as the nation's failure to recognize early on the significance of the microcomputer revolution reveals. The nation has simply not generated wholly new industries in the same manner as the United States. As of this writing, Japan is once again looking outward to identify them. Despite its many achievements since 1945, Japan's economy remains vulnerable and the sense of insecurity about the future that has underpinned the nation's modern outlook has not disappeared.[12]

With the end of the Cold War, the world has not exactly come full circle. Political conditions are more stable and less dangerous than they were during the late forties and the fifties. The market has won the economic argument in the Cold War, and capitalism is no longer as tainted as it was during the era of decolonization. The aim of most nations not already part of the global economy is to join it. Yet the international economic order that has emerged in the decades since 1945 is potentially fragile. As this study shows, its creation required sustained political commitment in the face of challenge.

The test of any established order is its ability to adapt to change, whether expected or unexpected. After a long period of concern about inflation, there is an echo of the 1930s in the currency crises of the 1990s. Foreign economic interests make convenient scapegoats in hard times, yet interdependence by its very nature increases public exposure to outside influence. In the wake of communism's collapse, the world faces the challenges of integrating both the former Communist powers and the world's poor nations into the global economy and political order. To an extent that will become evident only after the fact, this transition represents uncharted territory. Controversies concerning energy supplies, the environment, and the problems created by differential rates of growth are likely to accompany continued economic development. What will remain constant is the need for global leadership in dealing with them. The world will do well if it can match the record of the United States and Japan during the years after the Pacific War.

APPENDIX
Treaty of Friendship, Commerce, and Navigation between the United States and Japan, 1953 (Excerpts)

ARTICLE VII

1. Nationals and companies of either Party shall be accorded national treatment with respect to engaging in all types of commercial, industrial, financial and other business activities within the territories of the other Party, whether directly or by agent or through the medium of any form of lawful juridical entity. Accordingly, such nationals and companies shall be permitted within such territories (a) to establish and maintain branches, agencies, offices, factories, and other establishments appropriate to the conduct of their business; (b) to organize companies under the general company laws of such other Party, and to acquire majority interests in companies of such other Party; and (c) to control and manage enterprises which they have established or acquired. Moreover, enterprises which they control, whether in the form of individual proprietorships, companies, or otherwise, shall, in all that relates to the conduct of the activities thereof, be accorded treatment no less favorable than that accorded like enterprises controlled by nationals and companies of such other Party.

2. Each Party reserves the right to limit the extent to which aliens may within its territories establish, acquire interests in, or carry on public utilities enterprises or enterprises engaged in shipbuilding, air or water transport, banking involving depository or fiduciary functions, or the exploitation of land or other natural resources. However, new limitations imposed

---

Source: Department of State, "Treaty of Friendship, Commerce, and Navigation between the United States of America and Japan," TIAS no. 2863, 2 April 1953, *USTIA*, vol. 4, pt. 2.

by either Party upon the extent to which aliens are accorded national treatment, with respect to carrying on such activities within its territories, shall not be applied against enterprises which are engaged in such activities therein at the time such new limitations are adopted and which are owned or controlled by nationals and companies of the other Party. Moreover, neither party shall deny to transportation, communications and banking companies of the other Party the right to maintain branches and agencies to perform functions necessary for essentially international operations in which they are permitted to engage.

3. The provisions of paragraph 1 of the present Article shall not prevent either party from prescribing special formalities in connection with the establishment of alien-controlled enterprises within its territories; but such formalities may not impair the substance of the rights set forth in said paragraph.

4. Nationals and companies of either party, as well as enterprises controlled by such nationals and companies, shall in any event be accorded most-favored-nation treatment with reference to the matters treated in the present Article.

ARTICLE XII

1. Nationals and companies of either party shall be accorded by the other Party national treatment and most-favored-nation treatment with respect to payments, remittances and transfers of funds or financial instruments between the territories of the two Parties as well as between the territories of such other party and of any third country.

2. Neither party shall impose exchange restrictions as defined in paragraph 5 of the present Article except to the extent necessary to prevent its monetary reserves from falling to a very low level or to effect a moderate increase in very low monetary reserves. It is understood that the provisions of the present Article do not alter the obligations either party may have to the International Monetary Fund or preclude the imposition of particular restrictions whenever the Fund specifically authorizes or requests a Party to impose such particular restrictions.

3. If either Party imposes exchange restrictions in accordance with paragraph 2 above, it shall, after making whatever provision may be necessary to assure the availability of foreign exchange for goods and services essential to the health and welfare of its people, make reasonable provision for the withdrawal, in foreign exchange in the currency of the other Party, of:

(a) the compensation referred to in Article VI, paragraph 3, of the present Treaty, (b) earnings, whether in the form of salaries, interest, dividends, commissions, royalties, payments for technical services, or otherwise, and (c) amounts for amortization of loans, depreciation of direct investments, and capital transfers, giving consideration to special needs for other transactions. If more than one rate of exchange is in force, the rate applicable to such withdrawals shall be a rate which is specifically approved by the International Monetary Fund for such transactions or, in the absence of a rate so approved, an effective rate which, inclusive of any taxes or surcharges on exchange transfers, is just and reasonable.

4. Exchange restrictions shall not be imposed by either Party in a manner unnecessarily detrimental or arbitrarily discriminatory to the claims, investments, transport, trade, and other interests of the nationals and companies of the other Party, or to the competitive position thereof.

5. The term "exchange restrictions" as used in the present Article includes all restrictions, regulations, charges, taxes, or other requirements imposed by either Party which burden or interfere with payments, remittances, or transfers of funds or of financial instruments between the territories of the two Parties.

PROTOCOL

6. Either Party may impose restrictions on the introduction of foreign capital as may be necessary to protect its monetary reserves as provided in Article XII, paragraph 2.

15. During a transitional period of three years from the date of the coming into force of the present Treaty, Japan may continue to apply existing restrictions on the purchase by aliens, with yen, of outstanding shares in Japanese enterprises.

NOTES

Abbreviations

AmEmb	American Embassy (followed by location)
a-m	aide-mémoire
AWF	Ann Whitman File (Dwight D. Eisenhower Papers), Eisenhower Library
BFEA	Bureau of Far Eastern Affairs, U.S. Department of State
CF	Confidential File
DA	Dean Acheson
DDE	Dwight D. Eisenhower
DDEL	Dwight D. Eisenhower Library, Abilene, Kansas
desp	Foreign Service despatch (U.S. Department of State)
DF	Record Group 59: U.S. Department of State Decimal File, National Archives, Washington, D.C.
DOS	Department of State
DSB	*Department of State Bulletin*
FAOHP	Foreign Affairs Oral History Program, Lauinger Library, Georgetown University, Washington, D.C.
FO	Foreign Office (United Kingdom)
FRUS	*Foreign Relations of the United States*
FY	fiscal year
HST	Harry S Truman
HSTL	Harry S Truman Presidential Library, Independence, Missouri
ITF	Record Group 43: Department of State International Trade Files, National Archives, Washington, D.C.
JFD	John Foster Dulles
JFMA	Declassified Diplomatic Records on Microfilm, Japan Foreign Ministry Archives, Tokyo
JMA	John M. Allison
memcon	memorandum of conversation
MSP	Mutual Security Program
NA	National Archives, Washington, D.C.
NYT	*New York Times*
OCB	Operations Coordinating Board

OH   oral history interview (followed by location and person)
ONA   Office of Northeast Asian Affairs, U.S. Department of State
OSA   Office of the Special Assistant (in the White House Office)
PPP: DDE   *Public Papers of the Presidents: Dwight D. Eisenhower* (including year)
PRO   Public Record Office, Kew, England
RG   Record Group (of records at the National Archives, Washington, D.C.)
SOD   Secretary of Defense
SOS   Secretary of State
TC   United States Tariff Commission
tel   telegram
USIA   United States Information Agency
USTIA   *United States Treaties and Other International Agreements*
WHCF   White House Central File (Eisenhower Records as President, 1953–61)
WHO   White House Office
YS   Yoshida Shigeru

Note: Archival manuscript correspondence is in the form of a memorandum unless otherwise indicated.

Chapter One

1. Acheson, *Present at the Creation*. An expression of the prevailing view that high tariffs and other macroeconomic policy failures led to disaster in the 1930s is Kindleberger, *The World in Depression*.

2. Borden, *Pacific Alliance*, 124.

3. LaFeber, *The Clash*, 296–324.

4. The 1934–36 average of Japan's share of U.S. foreign trade was 9 percent for U.S. exports and 7.2 percent for U.S. imports. In 1950, these figures were 4.1 and 2.1 percent respectively. By 1955 they had increased to 4.4 and 3.8 percent respectively. In 1960 they reached 7.1 and 7.8 percent respectively. The upward trend continued. In 1970 Japan consumed 10.8 percent of U.S. exports and provided 14.9 percent of U.S. imports. Source: Hunsberger, "Japan-United States Trade," 122.

5. Dower, *Empire and Aftermath*, 273–414; Borden, *Pacific Alliance*, 137–222; Schaller, *The American Occupation of Japan*, 77–163; and Schonberger, *Aftermath of War*, 134–235.

6. NSC 13/2, 7 Oct. 1948, FRUS, 1948, 6:857–62.

7. Borden, *Pacific Alliance*, 98–102; Schonberger, *Aftermath of War*, 206–35; and Tucker, "American Policy toward Sino-Japanese Trade."

8. Quoted in Dower, *Empire and Aftermath*, 316.

9. Chen, *China's Road to the Korean War*, 121. For translations of the Chinese documents, see Zhang and Chen, *Chinese Communist Foreign Policy and the Cold War in Asia*. Other recent studies include Zhang, *Deterrence and Strategic Culture*;

Westad, *Cold War and Revolution*; Garver, "Polemics, Paradigms, Responsibility"; and Christiansen, "A 'Lost Chance' for What?" Earlier works focusing on American misperception include Schaller, *The United States and China*; and Warren I. Cohen, *America's Response to China*, 179–83.

10. Buckley, *US-Japan Alliance Diplomacy*, 27–98; Ishii, *Reisen to Nichibei Kankei* [The Cold War and Japan-American relations]; Dower, *Empire and Aftermath*, 415–92; Shimizu, "Creating People of Plenty: The United States and Japan's Economic Alternatives, 1953–58"; and Imai, "Trade and National Security: Japanese-American Relations in the 1950s."

11. On GNP: Ohkawa and Rosovsky, "A Century of Economic Growth," 89; Jerome B. Cohen, *Japan's Postwar Economy*, 47 (BOJ and Economic Planning Agency data). Statistics on aid are from *Japan Economic Yearbook, 1956*, 31 (MOF data).

12. Jerome B. Cohen, *Japan's Postwar Economy*, 123 (MITI data); and BOJ, *Economic Statistics of Japan, 1961*, 259–62.

13. Lacking a merchant marine after the war, Japan also had to pay for carriage of its imports and exports on foreign vessels. Japan's merchant fleet (of vessels of 1,19 gross tons or more) in 1950 numbered 387, totaling 1,534,000 gross tons, as compared to 1,180 ships totaling 5,102,346 gross tons in 1939. Source: Hansen, *The World Almanac and Book of Facts for 1952*, 640.

14. Jerome B. Cohen, *Japan's Postwar Economy*, 14, 67. While world textile production increased from an average of 35,000 million square yards during the years 1936–38 to 45,400 million square yards in 1955, the volume of goods entering into world trade declined from 6,500 million square yards (in 1936–38) to 5,100 million square yards (in 1955). Data from the Cotton Board, Royal Exchange, Manchester.

15. American analysts were aware of Japan's poor competitive position abroad. See, for example, Clarence B. Randall report, Sept. 1956, *FRUS, 1955–57*, 9:31.

16. Eckes, *Opening America's Market*, 140.

17. The United States concluded twenty-one reciprocal trade agreements, reducing about 1,000 tariff rates. Under the MFN clause, a concession in one agreement also applied to trade with all other parties enjoying MFN status. See Bauer, Poole, and Dexter, *American Business and Public Policy*, 26; and Pastor, *Congress and the Politics of U.S. Foreign Economic Policy*, 84–101.

18. Bauer, Poole, and Dexter, *American Business and Public Policy*, 26. Even before the 1930s domestic support for high tariffs was not universal. Southerners historically tended to oppose high tariffs and the Democratic Party intermittently pressed for lower tariffs during the previous fifty years.

19. The most detailed study of U.S. tariff policy to 1930 is Eckes, *Opening America's Market*, 1–139. Eckes attempts to defend protectionism on economic grounds. Although silent on Japan, the chapter on the Smoot-Hawley tariff, which downplays its significance in causing the problems of the 1930s, is the most persuasive in the book.

20. Hull, cited by Dunn, *Peace-making and the Settlement with Japan*, 7.

21. Joint Statement by President Roosevelt and Prime Minister Churchill, 14 Aug. 1941, *FRUS, 1941*, 1:367–69.

22. Pastor, *Congress and the Politics of U.S. Foreign Economic Policy*, 96–101.
23. Ibid., 100.
24. Statistics cited in ibid., 96. See also Zeiler, "Managing Protectionism," 337–55.
25. Ostry, *The Post–Cold War Trading System*, 57–67. As Kindleberger later explained, "The United States would be held to the general rule; other countries would claim avoidance under saving clauses." Kindleberger, "U.S. Foreign Economic Policy, 1776–1976," 409.
26. Pastor, *Congress and the Politics of U.S. Foreign Economic Policy*, 99. GATT, U.S., and UN statistics.
27. Verdier, *Democracy and International Trade*, 204.
28. On U.S. efforts to secure MFN for Japan under GATT, see TAC-D 99/52, "Japan's Application for Accession to the GATT," file: Japan, box 287, ITF.
29. Kaufman, *Trade and Aid*, 93–94, 131–32. Useful surveys of literature on political economy and U.S. trade policy are Gilpin, *The Political Economy of International Relations*, 8–64; and Goldstein, *Ideas, Interests, and American Trade Policy*, 1–22.
30. Surveys of Japan's economic performance during the 1990s in perspective include Drifte, *Japan's Foreign Policy in the 1990s*, 15–48; and Katz, *Japan: The System That Soured*. For analysis of the relationship between the changes of the 1990s and changes in the overall structure of Japan's postwar economy, consult Nakatani, *Nihon Keizai no Rekishiteki Tenkan* [The Japanese economy's historical turning point]; and Noguchi, *1940-Nen Taisei* [The 1940s' system].
31. Eckes, *Opening America's Market*, xix.
32. Chalmers Johnson, *MITI*, 6. The collection of essays in Smitka, *Japan's Economic Ascent*, provides a useful survey of scholarship on the international aspects of Japan's economic development.
33. The classic account is Haitani, *The Japanese Economic System*.
34. Gordon, *The Evolution of Labor Relations in Japan*, 329–432.
35. Van Wolferen, *The Enigma of Japanese Power*, 43–49.
36. Chalmers Johnson, *MITI*, 17–34.
37. Ibid., 19.
38. Japanese writers similarly emphasize the role of the state (although not exclusively the bureaucracy) in Japan's postwar economic development. An engaging firsthand account by an economist is Tsuru, *Japan's Capitalism*, 90–118.
39. Wade, *Governing the Market*, 3–33. Japan has not been as lucky recently. Mistakes by government officials contributed to the wild inflation of Japan's economy during the 1980s as well as the subsequent collapse of the nation's financial system. Consult Wood, *The Bubble Economy*, 21–47.
40. Beason and Weinstein, "Growth, Economies of Scale, and Targeting in Japan, 1955–1990."
41. Hein, "In Search of Peace and Democracy."
42. Porter, *The Competitive Advantage of Nations*, 384–421.
43. Calder, *Strategic Capitalism*, 1–57; and Mason, *American Multinationals and Japan*, 101–98.

Chapter Two

1. *Congressional Record*, 82d Cong., 2d sess., 1951, 97, 5 Jan. and 14 June 1951, pt. 1:54–61, and pt. 5:6556–6603.
2. Memcon by JMA, 18 Jan. 1951, *FRUS, 1951*, 6:804–5.
3. The classic account is Dunn, *Peace-making and the Settlement with Japan*. More recent works that develop the points of American-Japanese disagreement include Dower, *Empire and Aftermath*, 369–414; Yoshitsu, *Japan and the San Francisco Peace Settlement*; Hosoya, *San Furanshisuko Kōwa e no Michi* [The path to the San Francisco Peace Treaty]; Schonberger, *Aftermath of War*, 236–78; Miyasato, "John Foster Dulles and the Peace Settlement with Japan"; Finn, *Winners in Peace*, 241–312; and LaFeber, *The Clash*, 257–95.
4. George Atcheson to MacArthur, 20 Mar. 1947, *FRUS, 1947*, 6:452; and memo by MacArthur, 21 Mar. 1947, ibid., 6:454–56. On Japanese planning and peace feelers, see Finn, *Winners in Peace*, 245–50; Weinstein, *Japan's Postwar Defense Policy, 1947–1968*, 15–31; and Yoshitsu, *Japan and the San Francisco Peace Settlement*, 1–23.
5. Walter B. Smith to SOS, 23 July 1947, *FRUS, 1947*, 6:473–74; memo by John P. Davies, 11 Aug. 1947 and memo by Kennan, ibid., 6:485–87; and NSC-13/2, 7 Oct. 1948, *FRUS, 1948*, 6:857–62.
6. Schaller, *The American Occupation of Japan*, 178–94.
7. Draft DOS position paper, attached to memo by John B. Howard to Butterworth, 9 Mar. 1950, *FRUS, 1950*, 6:1147.
8. Memo by Dean Rusk, 24 Jan. 1950, *FRUS, 1950*, 6:1131.
9. Butterworth to SOS, 18 Jan. 1950, ibid., 6:1117–29; memcon with MacArthur and William J. Sebald, by Butterworth, 5 Feb. 1950, ibid., 6:1133–35; and Howard to Charles A. Bohlen, 31 Mar. 1950, ibid., 6:1158–60.
10. Howard to Butterworth, 9 Mar. 1950, ibid., 6:1138–49; and Voorhees to SOS, 23 Mar. 1950, ibid., 6:1150–53.
11. Schaller, *The American Occupation of Japan*, 250.
12. Rusk to SOS, 18 Apr. 1950, *FRUS, 1950*, 6:1161. Emphasis in original.
13. On the relationship between Acheson and Truman, see McCullough, *Truman*, 751–58; Acheson, *Present at the Creation*; and McGlothlen, *Controlling the Waves*, 19–20. McGlothlen's fine work builds a persuasive case that the centerpiece of Acheson's Asian vision was the revival of Japan.
14. Hoopes, *The Devil and John Foster Dulles*, 16.
15. Ann Whitman (Eisenhower's personal secretary), cited by Donovan, *Confidential Secretary*, 133. On the scholarly view of Dulles, see Divine, "John Foster Dulles: What You See Is What You Get."
16. OH, U. Alexis Johnson, p. 52, 19 June 1975, HSTL; Warren I. Cohen, *Dean Rusk*, 54–55.
17. Memcon with JFD and Butterworth, by Howard, 7 Apr. 1950, *FRUS, 1950*, 6:1164. Emphasis in original. The Inter-American Treaty of Reciprocal Assistance opened for signature at Rio de Janeiro on 3 Sept. 1947. On Dulles's brief senatorial career, see, for example, Hoopes, *The Devil and John Foster Dulles*, 76–79.

18. Memcon with JFD and Butterworth, by Howard, *FRUS, 1950*, 6:1164.
19. JFD to SOS, 6 June and 19 July 1950, ibid., 6:1209, 1243–44.
20. The best introduction to Allison is his memoir, *Ambassador from the Prairie*.
21. JFD letter to MacArthur, 18 Mar. 1951, *FRUS, 1951*, 6:931.
22. To Dulles, China was a natural source of raw materials for Japan, particularly iron ore. Trade with China (subject to security restrictions) promised to reduce U.S. aid by about $75 million annually (JFD to SOS, 6 June 1950, *FRUS, 1950*, 6:1210, 1212).
23. JFD to Rusk, 22 Oct. 1951, *FRUS, 1951*, 6:1380; and memcon by Howard, 7 Apr. 1950, *FRUS, 1950*, 6:1162. On State-Defense differences, see memcon by Howard, 24 Apr. 1950, ibid., 6:1175–82.
24. Memo by JFD, 30 June 1950, *FRUS, 1950*, 6:1220–30; report by JFD, 3 July 1950, ibid., 6:1230–37.
25. Memo by MacArthur, 23 June 1950, ibid., 6:1227–28.
26. JFD to DA, 19 July 1950, ibid., 6:1243.
27. JFD to Paul Nitze, 20 July 1950, ibid., 6:1247; and memcon with Jiro Shirasu, by JFD, 4 Dec. 1952, *FRUS, 1952–54*, 14:1364.
28. Memo by PPS, 26 July 1950, *FRUS, 1950*, 6:1257.
29. JMA to Carter B. Magruder, 21 July 1950, ibid., 6:1250–54.
30. DOS concurred in Dulles's draft agreement of July 1950. On 8 September, Truman authorized "preliminary negotiations" based on the interdepartmental recommendation in JCS memo to SOD, 22 Aug. 1950, ibid., 6:1281.
31. On consultations with FEC nations, see *FRUS, 1950*, 6:1296–1325.
32. JFD to SOS, 8 Dec. 1950, ibid., 6:1359–60. The likely price of securing Japanese loyalty Dulles envisioned was essentially defense of Japan and adjacent islands, certain economic assurances, and a prompt restoration of Japanese sovereignty.
33. Memo for HST, 9 Jan. 1951, *FRUS, 1951*, 6:787–88. Johnson was a wealthy corporation lawyer from Clarksburg, West Virginia, and a former assistant secretary of war who was willing to head the effort to raise money for Truman's reelection in 1948 when no one else would consider the job. Truman's biographer David McCullough rates the decision to appoint Johnson as head of the Department of Defense as "woefully wrong" (*Truman*, 678, 990). Acheson attributed Johnson's erratic and hostile behavior ("beyond the peculiar to the impossible") to a brain malady that claimed Johnson's life after Truman asked him to resign (*Present at the Creation*, 441).
34. JCS to SOD, 12 Dec. 1951, *FRUS, 1951*, 6:1434.
35. Biographies of Yoshida include Dower, *Empire and Aftermath*; and Kōsaka, *Saishō Yoshida Shigeru* [Prime Minister Yoshida Shigeru].
36. Memo by YS, undated, *FRUS, 1951*, 6:834.
37. Dower, *Empire and Aftermath*, 377–400; and (for official U.S. thinking) memo by John M. Steeves, encl. with Sebald desp to DOS, 7 Jan. 1952, 794.5/1–752, DF.
38. Gallup Poll, *Washington Post*, 14 Sept. 1951. Of those Americans surveyed, 51 percent favored Japanese rearmament.
39. Memo by YS, undated, *FRUS, 1951*, 6:834.
40. Finn, *Winners in Peace*, 274–77. Much controversy surrounds the 29 January

1951 meeting between Yoshida, Dulles, and MacArthur. MacArthur told Dulles that rearmament was not advisable at the present time. Dulles called the meeting a "courtesy call." According to Yoshida, however, the meeting was more substantial. He had met with MacArthur prior to Dulles's arrival and at his request MacArthur agreed secretly to oppose demands for rearmament. Thus, the meeting was a disappointment for Dulles in this view (OH, YS, National Diet Library, Tokyo). Yoshida's miscalculation was to think that MacArthur's opinion would be decisive (Yoshitsu, *Japan and the San Francisco Peace Settlement*, 50–58).

41. Memo by the Government of Japan, "Initial Steps for Rearmament Program," 3 Feb. 1951, file: Japan, U.S. Policy, box 1, Records of the Director of the Office of Northeast Asian Affairs, Subject Files, 1945–53, RG-59, NA.

42. Unsigned draft of bilateral agreement, 5 Feb. 1951, *FRUS*, 1951, 6:856; and Dulles mission staff meeting minutes, 5 Feb. 1951, ibid., 6:857–58.

43. DOS, "Security Treaty between the United States of America and Japan," TIAS no. 2491, 8 Sept. 1951, *USTIA*, vol. 3, pt. 3.

44. During the negotiation of the Administrative Agreement of February 1952, for example, the United States insisted on, and got, complete jurisdiction over U.S. forces stationed in Japan (Sebald tel to JFD, 6 Feb. 1952, *FRUS*, 1952–54, 14:1137; memo by DOS, undated, ibid., 14:1202; and Yoshitsu, *Japan and the San Francisco Peace Settlement*, 83–99).

45. JFD mission staff meeting minutes, 5 Feb. 1951, *FRUS*, 1951, 6:858.

46. Memo by JMA, 11 Jan. 1951, ibid., 6:790.

47. McCullough, *Truman*, 793. Dulles suggested to President Truman in 1950 that MacArthur should be retired before he caused trouble.

48. Memo by JFD, 12 Apr. 1951, *FRUS*, 1951, 6:975–76.

49. Dunn, *Peace-making and the Settlement with Japan*, 136; and (for the quotation) memcon by DA, 3 May 1951, *FRUS*, 1951, 6:1038.

50. JFD statement and draft treaty, 15 Aug. 1951, *DSB* 25 (27 Aug. 1951): 346–54.

51. Dunn, *Peace-making and the Settlement with Japan*, 172–86. Senators John J. Sparkman (D.-Ala.) and Alexander Wiley (R.-Wis.) signed the peace treaty for the United States. Senator Wiley and Senator Styles Bridges (R.-N.H.) signed the security treaty.

52. NIE 19, 20 Apr. 1951, box 253, President's Secretary's Files, HST Papers, HSTL.

53. Ibid.; and SE-13, Probable Developments in the World Situation through Mid-1953, 24 Sept. 1951, reprinted in Warner, *CIA Cold War Records*, 412, 418.

54. NIE 52, 29 May 1952, box 253, PSF, HST Papers, HSTL.

55. Ibid.

56. NSC 125/2, 7 Aug. 1952, *FRUS*, 1952–1954, 14:1302–8.

57. Ibid., 14:1306.

58. Report by Bureau of the Budget on the PSB, 21 Apr. 1952, p. 3, folder: PSB D-1, box 1, PSB Working Files, 1951–53, RG-59, NA. On the connections between operations abroad and NSC policy, see Walter B. Smith report to NSC, 23 Apr. 1953, reprinted in Warner, *CIA Cold War Records*, 457–62; and on the PSB and Japan, see Ishii, "Reisen no Shinri-teki Sokumen to Nihon" [Cold War psychological strategy and Japan].

59. James E. Webb to Gordon Gray, 9 Oct. 1951, folder: PSB D-27, box 4, PSB Working Files, 1951–53, RG-59, NA.

60. PSB D-27, pp. 5, 12, Psychological Strategy Program for Japan, 30 Jan. 1953, ibid.

61. Ibid., 13, 19.

62. Ibid., 14, 20–21. The PSB was particularly interested in finding examples of liberal thinkers who had formerly espoused Communist doctrine and renounced it.

63. NSC 5509, 31 Dec. 1954, Part 6—the USIA Program, FRUS, 1955–57, 9:504–21; and Frank B. Tenny to Robert McClurkin, 4 Nov. 1955, OCB 091.Japan (file no. 3), box 48, OCB Central File Series, NSC Staff Papers, WHO, DDEL.

64. Schaller, Altered States, 135–36. CIA records remain unavailable but the contours of the agency's activities in Japan are now understood.

65. PSB D-31, A Strategic Concept for a National Psychological Program with particular reference to Cold War Operations under NSC 10/5, 26 Nov. 1952, box 5, PSB Working Files, 1951–53, RG-59, NA.

66. Appendix to PSB D-27, pp. 20–21, box 4, PSB Working Files, RG-59, NA.

67. Jonas, The United States and Germany, 286–98. In 1955, when West Germany formally became a member of NATO, the Germans promised to create an army of 500,000 men. Compulsory military service became law the next year. Still, the Federal Republic's army grew slowly, reaching only 230,000 by the decade's end.

68. See, for example, JMA desp to DOS, 30 Mar. 1956, 611.94/3-3056, DDF.

69. Kataoka, introduction to Creating Single-Party Democracy, 1–33; Stockwin, Japan, 58–74.

70. Douglas MacArthur II to JFD, 25 May 1957, FRUS, 1955–57, 23:325–26, 330. Emphasis in original.

Chapter Three

1. Jonas, The United States and Germany, 263; and Churchill and Roosevelt joint statement, 14 Aug. 1941, FRUS, 1941, 1:367–69.

2. Hull, Memoirs, 2:1314–15; and Leffler, "The American Conception of National Security." On Hull, see also Butler, Cautious Visionary.

3. Jonas, The United States and Germany, 273–86; and Schwartz, America's Germany, 17–31. For detailed analysis, consult Eisenberg, Drawing the Line.

4. Schonberger, Aftermath of War, 11–39. Grew retired when the war ended.

5. SWNCC-150/4/A, Basic Initial Post-Surrender Policy for Japan, 29 Aug. 1945, SCAP, Political Reorientation of Japan, 2:423–26. Planning was incomplete when Japan surrendered. Complete instructions were sent to SCAP in November. See note 7.

6. Proclamation Defining Terms for Japanese Surrender, 26 July 1945, DSB 13 (July 29, 1945): 137–38.

7. JCS-1380/15, Basic Initial Post-Surrender Directive to SCAP for the Occupation and Control of Japan, 3 Nov. 1945, Political Reorientation of Japan, 2:433–34.

8. On the Occupation reforms, consult Ward and Sakamoto, Democratizing Japan; Schonberger, Aftermath of War; and Dower, Empire and Aftermath, 273–470.

9. Jonas, *The United States and Germany*, 275–86; and Smith, *Lucius D. Clay*, 350–55. Clay's aim in 1946 was to prod France to cooperate with plans for a quadripartite economic policy for Germany, but the State Department used the occasion to question Soviet intentions regarding Germany. On U.S. attitudes toward Japan at the war's end and U.S. policy, see Pauley to HST, 6 Dec. 1945, *FRUS*, 1945, 6:1004–9.

10. Pauley, *Report on Japanese Reparations*, reference 1-a. This full report, dated April 1946, was not completed until November 1946. It was released to the public in July 1948. Its recommendations, however, had long circulated within the government.

11. U.S. policy in 1946 is described in Atcheson to SOS, 23 Jan., SWNCC-236/10, 30 Apr. 1946, and subsequent revisions, *FRUS*, 1946, 8:474–76, 493–504, 574–78.

12. Pauley letters to William Clayton (30 Apr.), Willard L. Thorp (18 Sept.), and SOS, *FRUS*, 1946, 8:506–7, 567–69, 601–4; and JCS directive no. 75 to SCAP, 4 Apr. 1947, *FRUS*, 1947, 6:376–80.

13. SCAPIN-244, Dissolution of Holding Companies, 6 Nov.1945, and SCAPIN-1079, Ordinances and Regulations Affecting Holding Company Liquidation Commission, 23 July 1946, are reprinted in JCAP, *Political Reorientation of Japan*, 2:265–68. The best introductions are Bisson, *Zaibatsu Dissolution in Japan*; and Hadley, *Antitrust in Japan*.

14. U.S. Mission on Japanese Combines, *Report of the Mission on Japanese Combines*; Edwards, "The Dissolution of the Japanese Combines," 227–40.

15. Hadley, "Trust Busting in Japan," 431.

16. SWNCC-302/4 (FEC 230) is reprinted in Hadley, *Antitrust in Japan*, 495–515. For analysis, see pp. 107–46.

17. Davies memo, 11 Aug. 1947, *FRUS*, 1947, 6:485–86.

18. Statistics on industrial production are from Jerome B. Cohen, *Japan's Postwar Economy*, 47. U.S. aid to Japan during the Occupation totaled $192.8 million in 1945 and 1946, $404.4 million in 1947, $461 million in 1948, $534.8 million in 1949, $361.3 million in 1950, $156.7 million in 1951, and $0.5 million in 1952 (*Japan Economic Yearbook*, 1956, 31). Statistics on inflation are from Tsuru, *Japan's Capitalism*, 45.

19. Kennan memo (PPS/10), 14 Oct. 1947, *FRUS*, 1947, 6:537, 542. On Draper and his background as a Wall Street banker before the war and his service in Germany, see Schonberger, *Aftermath of War*, 161–63.

20. For Kennan's report of 25 Mar. 1948 (PPS/28), together with memoranda of his conversations with MacArthur and explanatory notes, see *FRUS*, 1948, 6:691–719. Throughout the period Kennan also participated—albeit to less effect—in the debate within the executive branch over policy toward Germany. On the U.S. effort to tie West Germany economically to the West, particularly the role of High Commissioner James J. McCloy (Clay's successor), see Schwartz, *America's Germany*, 33–45, 185–209.

21. On the Japan Lobby and Kern, see Schonberger, *Aftermath of War*, 134–60; and Schonberger, "The Japan Lobby in American Diplomacy, 1947–1952," 327–59.

22. Strike to Kenneth Royall, 30 Apr. 1948, *FRUS*, 1948, 6:970–71. Although SCAP concurred with the new recommendations, DOS reception to them was cool, owing largely to concern about allied opinion. See, for example, Charles E.

Saltzman memos, 5 June and 15 Sept. 1948, ibid., 6:973–77, 1015–16. Yen statistics are from Tsuru, *Japan's Capitalism*, 39.

23. Statistics are from Hadley, *Antitrust in Japan*, 167, 180. On Draper see Schonberger, *Aftermath of War*, 161–98. On Kennan, see Schaller, *The American Occupation of Japan*, 122–40. MacArthur responded to public criticism in letters to J. H. Gipson and Senator Brian McMahon, 28 Jan. and 1 Feb. 1948, *PRJ*, 2:780–83.

24. NSC 13/2, 7 Oct. 1948, *FRUS*, 1948, 6:858, 861.

25. Ibid., 860–61.

26. NSC 13/3, 6 May 1949, *FRUS*, 1949, 7:735–36. On GATT: TAC-D 99/52, "Japan's Application for Accession to the GATT," file: Japan, box 287, ITF.

27. Dulles mission memo, 5 Feb. 1951, *FRUS*, 1951, 6:853.

28. JFD memo, 6 June 1950, *FRUS*, 1950, 6:1207–12; and Kennan to JFD, 20 July 1950, ibid., 6:1248–50.

29. Dulles mission memo, 5 Feb. 1951, *FRUS*, 1951, 6:849–55; and memcon by Robert Fearey, 7 Feb. 1951, ibid., 6:869.

30. Memcon by DA, 2 Apr. 1951, ibid., 6:964.

31. On British policy during the Occupation, consult Buckley, *Occupation Diplomacy*.

32. British a-m, 12 Mar. 1951, *FRUS*, 1951, 6:910; and JMA to JFD, 5 Apr. 1951, ibid., 6:961–64.

33. British a-m, 12 Mar. 1951, ibid., 6:911.

34. Xiang, *Recasting the Imperial Far East*, 3–33; and Dimbleby and Reynolds, *An Ocean Apart*, 196–217.

35. *Parliamentary Debates*, Commons, 5th ser., vol. 485 (1951), Written Answers, cols. 242–43. British concerns relating to the peace treaty are reflected in parliamentary speeches. See ibid., cols. 1955–64.

36. Walter S. Gifford to SOS, 26 Feb. 1951, *FRUS*, 1951, 6:896–97.

37. On the Canberra Conference, see Buckley, *Occupation Diplomacy*, 153.

38. Canberra Conference communiqué, reprinted in Dunn, *Peace-making and the Settlement with Japan*, 68; Andrew B. Foster, Chargé in Australia, to SOS, 13 May 1949, *FRUS*, 1949, 7:744–46; and memcon by JFD, 29 July 1950, *FRUS*, 1950, 6:1261–62.

39. Arthur R. Ringwalt letter to JMA, 23 May 1950, *FRUS*, 1950, 6:1201–2.

40. U.K. a-m, 12 Mar. 1951, *FRUS*, 1951, 6:913. On the support of U.S. business and labor for MFN, see Dunn, *Peace-making and the Settlement with Japan*, 157–59. On U.K. economic policy toward Japan, see Yokoi, "Searching for a Balance," 48–82.

41. DOS, "Treaty of Peace with Japan," TIAS no. 2490, and "Security Treaty between the United States of America and Japan," TIAS no. 2491, 8 Sept. 1951, *USTIA*, vol. 3, pt. 3. On French demands, see memcon by JFD, 11 June, and French Ambassador to DOS, 24 July 1951, *FRUS*, 1951, 6:1115–16, 1220–21. Western Europeans imported considerably more from Japan than they exported; hence their lack of enthusiasm for concessions. See Akaneya, *Nihon no Gatto Kanyū Mondai* [The problem of Japanese accession to GATT], 98–102. Akaneya also makes extensive use of Australian records.

42. *Parliamentary Debates*, Commons, 5th Ser., vol. 494 (1951–52), cols. 1000–1004.

43. Ibid., vol. 491 (1951), cols. 574–81; and ibid., vol. 494 (1951–52), Written Answers, col. 328.

44. Memcon by DA, 2 Apr. 1951, *FRUS, 1951*, 6:964; U.K. a-m, 12 Mar. 1951, ibid., 6:913; U.S. a-m, ibid., 6:924–25; and memcon by Fearey, 2 Feb. 1951, ibid., 6:840. Japan lost over two-thirds of its oceangoing shipping in the war. Many of the raw materials for rebuilding the industry had to be imported.

45. For the British demands, see U.K. a-m, 12 Mar. 1951, ibid., 6:911–14. On these issues and the question of fisheries, see Dunn, *Peace-making and the Settlement with Japan*, 160–71.

46. DOS memo, 11 Sept. 1950, *FRUS, 1950*, 6:1297.

47. JFD letter to MacArthur, 15 Nov. 1950, ibid., 6:1350; memcon by JFD, 19 Dec. 1950, ibid., 6:1373; JFD letter to MacArthur, 2 Mar. 1951, *FRUS, 1951*, 6:902–3.

48. JFD tel to MacArthur, 12 Mar. 1951, ibid., 6:909.

49. Memcons by Stanton Babcock, 27 Sept. and 19 Oct. 1950, *FRUS, 1950*, 6:1309, 1325; Burmese Embassy note to DOS, 27 Aug. 1951, *FRUS, 1951*, 6:1281.

50. On Quirino's position: memcon by JFD, 12 Feb. 1951, *FRUS, 1951*, 6:881–82. Dulles's view: JFD letter to MacArthur, 2 Mar. 1951, 6:901. Myron Cowen, the American ambassador, recommended "some Japanese gesture" to win the Philippines' goodwill (tel to JFD, 15 Mar. 1951, ibid., 6:927–28).

51. U.K. a-m, 12 Mar. 1951, and Fearey memo, 17 Feb. 1951, ibid., 6:912, 886.

52. Memcons by Fearey, 18 and 23 Apr. 1951; and Japanese government memos, 23 Apr. 1951, ibid., 6:987, 1007, 1010–11.

53. The treaty provision was nevertheless heavily qualified (in Article 16): Japanese assets in neutral countries were to be turned over to the International Committee of the Red Cross for distribution to the appropriate agencies for the benefit of soldiers who had suffered undue hardships while prisoners of war of Japan.

54. Memcon by Richard B. Finn, 25 June and tel, Sebald to SOS, 2 July 1951, *FRUS, 1951*, 6:1145, 1171–73.

55. Elmer Staats to James Lay Jr., 28 Oct. 1954, *FRUS, 1952–54*, 14:1760. For the text of Japan's agreements with Burma, see *Contemporary Japan* 23 (1955): 424–29.

56. On the connections between Japan, Southeast Asia, and the origins of the U.S. commitment in Vietnam, see Rotter, *The Path to Vietnam*; Borden, *Pacific Alliance*, 191–222; and McGlothlen, *Controlling the Waves*, 23–49, 163–206. On Japan's postwar trade with Southeast Asia, consult Imai, "Trade and National Security," 290–333.

57. BOJ, *Economic Statistics of Japan*, 1961, 251, 253.

58. Perry, Stanley, and Thomson, *Sentimental Imperialists*, 220.

59. Xiang, *Recasting the Imperial Far East*, vii–ix, 209–38. On Foreign Office disillusionment with U.K. policy toward China in 1951, see especially FC 1027/3 (FO 371/92233), and FC 1048/48 (FO 371/92234), PRO. Numerous PRO files detail the difficulties British commercial and banking interests faced in their dealings with the Communist government. See, for example, FO 371/99304, PRO.

60. U.K. a-m, 30 Mar. 1951; JMA to JFD, 16 May 1951; Sebald tel to SOS, 19 May 1951; memcon with Chinese Ambassador Wellington Koo, by JFD, 29 May 1951; and tel, DA to Embassy in ROC, 21 June 1951, *FRUS, 1951*, 6:953, 1043, 1050, 1052, 1135.

61. Text of joint Anglo-American statement, ibid., 6:1134; tel, DA to AmEmb ROC, 21 June 1951, ibid., 6:1135.

62. Allison, *Ambassador from the Prairie*, 165; YS letter to JFD, 6 Aug. 1951, *FRUS, 1951*, 6:1242.

63. Yoshida, "Japan and the Crisis in Asia," 179; and Dower, *Empire and Aftermath*, 400–404. On Japanese opinion, see Imai, "Trade and National Security," 235–57.

64. Ed. note, *FRUS, 1951*, 6:1347.

65. YS letter to JFD, 24 Dec. 1951, ibid., 6:1466–67; JFD memo, 26 Dec. 1951, ibid., 6:1467–70; FO tel to Washington, 16 Jan. 1952, FO 371/99403, PRO; Zhang Hanfu (Chang Han-fu) statement, *People's China*, 1 Feb. 1952, 11–12; and Dower, *Empire and Aftermath*, 400–414. On the "Yoshida letter" controversy, start with Buckley, *Occupation Diplomacy*, 174–77; Warren I. Cohen, "China in Japanese-American Relations," 36–43; and especially Yokoi, "Searching for a Balance," 72–80.

66. The Japan-ROC agreements are reprinted in *China Handbook, 1952–53*, 154–60.

67. Reston, *Deadline*, 231; *Congressional Record*, 82d Cong., 2d sess., 1952, 98, pt. 2:2594; JFD memo, 21 Mar. 1952, *FRUS, 1952–54*, 14:1217.

68. Fred Christoph memo to Chief of the Trade Agreements Branch, 6 Nov. 1950, subseries 1, The Problem of Japanese Entry into GATT, 1949–51, pp. 54–56, reel E-0010, Public Release Series no. 10, JFMA. These records show clearly that U.S. officials assisted Japan to prepare for accession to GATT. See also Akaneya, *Nihon no Gatto Kanyū Mondai*, 83–118.

69. Bertha Merdian to Vernon L. Phelps, 31 Mar. 1952, folder: Japan, box 287, ITF.

70. Geneva tel to FO, 4 Oct. 1951, UEE218/8, FO 371/92025, PRO; and FO minutes, various dates, UEE67/12, FO 371/98985, PRO.

71. FO draft tel to Geneva, 27 Sept. 1951, UEE218/2, FO 371/92025, PRO.

72. GATT press release, 4 Oct. 1951, UEE281/6, ibid. At British insistence the GATT Secretariat "made clear" to Japan that, the invitation was "in no way to be interpreted as having any bearing on the ultimate accession of Japan" to GATT.

73. Leddy memo to Thorp, undated, attached to Leonard Weiss memo to Leddy, 17 Mar. 1952, folder: Japan, box 287, ITF; and Frank C. Nash letter to Thorp, 28 Aug. 1952, 460.509/8-2852, DF.

74. Leddy memo to Thorp, undated, folder: Japan, box 287, ITF, and table attached to TAC Paper, TAC-D 99/52, Aug. 1952, folder: Japan, box 287, ITF.

75. Leddy to Thorp, 18 Mar. 1952, folder: Japan, box 287, ITF.

76. Hoopes, *The Devil and John Foster Dulles*, 124–33.

77. Kenneth T. Young to JMA, 25 Sept. 1952, *FRUS, 1952–54*, 14:118–19; Akaneya, *Nihon no Gatto Kanyū Mondai*, 86.

78. TAC paper, TAC-D 99/52, folder: Japan, box 287, ITF.

79. Carl D. Corse to the president, 20 Aug. 1952, *FRUS, 1952–54*, 14:116. The Interdepartmental Committee on Trade Agreements, commonly known as the

Trade Agreements Committee, was formed in 1934 to make recommendations to the president on trade agreements. It included representatives from the Departments of State, Agriculture, Interior, Labor, Defense, and Treasury, as well as the Mutual Security Administration and the Tariff Commission.

80. Young to JMA, 25 Sept. 1952, *FRUS, 1952–54*, 1:118. Owing in part to domestic opposition to GATT, the United Kingdom was unable to offer de jure MFN treatment to Japan. See a-m, British Embassy to DOS, 22 Sept. 1952, file: Japan, box 287, ITF.

81. Young to JMA, 25 Sept. 1952, *FRUS, 1952–54*, 1:118–19; and on the resolution, press release GATT/83, 14 Oct. 1952, UEE67/108, FO 371/98988, PRO. On U.K. policy regarding the intersessional committee, see Yokoi, "Searching for a Balance," 129–45.

82. *Manchester Guardian*, 11 Oct. 1952. The *Guardian* was generally critical of the government's policy of delaying on Japanese accession. The *Economist*, the *Times*, and the *Financial Times* covered Japanese accession in fair, if less enthusiastic, fashion. Opponents, from the *Daily Express* to backbenchers, were more vocal and sensational.

83. David K. E. Bruce tel to AmEmb Tokyo, 17 Oct. 1952, 394.31/10-1752, DF; U.K. Delegation tel to FO, 8 Oct. 1952, UEE67/95, FO 371/98988, PRO; and tel, Robert Murphy to SOS, 13 Oct. 1952, 394.31/10-1352, DF; and Akaneya, *Nihon no Gatto Kanyū Mondai*, 191.

Chapter Four

1. NSC 68, 14 Apr. 1950, *FRUS, 1950*, 1:234–92. On NSC 68 in strategic context, see Gaddis, *Strategies of Containment*, 89–126.

2. Gaddis, *Strategies of Containment*, 113; U.S. Office of the Federal Register, *The Economic Report of the President to the Congress, February 1982*, 85. Congress authorized $48.2 billion for defense for fiscal 1951, a 257 percent increase over the original White House request of $13.5 billion before the war.

3. Asahi Shimbun, *The Pacific Rivals*, 193, 195. Assigning the number 100 to the level of Japanese industrial production in 1955, the BOJ estimated that production rose from 48.6 in 1950 to 85.8 in 1953. BOJ, *Economic Statistics of Japan, 1961*, 213. For analysis, see Borden, *Pacific Alliance*, 143–49; Schaller, *The American Occupation of Japan*, 288–97; Nakamura, *The Postwar Japanese Economy*, 41–48; and Hein, *Fueling Growth*, 213–23. Hein also emphasizes the war's role in Japan's shift from coal to oil.

4. Dodge, quoted in Borden, *Pacific Alliance*, 148.

5. Dingman, "The Dagger and the Gift," 45. Dingman downplays the impact of the Korean War altogether, calling it a "secondary, not a primary, event in modern Japanese history," at least in comparison with the Pacific War.

6. A fine summary of such views is Uchino, *Japan's Postwar Economy*, 75–77.

7. U. Alexis Johnson to Livingston Merchant, 29 Dec. 1950, *FRUS, 1950*, 6:1393–98.

8. Borden, *Pacific Alliance*, 149–58; and Imai, "Trade and National Security," 74–

8, 9. Imai details the expenditures in Japan and their impact on Japanese defense production.

9. Dower, "Peace and Democracy in Two Systems," 13; Havens, *Fire Across the Sea*, 92–96. Estimates vary, but Japan earned about $1 billion per year from 1966 to 1971. See Schaller, *Altered States*, 198–99.

10. Ienaga, *The Pacific War, 1931–1945*.

11. The scholarly literature on export controls focuses mostly on Europe. The pathbreaking study was Adler-Karlsson, *Western Economic Warfare, 1947–1967*. More recent works include Funigiello, *American-Soviet Trade in the Cold War*; Mastanduno, "Trade as a Strategic Weapon: American Alliance Export Control Policy in the Early Postwar Period"; and Spaulding, "'A Gradual and Moderate Relaxation.'" On Asia consult Hufbauer, Schott, and Elliott, *Economic Sanctions Reconsidered: History and Current Policy*, 2:100–115; and Katō, *Amerika no Sekai Senryaku to Kokomu* [American global strategy and COCOM].

12. Harriman tel to Paul Hoffman, 5 Nov. 1949, *FRUS*, 1949, 5:169–71; and tel to DOS, 19 Nov. 1949, *FRUS*, 1949, 5:174. The initial CG members were the United States, the United Kingdom, France, Italy, and the Benelux nations. These member nations initially agreed to embargo 124 items on the U.S. 1A list. Later Norway, Denmark, Canada, and the Federal Republic of Germany also joined CG-COCOM. On the work of COCOM, see *FRUS*, 1950, 4:65.

13. NSC 41, 28 Feb. 1949, *FRUS*, 1949, 9:827. On Acheson's role, see McGlothlen, *Controlling the Waves*, 139–62. McGlothlen summarizes well the argument that Acheson separated the questions of U.S. diplomatic recognition of the PRC and Sino-Japanese trade. Whereas from January 1950 he shelved the question of recognition, for several months he persisted in attempting to facilitate trade between the PRC and Japan.

14. NSC 41, *FRUS*, 1949, 9:827–28.

15. Ibid., 9:828–29. U.S. business and mission interests were less important for their own sake than as "opportunities for maintaining a flow of useful information on China and for continuing American cultural influence in China."

16. Ibid., 9:829–30.

17. Ibid., 9:830–34.

18. The application of NSC policy (transmitted to SCAP as JCS 1724/21) in Japan was a very delicate issue because SCAP represented all of the FEC nations. See Thorp to (U. Alexis) Johnson, 25 May 1951, 400.949/5-2551, RG-59, NA. Originally top secret, this lengthy memo summarizes U.S. policy relating to Japanese export controls.

19. NSC 48/2, 30 Dec. 1949, *FRUS*, 1949, 7:1215–20. Differences between State and Defense remained unresolved, however, as each interpreted NSC-48/2 in its own way. The Pentagon, for example, regarded steam locomotives and steel rails as 1A goods, whereas State insisted that they be considered 1B items. See Louis Johnson letter to DA, 24 Mar. 1950, *FRUS*, 1950, 6:625–26; and letter, DA to Johnson, 28 Apr. 1950, ibid., 6:632–36. On 24 August the NSC agreed, with President Truman participating, not to permit the export of rails to the PRC (ed. note, ibid., 6:660).

20. In May 1949, for example, the Department of the Army informed SCAP that clearance from Washington was required for every proposal to export items on either the 1A or 1B lists. Arguing that this requirement unnecessarily restricted commerce, including trade in nonstrategic goods, SCAP requested greater authority to approve export proposals. On 13 January 1950, the Departments of State and the Army sent a policy guidance message in response to SCAP's requests. By the time SCAP obtained the autonomy to regulate Japanese trade in keeping with U.S. national security guidelines, however, those guidelines themselves had become more restrictive. On this conflict, see memo, Thorp to U. Alexis Johnson, 25 May 1951, 400.949/5-2551, DF; and report, "Trade Between Japan and China and Adjacent Communist Areas," 15 May, 1951, 493.94/5-1651, DF. For the January instructions, see Army tel to SCAP, 13 Jan. 1950, 493.94/1-1350, DF; and *FRUS, 1950*, 6:619–20.

21. SOS circular airgram to all diplomatic offices, 8 Mar. 1950, *FRUS, 1950*, 4:77–80; and letter, DA to Charles Sawyer, 8 June 1950, ibid., 6:638–40.

22. James E. Webb letter to Sawyer, 4 Oct. 1949, *FRUS, 1949*, 9:879. Additional controls, according to State, were to deny (1A) goods of direct military utility to the Chinese Communists; to prevent transshipment via China to other Communist states; and to demonstrate Western solidarity, including the ability to control trade in strategic goods. Anticipating British reluctance to restrict trade in 1B items, the Americans were willing to permit such exports that "could be justified in terms of normal civilian requirements." The United States urged that the British control and exchange information on shipments to China of only "a highly selected list of 1-B items" (about 50 in total).

23. The impact of U.S. pressure on U.K. policy is revealed in two lengthy minutes by R. H. Scott, 28–29 June 1950, FC1121/31, FO 371/83365, PRO.

24. Webb letter to Sawyer, 4 Oct. 1949 and DA circular tel, 11 Oct. 1949, *FRUS, 1949*, 9:879, 880; and DA circular tel, 14 Oct. 1949, ibid., 9:884. Export controls did not rank as either government's highest priority, but the secretary of state and the foreign secretary both followed closely the bilateral negotiations on the matter.

25. Documentation concerning approaches to third powers may be found in FO 371/83364 and 83365, PRO; and *FRUS, 1949*, 9:884–89. See also DA tel to AmEmb Belgium, 29 Mar. 1950, *FRUS, 1950*, 6:627–28.

26. Quotation from memcon by R. N. Magill, 9 Sept. 1949, *FRUS, 1949*, 9:874. See also British Embassy a-m to DOS, 12 Sept. 1949, ibid., 9:877. Given U.K. possessions in Asia, the control of petroleum products was much more important (than 1B items) to the United Kingdom in order to deny the Communist Chinese the ability to expand beyond their borders.

27. Thompson, "Nationalizing British Firms in Shanghai: The Politics of Hostage Capitalism in People's China, 1949–1957," 171.

28. Circular tel by DA, 11 Oct. 1949, *FRUS, 1949*, 9:882.

29. DOS to British Embassy, 30 Dec. 1949, *FRUS, 1949*, 9:901; Katō, "Kokomu kara Wassenā Goi e" [From COCOM to the Wassenaar Arrangement], 22–23. Katō emphasizes that direct U.S. pressure (usually by means of assistance programs) on the allies individually was more important in determining the level of control than any independent power of COCOM.

30. Quotations are from AmEmb London a-m to Minister of State, 7 July 1950, 460.509/7-1150, DF. For further documentation, see *FRUS 1950*, 4:80, 85, 96, 116.

31. Another estimate placed the loss at one-third of exports (to Eastern Europe) and over one-third of imports. See DOS paper, undated, and Philip C. Jessup memo to DA, 24 Aug. 1950, *FRUS, 1950*, 4:151, 178.

32. The quotation is drawn from DOS paper on "Trade between Japan and China and Adjacent Communist Areas," p. 4, 493.94/5-1651, DF.

33. Lewis E. Douglas tel to DOS, 28 June 1950, 493.009/6-2850, DF; memcon by Makins, 29 June 1950, FC1121/38A, FO 371/83365, PRO; and Douglas tel to DOS, 1 July 1950, *FRUS, 1950*, 6:642.

34. Minute by Scott, 29 June 1950, FC1121/31, FO 371/83365, PRO; and minute by C. T. Crowe, 3 Aug. 1950, FC1121/86, FO 371/83367, PRO.

35. R. M. Hadow to W. Strang, 30 June 1950, FC1121/78, FO 371/83367, PRO.

36. Minute by Crowe, FC1121/86, ibid. In substance, the decisions prohibited exports of materials on IL/I and IL/II and proposed adding oil to IL/I. Thus, the ministers did not extend control to the entire American 1B list, although they did provide for surveillance of such shipments.

37. Douglas tel to DOS, 14 July 1950, *FRUS, 1950*, 6:649; minute by R. S. Milward, 22 July 1950, FC1121/82; and minute by D. P. Aiers, FC1121/93, FO 371/83367, PRO.

38. Minute by Aiers, 4 Aug. 1950, FC1121/93, ibid.

39. Memo by the Minister of Defence, 29 Aug. 1950, FC1121/140, FO 371/83369, PRO. The report listed forty-five items, none of which then appeared on IL/I or IL/II. It did not recommend complete suspension of exports to China or oriental Russia; "small and reasonable quantities" of the items in question—including radio receiving sets, locomotives, gasoline engines, nitric acid, copper wire, magnesium, and equipment for mapmaking and map reproduction—were to be allowed.

40. Staff Working Paper, 16 Aug. 1950, attached to R. F. Pryce memo to Colonel Shepley, 17 Aug. 1950, 460.509/8-1750, DF.

41. Record of Actions by the NSC, 24 Aug. 1950, and tel DA to AmEmb London, 9 Sept. 1950, *FRUS, 1950*, 4:180, 186.

42. Webb tel to AmEmb France, 23 Sept. 1950, *FRUS, 1950*, 4:192. The text of the Cannon amendment is reprinted in ibid., 4:193.

43. Julius C. Holmes tel to SOS, 21 Nov. 1950, ibid., 4:241; and agreed minute, 19 Sept. 1950, ibid., 4:188. On the compromises, see Webb tel to AmEmb France, 22 Sept. 1950, and DOS report, undated, ibid., 4:191, 204.

44. Bohlen desp to DOS, 4 Dec. 1950, ibid., 4:234.

45. Agreed report on the London Tripartite Conversations on Security Export Control, 20 Nov. 1950, ibid., 4:236.

46. Dept. of Commerce report, 4 Dec. 1950, ibid., 6:672-73; memcon by Barbara Evans, 29 Nov. 1950, ibid., 6:667; and Treasury to NSC, 30 Nov. 1950, ibid., 6:670.

47. Memcon by Jessup, 14 Dec. 1950, ibid., 6:681-82. See also memcon, Thomas C. Blaisdell and Robert W. Barnett, 15 Dec. 1950, 493.009/12-1550, DF.

48. DA circular tel to all diplomatic offices, 16 Dec. 1950, *FRUS, 1950*, 6:682-83; and a-m, 15 Dec. 1950, 493.009/12-1550, DF.

49. U. Alexis Johnson to Merchant, 21 Dec. 1950, *FRUS, 1950*, 6:685-87. As soon

as conflict broke out in Korea, Acheson regarded the problem of Japan's trade with the PRC as being "disposed of for the time being." See memo by Barnett, Aug. 1950, ibid., 6:177.

50. Sources of quotations: "deplorable campaign" etc.: H. A. Graves letter to J. S. H. Shattock, 30 Dec. 1950, FC 1121/6, FO 371/92272, PRO; "virtual embargo": FO tel to Washington, 21 Dec. 1950, FC1121/157, FO 371/83370, PRO; and "this embargo": Washington tel to FO, 18 Dec. 1950, FC1121/157, PRO.

51. Willard L. Thorp to H. Freeman Matthews, 9 Feb. 1951, *FRUS, 1951*, 7:1900; and George Marshall letter to DA, 9 Apr. 1951, ibid., 7:1950. DOS recommended that the ceiling be lowered to 60 percent. Instead of relaxing controls, Defense Secretary Marshall insisted that the imperative was to "persuade other friendly countries to impose economic restrictions, parallel to our own, on all exports to Communist China." For context, see Tucker, *Taiwan, Hong Kong, and the United States, 1945–1972*, 197–216.

52. Ed. note, *FRUS, 1951*, 7:1893.

53. FO minute by Scott, 30 Dec. 1950, FC1027/3, FO 371/92233, PRO. The "useless" quotation is from memcon by Allen, 13 Feb. 1951, *FRUS, 1951*, 7:1912.

54. Memcon by Ward P. Allen and Barnett, 21 Feb. 1951, *FRUS, 1951*, 7:1927; memcon by James N. Hyde, 5 Apr. 1951, ibid., 7:1947; and DOS position paper, 26 Mar. 1951, ibid., 7:1958. See also memo for the files by F. D. Collins, 10 Apr. 1951, 493.009/4-1051, DF.

55. Commonwealth Relations Office tel to U.K. High Commissioners, 21 Feb. 1951, FC1027/40, FO 371/92234, PRO. The "delayed" quotation is from Gladwyn Jebb tel to FO, 23 Feb. 1951, FC1027/47, ibid.

56. Minutes by A. E. Franklin and J. O. Lloyd, 27 and 28 Feb. 1951, FC1027/48, ibid.

57. DA tel to U.S. Mission at the UN, 1 May 1951, *FRUS, 1951*, 7:1977; DA tel to AmEmb U.K., 5 May 1951, and ed. note, ibid., 7:1984.

58. Chen, *China's Road to the Korean War*, 213–20. See also Zhang, *Mao's Military Romanticism*, which recounts Chinese leaders' view of the Korean War. Chinese leaders were quick to criticize British participation in the blockade of the PRC and point to it as a reason for refusing to establish full diplomatic relations with the United Kingdom. See Thompson, "Hostage Capitalism in People's China," 179. Thompson drew extensively upon interviews of principals and confidential documents from the companies he studied.

59. Attachment to Thorp memo to Johnson, 25 May 1951, 500.949/5-2551, DF.

60. Memo by Special Committee on East-West Trade to the NSC, 9 Feb. 1951, *FRUS, 1951*, 1:1018–19; and NSC 104/2, 4 Apr. 1951, ibid., 1:1059–64. Controversy over licensing policy for Hong Kong and Macao, however, was not resolved until the next year. See NSC 122/1, 6 Feb. 1952, *FRUS, 1952–54*, 14:5–8.

61. Ed. note, *FRUS, 1951*, 1:1073; and Linder to DA, 20 June 1951, ibid., 1:1123.

62. Philip W. Bonsal tel to DA, 2 Aug. 1951, ibid., 1:1164–65.

63. Jack K. McFall letter to Frederick J. Lawton, ibid., 1:1202–3. Foreign Secretary Morrison, for example, criticized U.S. legislation as "extremely annoying." See also minutes of U.S. and U.K. Foreign Ministers, 11 Sept. 1951, ibid., 1:1184.

64. The "intelligent" quotation is from memo, Linder to DA, 20 June 1951, ibid., 1:1123. On the relations with Battle, see tel, DA to Embassy in France, 14 June 1951, and memo, Linder to DA, 20 June 1951, ibid., 1:1109, 1125.

65. From Jan. 1952 to Dec. 1956, Presidents Truman and Eisenhower approved twenty-nine cases of Category B shipments, involving seven countries and having a value of $19.3 million. The law entrusted administration of the act to the head of the Mutual Security Program (and its successors), and created a permanent staff to assist in its implementation ("The Strategic Trade Control System, 1948–1956: Ninth Semiannual Report to Congress on Operations under the Mutual Defense Assistance Control Act of 1951, 28 June 1957," DOS, *American Foreign Policy, Current Documents, 1956*, 1069).

66. Laurie Battle letter to Harriman, 29 Sept. 1952, *FRUS, 1952–54*, 1:896–900. On subsequent attention to export controls, see letter, Battle to JFD, 19 Feb. 1953, plus attached speech, 493.009/2-1953; and letter, Battle to Yasuo Takeyama (Chief of Bureau, *Nihon Keizai Shimbun*), 24 July 1953, 493.009/7-2453, DF.

67. On procedures, the transfer, and cooperation, see two despatches by Peyton Kerr to DOS, both dated 12 Feb. 1952, 400.949/2-1252, DF. On cooperation, see also Kerr desp to DOS, 25 Feb. 1952, 400.949/2-2552, DF; and Kerr desp to DOS, 18 Mar. 1952, 400.949/3-1852, DF. For extensive documentation on control procedures, see Frank A. Waring desp to DOS, 8 Apr. 1952, 400.949/4-852, DF.

68. Yoshida letter to Trygve Lie (Secretary General of the UN), June 1951, FJ1126/2, FO 371/92641, PRO.

69. Kerr desp to DOS, 18 Mar. 1952, p. 2, 400.949/4-852, DF.

70. The a-m, dated 28 Mar., is reprinted in DA tel to AmEmb Paris, 17 Apr. 1952, 400.949/4-1152, DF.

71. A copy of the Japanese a-m is attached to Waring desp to DOS, 27 May 1952, 493.949/5-2752, DF. The MITI revisions are detailed in Dudley Singer desp to DOS, 12 Aug. 1952, 460.509/8-1252, DF.

72. On Japanese business opinion, see Robert Murphy tel to DOS, 17 June 1952, 493.949/6-1752, DF. Division within the Japanese government is discussed in Kerr desp to DOS, 10 June 1952, 493.949/6-1052, DF. The Okazaki quotation is from Waring desp to DOS, 27 May 1952, 493.949/5-2752, DF.

73. The Foreign Ministry quote is from Waring desp to DOS, 16 July 1952, 493.949/7-1652, DF. See also Kerr desp to DOS, 19 Aug. 1952, 493.949/8-1952, DF; A. Guy Hope to Walter P. McConaughy, 29 Sept. 1952, 493.9431/9-2952, DF; and Waring desp to DOS, 10 July 1952, 493.949/7-1052, DF. On the PRC's peace offensive and how the intent was to break out of U.S.-imposed diplomatic isolation, see Radtke, *China's Relations with Japan, 1945–1983*. On the peace offensive in the context of Japan's foreign policy, see Shimizu, "Perennial Anxiety."

74. Young to Allison, 4 June 1952, 611.94/6-452, DF. A copy of the Kawazoe-Takamatsu study is attached.

75. The Yoshida quotation is from summary of telegrams, 24 June 1952, folder: May–June 1952, box 23, Naval Aide Files, HSTL. For a memcon with Ishikawa Ichirō, President of the Keidanren, see Kerr desp to DOS, 26 Nov. 1954, Kerr to DOS, 493.949/11-2654, DF. See also Kerr desp to DOS, 24 July 1952, 493.949/7-2452, DF.

76. Yukawa Morio to Haguiwara Tōru, Dec. 1951; Haguiwara letter to Yukawa 21 Jan. 1952; and Haguiwara letter to Yukawa, 19 Feb. 1952, pp. 3–12, Tai-Kyōsanken Yushutsu Tōsei, Iinkai Kankei Ikken [Coordinating Committee related], reel E-0015, Public Release Series 12 (1994), JFMA. On Japanese anxiety about a connection between COCOM and NATO, see proposal, drafted 12 May 1952, pp. 68–70, ibid. On informing the United States, see Foreign Minister tel to Haguiwara, 30 May 1952, p. 72, ibid.

77. Acheson tel to AmEmb Tokyo, 6 June 1952, 493.949/5-3052, DF; and memcon by C. Thayer White, 20 Oct. 1954, 493.949/10-2054, DF.

78. The "at a time" quotation is from Hemmendinger letter to Waring, 16 June 1952, 493.949/6-1652, DF; and the source for "formally concur" is from DA tel to AmEmb Tokyo, 6 June 1952, 493.949/5-3052, DF.

79. Foreign Minister tel to certain embassies, 21 June 1952, pp. 210–11, Tai-Kyōsanken Yushutsu Tōsei Iinkai Kankei Ikken, reel E-0015, Public Release Series 12, JFMA. For the text of the U.S. invitation, see pp. 257–58, ibid.

80. Hope to Troy L. Perkins, 9 June 1952, *FRUS*, *1952–54*, 14:1267; Hope to Perkins, 3 June 1952, ibid., 14:1266–67; and Young to JMA, 8 July 1952, 400.949/7-852, DF.

81. Robert McClurkin to JMA, 21 July 1952, *FRUS*, *1952–54*, 14:1287–88. For the text of the proposals given to the Japanese government, see pp. 289–90, Tai-Kyōsanken Tōsei Iinkai Kankei Ikken, reel E-0015, Public Release Series 12, JFMA.

82. McClurkin to JMA, 21 July 1952, *FRUS*, *1952–54*, 14:1287–88.

83. DA tel to certain embassies, 18 July 1952, 460.509/7-1852, DF.

84. The relevant part of the text of NSC 125/1 is reprinted in *FRUS*, *1952–54*, 14:1296. For the DOS view, see Linder to Acting Sec., 6 Aug. 1952, ibid., 14:1298–1300.

85. Young to U. Alexis Johnson, 4 Aug. 1952, ibid., 14:1292–94.

86. Murphy tel to DOS, 18 June 1952, 493.949/6-1852, DF; and Murphy tel to DOS, 22 July 1952, 460.509/7-2252, DF.

87. The quotation is from Murphy tel to DOS, 25 July 1952, 460.509/7-2552, DF. On the Japanese press, see also Waring desp to DOS, 16 July 1952, 460.509/7-1652, DF; Murphy tel to DOS, 14 July 1952, 460.509/7-1452, DF; and Kerr desp to DOS, 24 July 1952, 493.949/7-2452, DF.

88. On the British view, see Holmes tel to DOS, 22 July 1952, 460.509/7-2252, DF. On the French view, see Dunn to DOS, ibid.

89. For the British proposal: Holmes to DOS, 22 July 1952, ibid. On the Japanese view: Araki tel to Foreign Minister, 28 July 1952, pp. 328–31, reel E-0015, Public Release Series 12, JFMA; Araki tel to Foreign Minister 31 July 1952, pp. 357–58, ibid.; and Murphy tel to DOS, 1 Aug. 1952, 460.509/8-152, DF. For the final agreement: Young to U. Alexis Johnson, 4 Aug. 1952, *FRUS*, *1952–54*, 14:1293. The text of the meeting's results is reprinted on pp. 360–63, Tai-Kyōsanken Yushutsu Tōsei Iinkai Kankei Ikken, reel E-0015, Public Release Series 12, JFMA.

90. Charles Bohlen to JMA, 1 Aug. 1952, 460.509/8-152, DF; and NSC 125/2, 7 Aug. 1952, *FRUS*, *1952–54*, 14:1308.

91. Murphy tel to DOS, 1 Aug. 1952, 460.509/8-152, DF. The telegram conveys

Yukawa's comments. See also what appears to be a confidential Japanese proposal on the matter, pp. 308–9, Tai-Kyōsanken Yushutsu Tōsei Iinkai Kankei Ikken, reel E-0015, Public Release Series 12, JFMA.

92. Young to U. Alexis Johnson, 4 Aug. 1952, *FRUS, 1952–54*, 14:1292–93.

93. Ibid. DOS wrote the letter Takeuchi was to sign. See draft letter, Takeuchi to Linder, undated, 460.509/8-152, DF. On Linder's need for letters, see David Bruce tel to AmEmb Tokyo, 19 Aug. 1952, 460.509/8-1652, DF. The letters exchanged were dated 2 Aug. 1952, and are filed in 460.509/8-252, DF. Copies are reprinted on pp. 388, 408–9, and 410–11, Tai-Kyōsanken Yushutsu Tōsei Iinkai Kankei Ikken, reel E-0015, Public Release Series 12, JFMA. The separate agreement on the methods of control was still closed to researchers at the National Archives. A copy of a draft, apparently proposed by the Japanese, is reprinted on pp. 379–84, ibid.

94. On the four hundred goods and the items released, see David K. E. Bruce tel to Murphy, 15 Aug. 1952, 460.509/8-152, DF, and Bruce tel to AmEmb Tokyo 2 Aug. 1952, 460.509/8-252, DF.

95. Linder to the Acting Secretary, 6 Aug. 1952, *FRUS, 1952–54*, 14:1299.

96. For a summary of Yukawa's interpretation, see Murphy tel to DOS, 16 Aug. 1952, 460.509/8-1652, DF. The Takeuchi quotation is from memcon by White, 18 Aug. 1952, 460.509/8-1852, DF.

97. Letter, Frank C. Nash to Thorp, 28 Aug. 1952, 460.509/8-2852, DF.

98. Murphy tels to DOS, 29 Aug. 1952, 460.509/8-2952; 2 Sept. 1952, 460.509/9-252; and 5 Sept. 1952, 460.509/9-552, DF.

99. DA tel to certain diplomatic and offices, 19 Sept. 1952, *FRUS, 1952–54*, 14:1332–33.

100. Raymond Ludden letter to McConaughy, 3 Dec. 1952, 493.009/12-552, DF. A copy of the speech is attached. Earlier, the United States floated the idea—which the allies promptly rejected—of a total embargo against the PRC. See W. S. Anderson to Hope, plus attached draft recommendations, 14 Aug. 1952, 493.009/8-1452; and W. Sandifer to U. Alexis Johnson, 24 Nov. 1952, 493.009/11-2452, RG-59, NA.

Chapter Five

1. Reichard, "Eisenhower as President: The Changing View"; and Rabe, "Eisenhower Revisionism: A Decade of Scholarship."

2. Nixon, *Six Crises*, 161.

3. See, for example, Divine, *Eisenhower and the Cold War*, 154–55.

4. Greenstein, *The Hidden-Hand Presidency*, 57.

5. Divine, *Eisenhower and the Cold War*, 9.

6. Unlike Dulles, Dodge remained in touch with top Japanese leaders. More accurately, the Japanese sought to maintain contact with him. See, for example, Ikeda Hayato letter to Dodge, 14 Feb. 1953, folder: Japan, 1952–53, box 9, Dodge Files, DDEL.

McClurkin was deputy director, Office of Northeast Asian Affairs (ONA), to Sept. 1954; then director to Dec. 1956. Hemmendinger was the officer in charge of economic affairs, ONA, to Sept. 1954; then deputy director through 1957. Young was director, ONA, from Mar. 1952 to Sept. 1954. White served as the assistant to the officer in charge of economic affairs from Apr. 1951. Leddy was an international economist in the Bureau of Economic Affairs until Oct. 1955; thereafter he served as a special assistant in various capacities to the assistant secretary and deputy under secretary (for economic affairs). Weiss served in the Division of Commercial Policy during the period studied. Corse began his government career as an economic analyst for the department before the war. He served on several delegations in connection with the work of GATT from 1948 to 1952; from 1951 he was chief of the Trade Agreements and Treaties Division. Two women serving in the latter division through the 1955 tariff negotiations with Japan were Selma G. Kallis and Margaret H. Potter. Kallis worked as an international economist from 1951, and Potter headed the division's Trade Agreements Branch from 1952.

7. DDE, Annual Message to the Congress on the State of the Union, 2 Feb. 1953, PPP: DDE, 1953, 15.

8. DDE diary entry, 2 July 1953, Ferrell, *Eisenhower Diaries*, 244.

9. Ibid. On Eisenhower's social and political philosophy, see Griffith, "Dwight D. Eisenhower and the Corporate Commonwealth."

10. Eisenhower, *Crusade in Europe*, 476.

11. DDE, Remarks at the National Editorial Association Dinner, 22 June 1954, PPP: DDE, 1954, 585–90.

12. Cook, *The Declassified Eisenhower*.

13. DDE, State of the Union, 2 Feb. 1953, PPP: DDE, 1953, 14, 18–19, 21. The budget for FY 1954 that President Truman submitted totaled $78.6 billion. Of this amount, $55.5 billion was to be spent on the Department of Defense, the Mutual Security Administration, and the Atomic Energy Commission. The projected deficit totaled $9.9 billion (Eisenhower, *Mandate for Change*, 171–72).

14. Reedy, *The U.S. Senate*, 101.

15. On Eisenhower and the Old Guard, see Ambrose, *Eisenhower*, 36–103; and Reichard, *The Reaffirmation of Republicanism*. Ambrose uses the term "Old Guard" to describe heartland conservatives. Reichard describes them as "nationalists." The words are used interchangeably here. Eisenhower's account is *Mandate for Change*, 145–79, 243–95, 339–401.

16. U.S. Congress, House, Committee on Ways and Means, *Hearings on Simplification of Customs Administration*, 82d Congress, 1st sess., 1952, 206.

17. Hoopes, *The Devil and John Foster Dulles*, 124–33.

18. Acheson, *Present at the Creation*, 369. For two portraits of the so-called Georgetown establishment, see Merry, *Taking on the World*; and Yoder, *Joe Alsop's Cold War*.

19. Hoopes, *The Devil and John Foster Dulles*, 156–58. See also U.S. Congress, Senate, Committee on Foreign Relations, *Executive Sessions (Historical Series)*, 83d Cong., 1st sess., 1953, 65–108. On McCarthy and McCarthyism, consult Oshinsky, "*A Conspiracy So Immense*"; Schrecker, *No Ivory Tower*; and Carlton, *Red Scare!*.

20. DDE diary entry, 7 Feb. 1953, Ferrell, *Eisenhower Diaries*, 227.

21. Tananbaum, *The Bricker Amendment Controversy*.

22. A thoughtful account of law making during the fifties is Reedy, *The U.S. Senate*.

23. Eisenhower, *Mandate for Change*, 254.

24. On the Tariff Commission, see Kravis, "The Trade Agreements Escape Clause."

25. Eisenhower, *Mandate for Change*, 263. For the highly unfavorable DOS view of the Simpson bill, see Weiss to Leddy, 15 May 1953, folder: Trade Agreements Renewal, box 296, ITF.

26. U.S. Congress, House, Committee on Ways and Means, *Hearings: Trade Agreements Extension Act of 1953*, 83d Cong., 1st sess., 1953.

27. Reedy, *The U.S. Senate*, 88. Reedy was an aide to Lyndon Johnson (D.-Tex.) when Johnson was a senator during the fifties. Millikin's power and his mastery of the issues, however, are evident from memoranda of his conversations with administration officials.

28. The quotation is from Garraty, *Dictionary of American Biography, Supplement Six, 1956–1960*, 455. No biography of Millikin exists.

29. See, for example, DDE meeting with legislative leadership, 13 Dec. 1954, box 1, Legislative Meetings Series, AWF, DDEL.

30. On the absence of debate, see Aaronson, *Trade and the American Dream*, 61–113.

31. DDE to Cabinet Officers and the Administrators and Directors of the Executive Agencies, 6 Mar. 1953, box 3, DDE Diary Series, AWF, DDEL. Eisenhower ordered executive officials to make certain of "appropriate and timely consultation with Congressional leaders in all matters where this seems necessary or desirable" before presenting any item to his office. While Congress was in session the president held weekly meetings with the GOP leaders of both houses of Congress.

32. Taft, quoted by Adams, *Firsthand Report*, 21. Adams's account is corroborated by legislative leaders meeting minutes, 30 Apr. 1953, Legislative Meeting Series, box 1, DDE Papers, DDEL; and DDE diary entry, 1 May 1953, Ferrell, *Eisenhower Diaries*, 235–36. According to James T. Patterson, Taft's biographer, Taft's outburst on April 30 "may have tumbled from a body increasingly racked with pain." It was at this time that the cancer which would claim his life began to spread throughout his body, sapping his energy and causing him considerable pain (Patterson, *Mr. Republican*, 600). Statistics are from Eisenhower, *Mandate for Change*, 171–72.

33. DDE diary entry, 7 Feb. 1953, Ferrell, *Eisenhower Diaries*, 227.

34. On the Japanese presentation to DOS, see ed. note (excerpt of DOS tel to AmEmb Tokyo, 9 Apr. 1953), *FRUS*, 1952–54, 14:1409. Records pertaining to the Mutual Defense Assistance Agreement bringing Japan into the MSP are in 794.5 MSP, 1953–54, DF. The texts of the agreements, dated 8 Mar. 1954, are reprinted in *DSB* 30 (5 Apr. 1954): 518–25. Special procurements and the spending of U.S. forces (plus their dependents) constituted 37 percent of all foreign exchange receipts in 1952–53; as late as 1959–60 they still amounted to 11 percent (Chalmers Johnson, *MITI*, 200).

35. Young to Walter S. Robertson, 10 Apr. 1953, *FRUS*, 1952–54, 14:1409.

36. W. B. Smith tel to AmEmb Tokyo, 11 Apr. 1953, ibid., 14:1410–11.

37. DDE, Special Message to the Congress Recommending the Renewal of the Reciprocal Trade Agreements Act, 7 Apr. 1953, *PPP: DDE*, 1953, 163–65. On Eisenhower's foreign economic policy his first year, see Kaufman, *Trade and Aid*, 12–33.

38. JFD testimony, 4 May 1953, *DSB* 28 (25 May 1953):745. The Bureau of Far Eastern Affairs urged Dulles not to make a statement precluding some sort of trade negotiations with Japan. See memo, Robertson to Linder, 30 Apr. 1953, 394.31/4-3053, DF.

39. Public Advisory Board for Mutual Security, *A Trade and Tariff Commission in the National Interest*. Bell was president of the American Security and Trust Company, Washington, D.C., and former under secretary of the treasury. The Office of Northeast Asian Affairs contributed to the Bell report (Hemmendinger letter to Waring, 7 Nov. 1952, 394.31/11-752, DF).

40. Bauer, Pool, and Dexter, *American Business and Public Policy*, 32, 375–87; and DDE, News Conference, 22 July 1953, *PPP: DDE*, 1953, 506–7. Eisenhower did not intend to come out against the Simpson bill in public, even though it was at odds with his own program. At a press conference held shortly before the measure came up for a vote, a reporter friendly to the anti-Simpson forces asked the president for his views on the measure. Trapped, Eisenhower responded that he opposed the measure.

41. For Randall's views, consult his *A Creed for Free Enterprise*.

42. DDE to JFD, 15 Jan. 1953, box 2, DDE Diary Series, AWF, DDEL; and memcon JFD and Stassen, 17 Mar. 1953, box 1, Chronological Series, JFD Papers, DDEL.

43. For the announcement, see letter to the President of the Senate and the Speaker of the House of Representatives Recommending Establishment of a Commission on Foreign Economic Policy, 2 May 1953, *PPP: DDE*, 1953, 252–54. On the background, see DDE to the Secretary of the Treasury, 27 Mar. 1953, plus attached paper by Kline, 18 Mar. 1953, folder: President-Office File, box 10, Papers of George Humphrey, RG-56, NA.

44. Humphrey letter to DDE, 21 Apr. 1953, folder: President-Office File, Box 10, Papers of George Humphrey, RG-56, NA.

45. Gabriel Hauge and Arthur Flemming initially called for Speaker Martin to appoint four members, two from the House, two from outside; Vice President Nixon to appoint four members, two from the Senate, two from outside; and for the president to appoint five members including the chairman (Hauge to Adams, 25 Apr. 1953, folder: Carbon Copies to the White House Staff, box 1, Records of Gabriel Hauge, DDEL). The final agreement was for each to appoint five members. Eisenhower appointed Randall, Lamar Fleming Jr. (vice chairman), David J. McDonald, Cola G. Parker, Jess W. Tapp, John Hay Whitney, and John H. Williams. Nixon named Senator Millikin, Senator Bourke B. Hickenlooper (R.-Iowa), Senator Prescott Bush (R.-Conn.), Senator Harry F. Byrd (D.-Va.), and Senator Walter F. George (D.-Ga.). Martin appointed Rep. Reed, Rep. Simpson, Rep. John M. Vorys (R.-Ohio), Rep. Jere Cooper (D.-Tenn.), and Rep. Laurie C. Battle (D.-Ala.). On the legislative history, see ed. note, *FRUS*, 1952–54, 1:49–50.

46. Memcon with Takeuchi, plus attachments, 27 Apr. 1953, 394.31/4-2753, DF. See also Akaneya, *Nihon no Gatto Kanyū Mondai*, 167–70.

47. DOS, "Treaty of Friendship, Commerce, and Navigation between the United States of America and Japan," TIAS no. 2863, 2 Apr. 1953, *USTIA*, vol. 4, pt. 2.

48. JFD tel to AmEmb Tokyo, 3 Apr. 1953, 394.31/4-253, DF.

49. Eisenhower, *Mandate for Change*, 264. On the care with which Eisenhower reviewed escape clause cases, see OH, H. Roemer McPhee, pp. 29–31, DDEL.

50. DDE letter to Reed, 10 June 1954, *DSB* 28 (29 Jun. 1953): 929–30. On the lobbying, see, for example, Emanuel Celler letter to DDE, 23 May 1953; and Young letter to Grew, 13 May 1953, folder: C-4.2/3(a) Silk Scarves, box 2, Records of the Office of Northeast Asian Affairs, Alpha Numeric Files on Japan, 1953–55, RG-59, NA.

51. DA tel to AmEmb France, 14 Jan. 1953, *FRUS, 1952–54*, 1:127–28. Similar telegrams were sent to other capitals. On the effort to win over the French, for example, see tel 3986, Dunn to SOS, 16 Jan. 1953, 394.31/1-1653, DF.

52. FO minute by J. A. Snellgrove, 8 Jan. 1953, UEE38/7, FO 371/105031, PRO.

53. Dening letter to W. D. Allen, 15 Dec. 1954, UEE1021/122, FO 371/110162, PRO.

54. Annex III to paper, "Japan and the GATT," by President, Board of Trade, n.d., UEE38/4A, FO 371/105031, PRO.

55. FO minute by A. Leavett, 24 Dec. 1954, UEE1021/122, FO 371/110162, PRO.

56. Paper prepared by BT, "Japan and the G.A.T.T.," pp. 3, 6–7, 7 Jan. 1953, UEE38/4A, FO 371/105031, PRO. Emphasis in original.

57. FO minute on Cabinet Paper C(53)20 by D. A. H. Wright, 19 Jan. 1953, UEE38/10, ibid. FO views are also summarized in FO tel to Brussels, 23 Jan. 1953, UEE38/13, ibid.

58. Dening tel to FO, 27 Jan. 1953, UEE38/17, ibid; and Dening tel to FO, 30 Jan. 1953, UEE38/36, FO 371/105032, PRO.

59. Memcon, Attitude of Canada, Australia, and New Zealand, 23 Jan. 1953, UEE38/20, FO 371/105031, PRO.

60. Robert Murphy tel to SOS, 20 Jan. 1953, *FRUS, 1952–54*, 1:131–32.

61. FO tel to Washington, 26 Jan. 1953, UEE38/13, FO 371/105031, PRO.

62. FO tel to Washington, 28 Jan. 1953, UEE38/21, ibid; and Roger Makins tel to FO, 28 Jan. 1953, UEE38/31, FO 371/105032, PRO.

63. Stanley D. Metzger to Jack B. Tate, 25 Feb. 1953, *FRUS, 1952–54*, 1:152–54; and Snellgrove letter to Wright, 12 Feb. 1953, UEE38/63, FO 371/105033, PRO.

64. U.K. delegation tel to FO, 4 Feb. 1953, UEE38/41, FO 371/105032, PRO; and Ward tel to SOS, 4 Feb. 1953, 394.31/2-453, DF.

65. McClurkin to JMA and U. Alexis Johnson, 5 Feb. 1953, 394.31/2-553, DF; and Ward tel to SOS, 4 Feb. 1953, 394.31/2-453, DF. See also U.K. delegation tel to FO, 6 Feb. 1953, UEE38/51, FO 371/105032, PRO.

66. FO tel to Geneva, 5 Feb. 1953, UEE38/42, FO 371/105032, PRO; and Peter Thorneycroft letter to Anthony Eden, 2 Feb. 1953; and FO minute by Wright, 3 Feb. 1953, UEE38/49, ibid.

67. Ad Hoc Committee on Agenda and Intersessional Business, "Report on the Accession of Japan," p. 4, 13 Feb. 1953, UEE38/69, FO 371/105033, PRO.

68. McClurkin to JMA, 6 Mar. 1953, 394.31/2-2753, DF. Press excerpts are attached.

69. For a summary of the points at issue, see FO minutes by Wright, 21 July 1953, UEE38/134, FO 371/105035, PRO.

70. FO minute by C. W. Sanders (memcon with Haguiwara Tōru), 4 May 1953, UEE38/88, FO 371/105033.

71. JFD tel to AmEmb Tokyo, 3 Apr. 1953, 394.31/4-253, DF. On the Japanese response, see William T. Turner tel to SOS, 12 Apr. 1953, 394.31/4-1253, DF.

72. Walter S. Robertson to Linder, 30 Apr. 1953, 394.31/4-3053; and Walter K. Scott to JFD, 15 July 1953, 394.31/7-1353, DF. For background, see OH, Robertson, DDEL.

73. Ward tel to SOS, 6 May 1953, 394.31/5-653; Leonard Weiss tel to U.S. Consul, Geneva, 7 May 1953, 394.31/5-753; and JMA tel to SOS, 1 June 1953, 394.31/6-153, DF.

74. The Japanese records make clear that the immediate reason why Japan made the bid for temporary membership was the disappointment with the Eisenhower's decision to put a hold on tariff negotiations, the effect of which was to delay the chance of full accession for over another year. Tel, Araki Eikichi (ambassador in Washington) to Okazaki Katsuo (foreign minister), 4 Apr. 1953, pp. 255–56, subseries 5, The Problem of Japanese Entry to GATT, Feb.–Apr. 1953, reel E-0011, Public Release Series 10, JFMA. The text of the temporary membership proposal is on p. 334, subseries 6, The Problem of Japanese Entry to GATT, May–Aug. 1953, ibid. See also: tel, Araki to Okazaki, 25 July 1953, pp. 122–23, subseries 7, The Problem of Japanese Entry to GATT, July–Aug., 1953, ibid.; and letter Haguiwara to J. Melander (chairman of the contracting parties), 4 Aug 1953, pp. 228–31, ibid.

75. Johnson to SOS, 13 July 1953, 394.31/7-1353, DF. JFD's initials and "OK" appear in handwriting on the cover memo.

76. JFD tel to AmEmb Tokyo, 17 Aug. 1953, plus attachments, 394.31/8-1753, DF.

77. JFD letter to Reed, 1 Aug. 1953, 494.00/8-153; W. B. Smith to DDE, 20 Aug. 1953, plus attachments, 394.31/8-2053, DF. A handwritten note indicates DDE's approval on 26 August.

78. W. B. Smith to DDE, 21 Sept. 1953, plus attachments, 394.31/9-2153, DF. A handwritten note indicates DDE's approval on 23 September. The issue of extending tariff concessions concerned the life of concessions made in previous GATT negotiations. According to prior agreement, those concessions were due to expire at the end of 1953. DOS sought to win the other contracting parties' agreement to extend the life of those concessions for a period of twelve or eighteen months.

79. Makins tel to FO, 3 Sept. 1953, UEE38/168, FO 371/105036, PRO.

80. Young to U. Alexis Johnson, 8 Sept. 1953, 394.31/9-853; and W. B. Smith to Canberra, 14 Sept. 1953, 394.31/9-1453, DF.

81. U.K. delegation tel to FO, 23 Sept. 1953, UEE38/174, FO 371/105036, PRO.

82. U.K. delegation tel to FO, 17 Sept. 1953, UEE38/169, ibid.

83. Annex to Smith to DDE, 21 Sept. 1953, 394.31/9-2153, DF.

84. On Japan's proposal, see GATT documents L/107, 20 Aug. 1953, UEE38/158, and L/109, 24 Aug. 1953, UEE38/159, FO 371/105036, PRO. The U.S. position is explained in JFD circular to certain embassies and missions, 1 Dec. 1953, 394.31/12-153, DF.

85. For head counts, see, for example, Frank Lee tel to E. A. Cohen, 19 Oct. 1953, UEE38/206, FO 371/105038, PRO.

86. U.K. Delegation Geneva tel to FO, 26 Sept. 1953, UEE38/175, FO 371/105036; and U.K. delegation tel to FO, 29 Sept. 1953, UEE38/179, FO 371/105037, PRO.

87. U.K. delegation tel to FO, 29 Sept. 1953, UEE38/180, ibid.

88. Brown letter to Waugh, 24 Oct. 1953, *FRUS, 1952–54*, 1:166.

89. Waugh letter to SOS, 8 Mar. 1954, *FRUS, 1952–54*, 1:171–72; and paper on Japan and GATT, 31 Dec. 1954, UEE1022/1, FO 371/114927, PRO.

90. U.S. Commission on Foreign Economic Policy, *Report to the President and the Congress, January 1954*. Scholarly views include Bauer, Pool, and Dexter, *American Business and Public Policy*, 42; and Kaufman, *Trade and Aid*, 20–21. For DOS views on the Randall report, see White to McClurkin, 15 Feb. 1954, folder: Randall Commission, box 11, BFEA Records, 1954, RG-59, NA.

91. Randall diary entry, 6 Jan. 1954, Clarence B. Randall Journals, DDEL.

92. Nelson Aldrich letter to DDE, 4 Feb. 1954, folder: Randall Commission, box 11, BFEA Records, 1954, RG-59, NA.

93. U.S. Commission on Foreign Economic Policy, *Minority Report January 1954*, 2.

94. Randall diary entry, 6 Jan. 1954, Randall Journals, DDEL.

95. McClurkin to Robertson, 9 Feb. 1954, folder: Randall Commission, box 11, BFEA Records, RG-59, NA. The Bureau of Economic Affairs held similar views. See White to McClurkin, 15 Feb. 1954, ibid. For contemporary analysis, see Knorr and Patterson, *A Critique of the Randall Commission Report*.

Chapter Six

1. On the "1955 system," consult Dower, "Peace and Democracy in Two Systems."

2. DDE, "Memorandum Transmitting the Report of the Commission on Foreign Economic Policy," 23 Jan. 1954, *PPP: DDE, 1954*, 192–93; and DDE, "Special Message to the Congress on Foreign Economic Policy," 30 Mar. 1954, ibid., 352–63.

3. On the Kean bill's proviso, see memcon by C. Thayer White, 20 May 1954, file C-2.16, Box 2, BFEA, ONA Alpha Numeric Files on Japan, 1953–55, RG-59, NA. The Japan proviso specified that concessions must concern items in an agreement to which Japan was a party and that the president find that the concessions must be necessary to provide expanding export markets for Japan. The RTAA did not contain these restrictions.

4. Randall journal entry, 27 Feb. 1954, Randall Journals, DDEL.

5. On Eisenhower's involvement: Everett Drumright to SOS, 24 May 1954, file C-2.15b, box 2, BFEA, ONA Alpha Numeric Files on Japan, 1953–55, RG-59, NA. On Dulles: Robert McClurkin letter to Frank A. Waring, 10 June 1954, file C-2.15b, ibid; JFD to Thorsten V. Kalijarvi, 28 May 1954, and JFD to DDE, 28 May 1954, box 7, Chronological Series, JFD Papers, DDEL.

6. *Congressional Record*, 83d Cong., 2d sess., 1954, 100, pt. 6:8078.

7. PL 768, 83d Congress, was enacted 1 Sept. 1954. For the text see 68 stat. 1136.

8. Progress Report on the President's Foreign Economic Program, drafted by Paul H. Cullen, 15 Aug. 1955, *FRUS, 1955–57*, 9:3.

9. Report, "The 'Buy American Act': Reasons and Effects," file: "Buy American Act," box, 279, ITF.

10. Memcon by C. Arnold Fraleigh, 8 Dec. 1952, 400.1115/12-852, DF; and Kenneth T. Young to JMA, 6 Jan. 1953, plus attachments, file C-2, 11/1 "Buy American," box 2, ONA Alpha Numeric Files, 1953–54, RG-59, NA.

11. Memcon, Carl D. Corse and William C. Carpenter (sales manager, R. Thomas and Sons Co., Lisbon, Ohio), 24 June 1953, file C-2.11/1 "Buy American," box 2, ONA Alpha Numeric Files, 1953–54, RG-59, NA; memcon with White and Sawaki Masao, 21 July 1953, ibid.; White letter to A. Thomas Lloyd, 14 May 1954, ibid.; and minutes of cabinet meeting, 31 July 1953, box 2, Cabinet Series, AWF, DDEL. Nippon Gaisha Kaisha won a contract in 1953 to supply porcelain electrical insulators to Bonneville Power Administration for its dams along the Columbia River. A disproportionately large number of government purchases of imported items were for hydroelectric projects. The principal reason was that the American-made items were considerably more expensive (SOD Charles Wilson's comments, minutes of cabinet meeting, 10 July 1953, AWF, DDEL).

12. Japanese companies seeking U.S. government contracts, such as Nippon Gaisha Kaisha, usually did so with an American partner, and they did not hesitate to bring their concerns to the Eisenhower administration. See, for example, T. Haraguchi (director of Overseas Div., Hitachi, Ltd.) letter to Dodge, 15 Dec. 1954, box 2, Correspondence subseries, Dodge Series, CFEP (Chair) Records, DDEL. Hitachi was attempting to win a contract to supply electrical equipment for a dam along the Columbia River. The company sought to demonstrate its ability to meet the standards of the American market so as to impress potential customers in Asia as much as to crack the U.S. market.

13. Minutes of cabinet meetings, 29 May, 10 July, and 31 July 1953, box 2, Cabinet Series, AWF, DDEL. A copy of the draft executive order is attached to memo, JFD to Director of the Bureau of the Budget, 18 July 1953, 400.1115/7-1353, DF.

14. John M. Leddy to SOS, 26 Aug. 1953, 400.1115/8-2653, DF.

15. U.S. Commission on Foreign Economic Policy, *Report to the President and the Congress, January 1954*, 45; minutes of cabinet meetings, 18 Aug. and 20 Dec. 1954, box 3, Cabinet Series, AWF, DDEL. A copy of the executive order is enclosed in the folder for 10 December.

16. Statistics cited by Kaufman, *Trade and Aid*, 27–28.

17. Borden, *Pacific Alliance*, 183; and Kaufman, *Trade and Aid*, 26–29, 147–51.

18. Minutes of cabinet meeting, 19 Nov. 1954, box 4, Cabinet Series, AWF, DDEL; DOS, "Agreement on Agricultural Commodities between the United States of America and Japan," TIAS no. 3284, 31 May 1955, *USTIA*, vol. 6, pt. 2.

19. Minutes of cabinet meeting, 5 Nov. 1954, *FRUS, 1952–54*, 14:1770.

20. Statistics cited by Talbot and Kihl, "The Politics of Domestic and Foreign Policy Linkages in U.S.-Japanese Agricultural Policy Making," 329. On differences within the administration over rice for Japan, see Joseph S. Davis letter to Dodge,

30 June 1955, file: CFEP 505, PL 480 Rice to Japan (3), box 2, policy papers series, CFEP Records, DDEL; and Paul Cullen to Dodge, 19 Apr. 1955, file: CFEP 505, PL 480 Rice to Japan (4), ibid.

21. Talbot and Kihl, "The Politics of Domestic and Foreign Policy Linkages," 329.

22. From July 1954 to September 1978, PL 480 costs amounted to over $31.6 billion, and consisted of 262 metric tons of commodities shipped (ibid., 299). In 1960 about 26 percent of U.S. agricultural exports were shipped under PL 480 provisions. In 1970 the percentage stood at 14 percent, and by 1979 the figure had fallen to 3 percent (ibid., 300).

23. NSC 104/2, "U.S. Policies and Programs in the Economic Field Which May Affect the War Potential of the Soviet Bloc," 4 Apr. 1951, *FRUS*, 1951, 1:1059–64. Although many sternly worded policies are not implemented with vigor, the executive branch took economic defense very seriously, watching carefully for smugglers, for example. Consult Carl H. Boehringer desp to DOS 31 Aug. 1951, 493.94A234/8-351, DF; Walter P. McConaughy to Drumright, 15 Jan. 1954, and McConaughy to Robertson, 22 Dec. 1954, folder: "Trade," box 12, BFEA Records, 1954, RG-59, NA.

24. Spaulding, "'A Gradual and Moderate Relaxation,'" 231–32; and (on allied sentiment) NSC 152, "Review of Economic Defense Policy," 25 May 1953, *FRUS*, 1952–54, 1:968–81.

25. Okazaki, quoted in Waring desp to DOS, 31 July 1953, 493.949/7-3153, DF.

26. MITI moves to release items from control were in line with the September 1952 bilateral understanding. The U.S. Embassy followed these releases carefully. See, for example, letter plus attachments, Takeuchi Ryūji to McClurkin, 6 July 1953, 493.949/7-653, DF.

27. Dudley Singer desp to DOS, 20 Feb. 1953, 493.949/2-2053, DF. This despatch reviews the progress of negotiations under the bilateral understanding of September 1952. See also memcon with Takeuchi, 21 Feb. 1953, 493.009/2-1353, DF; and McClurkin to JMA, 2 Feb. 1953, *FRUS*, 1952–54, 14:1382–85.

28. In March 1953 Hoashi Kei, an influential politician on the left, expressed his views in an article, "In Defense of Japan–Red China Trade," published in the magazine *Shakai Shugi* (Socialism). For a translation, see Singer desp to DOS, 24 Mar. 1953, 493.94/3-2453, DF. On the second Sino-Japanese Trade Agreement, see Waring desp. to DOS, 22 July 1953, 493.9431/7-2253, DF.

29. Ralph J. Blake desp to DOS, 11 June 1953, 493.94/6-1153, DF.

30. One of the most persuasive advocates of expanded economic ties with China was Dr. Ōuchi Hyōe, economist and president of Hōsei University in Tokyo. See his "Road to Lasting Peace," *Nippon Times*, 2 Apr. 1953.

31. Local press clippings are reprinted in John M. Steeves desp to DOS, 27 Mar. 1953, 493.949/3-2753, DF. The embassy paid careful attention to the Japanese press reporting on this issue. See, for example, Singer desp to DOS, 6 Mar. 1953, 493.94/3-653, DF. The despatch reviews an article in the 1 Feb. 1953 issue of *Tōyō Keizai Shimpo* (Oriental economist) on Sakurai Hideo, managing director of the Tomoe Trading Company, who objected to restrictions on trade with the Chinese mainland.

32. For a review of the views of the Kansai Japan-China Trade Promotion Associa-

tion (*Kansai Nitchū-Bōeki Sokushin Kaigi*), see James V. Martin Jr. desp to DOS, 20 Jan. 1953, 493.94/1-2053, DF. DOS files contain numerous other such documents. On critics' doubts consult Peyton Kerr desp to DOS, 25 Feb. 1953, 493.94/2-2553, DF. The despatch reports on a round table conference recounted in the March 1953 issue of the magazine *Sekai* (World).

33. Memo of NSC meeting 8 Apr. 1953, *FRUS*, 1952–54, 14:1407; and DDE, Address before the National Editorial Association, 22 June 1954, ibid., 14:1663. After the armistice in Korea, Eisenhower expressed the point more forcefully. See memo by JFD, 10 Aug. 1953, ibid., 14:1488; and memo of NSC meeting, 19 Mar. 1953, box 4, NSC Series, AWF, DDEL. Førland and Spaulding also discuss Eisenhower's views in detail. Although export controls did not rank as a top priority, Eisenhower considered the matter important. He thought carefully about U.S. policy, and he consistently favored what he considered a moderate line.

34. Robertson to Walter B. Smith, 4 Mar. 1954, 493.509/3-454, DF; McCarthy letter to JFD, 6 May 1957, 493.509/5-1253, DF. Attached are excerpts of Dulles's testimony on mutual aid, including commentary by Senator H. Alexander Smith.

35. JFD letter to McCarthy, 6 May 1953, box 6, Chrono series, JFD Papers, DDEL. The war in Korea was the decisive factor in American policy. Reasoning that "Communist China is a military aggressor," the NSC simply excluded trade with the PRC from its review of policy in 1953 (NSC-152/2, 31 July 1953, *FRUS*, 1952–54, 1:1012).

36. Churchill, Speech to the House of Commons, 24 Feb. 1954, *Parliamentary Debates*, Commons, 5th ser., vol. 524 (1953–54), 582.

37. U.S. Special Rep. in Europe tel to DOS, 22 July 1954, *FRUS*, 1952–54, 1:1231. Statistics cited by paper, Executive Committee of the Economic Defense Advisory Committee to NSC, 30 June 1954, ibid., 1:1216; and memo of NSC meeting, 22 July 1954, ibid., 1:1233. Of the 478 items considered, the COCOM nations agreed to delete 220 from the control lists, maintain an embargo on 176, submit 24 to quantitative control, and add 55 items to the watch list. The embargo on three items (tinplate rolling mills, certain electric generators, and strategic ball bearings) remained in force while the negotiations on their status continued.

38. Memcon, DDE-Churchill, 4 Dec. 1953, *FRUS*, 1952–54, 5:174; FO minutes by C. T. Crowe, 21 May and 24 July 1954, FC1121/26 and F1121/33, FO 371/110275, PRO (for a survey of U.K. policy); Nelson Aldrich tel to DOS, 31 Mar. 1954, *FRUS*, 1952–54, 1:1143; and memo of NSC meeting, 1 Apr. 1954, ibid., 1:1144. The Chinese effort represented part of a broader "peace" offensive. See memo by J. E. Mellor, 24 June 1954, 493.0031/6-2454, DF. Attached is DOS Intelligence and Research Brief, no. 1634, 22 June 1954, "Chinese Communist Trade Overtures in Geneva." Much remains unknown about PRC's policy. On the "peace" offensive toward Japan, see Radtke, *China's Relations with Japan*, 102–6. DOS thought the primary Chinese aim was to wreck Western unity rather than to promote a greater volume of trade.

39. Kerr desp to DOS, 21 Oct. 1953, 493.949/10-2153, DF. On the items MITI released from control in 1953, see Kerr desp to DOS, 5 Jan. 1954, 493.949/1-554, DF.

40. Memcon by JFD, 10 Aug. 1953, *FRUS*, 1952–54, 14:1488; and JFD press conference, 3 Sept. 1954, ibid., 14:1500.

41. McClurkin to Robertson, 26 Oct. 1953, folder: Japan–July thru Dec. no. 2, box 6, BFEA Records, 1953, RG-59, NA.

42. Controls on trade with the PRC were aimed "at impeding the *industrialization* of China in addition to its direct war potential, while the European Soviet bloc controls are aimed at impeding only the development of that area's *war potential*." First Progress Report on NSC 125/3, 30 Aug. 1954, *FRUS*, 1952–54, 1:1252. Emphasis in original.

43. Memo of NSC meeting, 5 Nov. 1953, ibid., 1:272; memo of NSC meeting, 11 Mar. 1954, ibid., 1:387; JFD tel to AmEmb Tokyo, 26 Mar., 1954, 493.949/3-2654, DF; JMA tel to DOS, 1 Apr. 1954, *FRUS*, 1952–54, 14:1627–28; JFD to AmEmb Tokyo, 8 Apr. 1954, ibid., 14:1630–31; and McClurkin to Drumright, 24 Apr. 1954, ibid., 14:1634–35.

44. First Progress Report on NSC-125/3, 30 aug. 1954, *FRUS*, 1952–54, 1:1251.

45. Hessell Tiltman, "Truce Spurs Japanese Trade Pleas," *Washington Post*, 5 Sept. 1954; and William J. Jorden, "Tokyo Rebuffs Bid for Tie by Russians and Chinese," *NYT*, 13 Oct. 1954. Specifically, Japan refused to take the various measures demanded by the Communists (such as an exchange of trade missions, a transparent effort by the Chinese to establish a diplomatic presence in Japan) as the price of expanded trade.

46. Russell Porter, "Yoshida Warns of Red 'Peace Lie,' Calls for Relaxed Trade Barriers," *NYT*, 6 Nov. 1954.

47. Cabinet meeting minutes, 6 Aug. 1954, box 3, Cabinet Series, AWF, DDEL.

48. Ibid.

49. Ibid.

50. Ibid.

51. Memcon with Millikin, 24 Aug. 1954, 394.31/8-2454, DF. Millikin's letter of the same date is attached.

52. CED, "United States Tariff Policy," pp. 20–1, Nov. 1954, file: Business Advisory Committee, box 8, Humphrey Papers, RG-56, NA. Two members of the Research and Policy Committee did not support the report. A "preponderant majority" did (p. 20).

53. Cabinet meeting minutes, 18 Aug. 1954, box 3, Cabinet Series, AWF, DDEL; and memo, Hauge to Adams, 19 Aug. 1954, file: Trade Agreements—Japan (5), box 91, Subject Series, CF, WHCF, DDEL.

54. Memo, JFD to DDE, 6 Nov. 1954, file: Trade Agreements—Japan (12), box 91, Subject Series, CF, WHCF, DDEL.

55. *DSB*, 31 (22 Nov. 1954): 767–71.

56. Minutes of cabinet meeting, 6 Aug. 1954, box 3, Cabinet Series, AWF, DDEL.

57. FO minute by P. G. A. Wakefield, 21 June 1954, UEE1021/7, FO 371/110160, PRO; and Record of Discussions with the Cotton Industry Manchester, 18–19 Aug. 1954, UEE1021/32, ibid.

58. Note of meeting, BT, 30 June 1954, UEE1021/9, ibid.: record of meeting, DOS, 29 June 1954, UEE1021/10, ibid.; and FO minute by Crowe, 10 July 1954, UEE1021/12, ibid.

59. Note of a meeting, DOS, 8 July 1954, UEE1021/16, ibid. Emphasis in original.

60. FO minute by D. Wilson, 25 Aug. 1954, UEE 1021/39, FO 371/110160, PRO.
61. Roger Makins tel to FO, 1 Oct. 1954, UEE1021/50, FO 371/110161, PRO.
62. FO minute by Wilson, 7 Oct. 1954, UEE1021/53; and (on the French reaction) Gladwyn Jebb to FO, 23 Sept. 1954, UEE1021/47, ibid.
63. The texts of both the aide-mémoire and the proposed bilateral agreement with Japan are enclosed in FJ1152/81, FO 371/110161, PRO. The essential provisions of the treaty allowed either party to apply a discriminatory quota or custom duty on specific items of trade. On the press, see letter, Wilson to E. W. Meiklereid, 1 Nov. 1954, UEE1021/62, ibid. The quotation is from letter, J. W. Chadwick to Crowe, 24 Nov. 1954, UEE1021/103, FO 371/110162, PRO. The text of the 30 Nov. 1954 Japanese aide-mémoire rejecting the British proposal is enclosed in UEE1021/112, ibid. On Haguiwara's views, see FO minute by T. H. Sinclair, 15 Nov. 1954, UEE1021/100, ibid.
64. Memcon with Haguiwara, 26 Oct. 1954, 394.31/10-2554, DF.
65. Makins tel to FO, 10 Dec. 1954, UEE1021/113, FO 371/110162, PRO.
66. Makins tel to FO, 1 Oct. 1954, UEE1021/50, FO 371/110161, PRO.
67. A. L. Mayall letter to Dening, 4 Feb. 1955, UEE1022/32, FO 371/114927, PRO. On last-minute developments, see FO minute by Wilson, 14 Dec. 1954, UEE1021/114; and letter, Dening to W. P. Allen, 15 Dec. 1954, UEE1021/122, ibid.
68. Tokyo tel to FO, 30 Jan. 1955, UEE1022/19, FO 371/114927, PRO; Washington tel to FO, 1 Apr. 1955, UEE1022/72, FO 371/114928, PRO; and letter, I. P. Garran to Wilson, 14 Apr. 1955, UEE1022/101, FO 371/114929, PRO.
69. A. G. Kirk letter to Wilson, 16 Feb. 1955, UEE1022/41, FO 371/114927, PRO; Morton Bach desp to DOS, 17 Feb. 1955, 394.41/2-1755, DF; and Waugh to Acting SOS, 26 May 1955, FRUS 1955–57, 9:119. Documentation on negotiations with third parties is available in the decimal file 394.41, DF. U.S. officials were particularly disappointed with the Dutch decision as they had been counting on the Netherlands to participate.
70. U.S. Congress, House, Committee on Ways and Means, *Hearings: Trade Agreements Extension Act of 1955*, 84th Cong., 1st sess., 1955.
71. Bauer, Pool, and Dexter, *American Business and Public Policy*, 60; and Bauge, "Voluntary Export Restriction," 120–23. On how the business community and each political party were divided over RTAA renewal in 1955, see Watson, "The Tariff Revolution: A Study of Shifting Party Attitudes."
72. Bauer, Dexter, and Pool, *American Business and Public Policy*, 65.
73. DDE, Statement by the President upon Signing the Trade Agreements Extension Act, 21 June 1955, *PPP: DDE, 1955*, 615.
74. Washington tel to FO, 1 Apr. 1955, UEE1022/72, FO 371/114928, PRO; Garran letter to Wilson, 14 Apr. 1955, UEE1022/101, FO 371/114929, PRO; A. E. Percival letter to Wilson, 14 Apr. 1955, UEE1022/107, ibid.; and *Parliamentary Debates*, Commons, 5th ser., vol. 540 (1955), Oral Answers, cols. 4–5.
75. Kerr desp to DOS, 11 May 1955, 411.9441/5-1155, DF. A copy of the article is enclosed; the translation is the U.S. Embassy's. U.S. officials in Tokyo attempted successfully to clarify the content of the proposed measure to the Japanese government as well as business leaders such as Keidanren president Ishikawa Ichirō. Waring desp to DOS, 28 Apr. 1955, 411.9441/4-2855, DF.

76. JFD tel to AmEmb Tokyo, 28 Apr. 1955, 411.9441/4-2855, DF.

77. Japan granted concessions on 286 items involving 143 tariff classifications. Of these concessions, reductions affected $61.4 million in trade, bindings of statutory rates $139.8 million, and bindings of duty-free treatment $194.7 million in trade (1953 figures). Duties on goods coming into the United States were reduced on $81 million in trade, or about 2 percent of the total dutiable imports from all countries that year. On the trade with Japan, reductions in duty affected $59 million in imports, bindings of statutory rates $32 million, and duty-free bindings $40 million. Unless otherwise noted, all figures in this section are from the DOS, *General Agreement on Tariffs and Trade* (1955), 32–111. For a summary, see *DSB* 32 (27 June 1955): 1051–55. The countries participating in negotiations with Japan were Burma, Canada, Chile, Denmark, Dominican Republic, Finland, Germany, Greece, Indonesia, Italy, Nicaragua, Norway, Pakistan, Peru, Sweden, United States, and Uruguay.

78. Eckes, *Opening America's Market*, 172.

79. Ibid., 170, 173.

80. Minutes of first meeting between the delegations of the United States and Japan, 22 Feb. 1955, box 234, ITF.

81. Memcon, Waugh and Iguchi Sadao, 25 Apr. 1955, 394.41/4-2555, DF; and report to SOS by Woodbury Willoughby, n.d., attached to memo by Kalijarvi 394.41/1-1856, DF.

82. TAC-D 99/52, "Japan's Application for Accession to the General Agreement on Tariffs and Trade," 9 Sept. 1952, file: Japan, box 287, ITF.

83. A complete list of reductions in Japanese rates of duty (in 1953 values) is reprinted in U.S. Department of State, *General Agreement on Tariffs and Trade* (1955), 32–111.

84. A complete list of Japanese bindings is reprinted in ibid.

85. A complete list of U.S. reductions is reprinted in ibid.

86. For a complete list consult ibid. The duty on low-priced cotton cloth was reduced by about 25 percent. On cotton velveteens concessions included a reduction on plain-back velveteens from 31.25 to 25 percent. On twill-back velveteens the rate was reduced from $.25 per square yard (for a minimum of 22.5 to a maximum of 44 percent) to a rate of $.25 per square yard (with a minimum rate of 22.5 percent and a maximum of 30 percent). Concessions on cotton outerwear included a reduction in rate from 35 to 25 percent. That rate had been reduced from 45 to 35 percent under GATT at Geneva in 1948.

87. Documentation on last-minute appeals is in decimal file 394.41. See, for example, letter, Warren G. Magnuson to William C. Herrington, 31 Jan. 1955, 394.41/1-3155, DF.

88. Eckes, *Opening America's Market*, 170. On the U.S. side's opposition to Japanese demands, see especially the minutes to the twelfth and thirteenth meetings, 28 and 29 Mar. 1955, box 234, ITF.

89. Eckes, *Opening America's Market*, 174; and Chalmers Johnson, *MITI*, 217.

90. DOS, *General Agreement on Tariffs and Trade* (1955), 2–3.

91. Willoughby report, 394.41/1-1856, DF; and minutes to tenth meeting of delegations of the United States and Japan, 27 Mar. 1955, box 234, ITF.

92. Eckes, *Opening America's Market*, 175.

93. Ibid., 177.

94. Draft report by Brown, 9 Mar. 1955, *FRUS*, 1955–57, 9:96–97; and "U.S. Farm Props Anger Allied Nations and Impede U.S. Plans for Freer Trade," *Wall Street Journal*, 4 Mar. 1955. For scholarly analysis of the place of agriculture in U.S. foreign economic policy, see Kaufman, *Trade and Aid*, 26–29, 76–79; and Goldstein, *Ideas, Interests, and American Trade Policy*, 154–58.

95. Report by Joseph A. Camelio, 17 June 1955, attached to Marshall M. Smith letter to Waugh, 23 June 1955, 394.441/6-2355, DF.

96. Woodbury desp to DOS, 22 Mar. 1955, 394.41/3-2255, DF. The fourteen countries invoking Article 35 were Australia, Austria, Belgium, Brazil, Cuba, the Federation of Rhodesia and Nyasaland, France, Haiti, India, Luxembourg, the Netherlands, New Zealand, South Africa, and the United Kingdom.

97. FO minute by D. S. Laskey, 25 July 1955, UEE1022/174, FO 371/114931, PRO.

98. FO tel to Tokyo, 2 Aug. 1955, UEE1022/177, ibid.

99. Memcon, Shima Shigenobu and Kalijarvi, 10 Apr. 1956, 394.41/4-1056. DF.

100. About half of the $3.5 million of trade affected in the "fifty percent" category was in silk handkerchiefs and mufflers from Japan (the rate of duty was reduced from 60 to 50 percent). See "Results of the 1956 Tariff Negotiations under GATT," *DSB* 34 (25 June 1956): 1054–57; and DOS, *General Agreement on Tariffs and Trade, 1956*.

101. Memo, "Coton Textiles and the 1956 Tariff Negotiations," undated, file: Textiles, 1956, 1957, box 295, ITF.

102. "Slowing Down," *Times*, 8 June 1956; and paper by Eric Wyndham-White, attached to White letter to John M. Leddy, 18 July 1956, *FRUS*, 1955–57, 9:197–203.

103. The 40 percent figure was widely used at the time, cited, for example by the Japanese government at the beginning of the tenth session (GATT publication L/420, 11 Oct. 1955, UEE1022/211, FO 371/114933, PRO). Despite invoking the escape clause, the United Kingdom, Benelux, Austria, and India did extend MFN to Japan on an ad hoc basis. That is, they extended GATT tariff treatment to Japanese trade, but imposed (or reserved the right to impose) quotas. U.K. policy is summarized in Butterworth tel to DOS, 19 Sept. 1955, 394.41/9-1955, DF. Other powers' policy is described in accompanying telegrams.

104. Waring desp to DOS, 13 July 1956, p. 1, 394.41/7-1356, DF. This despatch is the best summary of Japan's Article 35 problem at middecade. Its conclusion: "the prospect for unqualified treatment is far from bright."

105. Memcon, Haguiwara and Corse, 24 Sept. 1955, and attached copy of statement by Haguiwara handed to Corse, 394.41/10-555, DF; and position paper for the tenth session, undated, file: tenth session, box 9, Office of the Legal Advisor, GATT Files, 1947–59, DF. One sticking point with the Article 23 formula was that many of the other CPs did not want to consent to it if it allowed the United States emergency measures to restrict access to the American market. State understandably opposed any proposal making emergency measures available to the other CPs but not the United States. The department also feared that the intersessional formula would actually worsen Japan's position, since it would give to CPs which had not invoked Article 35 a weapon that they did not then have.

106. S. H. Levine letter to W. Harpham, 18 Sept. 1956, FJ1151/94, FO371/121058, PRO. The file also contains documentation on the U.K. position during the negotiations.

107. On 25 April CFEP recommended, as part of its overall plan to assist the American cotton textile industry to meet international competition, that the administration step up its efforts to get other countries to extend MFN treatment to Japanese textiles. See ed. note, *FRUS, 1955–57*, 9:182. For complete documentation, see CFEP 538 files, box 7, Policy Papers Series, CFEP Records, DDEL.

108. Waring desp to DOS, 13 July 1956, p. 2, 394.41/7-1356, DF.

109. Ibid., 3. Emphasis in original.

110. Ibid., 1.

111. Enclosure no. 1, p. 2, ibid.

112. Waring desp to DOS, 13 July 1956, pp. 4–5, ibid.

113. Herbert Hoover Jr. circular airgram to various U.S. missions abroad, 30 July 1956, 394.41/7-3056, DF; Hoover circular airgram to the American Embassies in Vienna and Tokyo, 31 July 1956, 394.41/7-3156, DF; and report by the Chairman of the U.S. Delegation to the Twelfth Session of GATT (17 Oct.–30 Nov. 1957), p. 51, 394.41/11-1557, DF.

114. Nakamura, *The Postwar Japanese Economy*, 59. The main point is that "Japan's exports were able to expand with a high degree of elasticity in response to world trade expansion during the 1950s." Conversely, without the expansion in global commerce during the postwar era, Japan would not have been able to expand its exports as it did.

Chapter Seven

1. Encarnation, "Cross-Investment," 134. A "multinational corporation" is any corporation in which ownership, management, production, and marketing extend across several national jurisdictions, where this activity counted for a significant percentage of the firm's total sales, assets, earning, employment, and production. In contrast to "portfolio investment," which usually involves purchase of noncontrolling equities in a firm, "foreign direct investment" entails the establishment of a foreign subsidiary or the acquisition of a foreign firm. Whereas portfolio investment allows managerial control to rest with the borrower and liabilities incurred can be liquidated by means of repayment, direct investment involves establishing managerial control (usually at least 10 to 25 percent) over an operation in a foreign country and establishes a lasting economic and political relationship. See Gilpin, *U.S. Power and the Multinational Corporation*, 8–10.

2. Mason, *American Multinationals and Japan*, 151. Until about 1970, Japanese controls generally limited foreign participation in the domestic market to the licensing of technology to Japanese firms.

3. Ibid., 247.

4. Boyle, *Modern Japan*, 63–76.

5. Warner, *Anglo-Japanese Financial Relations*, 1–61.

6. Mason, *American Multinationals and Japan*, 11–25.

7. Ibid., 99.

8. Ibid., 105. Recipient companies paid the government of Japan in yen for expropriated assets. Payments were deposited in the Yokohama Specie Bank in special accounts under the name of the foreign investor. Over ¥360 million was deposited in the accounts as compensation for seized assets, two-thirds of which had been U.S.-owned.

9. Chalmers Johnson, *MITI*, 165, 173. According to Japanese estimates, only forty-two Ministry of Commerce and Industry officials were purged from office; SCAP records indicate that sixty-nine officials were investigated and that ten were removed.

10. Mason, *American Multinationals and Japan*, 105–14. The best survey of U.S. policy is Carl H. Boehringer to DOS, 8 Mar. 1951, 800.05194/3-851, DF. Copies of relevant SCAP instructions and cabinet orders are attached.

11. Boehringer to DOS, 8 Mar. 1951, 800.05194/3-851, DF. SCAPIN 1961 (14 Jan. 1949) was promulgated as Cabinet Order No. 51 (Concerning the Acquisition of Properties and/or Rights by Foreign Nationals) on 15 Mar. 1949. SCAPIN 1961/1 (21 Oct. 1949) was promulgated as Cabinet Order No. 3 (Concerning the Business Activities of Foreign Nationals) on 15 Jan. 1950. Initial instructions and Cabinet Order No. 51 did not establish clearly the general principles to guide policy toward foreign investment or provide sufficient protection to the foreign investor. Hence the subsequent instructions.

12. Boehringer to DOS, 8 Mar. 1951, 800.05194/3-851, DF; and Mason, *American Multinationals and Japan*, 150–61. The Japanese name for the FIL is *Gaishi ni kansuru hōritsu*, Law No. 163 of 1950.

13. The chief issue regarding protection of the foreign investor was expropriation, but that issue was not a sticking point in U.S.-Japanese investment relations. The FCN treaty of 1953 reaffirmed the principle of requiring prompt and adequate compensation to private parties in the case of expropriation of assets.

14. W. W. Diehl to DOS, 24 Apr. 1953, 611.944/4-2453, DF. Cabinet Order No. 51 of 1949 made possible the purchase of stock subject to validation by the MOF. The 130 cases allowed, however, were purchases of certain prescriptions by foreigners who received rights by virtue of stock held before the war.

15. Frank A. Waring to DOS, 18 July 1952, 811.05194/7-1852, DF.

16. Chalmers Johnson, *MITI*, 194. In Japanese the Foreign Exchange and Foreign Trade Control Law is *Gaikoku kawase oyobi gaikoku bōeki kanri hō*, Law No. 228 of 1949.

17. Ibid., 194, 213. Examples of such bureaucrats include Ishihara Takeo and Hirai Tomisaburō, both of whom became MITI vice ministers during the 1950s.

18. Ibid.; Waring to DOS, 23 June 1953, 811.05194/6-2353, DF; and (on outward investment), Arthur Blaser to DOS, 10 Oct. 1960, 800.05194/10-1060, DF.

19. Hein, *Fueling Growth*, 205–12. Between 1949 and 1952 the five leading Japanese oil companies signed contracts giving 50 percent control to their foreign partners. The tie up between Tōa Nenryō and Standard-Vacuum provided for 55 percent (p. 206). Statistics in text cited by Mason, *American Multinationals and Japan*, 144–45, 149.

20. Paper, "Present Status of Program for Negotiating Treaties of Friendship, Commerce, and Navigation," 20 Aug. 1953, file: FCN Treaties, box 285, ITF.

21. DOS, "Treaty of Friendship, Commerce, and Navigation between the United States of America and Japan," TIAS no. 2863, 2 Apr. 1953, *USTIA*, vol. 4, pt. 2.

22. Boehringer to DOS, 16 Aug. 1951, 611.944/6-1651, DF (draft treaties attached). On DOS-business consultations, see Young to JMA, 7 Apr. 1953, file: Japan—Jan. thru June (1), box 5, BFEA Records, 1953, RG-59, NA. U.S. business was optimistic about investment prospects in Japan in 1952. See AmEmb Tokyo desp no. 468, 5 Sept. 1952, box 50, Country and Area Files: Japan, RG-56, NA. The American Chamber of Commerce nevertheless pressed for revision of the FIL. See AmEmb Tokyo desp 134, 27 May 1952, box 53, Country and Area Files: Japan, RG-56, NA.

23. Charles N. Spinks to DOS, 20 Nov. 1951, 611.944/11-2051; and Waring to DOS, 16 July 1952, 611.944/7-1652, DF.

24. DA to U.S. Political Advisor Tokyo, 29 June 1951, 611.944/6-2951, DF.

25. Peyton Kerr to DOS, 7 Dec. 1951, 611.944/12-751; DA to U.S. Political Advisor Tokyo, 7 Jan. 1952, 611.944/1-752, DF; and Foreign Ministry paper, Nichibei Yūkō Tsūshō Kōkai Jōyaku ni Kansuru Mondaiten, n.d., pp. 169–83 (attached to Foreign Ministry proposal, approved 17 Feb. 1953, p. 167), subseries 2, Nichibei Yūkō Tsūshō Kōkai Jōyaku Kansuru Ikken [U.S.-Japan FCN Treaty-related], reel B-0053, Public Release Series 11 (1991), JFMA.

26. Mason, *American Multinationals and Japan*, 248–51. On the FCN treaty specifically, see *Nihon Keizai Shimbun*, 6 Feb. 1953; editorials, *Asahi Shimbun*, 8 and 10 Feb. 1953; and editorial, *Tōkyō Shimbun* 9 Feb. 1953.

27. Waring to DOS, 11 Dec. 1952, 611.944/12-1152, DF.

28. Waring to DOS, 7 Jan. 1953, including attachments, 611.944/1-753, DF.

29. Waring to DOS, 29 Jan. 1953, 611.944/1-2953, DF.

30. Waring to DOS, 17 Feb. 1953, 611.944/2-1753, DF.

31. Kerr to DOS, 14 Apr. 1953, 611.944/4-1453, DF.

32. Waring to DOS, 23 June 1953, 611.944/6-2353, DF.

33. Diehl to DOS, 24 Apr. 1953, 611.944/4-2453, DF.

34. Harold W. H. Burrows (vice president, Parke-Davis) letter to Waugh, 24 July 1953, 811.05194/7-2453; JFD to AmEmb Tokyo, 30 July 1953, 811.05194/7-3053, DF. Because the Ministry of Health and Welfare regulated the Japanese pharmaceutical industry, that ministry participated in the review of the Parke-Davis proposal.

35. Wesley C. Haraldson to DOS, 9 Oct. 1953, 811.05194/10-953 (Waring's letter of 5 Oct. is attached); Waring to DOS, 5 Nov. 1953, 811.05194/11-553 (Okumura's letter of 12 Oct. is attached); and Waring to DOS, 14 Dec. 1953, 811.05194/12-1453, DF. On the preference for national control of investment, industrial enterprise, and technology in Japan, even at the price of inefficiency, see Samuels, *"Rich Nation Strong Army,"* 33–78.

36. Waring to DOS, 24 Mar. 1954, *FRUS, 1952–54*, 14:1626. During the early fifties the U.S. Embassy desired greater FDI in Japan. Besides attending to the interests of U.S. business, U.S. officials sought to foster a more competitive environment in Japan, in part to enhance the international competitiveness of Japanese industry.

37. Wilkins, *Multinational Enterprise*, surveys the topic from 1914–70. Vernon,

Sovereignty at Bay, analyzes the implications. Discussion here also draws from Lee, "The Strength of the Currency," 1–100.

38. U.S. Department of Commerce, *The Multinational Corporation*, 7. Although about three thousand U.S. firms engaged in some form of foreign enterprise, only a few hundred were significant. The fifty largest of these controlled half of all FDI in 1968; the largest one hundred controlled 70 percent; and the largest three hundred controlled 90 percent.

39. Statistics from 1965 illustrate the significance of FDI's income as a share of the total for selected multinationals: General Motors, 10 percent; Chrysler, 25 percent; Radio Corporation of America, 5 percent; General Electric, 18 percent; IBM, 30 percent; Firestone Tire and Rubber, 26 percent; Goodyear, 34 percent; Dupont, 17 percent; Monsanto, 21 percent; Proctor and Gamble, 18 percent; International Harvester, 9 percent; Honeywell, 23 percent; Singer, 52 percent; National Cash Register, 47 percent; IBM, 30 percent; Minnesota Mining and Manufacturing, 30 percent; Otis Elevator, 35 percent; H. J. Heinz, 65 percent; and General Foods, 7 percent. Source: Bergsten, Horst, and Moran, *American Multinationals*, 11–13.

40. A useful survey of the international impact of multinational enterprise is Gilpin, *The Political Economy of International Relation*, 231–62.

41. Wilkins, *Multinational Enterprise*, 330.

42. U.S. Tariff Commission, *Implications of Multinational Firms for World Trade and Investment*, 2, 95–97; Economist Intelligence Unit, *Growth and Spread of Multinational Corporations*, 6–8.

43. *Business Week*, 18 May 1963, 58–62.

44. McCraw, *America versus Japan*, 1–35; Safarian, *Multinational Enterprise and Public Policy*, 236–82; and Calder, *Strategic Capitalism*, 1–57. For the contemporary perspective of the foreign investor, see Ballon, *Joint Ventures and Japan*.

45. Wilkins, *Multinational Enterprise*, 285–300; and Kaufman, *Trade and Aid*, 80–91. Specifically, during the war federal courts ruled that international cartel arrangements violated U.S. antitrust laws. Later, the Department of Justice looked with disfavor on further domestic expansion by a company once it reached a near monopolistic position or if a member of an oligopoly threatened to expand at considerable expense to its rivals.

46. Gowa, "Subsidizing American Corporate Expansion Abroad" 180–82.

47. DDE, "Recommendations Concerning United States Foreign Economic Policy," 30 Mar. 1954, *DSB* 30 (19 Apr. 1954): 602–7; DDE, "Foreign Economic Policy," 10 Jan. 1955, reprinted in U.S. Department of State, *American Foreign Policy: Current Documents 1950–1955*, 2950; and U.S. Commission on Foreign Economic Policy, *Report to the President and the Congress, January 1954*, 16–27.

48. Memo for Gabriel Hauge, 10 Feb. 1954, file: Randall Commission, box 11, BFEA Records, 1954, RG-59, NA.

49. Gowa, "Subsidizing American Corporate Expansion Abroad," 190. Gowa emphasizes that U.S. multinationals were particularly critical of aid programs for competing with private capital and for acting as a disincentive to foreign governments to clear away obstacles to private investment.

50. Ibid., 192–98. Emphasis added.

51. Caves, *Multinational Enterprise and Economic Analysis*, 22.

52. Gowa, "Subsidizing American Corporate Expansion Abroad," 195. On subsequent attention (in 1958–59), see Kaufman, *Trade and Aid*, 154–59; Randall letter to Robert Anderson, 30 Oct. 1957, file: CFEP, box 26, Records of Secretary Robert B. Anderson, RG-56, NA; and report, "Joint Committee to Study Tax Policy and Investment," 25 Oct. 1957, file: BAC, box 17, ibid. On U.S. Treasury's attitude, see memo of meeting, 12 Feb. 1959, *FRUS, 1958–60*, 4:318.

53. Kaufman, *Trade and Aid*, 64.

54. Ibid., 65–67. Evidence of administration thinking abounds. See, for example Legislative Leaders' Meeting, 14 Dec. 1954, AWF, DDEL; C. D. Jackson letter to Nelson Rockefeller, 10 Nov. 1955, ibid., 9:8–10 (Rockefeller forwarded the letter to DDE); DDE to JFD, 5 Dec. 1955, *FRUS, 1955–57*, 9:10–12; JFD to Humphrey, 16 Apr. 1956, ibid., 9:377–78. The priority of responding to "Soviet economic penetration" abroad is also reflected in the work of the Committee for Economic Development of the Business Advisory Council: Donald K. David (chairman, CED), "A Plan for Waging the Economic War," pamphlet attached to George A. Wyeth Jr. memo to all BAC members, 30 Oct. 1958, file: BAC, box 17, Anderson Records, RG-56, NA.

55. Kaufman, *Trade and Aid*, 95–175. That growing public and official interest in the Third World came at the expense of Japanese affairs is reflected in the 1955 book, *The New Dimensions of Peace*, by Chester Bowles. This survey of the challenges facing the United States devotes only 5 of its 391 pages to Japan. It discusses China and newly independent nations such as India in detail.

56. NSC 125/2, 7 Aug., 1952, *FRUS, 1952–54*, 14:1308; and NSC 5516/1, 9 Apr. 1955, *FRUS, 1955–57*, 23:61.

57. Consult Aguayo, *Dr. Deming*.

58. For the announcement, see "U.S. and Japan Sign Agreement for Technical Cooperation," *DSB* 32 (25 Apr. 1955): 701–2. This account draws from a report on the Productivity Program in Japan by the U.S. Operations Mission to Japan, 1 Aug. 1956, file: Far East Trip—Background Papers (3), Randall Series, box 2, CFEP (Chair) Records, DDEL; and Japan Productivity Center, *Seisansei Undō Sanjūnen Shi* [History of the thirty years of the productivity movement]. The internal historical context of Japan's import of management systems is explored in Tsutsui, "Rethinking the Paternalist Paradigm in Japanese Industrial Management."

59. The initial cost of the productivity program was $462,887 (FY 1955) and $950,000 (FY 1956). Local currency contributions by Japan totaled a yen equivalent of $621,370.

60. Statistics cited by Ostry, *The Post–Cold War Trading System*, 47. Kobayashi quoted in Kotkin and Kishimoto, *The Third Century*, 60. Kotkin and Kishimoto estimate that Japan spent about $2.7 billion between 1950 and 1970 under licensing and royalty agreements. On Japanese private initiative, see Ozawa, *Japan's Technological Challenge to the West*, 24–25.

61. Chalmers Johnson, *MITI*, 17; Ozawa, *Japan's Technological Challenge to the West*, 22. In 1960 the government shifted its screening policy from a "positive" to a "negative" standard. That is, the government approved technology purchase con-

tracts as long as they were not thought to have any detrimental effects on Japan's economy. Previously, the government approved them only on the basis of their "positive" contribution.

62. Ozawa, *Japan's Technological Challenge to the West*, ix. The historical roots of Japan's capacity to absorb, apply, and improve upon foreign technology is the subject of Howe, *The Origins of Japanese Trade Supremacy*. On the 1950s, see Ozawa (pp. 31–51).

63. Boston Consulting Group, "Trade between Japan and the United States," quoted in Ostry, *The Post–Cold War Trading System*, 48–49; (on Ford and GM) Mason, *American Multinationals and Japan*, 146–47; and Ozawa, *Japan's Technological Challenge to the West*, 27. In analysis of why U.S. firms were willing to license technology to Japanese concerns, Ozawa emphasizes market conditions, particularly the confidence of leading U.S. firms and interfirm competition in the United States. In an environment of rapid technological progress and heavy competition, technology has a short shelf life. This fact biases corporate decision making to sell it quickly to those who can make the most use of it and, hence, pay the highest royalties.

64. Kahn, *The Emerging Japanese Superstate*, 80. As Japan's economy flourished, especially during the 1960s, foreign firms increasingly preferred to invest in the Japanese market rather than simply conclude license agreements.

65. Waring desp to DOS, 24 Mar. 1954, FRUS, 1952–54, 14:1623. Details on the Studebaker case are in Kerr desp. to DOS, 18 Feb. 1955, 894.3331/2-1855.

66. Okazaki letter to JMA, 3 June 1954, reprinted in Parsons tel to DOS, 811.05194/6-354, DF.

67. Murphy to AmEmb Tokyo, 21 June 1954, 811.05194/6-2154, DF; and JMA letter to Okazaki, 20 July 1954, FRUS, 1952–54, 14:1682–84. On the relationship between JMA and Okazaki, see Allison, *Ambassador from the Prairie*, 41–42.

68. Details relating to the Singer-Pine case are summarized in memcon Frederic P. Rich (attorney for Japan Steel Works and Pine Sewing Machine) and C. F. Baldwin, 21 Sept. 1954, 811.05194/9-2154, DF, memcon Donald P. Kircher and Baldwin, 22 Sept. 1954, and memo by Kircher, 22 Sept. 1954, 811.05194/9-2254, DF. Quotations and statistics are drawn from the latter memo. Kircher and DOS exchanged information regularly, so the developments during the rest of the decade are documented in the same decimal file.

69. JMA letter to Okazaki, 16 Sept. 1954, attached to Kerr desp to DOS, 24 Sept. 1954, 811.05194/9-2454, DF.

70. Memcon with Suzuki, Baldwin, and Noel Hemmendinger, 28 Sept. 1954, 811.05194/9-2854, DF; and memcon, Suzuki and Hemmendinger, 30 Sept. 1954, 811.05194/9-3054, DF.

71. Memcon, Kircher and Hemmendinger, 28 Sept. 1954, 811.05194/9-2854, DF; and Hoover tel to AmEmb Tokyo, 15 Oct. 1954, 811.05194/10-1554, DF.

72. JMA tel to SOS, 27 Sept. 1954, 811.05194/9-2754, DF.

73. Memcon, Kircher and Hemmendinger, 6 Oct. 1954, 811.05194/10-654, DF; and Kircher letter to Hemmendinger, 17 Feb. 1954, 811.05194/2-1755, DF. The Committee for Reciprocity Information heard hearings in 1954 as required by law as the

administration prepared a list of tariff concessions for the 1955 Geneva negotiations. Although they witnessed predictable criticism against GATT, they were uneventful except as noted here. Records pertaining to the hearings are compiled in box 234, ITF.

74. Letter, Kircher to Kalijarvi, 17 Dec. 1954, 811.05194/12-1754, DF.

75. Memcon, Kircher and Hemmendinger, 28 June 1955, 811.05194/6-2855, DF; and Waugh letter to Kircher, 22 July 1955, 811.05194/7-855, DF.

76. The quotation is from Waring letter to C. Thayer White, 19 July 1954, 811.05194/7-1454, DF. From May 1950 through October 1955, the Japanese government approved a total of 488 applications (341 of which were by U.S. firms). The number rose from 14 in 1950 to 96 in 1951, 94 in 1952, and 143 in 1953. It then declined to 85 in 1954 and 57 in the first ten months of 1955. (Source: Harrison Lewis desp to DOS, 27 Dec. 1955, 800.05194/12-2755, DF.)

77. Hoover tel to AmEmb Tokyo, 7 Nov. 1955, 811.05194/11-455, DF; memcon, Kircher and Hemmendinger, 7 Nov. 1955, 811.05194/11-755; and Waring desp to DOS, 21 Nov. 1955, 811.05194/11-2155, DF.

78. Waring desp to DOS, 24 July 1956, 811.05194/7-2456, DF.

79. Paul E. Pauly desp to DOS, 28 Jan. 1957, 811.05194/1-2857, DF.

80. Tel, Herter to AmEmb Tokyo, 5 July 1957, 811.05194/7-557, DF; and MacArthur II tel to SOS, 18 Sept. 1957, 811.05194/9-1857, DF.

81. Ben H. Thibodeaux desp to DOS, 22 Aug. 1958, 811.05194/8-2258, DF.

82. MacArthur II tel to SOS, 22 July 1959, 811.05194/7-2259, DF.

83. Memcon, MacArthur II and Ikeda, 9 July 1959, attached to William Leonhart letter to William Bane, 17 July 1959, FRUS, 1958–60, 28 (supplement): document no. 489; MacArthur II tel to DOS, 27 Aug. 1955 (recounting conversation with Japanese foreign minister Fujiyama Aiichirō), FRUS, 1958–60, 28:215–17; and memcon, Mizuta Mikio (Japanese finance minister) and C. Douglas Dillon, 30 Sept. 1960, ibid., 28:412.

84. MacArthur II tel to SOS, 10 Oct. 1959, 811.05194/10-1059, DF.

85. Pearl, "Liberalization of Capital in Japan." On American officials' discovery of bureaucratic reluctance to change, see, for example, Andrew B. Wardlaw desp to DOS, 21 Jan. 1960, 494.116/1-2160, DF. The despatch recounts a conversation between embassy officers and Koide Eiichi, director of the Heavy Industry Bureau of MITI.

86. *Ekonomisuto*, 8 June 1976, 82–89.

87. Mason, *American Multinationals and Japan*, 161–73 (on Coca-Cola).

Chapter Eight

1. Nakamura, *The Postwar Japanese Economy*, 49.
2. NSC 5516/1, 9 Apr. 1955, FRUS, 1955–57, 23:58.
3. Summary of Japan's proposal for a mutual defense treaty, July 1955, ibid., 23:79–80; Herbert Hoover Jr., tel to AmEmb Tokyo, 26 May 1956, ibid., 23:179; and memcon with Foreign Minister Shigemitsu Mamoru, 31 Aug. 1955, ibid., 23:111–13 (on security treaty revision, Japanese-Soviet relations, and Sino-Japanese trade respectively).

4. On discord flowing from discussion of the security treaty revision and Sino-Japanese trade, see memcon with JFD and Shigemitsu, 30 Aug. 1955, ibid., 23:97–99; and memcon with Kishi Nobusuke, 21 June 1957, ibid., 23:408. Although Ambassadors Allison and Douglas MacArthur II recommended clemency for Japan's aging war criminals (e.g., MacArthur II letter to Christian Herter, 20 Sept. 1957, ibid., 23:484), the issue was not settled until December 1958 (documentation in 694.0026, DF).

5. OCB, Progress Report on NSC 5516/1, 6 Feb. 1957, box 15, OSA/NSC, WHO, DDEL. This report, for example, concluded that Japan was "no longer as closely aligned with the United States as it was when NSC 5516/1 was approved" (p. 1).

6. AmEmb Tokyo desp to DOS, 21 Sept. 1956, 611.94/9-2156, DF. This report was widely circulated within the executive branch.

7. The incident concerned the public controversy over criminal jurisdiction for U.S. serviceman William S. Girard, who mortally wounded a Japanese woman with a grenade launcher on 30 Jan. 1957. For documentation, see FRUS, 1955–57, 23:292–426.

8. JMA desp to DOS, 30 Mar. 1956, 611.94/3-3056, DF; and paper, "Reappraisal of United States Policies toward Japan," attached to Robertson to JFD, 28 Mar. 1958, FRUS, 1958–60, 28 (supplement): document no. 439.

9. Chalmers Johnson, MITI, 217.

10. The worry that faster growth would exacerbate Japan's trade deficit faded by the 1960s. On this point, see Kanamori, "Economic Growth and the Balance of Payments."

11. Embassy political reports (794.00, DF) cover the specific incidents in detail. In one example, Japanese police and left-wing demonstrators clashed over surveys to extend a military airfield near Tachikawa (the so-called Sunakawa incidents). See AmEmb Tokyo desp to DOS, 19 Nov. 1956, 794.00/11-1956, DF.

12. Kataoka, The Price of a Constitution, 101–211.

13. Memcon, Walter Robertson and Ishibashi Tanzan, 19 Dec. 1956; and memcon, JFD and Kishi, 20 June 1957; and memcon, JFD and Fujiyama Aiichirō, 23 Sept. 1957, FRUS, 1955–57, 23:236–37, 398–99, 496, respectively. After Hatoyama, Japan's prime ministers were Ishibashi (Dec. 1956 to Feb. 1957) and Kishi (Feb. 1957 to July 1960).

14. Memcon, JFD and Hatoyama, 19 Mar. 1956, ibid., 23:169. Intelligence estimates concluded that a Socialist victory was unlikely, and that a Socialist government would move more slowly in a neutralist direction than the party's platform demanded. See NIE 41–54, 10 Aug. 1954, FRUS, 1952–54, 14:1448; and NIE 41–55, 10 Oct. 1955, FRUS, 1955–57, 23:132–33; and NIE 41–58, 23 Dec. 1958, FRUS, 1958–60, 18:114–16.

15. That high-level U.S. support for Kishi, and Kishi's solicitation of that backing long before the LDP was even organized, is obvious from the U.S. Embassy's political reports (e.g., AmEmb Tokyo to DOS, 4 Jan. 1955, 794.00/1-455, DF); and Ambassador MacArthur's correspondence. See his telegrams of 17 Apr. 1957 (urging support for Kishi), and 18 Oct. 1957 (on Kishi's political problems), both to DOS, FRUS, 1955–57, 23:277–79, 517–21. Dulles was the one who spoke (in 1957) of

making a "Big bet" with respect to "putting our money on" Kishi (memcon, JFD and Frank C. Nash, 5 June 1957, ibid., 23:329). George Morgan, embassy counselor, noted the failure of a "Kishi boom" to take hold (letter to Parsons, 14 Oct. 1957, ibid., 23:512). Without denying the existence of close connections between Kishi, U.S. leaders, and elusive figures such as Harry Kearn, the evidence does not bear out the claims (most recently expressed in Davis and Roberts, *An Occupation without Troops*, 124–40) that such secret associations were principally responsible for Kishi's rise to power or that they enabled the United States to dominate Japanese policy. Kishi's political ability matched his ambition, and he was able to impress the Eisenhower administration without such assistance. For their part, Dulles and Eisenhower also made their own decisions. Kishi nevertheless reached out to the U.S. Embassy early on during the postwar period (OH, William Hutchinson, FAOHP).

16. The biographical literature on Kishi is thin. Useful studies include Chalmers Johnson, *MITI*; Iwami, *Shōwa no Yōkai: Kishi Nobusuke* [The specter of Showa: Kishi Nobusuke]; and (for a sympathetic journalist's account), Kurzman, *Kishi and Japan*.

17. A fine survey of the industry's growth is Seki, *The Cotton Industry of Japan*.

18. CFEP Subcommittee Report on Cotton, 20 Apr. 1956, FRUS, 1955–57, 9:180.

19. Although significant, the fall of the yen was not wholly responsible for making Japanese goods competitive in the dollar area. The yen fell about 30 percent in terms of the U.S. dollar after Japan's decision to abandon the gold standard in Dec. 1931) (Bauge, "Voluntary Export Restriction," 29. On the other developments, see pp. 7–39).

20. Ibid., 45–49, 89. Total imports of cotton manufactures were less than 5 percent of domestic sales. Imports from Japan represented about 1 percent of domestic sales. Cotton manufactures as a percent of all imports remained relatively steady at about 2 percent (U.S. Department of Commerce data).

21. Voluntary restraint took two forms. Representatives of the two nations' industries concluded the cotton cloth agreement and the cotton velveteen and corduroy agreement (both in 1937). The Department of State and the Japanese government also signed the cotton rug and cotton hosiery agreements (1935 and 1936 respectively). For detailed analysis, see Bauge, "Voluntary Export Restriction," 50–91.

22. Jerome B. Cohen, *Japan's Economy in War and Reconstruction*, 392–93. Output of cotton cloth, for example, fell over 98 percent from 1937 to 1945, from 4,826 million square yards to 55 million square yards.

23. Letter, DDE to Martin, *DSB* 32 (7 Mar. 1955): 388.

24. U.S. tariff concessions are detailed in DOS, *General Agreement on Tariffs and Trade* (1955), 69–73.

25. Japan's share of all cotton textile imports rose from 20.3 percent in 1952 to 54.5 percent in 1956. This share declined for the rest of the decade, to 29 percent in 1960, before rising slightly in the 1960s (Bauge, "Voluntary Export Restriction," 100–101).

26. Ibid. Imports of cotton textiles never exceeded 2 percent of all U.S. imports during the 1950s. Japanese cotton textiles comprised .1 percent during the early fifties, rising to .7 percent in 1956, then falling to .5 percent in 1960.

27. Imports of Japanese cotton cloth jumped from 48 million square yards in 1954

to 100 million in 1955, and reached 143 million in 1956. In these two years, Japanese imports represented only 1.2 and 1.7 percent of domestic production respectively. But they represented about 75 percent of total imports. Imports of velveteens increased from 3.1 million square yards in 1954 to 6.8 million square yards in 1955. Imports of Japanese ginghams increased from 4 million square yards in 1954, to 33 million in 1955, and 77 million in 1956. As a share of U.S. production, imported Japanese ginghams totaled 3 percent, 14 percent, and 38 percent respectively for the same years. Japan's share of total gingham imports rose from 67 percent in 1954 to over 90 percent in 1955 and 1956. Source: Hunsberger, *Japan and the United States in World Trade*, 298–99.

28. U.S. Tariff Commission, *Annual Report*, 1957, 5–13.

29. CFEP report, "The Role of Imports in the Problems of the Cotton Textile Industry," undated (but obviously mid-1956), pp. 4, 8, file: CFEP 538 (4), box 7, Policy Papers Series, CFEP Records, DDEL.

30. Chase Smith (and cosignatories) letter to JFD, 28 Jan. 1955, 394.41/1-2855, DF.

31. Statistics are from CFEP report "The Role of Imports," p. 11. Unemployed textile workers faced unusual difficulties. One study of six locations in New England found that fewer than half of displaced workers were reemployed. Two-thirds of those who did find work were earning less than before. Source: summary of William H. Miernyk, *Inter-Industry Labor Mobility: The Case of the Displaced Textile Worker*, attached to letter, Humphrey to Miernyk, 7 Feb. 1955, box 5, Humphrey Papers, RG-56, NA. Miernyk was director of the Northeastern University Bureau of Business and Economic Research.

32. The proposal in question was Senator Frederick Payne's S.J. Resolution 236, of 11 Apr. 1956. The Japanese watched such developments carefully. See memcon, Shima Shigenobu and Howard L. Parsons, 20 Apr. 1956, file: CFEP 538 (5), box 7, Policy Papers Series, CFEP Records, DDEL. For the DOS position, see Thorsten V. Kalijarvi letter to Senator Harry F. Byrd, 26 June 1956, *FRUS, 1955–57*, 9:192–96.

33. Two amendments to a mutual security bill in the Senate in June and July 1956 would have imposed quotas on cotton textiles. The Senate passed the bill without amendments on 28 July. See ed. note, *FRUS, 1955–57*, 23:187.

34. Memcon, Tom Martin and J. M. C. Hand, 14 Sept. 1955, 394.41/10-455, DF.

35. For copies of the South Carolina and Alabama laws and copy of a similar law proposed (but not enacted) in Louisiana, see file: Textiles, 1956, 1957, box 295, ITF.

36. Foreign diplomats detected Dulles's flexibility at the time. See FO tel to Washington, 4 Nov. 1954, UEE1021/88, FO371/110162, PRO.

37. Dulles's views on escape clause recommendations are reflected in his opposition to increasing the tariff on imported bicycles. See JFD letter to DE, 10 Aug. 1955, *FRUS, 1955–57*, 9:142–43.

38. Memcon, JFD and Shigemitsu (third meeting), 31 Aug. 1955, ibid., 23:112–13.

39. Memcon, Isaiah Frank, Parsons, and Herbert V. Prochnow with Iguchi Sadao and Otabe Kenichi, 7 Dec. 1955, and attached letter from Shigemitsu to JMA, 30 Nov. 1955, 411.944/12-755, DF; and memcon by S. Nehmer, 30 Nov. 1955, 400.949/11-3055, DF. On 9 November, Japanese officials suspended the validation of export contracts for certain cotton cloth, velveteens, and corduroy. This suspension

was then extended to all types of cotton primary products and blouses. The restrictions limited 1956 exports of cotton cloth to the 1955 level, although the latter figure was disputed. Tokyo claimed 150 million square yards; the U.S. Embassy estimated that the 1955 level was between 120 million and 130 million yards. Following widespread protest against the "$1 blouse" imported from Japan, Japanese blouses were to be limited to 2.5 million dozens (500,000 dozen had already been approved; 500,000 blouses under new contracts were to be shipped each quarter). The Japanese Embassy also informed DOS that the Japanese government was considering a "link system," whereby companies wishing to export cotton textiles to the U.S. market would have to import some American raw cotton.

40. JFD letter to Senator Margaret Chase Smith, 1 Dec. 1955, 411.944/11-2155, DF.

41. Memcon, Frank, Parsons, and Prochnow with Iguchi and Otabe, 7 Dec. 1955, 411.944/12-755, DF. Ambassador Iguchi explained that his government's plan was simply to achieve a level of $2.5 billion of exports to the United States as part of a new six-year plan. The plan's modest aim required that Japan maintain the 1955 level of exports to the United States (about $432 million, of which cotton textiles counted for about $60 million). Even though cotton textile exports held steady as planned, total Japanese exports for the period were actually double this projected figure.

42. If U.S. dominance of the world market in 1946 and 1947 was unusual, several factors such as poor weather cut sharply into sales in early 1955. CFEP report, "The Role of Imports," p. 18.

43. *U.S. News and World Report*, 1 June 1956, pp.109–10; and *Wall Street Journal*, 29 May 1956. One result of consolidation was that the industry's rate of increase in productivity was higher than the rate of U.S. industry as a whole (*Survey of Current Business*, Sept. 1955, p. 4).

44. CFEP report, "The Role of Imports," pp. 11–14. The rate of tax on capital gains was 25 percent, compared with the top rate of 92 percent on personal income. Of plants acquired and then liquidated for the purpose of securing a tax credit, the report cites the cases of the Cleveland Worsted Mills, and eleven of the American Woolen Company's fifteen plants which were acquired by Textron, Inc.

45. Prochnow to Gabriel Hauge, 15 Feb. 1956, 411.944/2-356, DF.

46. Stanley D. Metzger to Thibodeaux, 29 Feb. 1956, 411.944/3-256, DF.

47. "Exchange of Notes on State Legislation Regarding Japanese Textiles," DSB 34 (30 Apr. 1956): 728–29.

48. JFD letter to George Ball Timmerman Jr., 17 Apr. 1956, FRUS, 1955–57, 9:177–78; JFD to DDE, 12 June 1957, ibid., 23:346–47; memo by MacArthur II, 18 June 1957, ibid., 23:361; and memcon, DDE and Kishi, 19 June 1957, ibid., 23:374. Except for the Southern Garment Manufacturers Association, which sponsored the anti-Japanese laws, the domestic industry generally favored removal of the discriminatory legislation. See report by Herbert N. Blackman (Department of Commerce), 12 July 1957, ibid., 9:254.

49. CFEP Report by Subcommittee on Cotton, 20 Apr. 1956, ibid., 9:182.

50. Memcon with Shima, 20 Apr. 1956, file: CFEP (6); and memo, Paul H. Cullen to Hauge, 21 May 1956, file: CFEP 538 (5), box 7, Policy Papers Series,

CFEP Records, DDEL. For the leak, see "U.S. Govt. Contacts Japanese to Negotiate about Quotas," *Daily News Record*, 11 May 1956.

51. Kishi and Eisenhower even discussed the discriminatory state laws when they met in 1957 (memcon, 20 June 1957, *FRUS*, 1955–57, 23: 399–400).

52. U.S. Tariff Commission, *Annual Report*, 1957, 4–13.

53. Memcon, Frank and Otabe, 31 Aug. 1956, 394.41/8-3156, DF.

54. Frank Waring desp to DOS, 9 Oct. 1956, 394.41/10-956, DF; and (on the wool quota) ed. note, *FRUS*, 1955–57, 9:220.

55. OH, MacArthur II, no. 3, p. 6, FAOHP.

56. DOS press release, 27 Sept. 1956, *DSB* 35 (8 Oct. 1956): 554–55.

57. Paper, "Actions by the ADMINISTRATION Concerning COTTON TEXTILES," n.d., file: Textiles, 1956, 1957, box 295, ITF.

58. Memo by McClellan, 7 Nov. 1956, file: Trade Agreements—Japan (17), box 92, CF, WHCF, DDEL.

59. Ibid.; and (for the quotation) Thibodeaux to Kalijarvi, 7 Dec. 1956, file: CFEP 538 (3), box 7, Policy Papers Series, CFEP Records, DDEL.

60. Memo by McClellan, 7 Nov. 1956, file: CFEP 538 (3), box 7, Policy Papers Series, CFEP Records, DDEL. The TC recommended (with one dissenting vote) that the duty on plain-back velveteens to be increased to 46 ⅞ percent ad valorem, and for the duty on twill-back velveteens to be increased to 56 ¼ percent ad valorem (U.S. Tariff Commission, *Annual Report*, 1957, 9). Yukawa Morio of the Foreign Ministry replied, "the basis for continuing conversations would be lost with disastrous economic and political effect on relations between two countries" (AmEmb Tokyo to SOS, 6 Dec. 1956, 411.944/12-656, DF).

61. U.S. Tariff Commission, *Annual Report*, 1957, 9–11; DOS press release, 16 Jan. 1957, *DSB* 36 (11 Feb. 1957): 218–19. The Japanese VER was highly specific. The overall limit of 235 million square yards was subdivided into five major groups limited as follows: (1) cotton cloth, 113 million square yards; (2) made-up goods, usually included in U.S. cotton broad woven goods production, 30 million square yards; (3) woven apparel, 71 million yards; (4) knit goods, 12 million square yards; and (5) miscellaneous cotton textiles, 9 million square yards. Within the overall annual total, the limit for any group was not to exceeded by more than 10 percent. These groups were then subdivided. For example, the sublimits for cotton cloth were as follows: ginghams, 35 million square yards; velveteens, 2.5 million square yards; and all other fabrics, 75.5 square million yards. The latter "all other fabrics" sublimit was then broken down into more precise categories including sheeting, shirting, twill, poplin, yarn-died fabrics, and other fabrics. The final paragraph of the Japanese announcement also explained that in case of "excessive concentration" of Japanese exports in a particular item or class of items or other problems occurred that the Japanese government and the U.S. government would consult to determine the most appropriate course of action.

62. Evidence on the replacement of Japanese cotton textile imports by similar imports from other sources abounds. Imports of cotton textiles from Hong Kong (including some garments made from Japanese fabrics) increased noticeably in 1957, as both U.S. and Japanese authorities noted with some concern. See John L.

Stegmaier desp to DOS, 24 Apr. 1957, 894.352-/4-2457, DF. The Japanese VER stabilized Japanese cotton texiles imports into the United States at about $70 million for five years (down from $86 million in 1856). Hong Kong's textiles exports rose from $1 million in 1956 to $64 million in 1960, or 1 percent of total imports in 1956 to 24 percent in 1960. One result was that Japan sought new outlets for its goods in Southeast Asia. Statistics cited by Bauge, "Voluntary Export Restriction," 140–42. See also Imai, "Trade and National Security," 189–234.

63. Memcon, Robertson and Ishibashi, 19 Dec. 1956, FRUS, 1955–57, 23:237.

64. Quotations are drawn from NIE 100–55, 11 Jan. 1955, ibid., 10:206–7, 208–9. If Japan dropped its controls to the COCOM level, the NIE estimated that Japanese exports to the PRC could rise from $40 million to about $100 million, possibly $150 million. The deputy director for intelligence, Joint Staff, however, disagreed with the conclusion that increased Sino-Japanese trade would not affect Japan's international orientation. He suggested instead that the needs of the Japanese and Chinese economies were complementary, and that increased trade would be to the Communist bloc's advantage.

65. Memcon (telephone), DDE and George Humphrey, 19 Apr. 1956, ibid., 10:339.

66. Samuel C. Waugh to Hoover, 21 Feb. 1955, ibid., 10:221.

67. Dodge to Robert Amory Jr., 7 Feb. 1955; CFEP 501/5, 24 Mar. 1955; A. C. Davis to Dodge, 23 Feb. 1955; and memo of discussion, NSC meeting, 6 Mar. 1957, FRUS, 1955–57, 10:216–17, 228–33, 223, 435. The quotation is from the memo by Davis.

68. Memcon, JFD, Robert Murphy, Waugh, and other DOS officials, 11 Aug. 1955; letter, JFD and Wilson, 28 June 1956, ibid., 10:250–54, 372–74. Some evidence suggests that despite general awareness of Japanese opinion on trade with China, the depth of that feeling, as reported by the U.S. Embassy in Tokyo, was not fully grasped by top DOS officials in Washington. See Waring letter to Howard L. Parsons, 9 Apr. 1957, 493.94/4-957, DF.

69. Memcon, JFD and Shigemitsu, 31 Aug. 1955, FRUS, 1955–57, 10:254.

70. Documentation on Japanese frustration with U.S. policy is voluminous. An example is AmEmb Tokyo desp to DOS, 21 Sept. 1956, 611.94/9-2156, DF. For analysis, see Shimizu, "Perennial Anxiety."

71. DOS officials noted the tendency of the Soviet bloc toward self-sufficiency (Waugh to Hoover, 21 Feb. 1955, FRUS, 1955–57, 10:221). The Japanese government offered numerous assurances that it did not intend to recognize the PRC, and successive prime ministers were careful not to break openly with the United States. U.S. officials were simply reluctant to take any chance. See memcon, Hoover and Kuraishi Tadao, 6 July 1956; and memcon, JFD and Tani Masayuki, 7 Sept. 1956, ibid., 23:184, 230.

72. Revealing studies of the CCP's catastrophic economic record are Becker, *Hungry Ghosts*; and Domenach, *The Origins of the Great Leap Forward*. The latter study focuses on Henan Province, which emerged as the national model of the Great Leap and then suffered more than most as the model failed.

73. JFD and Foreign Secretary Selwyn Lloyd reviewed the situation at Bermuda on 22 Mar. 1957, and exchanged notes the next day to the effect that they would

attempt to resolve Anglo-American differences (memcon, Bermuda, 22 Mar. 1957, and accompanying notes, *FRUS, 1955–57*, 10:434–38). On U.K. preferences, see John Hay Whitney tel to DOS, 14 May 1957, ibid., 10:452.

74. For the administration's halfhearted review of policy, see NSC 5704/1, 8 Mar. 1957; and a-m, 17 Apr. 1957, ibid., 10:428–31, 445–46.

75. On British policy, see ed. note, ibid., 10:466. On Dulles's views, see memcon, JFD and Kishi, 20 June, 1957, ibid., 23:400–1.

76. Memo, JFD to DDE, 16 May 1957, ibid., 10:455–56.

77. Memcon, DDE and Kishi, 19 June 1957, ibid., 23:375.

78. Thibodeaux desp to DOS, 26 June 1958, 493.94/6-2858, DF. Upon conclusion of the fourth trade agreement, Kishi discussed the issue privately with Ambassador MacArthur. Kishi explained that, "Japanese national opinion, including big business, small business, Conservative members of the Diet, to say nothing of Socialists, was so great that it was not . . . possible to disapprove [the] agreement." (MacArthur II tel to SOS, 12 Mar. 1958, *FRUS, 1958–60*, 28 (supplement): doc. no. 433). See also Shimizu, "Perennial Anxiety," 247–48.

79. Thibodeaux desp to DOS, 26 June 1958, 493.94/6-2858, DF; Herter to AmEmb Taibei, 14 Mar. 1958, 493.9441/3-1458, DF; and JFD to AmEmb Taibei, 26 Mar. 1958, 493.9441/3-2658, DF.

80. MacArthur II tel to SOS, 25 Mar. 1958, *FRUS 1958–60*, 28 (supplement): doc. no. 436.

81. MacArthur II tel to SOS, 28 Mar. 1958, 493.9441/3-2858, DF; and MacArthur II to SOS, 4 Apr. 1958, 493.9441/4-458, DF.

82. Thibodeaux desp to DOS, 26 June 1958, 493.94/6-2858, DF.

83. *Japan Economic Yearbook*, 1960, 58.

84. Eckes, *Opening America's Market*, 175.

85. On renewal or reciprocal trade in 1958, see Kaufman, *Trade and Aid*, 113–31.

86. Memcon, JFD and Sinclair Weeks, 4 June 1957, *FRUS, 1955–57*, 9:244. Of fifteen cases in which the TC recommended protection, Eisenhower approved only four.

87. Letter, Lodge to DDE, 11 Jan. 1958, box 24, Administration Series, AWF, DDEL.

88. Kaufman, *Trade and Aid*, 113–29. According to Secretary Weeks, Kearns "carried the laboring oar" for the Department of Commerce. He met personally and spoke with 360 members of the House, every Republican senator, and ten Democratic senators (Weeks letter to DDE, 11 Aug. 1958, file: Weeks, Sinclair 1956–68 (1), box 38, Admin. Series, AWF, DDEL).

89. Economic Report of the President to Congress (Excerpts), 20 Jan. 1958, *DSB* 38 (10 Feb. 1958): 228–35.

90. Kaufman, *Trade and Aid*, 125–31.

91. Address by Thibodeaux, 13 Jan. 1959, 411.9441/2-2859, DF. Clippings of newspaper articles in English and Japanese covering the speech are enclosed.

92. Ishizaka Taizō, "Quality Improvement Aids Japan's Case," and Adachi Tadashi, "U.S. Trade Imbalance Endangers Economy," *Asahi Evening News*, 25 Mar. 1959.

93. Adachi, "U.S. Trade Imbalance Endangers Economy."

94. The quotations are from (in order) minutes of NSC meeting, 12 Sept. 1954, *FRUS, 1952–54*, 14:1723; and JFD tel AmEmb Tokyo, 10 Nov. 1954, 033.9411/11-1054, DF. On another occasion, Dulles said to the cabinet, "We don't need or want many of their items since they are really cheap imitations of our own goods" (JFD, quoted in James Hagerty Diary, file: August 1954, box 1, Hagerty Papers, DDEL).

95. Memcon, Ikeda-Robertson talks, first session, 5 Oct. 1953, attached to F. H. Hawley memo to McClurkin, 611.94/9-2953, DF. In response to Robertson's question inquiring into the percentage of Japan's prewar trade with China, Ikeda replied: "About 15% depending upon what parts of China are included. Its importance was more qualitative than quantitative. We were able to sell in China what we were not able to sell elsewhere, and to buy certain materials more cheaply."

96. The observer was the journalist Igor Oganesoff. For his article, a translation of the law, and commentary by the U.S. commercial attaché, see Paul E. Pauly desp to DOS, 11 June 1957, 400.949/6-1157, DF. On the significance of this focus on producing quality goods for export, see Ozawa, *Japan's Technological Challenge to the West*, 100–103.

97. Specific numbers of Japanese exports to the United States for 1959 include: garments ($206 million, up 38 percent over 1958), sewing machines ($52 million, up 20 percent), toys ($77 million, up 21 percent), optical goods, ($61 million, up 29 percent), and veneer or plywood ($76 million, up 38 percent). Exports of metals and metal goods rose 8 percent (to $401 million) and chemical fertilizers gained 21 percent (reaching $81 million). Source: *Japan Economic Yearbook*, 1960, 54–55.

98. U.S. Tariff Commission, *Annual Report*, 1958, 9–13; *Annual Report*, 1959, 11; and *Annual Report*, 1960, 11–12.

99. In 1957 flatware sales peaked at about $7.8 million, after which the Japanese government imposed controls and the U.S. economy slipped into a recession. During the same period U.S. consumption of such cutlery grew dramatically, rising from 11.6 million dozens in 1953 to 23.7 million dozens in 1957. Source for Japanese statistics: *Japan Economic Yearbook*, 1958, 146. Source for statistics on American consumption: U.S. Tariff Commission, *Stainless-Steel Table Flatware*; and memo by Shimoda Takeso, 27 Aug. 1959, 411.944/8-2659, DF.

100. Thibodeaux desp to DOS, 7 Feb. 1958, 411.944/2-758, DF.

101. U.S. Tariff Commission, *Annual Report*, 1958, 10–13. The commission recommended doubling the duty (from 30 percent ad valorem to 60 percent ad valorem) on umbrella frames valued $4 or less, and withdrawing the relevant tariff concession. On thermometers, the commissioners recommended withdrawing the tariff concession. Withdrawal would have raised the duty from 42.5 percent to 85 percent ad valorem.

102. MacArthur II tel to SOS, 20 Jan. 1958, 411.944/1-2058, DF; and MacArthur II tel to SOS, 3 Feb. 1958, 411.944/2-558, DF. On the initial Japanese proposal to limit exports of flatware, see memcon with Shimoda, 27 Dec. 1957, 411.944/12-2757, DF.

103. MacArthur II tel to SOS, 20 Jan. 1958, 411.944/1-2058, DF.

104. MacArthur was political advisor to DDE at SHAPE (Supreme Headquarters

Allied Powers Europe), and the coordinator of Secretary Dulles's trips to South Asia, the Middle East, and Southeast Asia.

105. George V. Allen letter to Hauge, 11 Feb. 1958, file: Trade Agreements—Japan (17), box 92, Confidential file, WHCF, DDEL.

106. Memcon, Asakai and Dillon, 5 June 1958, *FRUS, 1958–60*, 4:164–65.

107. Memcon, Thomas C. Mann and Shimoda, 21 Feb. 1958, 411.944/2-2158, DF; memcon, Mann and Shimoda 25 Feb. 1958, 411.944/2-2558, DF, and Asakai note to JFD, 5 Mar. 1958, 411.944/3-558, DF.

108. U.S. Tariff Commission, *Annual Report*, 1958, 10–12. On the problems with the flatware import statistics, see tel, MacArthur to SOS, 3 Feb. 1958, 411.944/2-358, DF. Japanese representatives also claimed, with some justification, that their flatware products (which used a low-cost 13 percent chrome alloy) represented an innovation that benefited the American consumer. Of the three cases, thermometers had the least political salience in Japan. Only about $232,000 in sales (in 1956) were at stake. On Japanese control of exports of thermometers and relevant statistics, see note, Asakai to JFD, 1 Apr. 1958, 411.9441/4-158, DF; and note by Japanese Embassy, 4 Aug. 1958, 411.944/8-458, DF.

109. U.S. Tariff Commission, *Annual Report*, 1959, 11.

110. U.S. Tariff Commission, *Annual Report*, 1960, 11–12. The quota affected flatware not over 10.2 inches in length and valued at under $3 per dozen pieces. It increased the duty on imports in excess of 69 million single units annually; for imports up to that amount, the rate of duty remained the same.

111. For DOS handling of complaints by three U.S. fountain pen companies, for example, see letter, Ben H. Brown Jr. to Senator Prescott Bush, 18 Nov. 1954, 411.9431/11-354/11-354, DF.

112. Report on bilateral consultations, Geneva 1956, p. 1 and appendix J, attached to Richard DeFelice to TAC, 28 Feb. 1957, 394.41/2-2857, DF.

113. Thibodeaux desp to DOS, 5 July 1957, 394.41/7-557, DF. During the first half of 1957 Japanese imports rose precipitously. A rise in the price of raw materials and an expansion in equipment and inventories were chiefly responsible. The Suez Crisis exacerbated the problem by encouraging the stockpiling of various commodities (in anticipation of a lasting conflict). The Japanese government responded in stages with various measures, but market forces were probably more significant in restoring a balance (*Japan Economic Yearbook, 1958*, 51–57). Products facing discriminatory treatment after 1957 also included sewing machines, raisins, and cheddar cheese.

114. Memcon, Ikeda and MacArthur II, 9 July 1959, attached to William Leonhart letter to David M. Bane, 17 July 1959, *FRUS, 1958–60*, 28 (supplement): doc. no. 490; memcon, Sato and MacArthur II, 11 Aug. 1959, ibid., 28 (supplement): doc. no. 490; and MacArthur II tel to DOS, 27 Aug. 1959, ibid., 28:214–18.

115. Thibodeaux desp to DOS, 13 Aug. 1959, 394.41/8-1359, DF. The ten items on the automatic approval list were lard, beef tallow, hides and skins, soybeans, iron and steel scrap, pig iron, copper alloy scrap, luan logs (a variety of pine timbers from the Philippines), gypsum, and abaca (a variety of hemp from the Philippines).

116. Herter tel to AmEmb Japan, 3 Oct. 1959; and MacArthur II letter to Herter, 8 Oct. 1959, *FRUS, 1958–60*, 28:221–22, 223–24.

117. Memcon, Dillon, MacArthur II, and Kishi, 27 Oct. 1959, *FRUS, 1958–60*, 28 (supplement): doc. no. 499.

118. Memcon, Otabe and Woodbury Willoughby, 15 Nov. 1957, 394.41/11-1557, DF; memcon, Charles W. Adair and others at DOS, 17 Jan. 1958, 394.41/1-1758, DF; and DOS a-m, 27 Feb. 1958, 394.41/2-2758, DF.

119. Editorials, *Tōkyō Shimbun*, 25 Oct. 1959; and *Nihon Keizai Shimbun*, 27 Oct. 1959. On the Japan Management Association, see "Change of Policy Urged on Eve of GATT Talks," *Asahi Evening News*, 20 Oct. 1959.

120. A good summary of the session is *Japan Economic Yearbook, 1960*, 62–63.

121. On U.S. handling of the issue, see MacArthur II tel to DOS, 20 Nov. 1959, 394.41/11-20, DF.

122. The measures are detailed in *Japan Economic Yearbook, 1960*, 63–65.

123. Economic Planning Agency, *Economic Survey of Japan, 1960–1961*, 69, 72.

Epilogue

1. A useful survey is Kunz, *Butter and Guns*.

2. Surveys include Ostry, *The Post–Cold War Trading System*, 67–95; and Gilpin, *The Political Economy of International Relations*, 171–230.

3. On energy and international relations in East Asia, consult Calder, *Pacific Defense*.

4. Hein, "In Search of Peace and Democracy;" and Morris-Suzuki, *A History of Japanese Economic Thought*, 131–63.

5. Chalmers Johnson, *MITI*, 305–24; and "Consider Japan," *Economist*, 1 and 8 Sept., 1962. The Japanese commonly regard 1955 as a great turning point. The years leading up to the recovery of that year are usually understood as a period of economic revival. Also, Japanese accounts often divide the subsequent era of "high-speed economic growth" into an early period (1955–65) and a later period (1965–73). On the "Japanese model" in broader political and social perspective, see Hein, "Free-Floating Anxieties."

6. Gowa, *Closing the Gold Window*.

7. Upham, *Law and Social Change in Postwar Japan*, 28–77.

8. Ostry, *The Post–Cold War Trading System*, 87.

9. The best introduction is McCraw, *America versus Japan*.

10. Japanese FDI in the US rose from $1.5 billion in 1980, to $5.3 billion in 1985, to $26.1 billion in 1990. Since then it has declined, falling to $13.8 billion in 1992, and rising to $17.3 billion in 1994. Source: Ostry, *The Post–Cold War Trading System*, 149.

11. Fine surveys are Wood, *The Bubble Economy*, and Katz, *Japan*.

12. On "insecurity" (*fuan*), see Samuels, "Rich Nation Strong Army," ix.

BIBLIOGRAPHY

Manuscript Sources

Japan

Tokyo
   Japan Foreign Ministry Archives
      Declassified Diplomatic Records on Microfilm, series 10–12 (1989–94)
   National Diet Library
      Oral Interview with Yoshida Shigeru

United Kingdom

Kew, England
   Public Record Office
      Record Class BT 241, Records of the Board of Trade
         Commercial and Export Division
      Record Class FO 371, General Records of the British Foreign Office

United States

Abilene, Kansas
   Dwight D. Eisenhower Library
      Joseph M. Dodge Papers
      John Foster Dulles Papers
      Dwight D. Eisenhower Papers as President (Ann Whitman File)
      Dwight D. Eisenhower Records as President (White House Central Files)
      James C. Hagerty Papers
      Gabriel Hauge Records
      Oral History Transcripts
         Sherman Adams
         Prescott Bush
         Douglas Dillon
         Dwight D. Eisenhower
         James Hagerty
         Gabriel Hauge

      H. Roemer McPhee
      Robert D. Murphy
      Walter S. Robertson
    Clarence B. Randall Journals, 1953–61
    U.S. Council on Foreign Economic Policy, Office of the Chairman Records
    U.S. Council on Foreign Economic Policy Records
    U.S. President's Commission on Foreign Policy (Randall Commission) Records
    White House Office, National Security Council Staff Papers
    White House Office, Office of the Special Assistant for NSC Affairs Records
    White House Office, Office of the Staff Secretary Records
Independence, Missouri
  Harry S Truman Library
    Dean G. Acheson Papers
    Oral History Interviews
      Dean G. Acheson
      W. Walton Butterworth
      U. Alexis Johnson
    Harry S Truman Papers
      President's Secretary's File
      White House Central Files
Washington, D.C.
  Lauinger Library, Georgetown University
    Foreign Affairs Oral History Program Oral Interviews
      Edwin Cronk
      Raymond Ewing
      Richard Finn
      William Hutchinson
      Larue Lutkins
      Douglas MacArthur II
      George Allen Morgan
      William Sherman
      Thomas Shoesmith
      John Steeves
      Ulrich Straus
      John Sylvester
      Philip Trezise
    J. Graham Parsons Papers
  National Archives of the United States
    Record Group 43: Department of State, International Trade Files
    Record Group 56: General Records of the Department of the Treasury
      Secretary George A. Humphrey Papers
      Secretary Robert B. Anderson Papers
      Central Files of the Office of the Secretary of the Treasury, 1950–56

Country and Area Files: Japan (reviewed at the Department of the Treasury)
GATT Records, 1947–59 (reviewed at the Department of the Treasury)
Records on U.S. Trade and Commercial Policy, 1952–59
    (reviewed at the Department of the Treasury)
Record Group 59: General Records of the Department of State
Decimal Files, 1950–60
Special Files
    GATT Records, Office of the Legal Advisor, 1947–59
    Japanese Peace Treaty Files of John Foster Dulles
    Psychological Strategy Board Working Files, 1951–53
    Records of the Bureau of Far Eastern Affairs, 1953
    Records of the Bureau of Far Eastern Affairs, 1954
    Records of the Bureau of Far Eastern Affairs, 1956–58
    Records of the Director of the Office of Northeastern Affairs
        (U. Alexis Johnson), Subject Files, 1945–53
    Records of the Office of Northeast Asian Affairs (Japan), Alpha Numeric
        Files on Japan, 1953–55
    Records of the Office of Northeast Asian Affairs, Japan Subject Files,
        1947–56

Published Official Documents

Japan

Bank of Japan. *Economic Statistics of Japan*, 1961.
Economic Planning Agency. *Economic Survey of Japan*, 1950–61.
Jūkagaku Kōgyō Tsūshinsha. *Gaikoku Gijutsu Dōnyū Yōran* [Handbook of imports of foreign technology], 1965–66.
Kajima, Morinosuke, ed. *Nihon Gaikōshi* [The diplomatic history of Japan]. Vol. 30, *Kowagō no Gaikō (II) Keizai (jō)* [Diplomacy of the peace treaty (II) economics (part 1)]. Tokyo: Kajima Kenkyūjo Shuppankai, 1972.
Ministry of Finance, ed. *Shōwa Zaiseishi* [Showa financial history]. Vol. 15, *Shūsen kara Kōwa made* [From the end of the war to the peace treaty]. Tokyo: Tōyō Keizai Shinpōsha, 1976.
Ministry of Foreign Affairs. *Statistical Survey of Economy of Japan*, 1962.
Office of the Prime Minister. *Japan Statistical Yearbook*, 1972.
———. *Japan Statistical Yearbook*, 1985.

Republic of China

China Handbook, 1952–53.

United Kingdom

Parliamentary Debates. Commons, 5th ser., 1947–56.

United States

Pauley, Edwin W. *Report on Japanese Reparations to the President of the United States, November 1945 to April 1946*. DOS Publication 3174, Far Eastern Series 25. Washington, D.C.: Government Printing Office, 1946.
Public Advisory Board for Mutual Security. *A Trade and Tariff Policy in the National Interest*. Washington, D.C.: Government Printing Office, 1953.
U.S. Commission on Foreign Economic Policy. *Minority Report, January 1954*. Washington, D.C.: Government Printing Office, 1954.
——. *Report to the President and the Congress, January 1954*. Washington, D.C.: Government Printing Office, 1954.
——. *Staff Papers Presented to the Commission on Foreign Economic Policy*. Washington, D.C.: Government Printing Office, 1954.
U.S. Congress. *Congressional Record*, 1950–60.
U.S. Congress. House. Committee on Ways and Means. *Hearings: Foreign Investment Incentive Act*. 86th Cong., 1st sess., 1959.
——. *Hearings: Foreign Trade Policy*. 85th Cong. 1st sess., 1957.
——. *Hearings: Organization for Trade Cooperation*. 84th Cong., 2d sess., 1956.
——. *Hearings: Private Foreign Investment*. 85th Cong., 2d sess., 1958.
——. *Hearings: Simplification of Customs Administration*. 82d Cong., 1st sess., 1952.
——. *Hearings: Trade Agreements Extension Act of 1953*. 83d Cong., 1st sess., 1953.
——. *Hearings: Trade Agreements Extension Act of 1955*. 84th Cong., 1st sess., 1955.
——. *Hearings: Trade Agreements Extension Act of 1958*. 85th Cong., 2d sess., 1958.
U.S. Congress. Joint Economic Committee. *Hearings: Foreign Economic Policy*, 85th Cong., 1st sess., 1955.
U.S. Congress. Senate. Committee on Finance. *Hearings: Foreign Investment Incentive Act of 1960*. 86th Cong., 2d sess., 1960.
——. *Hearings: Trade Agreements Act Extension*. 85th Cong., 2d sess., 1958.
——. *Hearings: Trade Agreements Extension*. 84th Cong., 1st sess., 1955.
——. *Hearings: Trade Agreements Extension Act of 1953*. 83d Cong., 1st sess., 1953. S. Rept. 472.
——. *Hearings: Trade Agreements Extension Act of 1955*. 84th Cong., 1st sess., 1955. S. Rept. 1838.
——. *Hearings: Trade Agreements Extension Act of 1958*. 85th Cong., 2d sess., 1958, S. Rept. 232.
——. Committee on Foreign Relations. *Executive Sessions (Historical Series)*. 83d Cong., 1st sess., 1953.
——. *Hearings on Japanese Peace Treaty and Other Treaties Pertaining to Security in the Pacific*. 82d Cong., 2d sess. 1952. Washington, D.C.: Government Printing Office, 1952.
U.S. Department of Commerce. *Historical Statistics of the United States: Colonial Times to 1970*. Part 2. Washington, D.C.: Government Printing Office, 1975.
——. *The Multinational Corporation*. Washington, D.C.: Government Printing Office, 1972.
——. *Statistical Abstract of the United States*, 1950–72.

U.S. Department of State. *American Foreign Policy: Current Documents, 1950–1955.* Washington, D.C.: Government Printing Office, 1956.
——. *American Foreign Policy: Current Documents.* 1957–60.
——. *Department of State Bulletin.* 1950–60.
——. *Foreign Relations of the United States.* 1941–60.
——. *General Agreement on Tariffs and Trade: Analysis of Protocol (Including Schedules) for Accession of Japan, Analysis of Renegotiations of Certain Tariff Concessions.* Publication no. 5881. Washington, D.C.: Government Printing Office, 1955.
——. *General Agreement on Tariffs and Trade: Analysis of United States Negotiations, Sixth Protocol of Supplementary Concessions, Geneva, 1956.* Washington, D.C.: Government Printing Office, 1956.
——. *Proceedings, Conference for the Conclusion and Signature of the Treaty of Peace with Japan, San Francisco, California, September 4–8, 1951.* Publication no. 4392. Washington, D.C.: Government Printing Office, 1951.
——. *United States Treaties and Other International Agreements.* Vols. 1–11 (1950–60). Washington, D.C.: Government Printing Office, 1952– 61.
U.S. Mission on Japanese Combines. *Report of the Mission on Japanese Combines.* Washington, D.C.: Government Printing Office, 1946.
U.S. Office of the Federal Register. *The Economic Report of the President to the Congress, February 1982.* Washington, D.C.: Government Printing Office, 1982.
——. *Public Papers of the Presidents of the United States: Dwight D. Eisenhower, 1953–1961.* Washington, D.C.: Government Printing Office, 1958–61.
——. *Public Papers of the Presidents of the United States: Harry S. Truman, 1950–1953.* Washington, D.C.: Government Printing Office, 1965–66.
U.S. Supreme Commander for the Allied Powers. *The Political Reorientation of Japan, September 1945–September 1948, Report of the Government Section of SCAP.* 2 vols. Washington, D.C.: Government Printing Office, 1949.
U.S. Tariff Commission. *Annual Report.* 1950–60.
——. *Implications of Multinational Firms for World Trade and Investment and for U.S. Trade and Labor.* Washington, D.C.: Government Printing Office, 1973.
——. *Stainless-Steel Table Flatware: Supplemental Report on Escape Clause Investigation No. 61.* Washington, D.C.: Government Printing Office, 1959.
Warner, Michael, ed. *CIA Cold War Records: The CIA under Harry Truman.* Washington, D.C.: CIA History Staff, Center for the Study of Intelligence, 1994.

Newspapers and Periodicals

Japan

Asahi Evening News
Asahi Shimbun
Economisuto
Japan Economic Yearbook
Mainichi Shimbun

Nihon Keizai Shimbun
Nippon Times
Sekai
Tōkyō Shimbun
Tōyō Keizai Shinpō
Yomiuri Shimbun

United Kingdom

Economist
Financial Times
Manchester Guardian
Times

United States

Business Week
Daily News Record
Foreign Affairs
Newsweek Magazine
New York Times
Survey of Current Business
Time Magazine
U.S. News and World Report
Wall Street Journal
Washington Post

Books

Aaronson, Susan Ariel. *Trade and the American Dream: A Social History of Postwar Trade Policy*. Lexington: University Press of Kentucky, 1996.
Acheson, Dean. *Present at the Creation: My Years in the State Department*. New York: W. W. Norton, 1969.
Adams, Sherman. *Firsthand Report: The Story of the Eisenhower Administration*. New York: Harper, 1961.
Adler-Karlsson, Gunnar. *Western Economic Warfare, 1947–1967: A Case Study in Foreign Economic Policy*. Stockholm: Almqvist and Wiksell, 1968.
Aguayo, Rafael. *Dr. Deming: The Man Who Taught the Japanese about Quality*. Secaucus, N.J.: Carol, 1990.
Akaneya, Tatsuo. *Nihon no Gatto Kanyū Mondai: Rejimu Riron no Bunseki Shikaku ni yoru Jirei Kenkyū* [The problem of Japanese accession to GATT: A case study in regime theory]. Tokyo: Tokyo University Press, 1992.
Allen, G. C. *Japan's Economic Recovery*. London: Oxford University Press, 1958.
Allison, John M. *Ambassador from the Prairie, or Allison Wonderland*. Boston: Houghton Mifflin, 1973.

Ambrose, Stephen E. *Eisenhower: The President*. New York: Simon and Schuster, 1984.
——. *Nixon: The Education of a Politician, 1913–1962*. New York: Simon and Schuster, 1987.
Asahi Shimbun, *The Pacific Rivals: A Japanese View of Japanese-American Relations*. New York: Weatherhill, 1972.
Ballon, Robert J., ed. *Joint Ventures and Japan*. Tokyo: Sophia University in cooperation with Tuttle, 1967.
Barnet, Richard J. *The Alliance*. New York: Simon Schuster, 1983.
Barnhart, Michael A. *Japan Prepares for Total War: The Search for Economic Security, 1919–1941*. Ithaca, N.Y.: Cornell University Press, 1987.
Bauer, Raymond A., Ithiel De Sola Pool, and Anthony Dexter. *American Business and Public Policy: The Politics of Foreign Trade*. 2d ed. Chicago: Aldine, Atherton, 1972.
Becker, Jasper. *Hungry Ghosts: Mao's Secret Famine*. London: J. Murray, 1996.
Bergsten, C. Fred, Thomas Horst, and Theodore H. Moran. *American Multinationals and American Interests*. Washington, D.C.: Brookings, 1978.
Bisson, Thomas A. *Zaibatsu Dissolution in Japan*. Berkeley: University of California Press, 1954.
Blaker, Michael. *The Politics of Trade: US and Japanese Policymaking for the GATT Negotiations*. New York: East Asian Institute, 1978.
Bohlen, Charles. *Witness to History, 1929–1969*. New York: Norton, 1973.
Borden, William S. *The Pacific Alliance: United States Foreign Economic Policy and Japanese Trade Recovery, 1947–1955*. Madison: University of Wisconsin Press, 1984.
Borg, Dorothy. *The United States and the Far Eastern Crisis of 1933–1938*. Cambridge, Mass.: Harvard University Press, 1964.
Bowles, Chester. *The New Dimensions of Peace*. New York: Harper and Brothers, 1955.
Boyle, John Hunter. *Modern Japan: The American Nexus*. Fort Worth, Tex.: Harcourt Brace, 1993.
Brands, H. W., Jr. *Cold Warriors: Eisenhower's Generation and American Foreign Policy*. New York: Columbia University Press, 1988.
Buckley, Roger. *Occupation Diplomacy: Britain, the United States, and Japan, 1945–1952*. Cambridge: Cambridge University Press, 1982.
——. *US-Japan Alliance Diplomacy, 1945–1990*. Cambridge: Cambridge University Press, 1992.
Buhite, Russell D. *Soviet-American Relations in Asia, 1945–1954*. Norman: University of Oklahoma Press, 1981.
Butler, Michael A. *Cautious Visionary: Cordell Hull and Trade Reform, 1933–37*. Kent, Ohio: Kent State University Press, 1998.
Calder, Kent E. *Pacific Defense: Arms, Energy, and America's Future in Asia*. New York: William Morrow, 1996.
——. *Strategic Capitalism: Private Business and Public Purpose in Japanese Industrial Finance*. Princeton: Princeton University Press, 1993.

Campbell, James Creighton. *Contemporary Japanese Budget Politics*. Berkeley: University of California Press, 1977.
Carlton, Don. *Red Scare!: Right-wing Hysteria, Fifties Fanaticism, and Their Legacy in Texas*. Austin: Texas Monthly Press, 1985.
Caves, Richard E. *Multinational Enterprise and Economic Analysis*. Cambridge: Cambridge University Press, 1982.
Chen, Jian. *China's Road to the Korean War: The Making of the Sino-American Confrontation*. New York: Columbia University Press, 1994.
Cohen, Bernard. *The Political Process and Foreign Policy: The Making of the Japanese Peace Settlement*. Princeton: Princeton University Press, 1957.
Cohen, Jerome B. *Japan's Economy in War and Reconstruction*. Minneapolis: University of Minnesota Press, 1949.
——. *Japan's Postwar Economy*. Bloomington: Indiana University Press, 1958.
——, ed. *Pacific Partnership: United States-Japan Trade*. Lexington, Mass.: Lexington Books, 1972.
Cohen, Warren I. *America's Response to China: An Interpretive History of Sino-American Relations*. 3d ed. New York: John Wiley, 1990.
——. *Dean Rusk*. Totowa, N.J.: Cooper Square Publishers, 1980.
Cook, Blanche W. *The Declassified Eisenhower: A Divided Legacy of Peace and Political Warfare*. Garden City, N.Y.: Doubleday, 1981.
Crowley, James B. *Japan's Quest for Autonomy: National Security and Foreign Policy, 1930–1938*. Princeton: Princeton University Press, 1966.
Curtis, Gerald L. *The Japanese Way of Politics*. New York: Columbia University Press, 1988.
Davis, Glenn, and John G. Roberts. *An Occupation without Troops: Wall Street's Half-Century Domination of Japanese Politics*. Tokyo: Tuttle, 1996.
Dimbleby, David, and David Reynolds. *An Ocean Apart: The Relationship between Britain and America in the Twentieth Century*. New York: Random House, 1988.
Divine, Robert A. *Eisenhower and the Cold War*. New York: Oxford University Press, 1981.
Domenach, Jean-Luc. *The Origins of the Great Leap Forward: The Case of One Chinese Province*. Translated by A. M. Berret. Boulder, Colo.: Westview, 1995.
Donovan, Robert J. *Confidential Secretary: Ann Whitman's 20 Years with Eisenhower and Rockefeller*. New York: E. P. Dutton, 1988.
Dower, John W. *Empire and Aftermath: Yoshida Shigeru and the Japanese Experience, 1878–1954*. Cambridge, Mass.: Council on East Asian Studies, Harvard University, 1979.
Drifte, Reinhard. *Japan's Foreign Policy in the 1990s: From Economic Superpower to What Power?* London: Macmillan, 1996.
Dunn, Frederick S. *Peace-making and the Settlement with Japan*. Princeton: Princeton University Press, 1963.
Eckes, Alfred E., Jr. *Opening America's Market: U.S. Foreign Trade Policy since 1776*. Chapel Hill: University of North Carolina Press, 1995.
Economist Intelligence Unit. *The Growth and Spread of Multinational Enterprise*. London: Economoist Intelligence Unit, 1971.

Eisenberg, Carolyn Woods. *Drawing the Line: The American Decision to Divide Germany.* New York: Cambridge University Press, 1996.
Eisenhower, Dwight D. *Crusade in Europe.* Garden City, N.Y.: Doubleday, 1948.
——. *The White House Years: Mandate For Change, 1953–1956.* Garden City, N.Y.: Doubleday, 1963.
——. *The White House Years: Waging Peace, 1956–1961.* Garden City, N.Y.: Doubleday, 1965.
Feis, Herbert. *Contest over Japan.* New York: Norton, 1967.
Ferrell, Robert H., ed. *The Eisenhower Diaries.* New York: Norton, 1981.
Finn, Richard B. *Winners in Peace: MacArthur, Yoshida, and Postwar Japan.* Berkeley: University of California Press, 1992.
Funigiello, Philip J. *American-Soviet Trade in the Cold War.* Chapel Hill: University of North Carolina Press, 1988.
Gaddis, John Lewis. *Strategies of Containment: A Critical Appraisal of Postwar American National Security Policy.* New York: Oxford University Press, 1982.
Garon, Sheldon. *The State and Labor in Modern Japan.* Berkeley: University of California Press, 1987.
Garraty, John A., ed. *Dictionary of American Biography, Supplement Six, 1956–1960.* New York: Charles Scribner's Sons, 1980.
Gibney, Frank. *Japan: The Fragile Superpower.* Rutland, Vt.: Charles E. Tuttle, 1975.
Gilpin, Robert. *The Political Economy of International Relations.* Princeton: Princeton University Press, 1988.
——. *U.S. Power and the Multinational Corporation: The Political Economy of Foreign Direct Investment.* New York: Basic Books, 1975.
Goldstein, Judith. *Ideas, Interests, and American Trade Policy.* Ithaca, N.Y.: Cornell University Press, 1993.
Gordon, Andrew. *The Evolution of Labor Relations in Japan: Heavy Industry, 1853–1955.* Cambridge, Mass.: Council on East Asian Studies, Harvard University, 1988.
Gowa, Joanne. *Closing the Gold Window: Domestic Politics and the End of Bretton Woods.* Ithaca, N.Y.: Cornell University Press, 1983.
Greenstein, Fred I. *The Hidden-Hand Presidency: Eisenhower as Leader.* New York: Basic Books, 1982.
Guhin, Michael. *John Foster Dulles: A Statesman and His Times.* New York: Columbia University Press, 1972.
Hadley, Eleanor. *Antitrust in Japan.* Princeton: Princeton University Press, 1970.
Haitani, Kanji. *The Japanese Economic System: An Institutional Overview.* Lexington, Mass.: D. C. Heath, 1976.
Halberstam, David. *The Reckoning.* New York: William Morrow, 1986.
Hansen, Harry, ed. *The World Almanac and Book of Facts for 1952.* New York: New York World Telegram, 1952.
Hashimoto, Jurō. *Sengo no Nihon Keizai* [Japan's postwar economy]. Tokyo: Iwanami Shinsho, 1995.
Havens, Thomas R. H. *Fire Across the Sea: The Vietnam War and Japan, 1965–1975.* Princeton: Princeton University Press, 1987.

Hein, Laura E. *Fueling Growth: The Energy Revolution and Economic Policy in Postwar Japan.* Cambridge, Mass.: Council on East Asian Studies, Harvard University, Publications, 1990.

Hogan, Michael. *The Marshall Plan: America, Britain, and the Reconstruction of Western Europe, 1947–1952.* Cambridge: Cambridge University Press, 1987.

Hoopes, Townsend. *The Devil and John Foster Dulles.* Boston: Atlantic-Little, Brown, 1973.

Hosoya, Chihiro. *San Furanshisuko Kōwa e no Michi* [The path to the San Francisco Peace Treaty]. Tokyo: Chūō Kōronsha, 1984.

——, ed. *Nichibei Kankei Tsūshi* [Survey of Japanese-U.S. relations]. Tokyo: Tokyo University Press, 1995.

Howe, Christopher. *The Origins of Japanese Trade Supremacy: Development and Technology in Asia from 1540 to the Pacific War.* Chicago: University of Chicago Press, 1996.

Hufbauer, Gary Clyde, Jeffrey J. Schott, and Kimberly Ann Elliott. *Economic Sanctions Reconsidered: History and Current Policy.* 2d ed. Washington, D.C.: Institute for International Economics, 1990.

Hull, Cordell. *Memoirs.* New York: Macmillan, 1948.

Hunsberger, Warren S. *Japan and the United States in World Trade.* New York: Harper and Row, 1964.

Ienaga, Saburō. *The Pacific War, 1931–1945.* New York: Pantheon, 1975.

Immerman, Richard H., ed. *John Foster Dulles and the Diplomacy of the Cold War.* Princeton: Princeton University Press, 1990.

Iriye, Akira. *Across the Pacific: An Inner History of American-East Asian Relations.* New York: Harcourt, Brace and World, 1967.

——. *China and Japan in the Global Setting.* Cambridge, Mass.: Harvard University Press, 1992.

Iriye, Akira, and Warren I. Cohen, eds. *The United States and Japan in the Postwar World.* Lexington: University Press of Kentucky, 1989.

——. *The Great Powers in East Asia: 1953–1960.* New York: Columbia University Press, 1990.

Ishii, Osamu. *Reisen to Nichibei Kankei: Pātonāshippu no Keisei* [The Cold War and Japanese-American relations: Formation of a partnership]. Tokyo: Japan Times, 1989.

Iwami, Takao, ed. *Shōwa no Yōkai: Kishi Nobusuke* [Specter of Showa: Kishi Nobusuke]. Tokyo: Asahi Sonorama, 1994.

Johnson, Chalmers. *MITI and the Japanese Miracle: The Growth of Industrial Policy, 1925–1975.* Stanford: Stanford University Press, 1982.

Johnson, U. Alexis. *The Right Hand of Power.* Englewood Cliffs, N.J.: Prentice-Hall, 1984.

Jonas, Manfred. *The United States and Germany: A Diplomatic History.* Ithaca, N.Y.: Cornell University Press, 1984.

Kahn, Herman. *The Emerging Japanese Superstate: Challenge and Response.* Englewood Cliffs, N.J.: Prentice Hall, 1970.

Kataoka, Tetsuya. *The Price of a Constitution: The Origin of Japan's Postwar Politics*. New York: Taylor and Francis, 1991.
——, ed. *Creating Single-Party Democracy: Japan's Postwar Political System*. Stanford, Calif.: Hoover Institution, 1992.
Katō, Yōko. *Amerika no Sekai Senryaku to Kokomu* [American global strategy and COCOM]. Tokyo: Yūshindō, 1992.
Katz, Richard. *Japan: The System That Soured: The Rise and Fall of the Japanese Economic Miracle*. Armonk, N.Y.: M. E. Sharp, 1998.
Kaufman, Burton I. *Trade and Aid: Eisenhower's Foreign Economic Policy, 1953–1961*. Baltimore: Johns Hopkins University Press, 1982.
Kennan, George F. *Memoirs, 1925–1950*. Boston: Little, Brown, 1967.
Kindleberger, Charles P. *The World in Depression, 1929–1939*. Berkeley: University of California Press, 1973.
Knorr, Klaus, and Gardner Patterson. *A Critique of the Randall Commission Report*. Princeton: International Finance Section and Center of International Studies, Princeton University, 1954.
Koen, Ross. *The China Lobby in American Politics*. New York: Harper and Row, 1974.
Komiya, Ryūtaro, ed. *Postwar Economic Growth in Japan*. Translated by Robert S. Ozaki. Berkeley: University of California Press, 1966.
Kōsaka, Masataka. *100 Million Japanese: The Postwar Experience*. Tokyo: Kōdansha, 1972.
——. *Saishō Yoshida Shigeru* [Premier Yoshida Shigeru]. Tokyo: Chūō Kōronsha, 1968.
Kotkin, Joel, and Yoriko Kishimoto. *The Third Century: America's Resurgence in the Asian Era*. New York: Crown Publishers, 1988.
Kunz, Diane B. *Butter and Guns: America's Cold War Economic Diplomacy*. New York: Free Press, 1997.
Kurian, George Thomas. *Datapedia of the United States, 1790–2000*. Lanham, Md.: Bernan Press, 1994.
Kurzman, Dan. *Kishi and Japan: The Search for the Sun*. New York: Ivan Obolensky, 1960.
Kyogoku, Jun-ichi. *The Political Dynamics of Japan*. Translated by Nobutaka Ike. Tokyo: University of Tokyo Press, 1987.
LaFeber, Walter. *The Clash: A History of U.S.-Japan Relations*. New York: W. W. Norton, 1997.
Leffler, Melvyn P. *A Preponderance of Power: National Security, the Truman Administration, and the Cold War*. Stanford: Stanford University Press, 1992.
Levi, Werner. *Australia's Outlook on Asia*. Sydney: Angus and Robertson, 1958.
Lisagor, Nancy, and Frank Lipsius. *A Law unto Itself: The Untold Story of Sullivan and Cromwell*. New York: William Morrow, 1988.
Lockwood, William W., ed. *The State and Economic Enterprise in Japan: Essays in the Political Economy of Growth*. Princeton: Princeton University Press, 1965.
McCraw, Thomas K., ed. *America versus Japan*. Boston: Harvard Business School Press, 1986.

McCullough, David S. *Truman*. New York: Simon and Schuster, 1992.
McGlothlen, Ronald. *Controlling the Waves: Dean Acheson and U.S. Foreign Policy in Asia*. New York: Norton, 1993.
Maier, Charles S. *Recasting Bourgeois Europe: Stabilization in France, Germany, and Italy after World War I*. Princeton: Princeton University Press, 1975.
Mason, Mark. *American Multinationals and Japan: The Political Economy of Japanese Capital Controls, 1899–1980*. Cambridge, Mass.: Council on East Asian Studies, Harvard University, 1992.
Mayers, David Allan. *Cracking the Monolith: U.S. Policy against the Sino-Soviet Alliance, 1949–1955*. Baton Rouge: Louisiana State University Press, 1986.
Merry, Robert W. *Taking on the World: Joseph and Stewart Alsop—Guardians of the American Century*. New York: Viking, 1996.
Morris-Suzuki, Tessa. *A History of Japanese Economic Thought*. London: Routledge, 1989.
Mosley, Leonard. *Dulles: A Biography of Eleanor, Allen, and John Foster Dulles and Their Family Network*. New York: Dial Press, 1978.
Murphy, Robert. *Diplomat among Warriors*. Garden City, N.Y.: Doubleday, 1964.
Nagai, Yōnosuke, and Akira Iriye, eds. *The Origins of the Cold War in Asia*. New York: Columbia University Press, 1977.
Nakamura, Takafusa. *The Postwar Japanese Economy: Its Development and Structure*. Tokyo: University of Tokyo Press, 1981.
Nakatani, Iwao. *Nihon Keizai no Rekishiteki Tenkan* [The Japanese economy's historical turning point]. Tokyo: Tōyō Keizai Shinpōsha, 1996.
Nixon, Richard. *RN: The Memoirs of Richard Nixon*. New York: Grosset and Dunlap, 1978.
——. *Six Crises*. New York: Doubleday, 1962.
Noguchi, Yukio. *1940-Nen Taisei* [The 1940s' system]. Tokyo: Tōyō Keizai Shinpōsha, 1995.
Nolte, Sharon. *Liberalism in Modern Japan: Ishibashi Tanzan and His Teachers, 1905–1960*. Berkeley: University of California Press, 1987.
Oshinsky, David M. *"A Conspiracy So Immense": The World of Joe McCarthy*. New York: Free Press, 1983.
Ostry, Sylvia. *The Post–Cold War Trading System: Who's on First?* Chicago: University of Chicago Press, 1997.
Ozawa, Terutomo. *Japan's Technological Challenge to the West, 1950–1974: Motivation and Accomplishment*. Cambridge, Mass.: MIT Press, 1974.
Packard, George R. *Protest in Tokyo: The Security Treaty Crisis of 1960*. Princeton: Princeton University Press, 1966.
Parmet, Herbert S. *Eisenhower and the American Crusades*. New York: Macmillan, 1972.
Passin, Herbert, ed. *The United States and Japan*. Englewood Cliffs, N.J.: Prentice-Hall, 1966.
Pastor, Robert A. *Congress and the Politics of U.S. Foreign Economic Policy, 1929–1976*. Berkeley: University of California Press, 1980.

Patterson, James T. *Mr. Republican: A Biography of Robert A. Taft.* Boston: Houghton Mifflin, 1972.
Perry, John Curtis, Peter W. Stanley, and James C. Thomson Jr. *Sentimental Imperialists: The American Experience in East Asia.* New York: Harper and Row, 1981.
Porter, Michael E. *The Competitive Advantage of Nations.* New York: Free Press, 1990.
Pruessen, Ronald. *John Foster Dulles: The Road to Power.* New York: Free Press, 1982.
Radtke, Kurt Werner. *China's Relations with Japan, 1945–1983: The Role of Liao Chengshi.* Manchester: Manchester University Press, 1990.
Randall, Clarence B. *A Creed for Free Enterprise.* Boston: Little Brown, 1952.
Reedy, George E. *The U.S. Senate: Paralysis or a Search for Consensus?* New York: Crown, 1986.
Reese, Trevor R. *Australia, New Zealand, and the United States: A Survey of International Relations, 1941–1968.* London: Oxford University Press, 1969.
Reichard, Gary W. *The Reaffirmation of Republicanism: Eisenhower and the Eighty-third Congress.* Knoxville: University of Tennessee Press, 1975.
Reischauer, Edwin O. *The United States and Japan.* 3d ed. New York: Viking, 1965.
Reston, James. *Deadline: A Memoir.* New York: Random House, 1991.
Rotter, Andrew J. *The Path to Vietnam: Origins of the American Commitment to Southeast Asia.* Ithaca, N.Y.: Cornell University Press, 1987.
Rovere, Richard H. *Affairs of State: The Eisenhower Years.* New York: Harcourt, Brace, 1956.
———. *Senator Joe McCarthy.* New York: Harcourt Brace Jovanovich, 1959.
Safarian, A. E. *Multinational Enterprise and Public Policy: A Study of the Industrial Countries.* Aldershot: E. Elgar, 1993.
Samuels, Richard J. *"Rich Nation Strong Army": National Security and the Technological Transformation of Japan.* Ithaca, N.Y.: Cornell University Press, 1994.
Scalapino, Robert A., ed. *The Foreign Policy of Modern Japan.* Berkeley: University of California Press, 1977.
Schaller, Michael. *Altered States: The United States and Japan since the Occupation.* New York: Oxford University Press, 1997.
———. *The American Occupation of Japan: The Origins of the Cold War in Asia.* New York: Oxford University Press, 1985.
———. *Douglas MacArthur: The Far Eastern General.* New York: Oxford University Press, 1989.
———. *The United States and China in the Twentieth Century.* New York: Oxford, 1979.
Schonberger, Howard B. *Aftermath of War: Americans and the Remaking of Japan, 1945–1952.* Kent, Ohio: Kent State University Press, 1989.
Schrecker, Ellen W. *No Ivory Tower: McCarthyism in the Universities.* New York: Oxford University Press, 1986.

Schwartz, Thomas Alan. *America's Germany: John J. McCloy and the Federal Republic of Germany.* Cambridge, Mass.: Harvard University Press, 1991.
Seki, Keizō. *The Cotton Industry of Japan.* Tokyo: Japan Society for the Promotion of Science, 1956.
Shigemitsu, Mamoru. *Japan and Her Destiny: My Struggle for Peace.* Translated by Oswald White. London: Hutchinson, 1958.
Smith, Jean Edward. *Lucius D. Clay: An American Life.* New York: Henry Holt, 1990.
Smitka, Michael, ed. *Japanese Economic History, 1600–1960.* Vol. 5, *Japan's Economic Ascent: International Trade, Growth, and Postwar Reconstruction.* Hamden, Conn: Garland, 1998.
Stockwin, J. A. A. *Japan: Divided Politics in a Growth Economy.* 2d ed. New York: Norton, 1982.
———. *The Japanese Socialist Party and Neutralism: A Study of a Political Party and Its Foreign Policy.* London: Melbourne University Press, 1968.
Tananbaum, Duane. *The Bricker Amendment Controversy: A Test of Eisenhower's Political Leadership.* Ithaca, N.Y.: Cornell University Press, 1988.
Thayer, Nathaniel. *How the Conservatives Rule Japan.* Princeton: Princeton University Press, 1969.
Truman, Harry S. *Memoirs.* Garden City, N.Y.: Doubleday, 1955.
Tsuru, Shigeto. *Japan's Capitalism: Creative Defeat and Beyond.* Cambridge: Cambridge University Press, 1993.
Tucker, Nancy Bernkopf. *Patterns in the Dust: Chinese-American Relations and the Recognition Controversy, 1949–1950.* New York: Columbia University Press, 1983.
———. *Taiwan, Hong Kong, and the United States, 1945–1972: Uncertain Friendships.* New York: Twayne, 1994.
Uchino, Tatsurō. *Japan's Postwar Economy: An Insider's View of Its History and Future.* Translated by Mark A. Harbison. Tokyo: Kōdansha, 1983.
Upham, Frank K. *Law and Social Change in Postwar Japan.* Cambridge, Mass.: Harvard University Press, 1987.
Utley, Jonathan G. *Going to War with Japan, 1937–1941.* Knoxville: University of Tennessee Press, 1985.
van Wolferen, Karel. *The Enigma of Japanese Power: People and Politics in a Stateless Nation.* New York: Knopf, 1989.
Verdier, Daniel. *Democracy and International Trade.* Princeton: Princeton University Press, 1994.
Vernon, Raymond. *Sovereignty at Bay: The Spread of U.S. Multinational Enterprise.* New York: Basic Books, 1971.
———. *Storm over the Multinationals: The Real Issues.* Cambridge, Mass.: Harvard University Press, 1978.
Wade, Robert. *Governing the Market: Economic Theory and the Role of Government in East Asia.* Princeton: Princeton University Press, 1990.
Ward, Robert E., and Yoshikazu Sakamoto, eds. *Democratizing Japan: The Allied Occupation.* Honolulu: University of Hawaii Press, 1987.

Warner, Fred. *Anglo-Japanese Financial Relations: A Golden Tide.* Oxford: Basil Blackwell, 1991.
Weinstein, Martin E. *Japan's Postwar Defense Policy, 1947–1968.* New York: Columbia University Press, 1971.
Welfield, John. *An Empire in Eclipse: Japan in the Postwar American Alliance System: A Study in the Interaction of Domestic Politics and Foreign Policy.* London: Athlone Press, 1988.
Westad, Odd Arne. *Cold War and Revolution: Soviet-American Rivalry and the Origins of the Chinese Civil War.* New York: Columbia University Press, 1993.
Wilkins, Mira. *The Maturing of Multinational Enterprise: American Business Abroad from 1914 to 1970.* Cambridge, Mass.: Harvard University Press, 1974.
Wood, Christopher. *The Bubble Economy: The Japanese Economic Collapse.* London: Sidgwick and Jackson, 1992.
Xiang, Lanxin. *Recasting the Imperial Far East: Britain and America in China, 1945–1950.* Armonk, N.Y.: M. E. Sharpe, 1995.
Yamamura, Kozo. *Economic Policy in Postwar Japan: Growth versus Economic Democracy.* Berkeley: University of California Press, 1967.
Yoder, Edwin M., Jr., *Joe Alsop's Cold War: A Study of Journalistic Influence and Intrigue.* Chapel Hill: University of North Carolina Press, 1995.
Yoshida, Shigeru. *The Yoshida Memoirs: The Story of Japan in Crisis.* Translated by Kenichi Yoshida. Boston: Houghton Mifflin, 1962.
Yoshitsu, Michael. *Japan and the San Francisco Peace Settlement.* New York: Columbia University Press, 1983.
Zhang, Shuguang. *Deterrence and Strategic Culture: Chinese-American Confrontation, 1949–1958.* Ithaca, N.Y.: Cornell University Press, 1992.
——. *Mao's Military Romanticism: China and the Korean War, 1950–1953.* Lawrence: University of Kansas Press, 1995.
Zhang, Shuguang, and Jian Chen, eds. *Chinese Communist Foreign Policy and the Cold War in Asia: New Documentary Evidence. 1944–1950.* Chicago: Imprint, 1996.

Articles, Papers, and Dissertations

Bauge, Kenneth L. "Voluntary Export Restriction as a Foreign Commercial Policy with Special Reference to Japanese Cotton Textiles, 1930–1962." Ph.D. dissertation, Michigan State University, 1967.
Beason, Richard, and David Weinstein. "Growth, Economies of Scale, and Targeting in Japan, 1955–1990." Harvard Institute of Economic Research, Discussion Paper 1644, 1993.
Brands, H. W., Jr. "The United States and the Reemergence of Independent Japan." *Pacific Affairs* 59 (Fall 1986): 387–401.
Christiansen, Thomas J. "A 'Lost Chance' for What? Rethinking the Origins of the U.S.-PRC Confrontation." *Journal of American-East Asian Relations* (Fall 1995): 249–78.
Cohen, Warren I. "China in Japanese-American Relations." In *The United States*

and Japan in the Postwar World, edited by Warren I. Cohen and Akira Iriya, 36–43. Lexington: University Press of Kentucky, 1989.

Dingman, Roger. "The Dagger and the Gift: The Impact of the Korean War on Japan." *Journal of American-East Asian Relations* 2 (Spring 1993): 29–55.

Divine, Robert A. "John Foster Dulles: What You See Is What You Get." *Diplomatic History* 15 (Spring 1991): 277–85.

Dower, John W. "Peace and Democracy in Two Systems: External Policy and Internal Conflict." In *Postwar Japan as History*, edited by Andrew Gordon, 3–33. Berkeley: University of California Press, 1993.

Edwards, Corwin D. "The Dissolution of the Japanese Combines." *Pacific Affairs* 19 (3 September 1946): 227–40.

Encarnation, Dennis J. "Cross-Investment: A Second Front of Economic Rivalry." In *America versus Japan*, edited by Thomas K. McCraw, 117–49. Boston: Harvard Business School Press, 1986.

Førland, Tor Egil. "'Selling Firearms to the Indians': Eisenhower's Export Control Policy, 1953–1954." *Diplomatic History* 15 (Spring 1991): 221–44.

Forsberg, Aaron. "After the Occupation: America and the Resurgence of Postwar Japan." Ph.D. dissertation, University of Texas at Austin, 1992.

———. "Eisenhower and Japanese Economic Recovery: The Politics of Integration with the Western Trading Bloc, 1952–1955." *Journal of American-East Asian Relations* 5 (Spring 1996): 57–75.

———. "The Politics of GATT Expansion: Japanese Accession and the Domestic Political Context in Japan and the United States, 1948–1955." *Business and Economic History* 27 (Fall 1998): 185–95.

Garver, John W. "Polemics, Paradigms, Responsibility, and the Origins of the U.S.-PRC Confrontation in the 1950s." *Journal of American-East Asian Relations* 3 (Spring 1994): 1–34.

Gowa, Joanne. "Subsidizing American Corporate Expansion Abroad: Pitfalls in the Analysis of Public and Private Power." *World Politics* 37 (January 1985): 180–203.

Griffith, Robert. "Dwight D. Eisenhower and the Corporate Commonwealth." *American Historical Review* 87 (February 1982): 87–123.

Hadley, Eleanor. "Trust Busting in Japan." *Harvard Business Review* 26 (July 1948): 425–40.

Hein, Laura E. "Free-Floating Anxieties on the Pacific: Japan and the West Revisited." *Diplomatic History* 20 (Summer 1996): 411–37.

———. "In Search of Peace and Democracy: Japanese Economic Debate in Political Context." *Journal of Asian Studies* 53 (August 1994): 752–78.

Hollerman, Leon. "International Economic Controls in Occupied Japan." *Journal of Asian Studies* 38 (August 1979): 707–19.

Hunsberger, Warren S. "Japan-United States Trade—Patterns, Relationships, Problems." In *Pacific Partnership: United States-Japan Trade*, edited by Jerome B. Cohen, 117–48. Lexington, Mass.: Lexington Books, 1972.

Imai, Noboru. "Trade and National Security: Japanese-American Relations in the 1950s." Ph.D. dissertation, Columbia University, 1995.

Ishii, Osamu. "China Trade Embargo and America's Alliance Management in the 1950s: The Japan Case." *Hitotsubashi Journal of Law and Politics* 20 (February 1992): 23–31.

———. "Reisen no Shinri-teki Sokumen to Nihon" [Cold War psychological strategy and Japan]. *Hiroshima Hōgaku* 9 (December 1985): 21–38.

Japan Productivity Center. *Seisansei Undō Sanjūnen Shi* [The history of thirty years of the productivity movement]. Tokyo: Japan Productivity Center, 1985.

Kanamori, Hisao. "Economic Growth and the Balance of Payments." In *Postwar Economic Growth in Japan*, edited by Ryūtaro Komiya, 79–94. Translated by Robert S. Ozaki. Berkeley: University of California Press, 1966.

Katō, Yōko. "Kokomu kara Wassenā Gōi e: 'Atarashii Reisenshi' to Konnichi no Yushutsu Kisei" [From COCOM to the Wassenaar Arrangement: The "new Cold War history" and present-day export controls]. *Kokusai Mondai* [International affairs], no. 401 (August 1998): 16–30.

Kindleberger, Charles P. "U.S. Foreign Economic Policy, 1776–1976." *Foreign Affairs* 55 (January 1977): 395–417.

Kravis, Irving B. "The Trade Agreements Escape Clause." *American Economic Review* 44 (June 1954): 319–38.

Lee, Jonathan A. "'The Strength of the Currency': The Multinationalization of American Business, the Balance of Payments Problem, and United States Foreign Economic Policy in the 1960s." Ph.D. dissertation, University of Texas at Austin, 1996.

Leffler, Melvyn. "The American Conception of National Security and the Beginnings of the Cold War, 1945–48." *American Historical Review* 89 (April 1984): 346–81.

McMahon, Robert J. "The Cold War in Asia: Toward a New Synthesis?" *Diplomatic History* 12 (Summer 1988): 307–27.

Maier, Charles S. "The Two Postwar Eras and the Conditions for Stability in Twentieth-Century Western Europe." *American Historical Review* 86 (April 1981): 327–52.

Mastanduno, Michael. "Trade as a Strategic Weapon: American Alliance Export Control Policy in the Early Postwar Period." *International Organization* 42 (Winter 1988): 121–50.

Meade, J. E. "Japan and the General Agreement on Tariffs and Trade." *Three Banks Review* 34 (June 1957): 3–32.

Miyasato, Seigen. "John Foster Dulles and the Peace Settlement with Japan." In *John Foster Dulles and the Diplomacy of the Cold War*, edited by Richard H. Immerman, 63–92. Princeton: Princeton University Press, 1990.

Nanto, Dick. K. "The United States Role in the Postwar Economic Recovery of Japan." Ph.D. dissertation, Harvard University, 1977.

Ohkawa, Kazushi, and Henry Rosovsky. "A Century of Economic Growth." In *The State and Economic Enterprise in Japan: Essays in the Political Economy of Growth*, edited by W. W. Lockwood, 86–103. Princeton: Princeton University Press, 1965.

Pearl, Allan. "Liberalization of Capital in Japan," *Harvard International Law Journal* 13 (Winter 1972): 59–87, Part I; and (Spring 1972): 245–70, Part II.

Rabe, Stephen. "Eisenhower Revisionism: A Decade of Scholarship." *Diplomatic History* 17 (Winter 1993): 97–115.

Reichard, Gary W. "Eisenhower as President: The Changing View." *South Atlantic Quarterly* 77 (Summer 1978): 266–81.

Schonberger, Howard B. "The Japan Lobby in American Diplomacy, 1947–1952." *Pacific Historical Review* 46 (August 1977): 327–59.

———. "Peacemaking in Asia: The United States, Great Britain, and the Japanese Decision to Recognize Nationalist China, 1951–1952." *Diplomatic History* 10 (Winter 1986): 59–73.

Shimizu, Sayuri. "Creating People of Plenty: The United States and Japan's Economic Alternatives, 1953–58." Ph.D. dissertation, Cornell University, 1991.

———. "Perennial Anxiety: Japan-U.S. Controversy over Recognition of the PRC, 1952–1958," *Journal of American-East Asian Relations* (Fall 1995): 223–48.

Spaulding, Robert Mark, Jr., "'A Gradual and Moderate Relaxation': Eisenhower and the Revision of American Export Control Policy, 1953–1955." *Diplomatic History* 17 (Spring 1993): 223–49.

Talbot, Ross B., and Young W. Kihl. "The Politics of Domestic and Foreign Policy Linkages in U.S.-Japanese Agricultural Policy Making." In *U.S.-Japanese Agricultural Trade Relations*, edited by Emery N. Castle and Kenzo Hemmi, with Sally A. Skillings, 275–338. Washington, D.C.: Resources for the Future, 1982.

Thompson, Thomas N. "Nationalizing British Firms in Shanghai: The Politics of Hostage Capitalism in People's China, 1949–1957." In *Transnationalism in World Politics and Business*, edited by Forest L. Grieves, 166–90. New York: Pergamon Press, 1979.

Tsutsui, William M. "Rethinking the Paternalist Paradigm in Japanese Industrial Management." *Business and Economic History* 26 (Winter 1997): 561–72.

Tucker, Nancy Bernkopf. "American Policy toward Sino-Japanese Trade in the Postwar Years: Politics and Prosperity." *Diplomatic History* 8 (Summer 1984): 183–208.

Uchida, Katsutoshi. "Japan's Foreign Trade after the War." *Bulletin of University of Osaka Prefecture* 1 (1957): 117–32.

Watson, Richard A. "The Tariff Revolution: A Study of Shifting Party Attitudes." *Journal of Politics* 18 (November 1956): 678–701.

Yasuhara, Yoko. "Japan, Communist China, and Export Controls in Asia, 1948–52." *Diplomatic History* 10 (Winter 1986): 75–89.

———. "Japanese Export Controls, COCOM, and the United States: A Historical Perspective." In *U.S. and Japanese Nonproliferation Export Controls: Theory, Description, and Analysis*, edited by Gary K. Bertsch, Richard T. Cupitt, and Takehiko Yamamoto, 87–101. New York: University Press of America, 1996.

Yokoi, Noriko. "Searching for a Balance: Britain's Trade Policy towards Japan,

1950–1954." Ph.D. dissertation, London School of Economics and Political Science, 1998.
Yoshida, Shigeru. "Japan and the Crisis in Asia." *Foreign Affairs* 29 (January 1951): 171–81.
Zeiler, Thomas W. "Managing Protectionism: American Trade Policy in the Early Cold War." *Diplomatic History* 22 (Summer 1998): 337–60.

INDEX

Acheson, Dean, 2; and Japanese peace settlement, 31, 32, 33, 34, 44; and Sino-Japanese trade, 32, 33, 87, 94; background of, 34; and John Foster Dulles, 34, 35, 78; and export controls, 94, 259 (n. 24); and Red Scare, 117; and foreign policy decision making, 125
Adachi Tadashi, 221
Adenauer, Konrad, 39, 49, 50
Afghanistan, 186
Agricultural exports, U.S., 141–43, 159, 162–63, 202, 209
Agricultural imports, Japanese, 15, 16, 88, 142–43, 158. *See also specific commodities*
Agricultural policy, U.S., 163
Agricultural Trade and Development Assistance Act (PL 480), 141–43
Agriculture, U.S. Department of, 142, 212
Aircraft, 158; manufacturing, 63, 68
Aldrich, Winthrop, 133
Allison, John M.: and peace with Japan, 37, 38, 65–74 passim; as ambassador to Japan, 115, 129; and foreign investment in Japan, 190, 193–94; evaluation of U.S.-Japanese relations at middecade by, 201–2
Alsop, Joseph, 149
"American alliance," xi–xii; economic advantages for Japan of, 4–9, 65–72, 84–85, 113–15, 137, 150–68 passim; 187–97, 218; demands on Japan of, 9–10, 39–41, 46–47, 49–50, 74–76, 84, 85, 102, 104–12, 138, 145–47, 208–18, 222–25; enduring power of, 10–11, 234. *See also* Bilateralism; Japan: rearmament of; National security policy, U.S.; U.S.-Japanese Relations; U.S.-Japan Security Treaty
American Chamber of Commerce in Japan, 175, 220
Anderson, Samuel, 149
Anglo-American relationship, 65–70, 73–81, 89–99
Anti-Communism. *See* Communism, threat of; Containment policy; Export controls; National security policy, U.S.; Sino-American antagonism; U.S.-Japan Security Treaty
Antidumping laws, 140
Anti-Japanese: protest, 126, 153, 207–8, 209, 210–11, 218; laws of U.S. states, 208, 210, 211, 287 (n. 35), 288 (n. 48), 289 (n. 51)
Antitrust: reforms in occupied Japan, 59–60; reform reversal, 63–64; and Japanese VER, 209, 210; and multinational enterprise, 281 (n. 45)
ANZUS Pact, 43, 44, 70, 130
Army, U.S. Department of, 88, 259 (n. 20)
Asakai Koichirō, 224
Asian currency crisis (1990s), 26
Atlantic Charter, 19, 54
Atlee, Clement, 92

315

Atomic bomb, 55, 56
Atomic energy materials, 97
Australia: and peace with Japan, 43, 44, 68, 70; and Japanese membership in GATT, 79, 127, 130, 131, 151; and Article 35, 166–67; and trade with Japan, 167
Automobile Manufacturing Industry Law (1936), 171
Automobiles and the automobile industry, 6, 156–58, 190, 206, 229, 231. See also specific companies

Balance-of-payments: of Japan, 5, 85–86, 114, 145, 156, 161, 176, 195, 226, 238; Japanese crises of, 5, 156, 162, 195, 203, 206, 293 (n. 113); as justification for Japanese protectionism, 161–62, 176, 193, 195, 197, 203, 225–26, 230–31; and U.S. tolerance of Japanese restrictions, 170, 172–74, 176–77, 195, 197, 203 226; and protocol to FCN Treaty, 176, 243; of United States, 185, 202, 238
Bank for International Settlements, 69–70
Bank of Japan, 84, 178
Battle, Laurie C., 100, 101, 106
Battle Act (1951), 100, 101, 102, 103; 262 (n. 65); Lists, 101, 102, 103
Beason, Richard, 26
Belgium, 89, 92, 277 (n. 96)
Bell, Daniel W., 123
Bell Commission, 122–23
Benelux nations, 152, 166
"Berry amendment," 141
Berthoud, Eric, 108
Bevin, Ernest, 66, 94,
B. F. Goodrich, 171
Bilateralism: in U.S.-Japanese relations, 10–11, 168, 200, 230, 234, 228; and Japanese peace settlement, 39, 43, 65; and export controls, 89, 102, 108–9, 110, 111, 259 (n. 29)
Bipartisanship, U.S.: in foreign policy,

2, 21–22, 30, 33–35, 45, 78; and consensus on Japan, 30, 114; decline of, 117
Bireley's, 193
Blouses, 209, 211, 286–87 (n. 27)
Board of Trade, U.K.: and Japanese Peace Treaty, 67, 69; opposes Japanese membership in GATT, 77; opposes MFN for Japan without restrictions, 126–28; and Article 35, 152
Boggs, Hale, 185
Bohlen, Charles E., 94
Borden, William S., 12, 142
Bradley, Omar, 37
Brazil, 166–67, 183
Bretton Woods system, 19, 236
Bricker, John, 117, 118
Bridges, Styles, 251 (n. 51)
British Petroleum, 183
Brown, Winthrop, 127, 131
Bubble economy, 26, 238
Business Advisory Council, 185, 282 (n. 54)
Burma: and reparations issue, 58, 70, 72; peace treaty with Japan of, 72; and GATT, 131; and trade with Japan, 143, 152
Butterworth, W. Walton, 32, 33, 87
"Buy American" policy, revision of, 132, 134, 140–41, 271 (n. 15); and Japan, 141, 271 (nn. 11, 12)
Byrd, Harry, 153

Calder, Kent, 27
Caltex, 175, 279 (n. 19)
Cambodia, 89
Camelio, Joseph A., 164
Camphor, 162
Canada, 104, 106–7, 110, 151
Canberra Conference, 67–68
Cannon, Clarence, 94
Capital controls. See Balance-of-payments: as justification for Japanese protectionism; Foreign direct investment; Foreign Investment Law

Capitalism, varieties of, 8, 200, 230, 236
Capital liberalization, 189, 195–97
Carnauba wax, 166
Caves, Richard E., 185
Celanese Corporation, 178
Central Intelligence Agency, 48, 252 (n. 64)
Ceylon, 67
Chase Smith, Margaret, 209
Chemicals industry, 17, 58, 95, 222
Chen, Jian, 13, 99
Chiang Kai-shek, 31, 73, 217
China: collapse of nationalist rule, 31, 60; U.S. aid to, 31; and Japanese peace settlement. *See* People's Republic of China, Republic of China; Sino-Japanese Trade
"China differential," 147; end of, 217, 290 (n. 64)
China market: as an object of Japanese attention, 9–10, 102–3, 104, 107, 144–45, 214, 215–16, 217, 236, 291 (n. 78); Cold War disruption of, 15–16; prewar, 16, 221, 292 (n. 94); limits of, 145, 150, 216, 218. *See also* Export Controls; Sino-American antagonism; Sino-American trade; Sino-Japanese trade; Sino-Soviet alliance
Chinaware, 17, 78, 160, 161
CHINCOM, 108, 110, 264 (n. 100)
Chinese Communist Party (CCP), 32, 87
Chrysler Corporation, 179
Churchill, Winston, 19, 146
Clay, Lucius D., 2, 57, 60, 61
Coal, coking, 16, 96, 102
Cobdenism, 163
Coca-Cola Company, 169, 172, 178, 193, 196
Cocoa, 166
COCOM: formation of, 87, 105, 258 (n. 12); level of controls of, 97, 100; Japan's desire to join equal to Western allies', 104; Japanese admission to, 105–11; Far East-COCOM proposal, 106–7; and CHINCOM, 108, 110, 264 (n. 100); revision of control lists of, 146–47, 273 (n. 37); and "China Differential," 147, 217, 290 (n. 64)
Coffee, 166
Cold War: as backdrop for U.S. policy, xi–xii, 3, 21–22, 29–51 passim, 60–65, 139–40, 186, 200–204, 224; prompts American interest in Japanese economic recovery, 3–4, 12, 53; distracts from varieties of capitalism, 8; prompts American demands on Japan, 9–10, 39–43, 95–111 passim; divides Asia, 13, 15, 80–81, 83–112 passim. *See also specific issues*
Collective security, 40, 43, 116
Colombo Conference, 68
Commerce, U.S. Department of: and export controls, 86, 95, 96, 106, 214; and "Buy American" revision, 140–41; and Japanese access to U.S. market, 149; and FDI, 185; and Japan's VER on cotton textiles, 211–13; and RTAA renewal, 219, 220
Committee for Economic Development, 150
Committee for Reciprocity Information (U.S.), 194, 283–84 (n. 73)
Commodity Credit Corporation, 143
Commonwealth nations: and Japanese Peace Treaty, 65, 68; and Japanese revival, 67, 68; opposition to Japanese membership in GATT of, 76, 79, 135; U.S. attention to, 79; and export controls, 89; and imperial preferences, 151
Commonwealth Relations Office, U.K., 128
Communism, 8; threat of, 139–40. *See also* Red Scare
Competitiveness, economic, 27, 162
Competitiveness, low-wage, 126, 228
Congo Basin Treaties (1919), 69–70
Congress, U.S.: and foreign trade policy, 16–17, 20, 21, 22; and the Japanese

Index 317

peace settlement, 29–30, 36, 39, 40, 45, 75–76, 251 (n. 51); and defense spending, 83, 84, 85; and export control legislation, 94, 99–101; and Sino-Japanese trade, 104; Republican insurgency of 1953 in, 116–25 passim; and fiscal policy, 118–19; and reciprocal trade, 119–21, 122–24, 138–40, 153–55, 219, 220; and PL 480, 141–43; and trade friction, 206–7, 208, 209, 210, 228, 287 (nn. 32, 33). support of for export controls, 210, 215, 216–17; *See also* Senate, U.S., Finance Committee

Conservatives. *See* Economic nationalists; Old Guard
Consolidated Textile Company, 207
Consultative Group-Coordinating Committee. *See* COCOM
Containment policy, 31, 32, 33; criticism of by Republicans, 29; prolongs Occupation of Japan, 31; Korean War bolstering of, 83–85; Eisenhower's criticism of, 116. *See also* National security policy, U.S.
Cooper, Jere, 153
Copying of designs, 151, 221
Copyright, 69, 126
Corse, Carl D., 115
Cotton: raw, 95, 158, 209; knitgoods, 102; cloth, 206, 209, 213, 286–87 (n. 27); outerwear, 207
Cotton textiles: in trade negotiations, 78, 160–61, 165, 276 (n. 86), 277 (n. 100); and "Buy American" policy, 141; background of U.S. and Japanese industries of, 204–6; as foreign exchange earner for Japan, 206; Eisenhower administration and, 206–13, 230; middecade surge in Japanese exports of, 207, 286–87 (nn. 20, 25, 26, 27); Japanese VERs on, 209, 212–13, 286 (n. 21), 287–88 (n. 39), 288 (n. 41), 289 (n. 61); Japanese textiles blamed for U.S. industry problems, 210–11, 288 (nn. 42, 43, 44); Hong Kong exports of, 213, 289–90 (n. 62). *See also specific goods*

Council on Foreign Economic Policy, (CFEP, U.S.), 186; evaluation of cotton textiles problem by, 205, 278 (n. 107); endorses Japanese VER on cotton textiles, 211; supports maintaining export controls, 214
Cuba, 166
Currency convertibility, 6, 181, 202, 226
Customs simplification, 115, 140
Czechoslovakia, 86, 131

Davies, John P., 60
Deconcentration Review Board, 63
Defense, U.S. Department of: and peace with Japan, 31–32, 33, 37, 39; and Japanese export controls, 106, 107, 108, 110, 214–15, 258 (n. 19), 261 (n. 51); and NSC 125/2, 108; *See also* Joint Chiefs of Staff, U.S.
Deming, W. Edwards, 187
Democratic Party, U.S.: and foreign policy, 17–18, 116; leadership of, 116, 138, 153, 154, 219, 220; and Red Scare, 118; and protectionism, 153–54. *See also* Bipartisanship
Dening, Esler, 73, 74, 127, 152
Development Loan Fund, 187
Development loans, 143
Dewey, Thomas E., 117
Diehl, W. W., 177
Dienbienphu, 139
Dillon, C. Douglas, 196, 219, 224, 228
Dingman, Roger, 85, 257 (n. 5)
Dodge, Joseph M.: and Dodge Plan, 12, 64; on Japan's economy, 85; as budget director, 114–15; and foreign aid, 186; as chairman of CFEP, 186, 214; and export controls, 214; and Japanese leaders, 264 (n. 6)
Dollar area, 15, 16, 145, 226
Dollar-gap, 132, 150. *See also* Balance-of-payments

Dow Chemical, 183
Dower, John W., 12
Draper, William H, 61, 62, 63
Dulles, John Foster: and Congress, 29–30, 36, 39, 40, 45, 74, 75–76, 122, 139, 153, 216–17, 219, 290–91 (n. 73); appointment of, 30, 33; negotiation of peace and security treaties by, 30, 35–45, 53–54, 65–76, 81, 250 (nn. 30, 32); background of, 34, 35; reputation of, 34, 35; distrust of for Soviet Union, 36; initial view of Sino-Japanese trade, 37, 250 (n. 22); and bilateralism, 39, 65, 66–76 passim; and economic clauses of peace treaty, 65–72; and reparations, 70–72; and peace between Japan and China, 73–76; as secretary of state, 114–15; and 1952 GOP platform, 117; support of for reciprocal trade, 122–23, 139, 153, 219, 287 (nn. 36, 37); and Walter Robertson, 129; and "Buy American" policy, 141; and restriction of Sino-Japanese trade, 145, 146, 147, 214, 215, 216–17; and tariff negotiations, 148, 149; and Japanese entry into GATT, 150, 151; and foreign investment, 194; resignation of, 195; and trade friction, 207–21 passim; and Japanese cotton textiles VER, 209; protests discriminatory U.S. state laws, 210; criticizes Japanese product quality, 221, 292 (n. 94); and underestimation of Japan, 235; and Kishi Nobusuke, 286–87 (n. 15)
Dulles-Morrison Agreement, 74
Dumping, 126, 140
Dyestuffs, 102, 105

East-West Trade. *See* Export Controls
Eckes, Alfred E., Jr., 17, 23, 24, 156–63, 247 (n. 19)
Economic nationalists, 118–23, 127, 132–35, 148, 219–20
Economic Stabilization Board (Japan), 174

Edwards, Corwin D., 59, 60
Egypt, 186
Eisenhower, Dwight D., 4, 8, 112; and Japanese admission to GATT, 4, 114; and relations with Japan, 114–15; "hidden-hand" leadership of, 114–15, 266 (n. 31), 267 (n. 40); and reciprocal trade renewal, 115, 122–24, 135, 137, 138–40, 154, 219–20; and foreign investment, 115, 184–85; economic and political philosophy of, 115–16; fiscal conservatism of, 116; and foreign aid, 116, 186–87; conflict with Republican Old Guard of, 116–24; and escape clause cases, 124–25, 224–25; and decision-making process on trade, 138–39; and export controls, 145, 146, 214, 216–17, 273 (n. 33); and expanding Japanese trade foreign, 145, 148–49; and Third World, 186–87; and trade friction with Japan, 206–7, 211
Eisenhower administration, 3, 4, 5, 8, 30, 50; and Japanese membership in GATT, 4, 24, 113–14, 125, 129–31, 150–52, 167; continuity with Truman administration of, 113–15; basic policies of, 114–16, 121–25; and foreign investment, 115; and reciprocal trade renewal, 115, 120–21, 122–24, 137, 138–40, 218–20, 132–34, 135, 153–55, 167; and "Buy American" policy, 140–41; and agricultural trade, 141–43; and export controls, 144–48, 213–18, 273 (nn. 33, 35 37), 274 (n. 42); and tariff negotiations, 148–50, 155–65; and Japan's Article 35 problem, 165–67; and foreign investment, 184–85, 190–97; and foreign assistance, 186–87, 188; and relations with Japan, 200–203; and controversy over textiles, 206–13; and trade friction, 206–31 passim. *See also specific agencies, departments, issues, and persons*

Index 319

Electronics, consumer: 6, 27, 162, 222, 231; televisions, 158, 226; transistor radios, 222
Embargo of PRC and North Korea. *See* Export controls
Escape clause. *See* Reciprocal Trade Agreements Act—escape clause
Exchange rate, 61, 64
Exchequer, U.K. Office of, 128
Executive branch, U.S., 2, 120. *See also specific agencies, committees, and departments*
Export controls, 4, 9–10, 15, 84; legacy of, 4, 9, 84, 111–12, 147–48, 200, 215–16, 236; Korean War strengthening of, 84, 91–112 passim; international lists of, 86–87, 88, 93, 94, 95, 97, 100, 105; background of U.S., 86–89; multilateral aspects of, 89, 91–111 passim; estimated trade involved in, 91, 95, 214, 260 (n. 31), 290 (n. 64); and Japanese independence, 101–2; and bilateral U.S.-Japanese understanding, 102, 105–11, 146–47; Japanese views of, 102–4, 107, 109–10, 144–45, 146, 147, 216, 217, 218, 236; complexity of, 105; U.S. commitment to maintaining, 109–12, 143–44, 214–16, 264 (n. 100), 272 (n. 23), 274 (n. 42); Eisenhower administration and, 144–48, 213–18. *See also* COCOM; Congress, U.S.: and export control legislation; Sino-Japanese trade
Export-Import Bank, 143
Export trade, Japanese, 16–17, 206–7, 208–25 passim, 292 (n. 97); westward reorientation of, 4, 15–16, 80–81, 167–68, 230–31, 236
Expropriation, 171–72, 279 (nn. 8, 13)
European Economic Community, 76, 181, 202

"Fall" of China, 29, 73; and U.S. Department of State, 115

Far Eastern Commission (FEC), 31, 39, 58, 60, 63, 64, 99
FCN Treaty. *See* U.S.-Japan Treaty of Friendship, Commerce, and Navigation
Finland, 152
Fiscal policy, 115–16, 118, 121–22, 265 (n. 13)
Flatware, 161, 222, 223, 225, 292 (n. 99), 293 (n. 108, 110)
Ford Motor Company, 6, 171, 179, 189
Fordney-McCumber Tariff (1922), 18
Foreign aid, 61, 116, 186–87, 253 (n. 18)
Foreign direct investment (FDI), 6–7, 8; low level in Japan of, 169–70, 197; Japanese attitude toward, 170–78, 187–97 passim; significance of Japanese restrictions on, 177–78, 197, 238; postwar increase in, 179–81; passive role of U.S. government in, 183–84; legacy of, 237, 238, 239; definition of, 278 (n. 1). *See also* Multinational enterprise
Foreign economic policy, U.S.: background of, 2, 17–21, 133; interconnection between economic and security policies in, 4, 12, 17, 46–47, 53, 64, 65, 68, 82–83, 84–89, 111–12, 113–14, 139–40, 163–64, 186–87, 208, 228, 230; Japan as test of emerging order and, 3, 22, 163–64, 236–37; and the postwar trading system, 234–37. *See also specific issues and policies*
Foreign Exchange and Foreign Trade Control Law (Japan), 174
Foreign Exchange Control Board (Japan), 174, 175
Foreign Investment Commission (Japan), 173, 175
Foreign Investment Council (Japan), 175, 194, 196
Foreign Investment Law (Japan), 173–74, 176, 193
Foreign markets: Japan's need for, 16–17, 72, 111, 122, 137, 156, 213, 224

Foreign Office, U.K.: and invocation of GATT Article 35, 126–27, 152; and negotiation of the Japanese peace treaty, 66–76 passim; and China policy, 73–76; favors Japanese membership in GATT, 77, 126–27, 128, 135, 151, 152; and export controls, 89–99 passim, 259 (n. 24), 290–91 (n. 73); supports Japanese admission to COCOM, 108; and commercial treaty, 166

Forrestal, James, 31, 62

"Fortress-America," 133

"Fourth-round" of tariff negotiations, 138, 164–65, 167

France, 44, 49, 148; and Japanese membership in GATT, 79; and export controls, 89, 92, 93, 94, 105, 106, 107; and Japanese membership in COCOM, 106, 107, 108

Free trade. See Internationalism; Trade liberalization

Fujiyama Aiichirō, 227

General Agreement on Tariffs and Trade (GATT), 4, 5; Article 35, 5, 126–27, 152, 164–67, 208, 228–29, 277 (nn. 96, 103, 104, 105); launching of, 20, 21, 22; U.S. support for Japanese admission to, 20, 77–78, 79, 80,114, 127 135, 129–31; opposition to Japanese admission to, 24, 76–77, 79, 80, 120, 121, 125–27, 135; Japanese anxiety regarding, 79, 128, 129; Japan's application for membership, 79–80, 124, 129; criticism of, 120, 121, 125–26, 128; intersessional committee on Japanese membership in, 125–28; Article 19, 126, 127; Article 23, 127, 131, 165, 277 (n. 105); and provisional membership for Japan, 129–31; and Japanese tariff negotiations, 140, 148–65 passim, 199; full Japanese membership in, 164, 167; and Japan's Article 35 problem, 165–67, 228, 229; Tokyo session of, 227–29; legacy of, 235, 237. See also Most-favored-nation status

General Electric, 171, 179

General Foods, 177, 178, 179, 193

General Motors, 171, 179, 189

Geneva Conference (1954), 146, 147

Geneva Tariff Negotiations: in 1955, 155–64; in 1956, 164–65, 167, 276 (nn. 77, 86), 277 (n. 100)

George, Walter, 154, 155

George amendment, 154–55, 157

Germany: U.S. relations with West, 2, 3, 5, 30, 49, 50; and U.S. strategy, 2, 3, 12; Occupation of, 2, 12, 57, 60, 253 (n. 9); and GATT, 22, 24; creation of the Federal Republic of, 31, 39, 60, 64; rearmament of West, 49, 252 (n. 67); U.S. planning for Occupation of, 55, 56, 57; and reparations of, 57; postwar economic integration of West, 76; prewar nationalism of, 133

Gingham, 211, 213

Globalized production, 179

Government and Relief in Occupied Areas (GARIOA), 66

Government-business relationship, 172, 174–77, 183–90, 196–97, 208–30 passim. See also Japan: industrial model of

Gowa, Joanne, 185

Gray, Gordon, 47

Great Depression: influence of on postwar U.S. leaders, 2, 133; and trade policy, 18; and "Buy American" policy, 140; impact of on U.S.-Japan trade relations, 205–6, 286 (nn. 19, 21)

Greater East Asian Co-Prosperity Sphere, 72

Great Leap Forward, 216, 290 (n. 72)

Greece, 152

Greenstein, Fred I., 114

Grew, Joseph, 55, 56, 252 (n. 4)

Growth, high-speed, xii–xiii, 24–27, 199, 203, 222, 233, 234, 278 (n. 114), 294 (n. 5)

Guatemala, 48

Index 321

Hadley, Eleanor, 59
Haguiwara, Tōru, 105; 211; and GATT matters, 128, 151–2, 157, 164, 166
Haiti, 166
Halleck, Charles, 121
Harriman, W. Averell, 86
Harris, Townsend, 170
Hatoyama, Ichirō, 50, 194, 201, 203–4, 216, 236, 285 (n. 13)
Hauge, Gabriel, 224
Hayashi, Shintarō, 196
Hemmendinger, Noel, 115
Herter, Christian A., 196, 219
"Hidden-hand" leadership, 114–15, 138–39
Hiroshima, 56
Hoffmann, Paul, 123
Holding Company Liquidation Commission, 60, 63
Hong Kong, 73, 74; and export controls, 89, 90, 92, 93, 95, 96, 97, 261 (n. 51); and textiles, 213, 289–90 (n. 62)
Hoover, Herbert, 55, 140
"Hostage capitalism," 90, 261 (n. 58)
Hull, Cordell, 17, 18, 19, 54, 57, 63, 208
Humphrey, George, 122–24, 141, 145, 149, 185
Humphrey, Hubert H., 142
Hurley, Patrick, 129

Ichimada Naoto, 178
Iguchi Sadao, 105, 209
Ikeda Hayato, 178, 221, 227, 233, 292 (n. 95)
Import trade: Japan, 13–16, 225–31; 293 (n. 115). *See also* Agricultural imports: Japanese; Raw materials imports: Japanese
Import quotas, 114, 131, 227
India, 4, 50, 48, 97, 166, 186
Indonesia, 43, 67, 72, 89, 131, 186, 183
Industrial Bank of Japan, 27
"Industrial policy," 25, 26, 27
Industry: higher-value-added, 17, 134, 162–63, 206, 222 (*see also* Industry, light); Japanese heavy, 206, 222
Industry, light: Japanese, 17, 144, 162; U.S., 23, 119, 122, 134, 163, 222
Inflation (Japan), 61, 85
Inter-American Development Bank, 187
Interior, U.S. Department of, 141
International Business Machines, 172, 183
International Development Association, 187
International economic order: influence of Cold War on, xi–xii, 3, 21–22, 29–51 passim, 60–65, 139–40, 186, 200–204, 224; ideological background of, 2, 133; Japan as test of, 3, 22, 163–64, 236–37; interconnection between economic and security relationships in, 4, 12, 17, 46–47, 53, 64, 65, 68, 82–83, 84–89, 111–12, 113–14, 139–40, 163–64, 186–87, 208, 228, 230; basic institutions of, 19–22; and the postwar trading system, 234–37. *See also specific events, institutions, issues, and policies*
Internationalism, 2, 117–18
International Monetary Fund, 19
International Trade Organization (ITO), 19, 20, 23, 121, 235
Iran, 48
Iron: ore, 15, 96, 102; galvanized sheets of, 102, 105
Ishibashi Tanzan, 203, 204, 216, 236, 285 (n. 13)
Ishikawa Ichirō, 275 (n. 75)
Ishizaka Taizō, 220, 221
Italy, 148, 162

Japan: bureaucracy in, 6–8, 25–27, 169–97, passim, 202–3, 204, 222, 248 (n. 38), 284 (n. 85); Productivity Programs of, 7, 187–88; industrial model of, 8, 25, 26–27, 236, 238; economic competitiveness of, 9, 22, 126, 149,

153–54, 207–25 passim, 235–38; trade deficit of, 12, 13, 61, 114, 148, 156, 293 (n. 113) (*see also* Balance-of-payments); rearmament of, 12, 38, 40, 41, 42, 49, 250–51 (no. 40); industrial production in, 13, 61, 257 (n. 3); business in, 25–27, 104, 144–45, 173, 182–83, 192, 194, 220–21, 222 (*see also specific firms*); demilitarization of, 41, 49; emperor of, 56; democratization of, 56–64; inflation in, 61, 85; anxiety of regarding foreign markets, 167; heavy industry in, 206, 222
— economic recovery of: as an objective of U.S. policy, 1–3, 12, 45, 46, 50, 113–14, 136, 137–38, 172, 208; unexpectedness of, 199, 222, 233, 234; distracts Eisenhower administration, 202; leads to trade friction, 195–96, 206–31 passim
— Occupation of: postwar conditions during, 2, 12, 13; reversal of reforms during, 12; U.S. economic aid during, 13, 253 (n. 18); U.S. planning for, 55–57; reforms during, 57–64; *See also* Reverse course; Supreme Command for the Allied Powers
— politics of, xii, 2, 41, 144–45, 202, 203–4, 216–17; Socialists in, 50, 75, 144, 203, 272 (n. 28), 285 (n. 14); Liberal Democratic Party in, 50, 203; Communists in, 75, 144; conservatives in, 103, 203–4, 234; Liberal Party in, 122, 194. *See also specific persons*
— reparations program of, 57–58; reversal of, 61–64; and the peace settlement, 70–72, 255 (n. 53)
— voluntary export restraint (VER) of, 8; during 1930s, 206, 208, 286 (n. 21); 1955–56 textiles, 209, 287–88 (n. 39), 288 (n. 41); as a solution to trade friction, 210–11; 1957 cotton textiles, 212–13, 289 (n. 61); subsequent, 223, 225; legacy of, 213, 218, 230
Japanese Embassy (Washington): and U.S. military purchases, 121–22; and entry into GATT, 124, 269 (n. 74)
Japanese "miracle," xii–xiii, 1, 24, 25–27
Japanese National Diet, xii, 110, 145, 171, 173, 174, 222
Japanese Peace Treaty (1951), xi, 4, 30; as a separate peace, 30, 32, 73–76; Japanese desire for, 31; U.S. planning for, 31–39; negotiation of, 39–45, 65–76; ratification of, 45, 76, 78; economic clauses of, 65–72; and reparations issue, 70–72; and China issue, 73, 74, 75; and "bilateral treaty" with ROC, 75–76. *See also* ANZUS Pact; U.S.-Japan Security Treaty
Japan External Trade Association, 196
Japan Lobby, 62, 63
Japan Management Association, 229
Japan Steel Works, Ltd., 192
Jenner, William, 76, 117
Johnson, Chalmers, 25–26, 174, 189
Johnson, Louis, 31, 37, 39, 250 (n. 33)
Johnson, Lyndon, 153, 219, 220
Johnson, U. Alexis, 129
Joint Chiefs of Staff, U.S.: and peace with Japan, 31, 33, 38; and Japanese reparations, 57–58; and export controls, 88, 95, 214–15
Jonas, Manfred, 54
Justice, U.S. Department of, 59, 281 (n. 45)

Kahn, Herman, 190
Katayama Tetsu, 61
Kauffman, James Lee, 62
Kaufman, Burton I., 22
Kean, Robert W., 138
Kean bill, 138, 270 (n. 3)
Kearn, Harry F., 62
Kearns, Henry, 219, 291 (n. 88)
Keating, Kenneth, 119
Keidandren, 104, 173, 177, 188, 220, 275 (n. 75)
Kem, James P., 99, 100

Index 323

Kennan, George, 31, 32, 61–62, 253 (n. 75)
Kerr, Robert, 220
Kircher, Donald P., 192, 194
Kishi Nobusuke, xii; 203, 204, 216, 217, 228, 233, 234, 285–86 (n. 15), 289 (n. 51)
Kline, Allan B., 123
Knowland, William, 31, 75, 76, 117
Kobayashi Kōji, 188, 189
Korea: prewar Japanese presense in, 16; and GATT, 22; and export controls, 83–112 passim; *See also* North Korea; Republic of Korea (ROK)
Korean War, xii, 13, 29, 32, 37; impact on Japan's economy, xii, 4, 13, 16, 84–86, 95–99, 101–4, 108–12; impact on Japanese peace settlement, 38, 39; divides Asia, 84; impact on U.S. foreign policy, 84, 85, 87; bolsters export controls, 84, 91–112 passim; prompts stronger U.K. export controls, 92–93; and domestic PRC politics, 99; consequences of armistice of, 116, 121–22, 144–45, 146, 147

Labor-intensive industry. *See* Industry, light
Labor standards, 126
LaFeber, Walter, 9, 10
Laos, 89
Lancashire, 126
Latin America, 8
Leddy, John, 78, 115
Leffler, Melvyn, 55
Liberal Democratic Party (Japan), 50, 203
Linder, Harold P., 108–9, 110
Lodge, Henry Cabot, 138–39, 219

Macao, 89, 95, 96
MacArthur, Douglas, 2, 85; and Japanese peace settlement, 31, 37, 38, 42, 44, 250–51 (n. 40); firing of, 44; and U.S. postsurrender policy, 56; and Occupation reforms, 57–63; and the Korean War, 95, 96, 98
MacArthur, Douglas, II,: on ties with Japan, 50, 204, 285 (n. 4); and U.S.-Japanese economic friction, 196, 212, 217, 224
McCarthy, Joseph, 29, 33, 117, 118, 145, 215
McClellan, Harold C., 211–13
McClurkin, Robert J., 115
McDermott, Michael J., 122
Makins, Roger, 130
Malaysia, 58, 72
Mao Zedong, 216
Manchuria, 16, 87, 204
Marshall, George C., 29,39, 261 (n. 51)
Marshall Plan, 12, 60, 84, 123, 183, 188, 200
Martin, Joseph, 117, 121, 206, 211
Martin, Lester, 207
Mason, Mark, 169, 170, 196
Matsumoto, Shun'ichi, 130, 131
Menzies, Robert, 68
Mercantilism, 5–6, 26, 133, 162. *See also* Protectionism
Mexico, 183
Middle East, 8
Military bases: and U.S. strategy, 32, 33, 38; "incidents" of, 202, 203, 285 (nn. 7, 11)
Military purchases, 13, 14, 115, 121–22, 134
Millikin, Eugene, 117, 118, 119–20, 132, 134, 139, 266 (n. 27); and trade, 24, 119–20, 139, 154; and GATT, 120, 149; and foreign investment, 185
Mills, Wilbur, 153, 219
Ministry of Finance (Japan), 166; and FIL, 174–75; and FCN Treaty, 176–77; and U.S. foreign investment, 193
Ministry of Foreign Affairs (Japan), 102–12 passim; 166; and foreign investment, 178, 190–94
Ministry of Health and Welfare (Japan), 178, 280 (n. 34)

Ministry of International Trade and Industry (Japan), 7, 26, 26, 101, 102, 279 (nn. 9, 17), 284 (n. 85); and export controls, 146; and Article 35, 166, 272 (n. 26); and foreign investment, 174–75, 182, 188–90, 192, 195; and technology transfer, 188, 189, 190; and export inspection, 222
Minnesota Mining and Manufacturing Company, 179
Mitsubishi: zaibatsu, 58; Rayon Company, 178; equipment, 183; Shin-Mitsubishi Heavy Industries, 196
Mitsui zaibatsu, 58
"Morganthau Plan," 55
Morrison, Herbert, 66, 74, 75, 261 (n. 63)
Most-favored-nation (MFN) status, 22, 64, 65, 67, 68, 6, 126, 131
Mukai Tadaharu, 177
Multinational enterprise, 6–7; growth of, 179–83, 281 (nn. 38, 39); and Japan, 182–83, 196–97; passive role of government in, 183–84, 281 (nn. 45, 49); and technology transfer, 187–90, 282 (n. 60); and international economic order, 236–37
Murphy, Robert, 104, 106, 107
Mutual Defense Assistance Control Act of 1951. *See* Battle Act
Mutual Security Program (MSP), 122, 187, 266 (n. 34). *See also* Military purchases

Nagasaki, 56
National Cash Register, 188
National Intelligence Estimates, 45–46, 91, 214, 260 (n. 31), 285 (nn. 5, 14), 290 (n. 64)
National Security Council, U.S., policy papers of: NSC 13/2, 12, 64; NSC 125/2, 46–47, 108, 113, 187; NSC 68, 83, 257 (n. 2); NSC 34/1, 87; NSC 41, 87–89; NSC 48/2, 88; NSC 125/1, 107; NSC 152/3, 147; NSC 5516/1, 187, 201; NSC 152/2, 273 (n. 35)

National security policy, U.S.: and Japanese economic revival as a strategic objective of, 1–3, 12, 45, 46, 50, 113–14, 136, 137–38, 172, 208; role of West Germany and Japan in, 2, 3, 12; interconnection with foreign economic policy, 4, 12, 17, 46–47, 53, 64, 65, 68, 82–83, 84–89, 111–12, 113–14, 139–40, 163–64, 186–87, 208, 228, 230; and competing strategies of containment, 21, 31–33; and importance of lenient peace settlement with Japan, 36, 65, 68; strategic importance of Japan in, 45, 60–61, 64; and review of policy toward Japan, 46–47, 201. *See also* Export Controls; National Security Council, U.S., policy papers of
"National treatment": and Japanese Peace Treaty, 65, 70; and FCN Treaty, 176, 241–43; and foreign investment in Japan, 176–77. *See also* Singer Sewing Machine Company
NEC Corporation, 188
Netherlands, The, 58, 89, 92, 275 (n. 69). *See also* Benelux nations
Neutralism, 4, 50
New Zealand: and peace with Japan, 43, 44, 70, 79; and Japanese membership in GATT, 79, 127, 131, 151; and Article 35, 166. *See also* Commonwealth nations
Nikkeiren, 188
1950s as distinctive period, xi–xiii
"1955 system," 137
Nippon Gaisha Kaisha, Ltd., 141, 271 (nn. 11, 12)
Nisshō, 177, 188, 221
Nixon, Richard, 84, 114, 237
Nontariff barriers, 162–63, 225–31. *See also* Balance-of-payments: as justification for Japanese protectionism; Foreign Investment Law
Nonstrategic trade, 92, 96, 107, 109–10
North Atlantic Treaty Organization (NATO), 40, 105, 106, 120, 121

Index 325

North Korea, 13, 37, 83, 91; embargo of, 92, 93, 111. *See also* Export controls
Norway, 152

Oil, 15, 89, 92, 97, 259 (n. 26); companies, 89, 123, 175, 279 (n. 19); machinery, 95; lubricant products, 156, 158
Okano Kiyohide, 144
Okazaki Katsuo, 103, 110, 144, 190–91, 193
Okinawa, 50, 203
Okumura Katsuo, 178
Old Guard, 116–24
Organization for Trade Cooperation, 219
Ozawa, Terutomo, 189

Pacific security pact, 43
Pacifism, 41. *See also* Japan: demilitarization of
Parke-Davis Company, 177 178, 179, 190, 193
Parker Pen Company, 177
Parsons, J. Graham, 115
Partisan tension, U.S., 29, 30, 33; policy toward Japan unaffected by, 30, 33–35; *See also* Bipartisanship; Dulles, John Foster; Old Guard
Patent and trademark protection, 69, 171
Pauley, Edwin W., 57–58, 63
"Pay-as-you-go" financing, 85
People's Republic of China (PRC): and U.S. politics, 29–33, 35, 73, 115; U.S. containment of, 30–33, 73–76, 83–112 passim; criticizes Yoshida Letter, 75; entry into Korean War of, 95; "peace offensive" toward Japan, 103, 146–47; *See also* China market; Export controls; Sino-American antagonism; Sino-American trade; Sino-Japanese Trade; Sino-Soviet alliance
Peril-point provision. *See* Reciprocal Trade Agreements Act—peril-point provision
Perry, Matthew, 170
Peru, 131, 152
Philippines, 43, 44, 58, 70–72
Pine Sewing Machine Manufacturing Company, 192. *See also* Singer Sewing Machine Company
PL 480 (Agricultural Surplus Disposal Program), 141–43, 187, 272 (n. 22)
Policy Planning Staff (PPS), 31, 38, 60, 61
Porter Michael E., 27
Portfolio investment, 171, 278 (n. 1)
"Positive List," 86, 97. *See also* Export controls
Postwar trading system, 3–9, 17–24, 163, 179–80; 197, 230–31, 233–39
Potsdam Conference, 57
Potsdam Declaration, 56
Press: American, 62, 153, 202, 210; British, 80, 128, 165, 257 (n. 82); Japanese, 107, 145, 146, 155, 175, 192–93, 272 (n. 31)
Proctor and Gamble, 6, 179
Protectionism, 3, 8, 23; Japanese, 5–9, 25–27, 161–62, 176, 193, 195, 197, 203, 225–26, 230–31, 284 (n. 85), U.S. tolerance of, 9, 23–24, 170, 172–74, 176–77, 195, 197, 203, 226; domestic U.S. pressure for, 117–20, 123, 127, 132–35, 148–49, 153–54, 207–13, 218–31 passim. *See also* United Kingdom; and Japanese accession to GATT
Psychological Strategy Board (U.S.), 47, 48, 49, 252 (n. 62)
Public Advisory Board for Mutual Security (U.S.), 122–23
Public opinion, 3, 9, 22–24, *See also* Commonwealth nations; Congress, U.S.; Press; Protectionism; Western allies

Quality control, 221, 222
Quirino, Elpidio, 70–71

Radford, Arthur W., 214
Randall, Clarence B., 123–24, 132, 133, 134, 138–39
Randall Commission: creation of, 123–24, 267 (n. 45); report of, 132–35, 138, 141, 184
Raw materials imports: Japanese, 13, 15–17; from United States and dollar area, 15–16, 142–43, 158–59, 162–63; from Southeast Asia, 72; from China, 96, 103
Rayburn, Sam, 153–54
Reciprocal trade, early agreements for, 78, 247 (n. 17)
Reciprocal Trade Agreements Act (RTAA, 1934): passage of, 17–18; praise for, 22; criticism of, 22–24; Eisenhower supports renewal of, 115; domestic U.S. criticism of, 119, 120, 121, 122, 123, 132, 133, 135, 120, 132–33, 207; and Japanese anxiety about entry to GATT, 124, 128–29; one-year renewal (1953), 124; one-year renewal (1954), 137, 138–40; Trade Agreements Extension Act (1955), 153–55; limits of, 167; 1958 renewal of, 219–20, 225. *See also* General Agreement on Tariffs and Trade; Tariff Negotiations
—escape clause: origins, 20, 120; proposals regarding, 120, 127, 134, 220; and silk scarves, 124–25; and prewar Japanese imports, 206; and relief for cotton textiles industry, 207; and velveteens, 212–13; and ginghams application, 213; and flatware and other cases, 222–25, 292 (nn. 99, 101), 293 (nn. 108, 110)
—peril-point provision: origins of, 20, 21, 120; proposals regarding, 119, 134, 220; and tariff negotiations, 148, 161, 165, 207
Red Scare, 29, 99, 117–18
Reed, Daniel A., 117, 118–19, 120, 124, 132, 134, 139–40, 153

Reedy, George, 120, 266 (n. 27)
Reparations. *See* Japan—reparations program of
Republican Party, U.S.: and trade policy, 18, 19–22, 135; challenges containment policies, 29, 30; supports Nationalist Chinese, 74–76; Old Guard faction of, 77–76; Old Guard-internationalist split within, 116–18; and Eisenhower, 116–24, 135. *See also* Economic nationalists; *specific persons*
Republic of China (ROC): prewar Japanese presence in, 16; and Japanese industrial model, 26; and peace with Japan, 44, 74–76; and reparations, 70; and U.S. politics, 73–76, 104; and trade with Japan, 104, 143, 217–18; export controls of, 110; *See also* Chiang Kai-shek; China
Republic of Korea (ROK): North Korean attack on, 13, 37, 83, 91; and Japanese industrial model, 26; export controls of, 110. *See also* Korea
Reston, James, 76
Reverse course, 2, 12, 31–32, 41, 60–65
"Revisionism," 25–26
Rhodesia, 131, 151, 166
Rice, 143, 209
Rio Treaty (1947), 36
Robertson, Walter S., 129
Roosevelt, Franklin D., 2, 19, 54
Rusk, Dean, 33, 34

San Francisco Peace Conference (1951), 30, 44–45, 73
Sankyo Company, Ltd., 177
Satō Eisaku, 227, 228
Schaller, Michael, 12
Schonberger, Howard B., 12
Schuman, Robert, 94
Scott, R. H., 97
Section 22 (Agricultural Adjustment Act), 163
Senate, U.S.: ratifies Japanese Peace

Index 327

and Security Treaties, 45, 78; Finance Committee, 117, 120, 153–55, 185; leadership of, 117–18, 153; and GATT, 120; and trade, 139–40, 154, 209, 219–20
Sewing machines, 161, 191–96
Shigemitsu Mamoru, 209, 215
Shima Shigenobu, 211
Shipping, 69–70, 247 (n. 13), 255 (n. 44)
Silk: scarves, 124–5; raw, 161
Simpson, Richard, 117, 118, 119, 120, 122, 123, 124, 132, 134, 139, 153, 219
Singapore, 89, 92
Singer Sewing Machine Company, 171; and foreign investment in Japan, 191–96
Sino-American antagonism, 4, 13, 15, 31–33, 73–76, 84–112 passim
Sino-American trade, 87–89, 91, 95, 96, 110, 258 (n. 15), 274 (n. 42)
Sino-Japanese Trade, 12, 15–16, 37, 96, 272 (n. 26), 290 (n. 71); domestic Japanese pressure for, 9–10, 102–3, 104, 107, 144–45, 214, 215–16, 217, 236, 291 (n. 78); and Sino-Soviet "peace offensive," 103, 144, 274 (n. 45); See also CHINCOM; "China differential"; Export Controls: U.S. commitment to maintaining; State, U.S. Department of: encourages Sino-Japanese trade; State, U.S. Department of: reevaluates policy regarding Sino-Japanese trade
Sino-Japanese Trade Promotion Association, 103, 144
Sino-Soviet alliance, 33, 83, 89, 97, 103
Smith, H. Alexander, 31, 75, 76, 145
Smith, Walter B., 145
Smoot-Hawley Tariff Act (1930), 18, 78, 119, 247 (n. 19)
Sony, 183
South Africa, 79, 131, 151, 166
Southeast Asia: and Japanese peace settlement, 43, 67, 70–72; and reparations issue, 70–72; Japanese trade with, 72, 143, 150, 195, 213, 271 (n. 12); *See also specific countries*
South Korea. *See* Republic of Korea
Soviet bloc, 3, 21
"Soviet economic penetration," 186
Soviet Union: and peace with Japan, 31, 32, 44, 45; Sino-Soviet alliance, 33, 83, 89, 97; "peace offensive toward Japan," 103; and Third World, 186, 202; normalization of relations with Japan by, 201
Soybeans, 96, 102
Sparkman, John, 75, 251 (n. 51)
Standard-Vacuum, 175, 279 (n. 19)
Stassen, Harold, 123, 214
State, U.S. Department of: encourages Sino-Japanese trade, 12, 32, 87–88; and ITO, 20; and peace with Japan, 31–45 passim; and China policy, 32; and reparations, 59; and reversal of Occupation policies, 61–65, 253 (n. 22); supports Japanese membership in GATT, 77–80; approaches Dulles regarding Japanese trade negotiations, 78; reevaluates policy regarding Sino-Japanese trade, 87–89, 258 (nn. 12, 19); differs with Department of Defense on export controls, 88, 106–7, 258 (n. 19); presses allies to tighten controls on trade with the PRC, 89, 91, 92, 94–95, 259 (nn. 22, 24); and Sino-Japanese trade during Korean War, 95–97; and UN sanctions, 97–98; and export control legislation, 99–101; and Japanese membership in COCOM; continues pressure on Japan to maintain export controls, 103–11; 104–11; and bilateral understanding with Japan, 108–9; continuity of between Truman and Eisenhower administrations, 114–15, 164–65 (n. 6); as target of Republican attack, 118–19; and U.S. military purchases in Japan, 122; and U.S.-Japan FCN treaty, 124, 175–77; and inter-

328 Index

sessional committee on Japanese accession to GATT, 125, 127, 128; fears trade negotiations may exacerbate U.S. protectionism, 128; and 1953 RTAA renewal, 129, 266 (n. 25), 267 (nn. 38, 39); and provisional Japanese accession to GATT, 129–31; and 1954 RTAA renewal, 138, 139, 270 (n. 3); and "Buy American" policy, 141; and PL 480, 143; continues pressure on Japan regarding export controls, 146–47; and domestic U.S. criticism of GATT, 149; announces tariff negotiations with Japan, 150; and U.K. invocation of Article 35, 155; and 1955 TAEA, 155; and tariff negotiations, 155–65 passim; and Japan's Article 35 problem, 165, 167; favors expanded U.S. FDI, 185; urges Japanese capital liberalization, 190–96; and Singer-Pine case, 191–96; and cotton textiles, 208–13; and end of "China Differential," 214–18; and Japanese industrial model, 235. *See also* Policy Planning Staff; *specific persons*
State-War-Navy-Coordinating Committee, U.S., 55, 56, 58
Steel industry, 17, 58, 206
Stettinius, Edward, 55
Stimson, Henry, 55
Stock purchases, 176–77, 279 (n. 114)
Strategic materials. *See* Battle Act, Lists; COCOM; Export controls
Strike, Clifford, 63
Studebaker Corporation, 190, 193
Suez crisis, 114, 202, 293 (n. 113)
Supreme Command for the Allied Powers (SCAP): and demilitarization of Japan, 41; and reparations, 57–58, 71; and Occupation economic reforms, 57–64; and export controls, 88–89, 92, 96, 99, 101–2; and Japanese capital controls, 172–74; and foreign investment, 173; encourages revival of Japan's textile production, 206

Suzuki Gengo, 193
Sweden, 152
SWNCC-150/4/A, 56. *See also* U.S. postsurrender policies
SWNCC 302/4 (FEC 230), 60
Syria, 186

Tableware. *See* Flatware
Taft, Robert A., 29; 117–21, 266 (n. 32)
Taiwan Straits crisis, 114, 202
Takamatsu, Prince, 103
Takeuchi Ryūji, 109–10
Talmadge, Herman, 154
Tariff Commission, U.S.: proposals regarding, 119, 120, 127, 134, 220; and silk scarves escape clause case, 124–25; and dumping, 140; and tariff negotiations, 150, 161, 165; and prewar escape clause cases, 206; and trade friction over cotton textiles, 206–13; and velveteens case, 212, 213; and ginghams application, 213; and flatware and other escape clause cases, 222–25, 292 (nn. 99, 101), 293 (nn. 108, 110)
Tariff negotiations, 22, 269 (n. 78); postponed (1953), 122, 124, 128; Japanese press for, 128–29; Annecy-type, 129; U.S. decision to conduct, 139–40; 1955 Geneva, 155–64, 276 (n. 77), 276 (n. 86); Japanese style of, 157, 162, 164; 1956 Geneva, 164–66, 277 (n. 100); *See also* State, U.S. Department of; Tariff Commission, U.S.; *specific products*
Technology transfer, 7, 187–90, 282 (nn. 59, 60, 61), 283 (nn. 63, 64)
Textiles: industry, 17, 84, 204–6; machinery, 102; lace, 119, 165
Textiles in trade negotiations, 78, 160–61, 165, 276 (n. 86), 277 (n. 100)
Thailand, 143
Thermometers, clinical, 222, 225, 292 (n. 101), 293 (n. 108)
Thibodeaux, Ben H., 220, 222
Third World: distracts U.S. attention

from Japan, 8, 186–87, 202; as object of superpower attention, 186–87. *See also specific countries*
Thurmond, Strom, 220
Toyota automobiles, 84, 183
Trade Agreements Committee (TAC), U.S., 79, 130, 150, 256–57 (n. 79)
Trade Agreements Extension Act (1955), 153–55, 167. *See also* Reciprocal Trade Agreements Act
Trade liberalization: Japanese attitude toward, 4, 6, 128, 147–48, 155, 162, 190–97, 218–31 passim; and U.S. policy, 4, 17–24, 113–35 passim, 137–43, 150–67 218–31, 234–35; and U.S. expectations, 8, 235–37; scholarly debate regarding, 22–24; and Japanese Peace Treaty, 65–70; and Japanese membership in GATT, 76–81, 125–31, 148–68; domestic U.S. opposition to, 117–20, 123, 132–35, 138–39, 148–54, 206–13, 218–25, compared to collective security, 120–21; and accompanying shift of power to executive branch, 120; *See also* Foreign economic policy, U.S.; Reciprocal trade; Reciprocal Trade Agreements Act; United Kingdom: and Japanese accession to GATT
Trade sanctions, 97–99, 111
Treasury, U.S. Department of, 96, 140; and foreign investment, 185; report on U.S. business indifference to Japan, 189. *See also* Humphrey, George
Triangular negotiations (1955), 155, 162
Truman, Harry S, 2, 20, 57, 64, 85, 114, 120, 125; and Japanese peace settlement, 32, 44; and export controls, 41, 88, 89, 96, 99, 100; fires Douglas MacArthur, 44; directs review of policy toward Japan, 46; and Japanese membership in GATT, 79
Truman administration: and Cold War strategy, 3, 12, 21; and reciprocal trade, 19–21; and Japanese membership in GATT, 22, 24, 76–80, 125; and Japanese peace settlement, 29–45 passim; internal division of over peace with Japan, 31–32; containment policies of, 59–64, 84; and export controls, 85–111 passim; continuity of with Eisenhower administration, 114–15; agricultural policy of, 142. *See also specific agencies, departments, issues, and persons*
Truman Doctrine, 21
Tuna, 17, 156, 157, 161

Umbrella frames, 222, 225, 292 (n. 101), 293 (n. 108)
Underestimation of Japan, 189, 197, 200, 202, 235–36
Unemployment, 133, 149, 287 (n. 31)
United Kingdom, xi, 5, 24; and the Japanese Peace Treaty, 44, 58, 65, 66, 67, 68, 69, 70, 80; and Japanese reparations, 58, 70–71; postwar attitude toward Japan of, 66, 69, 126; opposes MFN for Japan, 67, 68, 69; policy regarding China, 73–76; postwar relationship with the United States, 73–99 passim; and export controls, 89–109 passim, 146, 216, 290–91 (n. 73); and Japanese accession to GATT, 125–28, 130, 131, 151–52, 164; and issue of bilateral commercial treaty with Japan, 148, 151, 164, 166; votes for Japanese accession, 164; and invocation of Article 35, 164, 165, 166, 167
United Nations, 39, 83, 97–99, 103, 111, 118
United States Embassy in Tokyo: and allied opinion of Japanese trade, 127; evaluation of U.S.-Japanese relations, 201–2; and textiles issue, 211–13; and Sino-Japanese trade, 218; and Japanese exports, 220; and flatware case, 223; and Japanese press, 272 (n. 31)

United States Information Agency (USIA), 48, 224
U.S. anxiety: about Japan's reliability as an ally, 30, 33, 45, 46, 49, 50, 200–204; about Japan's economy, 30, 45, 46, 49, 83, 148, 172
U.S. business in Japan, 7, 169, 171–72, 175, 177–78, 189–97, 202. *See also* Multinational enterprise; *specific firms*
U.S. establishment, 2, 34, 117
U.S.-Japanese relations: and growing bilateral interdependence, 8, 10–11, 50–51, 80–81, 102–3, 111–12, 167–68, 203–4, 228, 230–31, 234–35; and mutual frustration, 9–10, 49–50, 80–81, 200–203, 214–15, 233–34, 237–38, *See also specific issues*
U.S.-Japan Mutual Security Treaty (1960), xii, 4; protest against, xii, 233, 234
U.S.-Japan Security Treaty (1951), xi–xii; and administrative agreement (1952), 42, 251 (n. 44); negotiation of, 42–43; revision of, 114, 228
U.S.-Japan Treaty of Friendship, Commerce, and Navigation (1953), 4, 6; signing of, 124; negotiation of, 175–77; protocol to, 176; and U.S. foreign investment, 176–78, 191–93, 197
U.S. military spending in Japan, 13, 14, 84–86, 115, 122–22, 134, 258 (n. 9)
U.S. postsurrender policies, 2, 55–57
USSR. *See* Soviet Union

Vandenberg, Arthur, 33, 120
Vandenberg Resolution, 40
Van Wolferen, Karel, 25
Velveteens, 160, 161, 206, 211, 212, 213
Verdier, Daniel, 21–22
Versailles Treaty, 36
Vietnam, 72, 89
Vietnam War, 85, 258 (n. 9)
Volkswagen cars, 183

Voluntary export restraint (VER), 23, 206, 209–13, 222–25, 230
Voorhees, Tracy, 33

Wade, Robert, 26
Wake Island Conference, 85
War, 2, 133
War, U.S. Department of, 61
War criminal issue, 201, 204, 285 (n. 4)
Waring, Frank, 115, 178, 190, 220
Waugh, Samuel C., 151, 157
Ways and Means, U.S. House Committee on, 117–19, 122, 139, 185, 219
Weeks, Sinclair, 141, 149, 219
Weinstein, David, 26
Weiss, Leonard, 115
Western allies: attitude toward Japanese trade, 3, 24, 65, 67, 68, 76, 77, 152; economic competitiveness with United States, 3, 8, 9, 22–23, 236, 237, 238; and trade liberalization, 4, 5, 254 (n. 41); and Japanese peace settlement, 37–39, 65–71. *See also specific countries and institutions*
Western European market, 76, 147–48, 181, 189–90, 202. *See also* Currency convertibility
Wheat, 16, 209
Wherry, Kenneth S., 94
White, C. Thayer, 115
Wiley, Alexander, 251 (n. 51)
Wilson, Harold, 67
Wilson, Woodrow, 18
Wool, 15, 95, 167; yarn, 102; textiles, 141, 211
World Bank, 19, 187
World War II: economic impact on Japan of, 16–17; and Britain, 69; causes of, 133; impact on U.S. and Japanese textile industries, 206, 286 (n. 22)
Wyndham-White, Eric, 131

Xiang, Lanxin, 66–67

Index 331

Yoshida government: and military purchases, 122; and Japanese application for admission to GATT, 128–29; and relaxation of export controls, 144–47. *See also* Ministry of Finance; Ministry of Foreign Affairs; Ministry of International Trade and Industry

Yoshida Shigeru, 54, 190; and Japanese peace settlement, 37, 39, 40, 41, 42, 65–66, 71; background of, 40–41; reluctance of to rearm, 40–41; differs with United States over relations with China, 73–76; and "Yoshida letter," 75–76; and membership in GATT, 76, 77, 79, 80; and trade with China, 104, 144–47; and 1953 election, 122; weakening hold on power of, 144; visit to United States of, 147, 150, 153; fall of, 194, 203

Young, Kenneth T., 115

Yugoslavia, 186

Yukawa Morio, 102, 103, 105, 109, 110, 213

Zaibatsu, 173; dissolution of, 58, 59, 62, 63

www.ingramcontent.com/pod-product-compliance
Lightning Source LLC
Chambersburg PA
CBHW021341300426
44114CB00012B/1030